An Introduction to Homeland Security

A Compilation and Commentary on Key Doctrine and Policy

Edited by

Jeffrey P. Grossmann, JD

OSS Publishing Group

Published by OSS Publishing Group, New York, A Division of Order of the Sword and Shield Organization

ISBN-13: 978-1469985213
ISBN-10: 1469985217

You may contact OSS Publishing Group at **OSSPUB@gmx.com**

For Daphne, Cole, and Madlen

Contents

Preface

Developing college curriculum is an arduous task. Teaching within the curriculum model is even more problematic without adequate resources. Having many years of pragmatic leadership experience within a profession is a solid foundation for any teaching endeavor. Experience, however, is only one of the core ingredients of preparation. Undoubtedly, resource materials play a huge role in the teaching process.

Having the distinct honor (and pleasure) of creating program curriculum in an emerging academic discipline, I have encountered the challenge of developing course materials with limited or basic resources. In particular, the lack of commonality and agreement of even the essential components comprising the Homeland Security academic discipline has been frustrating to say the least. Although it is true that text and reference materials can approach the same subject matter from differing perspectives, it is uncomforting to see the lack of consistency among these efforts.

It is for this reason I have compiled this reference. I use the term "compiled" because I did not create these topics. I did not design these standards. I did not initiate these programs. I do think, however, that I contributed to the overall "process". Along with insightful commentary and historical perspective, I brought together these works in a very unique way. A way in which tells a story, the story of homeland security.

Each of these noteworthy government documents has been chosen for its unique content. The government, in particular the Department of Homeland Security (DHS), has done an extraordinary job in developing many of the systems, concepts, and schemes used in actual practice today. DHS has been a true leader on many educational fronts. Educating the United States and the world about terrorism has been no small undertaking. DHS should be commended for developing these resources, and sharing them in a thorough and judicious fashion.

I would like to thank DHS for providing the resources that made this project possible.

Introduction

This text reference is a compilation of key governmental doctrine in the subject area of homeland security. It is designed to provide an introductory foundation or framework necessary for the understanding of principles, formulas, theories, and general opinions associated with the United States Department of Homeland Security. It is intended to be the primary resource for any introductory course.

This text reference is divided into two parts. The first section focuses on the *foundations* of homeland security. The "what", "why", and "how" of the homeland security function are the driving themes contained in this segment. The second section concentrates on the *functions* of homeland security. Administration, mission, adversaries, and preventative measures are all included in the final sequence of this resource. In its entirety, the concept of homeland security is thoroughly explored.

Using materials compiled in this format allows the student to gain a broad understanding of the general concepts involved in homeland security, while focusing on department or agency-specific models. In addition, the theories, practices, and terminology, while specific to United States homeland security efforts, are quickly becoming industry and world standards.

Part I

Foundations of Homeland Security

- o Before Homeland Security
- o The History of the Department of Homeland Security
- o Defining Homeland Security
- o Statutory Authority
- o Organizational Structure
- o Partners in Homeland Security

President George W. Bush, Address to the Nation, September 11, 2001

"Good evening. Today, our fellow citizens, our way of life, our very freedom came under attack in a series of deliberate and deadly terrorist acts. The victims were in airplanes, or in their offices; secretaries, businessmen and women, military and federal workers; moms and dads, friends and neighbors. Thousands of lives were suddenly ended by evil, despicable acts of terror. The pictures of airplanes flying into buildings, fires burning, huge structures collapsing, have filled us with disbelief, terrible sadness, and a quiet, unyielding anger. These acts of mass murder were intended to frighten our nation into chaos and retreat. But they have failed; our country is strong. A great people has been moved to defend a great nation. Terrorist attacks can shake the foundations of our biggest buildings, but they cannot touch the foundation of America. These acts shattered steel, but they cannot dent the steel of American resolve. America was targeted for attack because we're the brightest beacon for freedom and opportunity in the world. And no one will keep that light from

shining. Today, our nation saw evil, the very worst of human nature. And we responded with the best of America ~ with the daring of our rescue workers, with the caring for strangers and neighbors who came to give blood and help in any way they could. Immediately following the first attack, I implemented our government's emergency response plans. Our military is powerful, and it's prepared. Our emergency teams are working in New York City and Washington, D.C. to help with local rescue efforts. Our first priority is to get help to those who have been injured, and to take every precaution to protect our citizens at home and around the world from further attacks. The functions of our government continue without interruption. Federal agencies in Washington which had to be evacuated today are reopening for essential personnel tonight, and will be open for business tomorrow. Our financial institutions remain strong, and the American economy will be open for business,

President George W. Bush addresses the nation from the Oval Office the evening of Sept. 11, 2001. White House Photo by Paul Morse.

as well. The search is underway for those who are behind these evil acts. I've directed the full resources of our intelligence and law enforcement communities to find those responsible and to bring them to justice. We will make no distinction between the terrorists who committed these acts and those who harbor them. I appreciate so very much the members of Congress who have joined me in strongly condemning these attacks. And on behalf of the American people, I thank the many world leaders who have called to offer their condolences and assistance. America and our friends and allies join with all those who want peace and security in the world, and we stand together to win the war against terrorism. Tonight, I ask for your prayers for all those who grieve, for the children whose worlds have been shattered, for all whose sense of safety and security has been threatened. And I pray they will be comforted by a power greater than any of us, spoken through the ages in Psalm 23: "Even though I walk through the valley of the shadow of death, I fear no evil, for You are with me." This is a day when all Americans from every walk of life unite in our resolve for justice and peace. America has stood down enemies before, and we will do so this time. None of us will ever forget this day. Yet, we go forward to defend freedom and all that is good and just in our world".

Editor's Comments

And with Executive Order 13228 of October 8, 2001, President George W. Bush officially introduced Homeland Security to the people of the United States...

In immediate and direct response to the events of September 11, 2001, President Bush used the authority granted to him under the Constitution and the laws of the United States to establish the Office of Homeland Security. Appointing Pennsylvania Governor Tom Ridge as the first Assistant to the President for Homeland Security, and head of the newly commissioned Office, President Bush was targeting a new and deadly threat. Large scale international terrorism had found its way to American shores.

The mission of the Office of Homeland Security is clear; to develop and coordinate the implementation of a comprehensive national strategy to secure the United States from terrorist threats or attacks. The functions of the Office are to coordinate the executive branch's efforts to **detect, prepare** for, **prevent, protect** against, **respond** to, and **recover** from terrorist attacks within the United States. With a main concentration in the areas of detection, preparedness, prevention, protection, response and recovery, and incident management, the Office of Homeland Security has embarked on a monumental endeavor. The Office's primary functions focus on working with executive departments and agencies, state and local governments, and private entities to ensure the adequacy of the new national strategy.

Office of the President of the United States
Securing the Homeland Strengthening the Nation
2002, (Excerpts)

A New National Calling: Homeland Security

The higher priority we all now attach to homeland security has already begun to ripple through the land. The Government of the United States has no more important mission than fighting terrorism overseas and securing the homeland from future terrorist attacks. This effort will involve major new programs and significant reforms by the Federal government. But it will also involve new or expanded efforts by State and local governments, private industry, nongovernmental organizations, and citizens. By working together we will make our homeland more secure.

Furthermore, as we pursue the goals of homeland security we will build an America better and stronger than it was before. Out of the crisis triggered by September 11 has emerged a renewed commitment by all Americans to their country. We will transform the adversity of September 11 into greater opportunities for the future. We will channel America's renewed civic spirit into concrete improvements in our society. We will find new and important ways to encourage citizens to be more alert and active in their communities. We will renovate our inadequate public safety systems – most importantly public health – and will enhance America's emergency management system. We will consider new organizational models for governing that are appropriate for the new century. We will promote the principles and practice of mutual aid across America. And we will provide leadership and technical assistance to our international partners who seek greater security in their own homelands.

The American people should have no doubt that we will succeed in weaving an effective and permanent level of security into the fabric of a better, safer, stronger America.

Standing upon the ashes of the worst terrorist attack on American soil September 14, 2001, President Bush pledges that the voices calling for justice from across the country will be heard. Responding to the Presidents' words, rescue workers cheer and chant, "U.S.A, U.S.A." White House Photo by Eric Draper.

Chapter 01

Before Homeland Security

"In this shrinking world, it is futile to seek safety behind geographical barriers. Real security will be found only in law and in justice."

President Harry S. Truman, April 16, 1945

**United States Department of Homeland Security
National Preparedness Task Force
Civil Defense and Homeland Security:
A Short History of National Preparedness Efforts
September 2006, (Excerpts)**

Introduction

From the air raid warning and plane spotting activities of the Office of Civil Defense in the 1940s, to the Duck and Cover film strips and backyard shelters of the 1950s, to today's all-hazards preparedness programs led by the Department of Homeland Security, Federal strategies to enhance the nation's preparedness for disaster and attack have evolved over the course of the 20th century and into the 21st.

Presidential administrations can have a powerful impact on both national and citizen preparedness. By recommending funding levels, creating new policies, and implementing new programs; successive administrations have adapted preparedness efforts to align with changing domestic priorities and foreign policy goals. They have also instituted administrative reorganizations that reflected their preference for consolidated or dispersed civil defense and homeland security responsibilities within the Federal government.

Programs were seldom able to get ahead of world events, and were ultimately challenged in their ability to answer the public's need for protection from threats due to bureaucratic turbulence created by frequent reorganization, shifting funding priorities, and varying levels of support by senior policymakers. This in turn has had an effect on the public's perception of national preparedness. Public awareness and support have waxed and waned over the years, as the government's emphasis on national preparedness has shifted.

An analysis of the history of civil defense and homeland security programs in the United States clearly indicates that to be considered successful, national preparedness programs must be long in their reach yet cost effective. They must also be appropriately tailored to the Nation's diverse communities, be carefully planned, capable of quickly providing pertinent information to the populace about imminent threats, and able to convey risk without creating unnecessary alarm.

The following narrative identifies some of the key trends, drivers of change, and lessons learned in the history of U.S. national preparedness programs. A review of the history of these programs will assist the Federal government in its efforts to develop and implement effective homeland security policy and better understand previous national preparedness initiatives.

Pre-Cold War Period (1917-1945)

World War I introduced a new type of attack: the use of strategic aerial strikes against an enemy's population to degrade its ability and will to wage war. German aerial bombardment of towns in countries such as France, Belgium, and Poland began in August 1914, and in the following year Kaiser Wilhelm authorized sustained bombing campaigns against military and civilian targets, particularly against England. From May through October of 1915, Germany launched seven air strikes against London alone. England, like most other nations at the time, did not have an organized civil defense program to aid citizens during such attacks. Individuals were forced to find their own way to safety, often taking refuge in the city's underground subway stations. By all assessments, the damage and casualty figures that resulted from these early bombing operations were comparatively insignificant, but they exerted a psychological toll on the British public. It became clear that civilian defense, involving a range of actions to protect the general public in the event of attack, would become a major fixture in future warfare.

Though the Axis and Allied powers continued to employ strategic bombing throughout World War I, leaders in the United States did not feel that the country was vulnerable to attack. They concentrated their public outreach on rallying support for the war effort. Much of this task was coordinated by the Council of National Defense, established on August 29, 1916 with the passage of an Army appropriations bill. The Council was a presidential advisory board that included the Secretaries of War, Navy, Interior, Agriculture, Commerce, and Labor; assisted by an Advisory Committee appointed by the President. Its responsibilities included "coordinating resources and industries for national defense" and "stimulating civilian morale."

The work of the Council escalated when the United States entered the war in 1917. In the same year, the Federal government asked State governors to create their own local councils of defense to support the National effort. However, the Council's activities continued to focus more on facilitating mobilization for the war than on protecting civilian resources. When hostilities ended, the Council shifted its efforts toward demobilization. Its operations were suspended in June, 1921.

For the remainder of the 1920s, the Federal government undertook little public outreach related to defense and security. However, the 1930s saw a revival of civil defense efforts, when aggressive actions and arms stockpiling in Europe fueled international concern. In 1933, President Franklin Roosevelt created by executive order the National Emergency Council (NEC) which consisted of the President, his Cabinet members, and the head of nearly every

Civil Defense logo circa 1939.

major Federal agency, commission, and board. The mission of the NEC included a variety of programs unrelated to civil defense; however, its duties also included coordination of emergency programs among all agencies involved in national preparedness.

As World War II ignited in Europe, Roosevelt reestablished the Council of National Defense in 1940. Once again States were asked to establish local counterpart councils.

Tensions among Federal, State and local governments began to rise about authority and resources.

The states claimed they were not given enough power to manage civil defense tasks in their own jurisdictions, and local governments asserted that State governments did not give urban areas proper consideration and resources. Non-attack disaster preparedness remained almost entirely the responsibility of States, while federal funding was reserved primarily for attack preparedness.

Mrs. Eleanor Roosevelt and Mayor Fiorello H. La Guardia on the occasion of Mrs. Roosevelt's being sworn in as Mayor La Guardia's assistant in the Office of Civilian Defense. Mrs. Roosevelt's title is Assistant Director of the Office of Civilian Defense. September 29, 1941. Photo credit: Library of Congress.

Because of extensive civilian bombing campaigns in Europe, concerns about possible attacks against the U.S. homeland increased. Mayor Fiorello La Guardia of New York City wrote a letter to President Roosevelt stating: "There is a need for a strong Federal Department to coordinate activities, and not only to coordinate but to initiate and get things going. Please bear in mind that up to this war and never in our history, has the civilian population been exposed to attack. The new technique of war has created the necessity for developing new techniques of civilian defense".

President Roosevelt responded to the increasing concern of the public and local officials by creating the Office of Civilian Defense (OCD) in 1941. The President delegated a number of responsibilities to the OCD by broadly interpreting civilian protection to include morale maintenance, promotion of volunteer involvement, and nutrition and physical education. The OCD oversaw unprecedented federal involvement in attack preparedness. As with the Council of National Defense, the OCD created corresponding defense councils at the local level.

The issue of whether the OCD should emphasize protective services, typically done at that time by men, or social welfare services, typically undertaken at that time by women, created tension from the office's inception. Director Fiorello LaGuardia referred to "non-protective" activities as "sissy stuff" and saw opportunities to build neighborhood militias. Pressured to focus on other non-protective areas such as neighborhood support, he appointed Eleanor Roosevelt to expand volunteer activities. The two leaders, with their radically divergent points of view, exemplified a conflict over the meaning and purpose of civil defense that would continue well into the cold war era.

OCD received criticism from Congress and the public on several fronts. It was called "pink" by influential politicians who disliked the program's broad reach and social development programs. Some believed the organization's tasks were better undertaken by the Department of War. One of OCD's early leaders, James Landis, recommended that the organization be abolished, since the threat of an attack on U.S. civilians had receded.

With the end of World War II, most U.S. officials agreed that the risk of an attack on the U.S. homeland was minimal. Roosevelt did not take Landis' suggestion, and the OCD continued to operate. While the OCD did not fulfill all of its ambitious goals, it did begin the development of concrete civil defense plans, including air raid drills, black outs, and sand bag stockpiling.

Truman Administration (1945-1953)

Soon after taking office, Harry Truman did follow Landis' advice and abolished the OCD, reflecting the widely held belief that the immediate threat of war had receded. Initially, civil defense was not a high priority in the Truman Administration, as troops began to return home and other war time offices were diminished in scale or disbanded altogether. The development of the atomic bomb, however, had opened up previously unthinkable risks. Increasing hostilities with the Soviet Union and their pursuit of a nuclear bomb threatened the United States.

In this context, Truman began to reexamine the national defense structure, reviewing the results of a set of commissions. In 1946, the U.S. Strategic Bombing Survey published its report evaluating the results of strategic bombing campaigns by imperial Germany and Japan against enemy civilian populations. The report indicated that civil defense plans could significantly mitigate the effects of strategic bombing. Specifically, mass evacuation plans for urban areas and shelters for those unable to leave the area could form components of a viable civil defense plan. In 1947, the War Department's Civil Defense Board, led by Major General Harold Bull, released a second report. The so-called Bull Report stated that civil defense is the responsibility of civilians, and the military should not be expected to get involved in

Civil Defense Poster, designed by Charles Tudor, and issued in two colors by the Office of War Information (OWI) between 1940 and 1946. Photo credit: Library of Congress.

such matters. According to the report, civil defense was best implemented locally, a concept referred to as "self-help". Still, the document did concede that the Federal government could provide the majority of necessary resources. Additionally, Congress passed the National

Security Act of 1947. Best known for the creation of the Central Intelligence Agency, the Act also created the National Security Resources Board (NSRB), which was initially responsible for mobilizing civilian and military support, as well as maintaining adequate reserves and effective resource use in the event of war.

From left to right, Russian Prime Minister Josef Stalin, President Harry S. Truman, and British Prime Minister Winston Churchill at the Potsdam Conference, Potsdam, Germany, July 17, 1945. Photo credit: U. S. Army, courtesy of Harry S. Truman Library.

Neither report resulted in substantial reforms to the Truman Administration's policies because civil defense continued to remain a low priority. However, as U.S.-Soviet relations became increasingly strained, President Truman began to implement civil defense policy reforms. These changes resulted, in part, from the strong recommendation of Colonel Burnet Beers, who was responsible for directing a study on future civil defense planning and operations to establish a civil defense unit in the Office of the Secretary of Defense (OSD). Truman acted promptly on this advice, establishing the Office of Civil Defense Planning (OCDP), whose purpose was to recommend a course for the creation of a permanent civil defense agency. After six months, the OCDP released its 300-page Hopley Report, which called for the creation of a Federal office of civil defense directly under the President or Secretary of Defense. The report additionally recommended that the Federal government provide civil defense guidance and assistance, but that State and local governments handle most of the operational responsibilities.

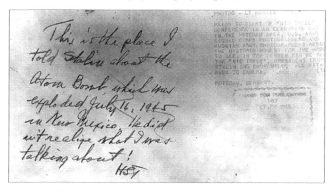

On the back of the photo of President Harry S. Truman, Winston Churchill, and Joseph Stalin at the Potsdam Conference, Truman wrote the following: "This is the place I told Stalin about the Atom Bomb, which was exploded July 16, 1945 in New Mexico. He didn't realize what I was talking about! HST", July 17, 1945. Photo credit: Harry S. Truman Library.

Reactions to the Hopley Report inside and outside government were generally negative. There were concerns about the cost and scope of civil defense. Many people feared its recommendations were too far-reaching and made unrealistic demands on the public and government. And there were concerns about military control. Some civilian groups thought the report called for transferring what should be a civilian responsibility to the military, which could lead to a "garrison state."

Truman ultimately chose to address the latter concern by assigning civil defense planning to the NSRB, a civilian agency. However, the NSRB did not receive the necessary resources or authority to carry out its mandate. As a result, the Board was moved to the Department of Defense (DOD), then shifted to the Executive Office of the President, and finally had its responsibilities transferred to the Office of Defense Mobilization in December of 1950.

The climate of civil defense changed dramatically with the successful Soviet test of a nuclear weapon in August of 1949. The United States lost its monopoly on nuclear weapons and the corresponding negotiating power that this entailed. Local officials began to demand from the Federal government a clear outline of what they were to do in crisis situations. The Truman Administration received criticism from local officials, a worried American public, and Congress for not taking firm action. In response, in 1950, the NSRB generated a new proposal called the Blue Book, which outlined a set of civil defense functions and how they should be implemented at each level of government. The Blue Book also recommended the creation of an independent Federal civil defense organization.

Truman agreed with many of the Blue Book recommendations, but held firm to his belief that civil defense responsibilities should fall mostly on the shoulders of the State and local governments. In response, Congress enacted the Federal Civil Defense Act of 1950, which placed most of the civil defense burden on the States and created the Federal Civil Defense Administration (FCDA) to formulate national policy to guide the States' efforts.

As planning began, policymakers struggled to define what was meant by national security. A key question was the appropriate level of readiness to be attained. At what readiness level would people have to surrender personal freedoms to state control? At what level of security would civil defense metamorphose into a garrison state, undermining the underlying purpose of protecting individual rights? The decision to assign civil defense responsibility to States and localities was intended partly as a safeguard against the garrison state.

Planners also struggled with a difficult political question: just how much support should government provide? Congressional resistance to paying for a comprehensive program, and concerns about establishing public dependency on government, led to adoption of a doctrine of "self help": individual responsibility for preparedness to minimize (not eliminate) risk. The idea of decentralized, locally controlled, volunteer-based civil defense was not new; in fact it was the foundation of the successful British civil defense effort in World War II. However, the decision to make self-help the basis of civil defense was also a political compromise, a way to balance conflicting views over the size, power, and priorities of the emerging postwar nation.

The FCDA led shelter building programs, sought to improve Federal and State coordination, established an attack warning system, stockpiled supplies, and started a well known national civic education campaign. In 1952, the FCDA joined with the Ad Council to release Korean War advertising to boost national morale. The FCDA specifically aimed to teach schoolchildren about preparedness, primarily through civil defense drills. In order to effectively educate the entire youth population, the FCDA commissioned a movie studio to produce nine civil defense movies that would be shown in classrooms across the nation – among them Duck and Cover. The movie, through its main character Bert the Turtle, showed children what to do when they saw "the flash of an atomic bomb." Newspapers and experts generally heralded the film as a positive and optimistic step toward preparedness. The New York Herald Tribune, for example, called the film "very instructive" and "not too frightening for children." Ultimately, the film was seen by millions of schoolchildren during the 1950s. The public education campaign throughout the decade promoted the idea that with preparation, a nuclear attack could be survivable.

An examination of the FCDA-led shelter-building initiative underscores some of the civil defense program's internal inconsistencies. The Federal Civil Defense Act of 1950 allocated significant funding to a shelter initiative. The law allowed the FCDA to develop shelter designs and make financial contributions to shelter programs. However, Congress stipulated that the Federal government could not finance the construction of new shelters. In communities across the country there was great debate over the necessity of the shelters, and Truman himself was not eager to spend government money on the program. Moreover, FCDA Administrator Millard Caldwell initiated a public relations fiasco when he misconstrued the shelter program as a means to protect every person in the country. A program that expansive was deemed to be too costly to receive sufficient political support; as a result, it never left the planning stages during the Truman Administration.

Contrary to the outlook offered by Duck and Cover and the other educational campaigns, early media reports about the possibility of nuclear war offered grim predictions concerning the aftermath of an attack. The scenarios were horrific, and the association of civil defense with death and destruction made not only home preparedness and sheltering, but the whole self-help preparedness concept, a tough sell.

The political, fiscal, and emotional crosscurrents were reflected in civil defense funding. Despite ambitious funding requests, actual appropriations to civil defense remained low throughout the Truman Administration, and throughout the 1950s. For example, from 1951 to 1953 Truman requested $1.5 billion for civil defense, but appropriations totaled only $153 million – 90 percent less than requested.

Despite these practical setbacks, the concept of civil defense as a purposeful approach to the protection of citizens from threats outside the Nation's borders began to take shape during Truman's presidency. Though each leader who followed would focus on different programs and approaches, civil defense remained an important initiative during the coming decades.

Eisenhower Administration (1953-1961)

President Dwight Eisenhower's approach to civil defense was quite different from his predecessor's. Eisenhower identified the enormous economic commitment required for military development as one reason not to undertake expensive civil defense programs. Additionally, Republicans in Congress were eager to curtail spending, as the party had publicly promised to balance the budget when Eisenhower took office. Though Eisenhower requested less funding than Truman, actual appropriations were virtually identical to appropriations under Truman.

In addition to economic concerns, world events contributed to Eisenhower's decision to support a mass evacuation policy, instead of the shelter program initiated under Truman. In 1953, the Soviets detonated a hydrogen nuclear bomb; and shortly thereafter, the effects of the initial U.S. hydrogen explosion were released to the American public. The blast and thermal effects of these new fusion nuclear weapons were so destructive that many experts argued that American cities would be doomed in the event of a nuclear attack, regardless of sheltering efforts. As a result, new FCDA Administrator Frederick Peterson urged Congress to scale back or completely eliminate the shelter program.

In strongly supporting mass evacuation, Peterson noted that successful execution would depend on sufficient warning time, proper training for civil defense officials, and regular public drills. Many of the responsibilities for evacuation would be borne at the State and local level, which appealed to Eisenhower's belief that the Federal government should not shoulder the entire burden for civil defense programs. Congress also was in favor of the shift in attention from shelters to evacuation. Yet some members, especially Congressman Chet Holifield of California, were adamantly opposed to reducing the shelter system. Holifield was the ranking member of the Joint Committee on Atomic Energy and later the chairman of the Military Operations Subcommittee. In support of a federally funded shelter system, he likened the idea of family built shelters to creating "an army or a navy or an air force by advising each one to buy himself a jet plane." As a well publicized champion for shelter building, Congressman Holifield consistently and persuasively articulated the benefits of shelter building to the American public.

Eisenhower receives a report from Lewis L. Strauss, Chairman of the Atomic Energy Commission, on the hydrogen bomb tests in the Pacific, March 30, 1954. Photo credit: Eisenhower Presidential Library.

In March of 1954, the United States detonated another thermonuclear bomb, called Bravo, on Bikini Atoll in the Marshall Islands. Due to a major wind shift, a large amount of radioactive fallout was released over a 7000 square mile area, ultimately poisoning the crew of a Japanese fishing boat in the area and even injuring personnel involved in the test. It did not take long for Congress and the public to turn their attention to the need for shelters to protect the citizenry from such lethal effects. The FCDA was in a tough position. They had just fought for evacuation policies, at the expense of the shelter option, and the Eisenhower Administration continued to support evacuation as the chief civil defense objective. Faced with this dilemma, FCDA Administrator Peterson redirected his policy toward an "evacuation to shelter" approach, whereby individuals would be evacuated from affected areas to shelters. He even proposed digging ditches along roadsides for those who could not get to shelters in time.

The Eisenhower Administration had just begun work on its massive federal highway program, connecting major cities and in the process providing a means for evacuation. Peterson clashed with the President on the program, arguing that Congress should divert some of the highway funding to support civil defense programs. He believed that the highways should be designed to lead only 30 to 40 miles outside of major cities to rural "reception areas." However, Peterson's clout did not match the President's, and thus no money was diverted from the highway program.

The FCDA received extensive criticism over the next few years for not developing a feasible plan for evacuating major cities. Congressman Holifield called FCDA efforts only a façade of civil defense programs. He also chastised the President for not taking more responsibility. At Holifield's request, in 1956 the House Committee on Government Operations held a series of hearings to discuss the viability of the FCDA. The "Holifield Hearings" constituted the largest examination of the civil defense program in U.S. history.

Holifield and his Committee concluded that the FCDA had been myopically focused on evacuation, which they termed "a cheap substitute for atomic shelter."The FCDA responded by presenting a National Shelter Policy, which proposed a $32 billion program for "federally subsidized self-help" (e.g. tax incentives or special mortgage rates to shelter-owning families). Taken aback by the cost of the proposal, Eisenhower convened the Gaither Committee (named for its first chairman, H. Rowan Gaither) composed of leading scientific, military, and business experts. The committee evaluated military readiness and concluded that the United States could not defend itself from a Soviet surprise attack on the homeland. While its report, released in 1957, emphasized funding anti-ballistic missile (ABM) defense systems, it also acknowledged that a fallout shelter system occupied a secondary position in deterrence, and to that end recommended adopting the FCDA shelter proposal. Two subsequent reports advanced similar ideas. In 1958, the Rockefeller Report, compiled by a board of experts and practitioners directed by Henry Kissinger, stated that civil defense was one aspect of a robust deterrent that should also include more investment in offensive military capabilities. That same year, a report published by the RAND Corporation emphasized the importance of civil defense as a powerful component of deterrence.

Despite these supporting reports, the FCDA shelter proposal continued to run counter to the views of top officials in the Eisenhower Administration. Secretary of State John Foster Dulles argued that the nation should focus resources on retaliation capabilities and curtail the shelter program. Military leaders also opposed the shelter program, fearing it would cut into defense spending. Eisenhower himself remained opposed to the massive shelter program. Instead of pursuing the National Shelter Policy, he instructed the FCDA to initiate much more limited actions, including research on fallout shelters, a survey of existing structures, and informing the public about shelters.

Holifield and other legislators were outraged that the President would disregard the findings of three separate committees. Supporters of the shelter system publicly expressed disappointment with the Eisenhower administration, and Holifield commented that civil defense was in a "deplorable" state during this period. Finally, in the face of strong criticism,

Eisenhower largely dissolved the FCDA to make way for the short-lived Office of Civil and Defense Mobilization (OCDM), which began the bulk of its work during the Kennedy presidency.

It bears noting that for all of his public opposition to massive sheltering programs, in the middle of his tenure Eisenhower secretly commissioned the building of an underground bunker in West Virginia that would serve as a safe haven for top members of Congress, in the event of a catastrophe. The project was similar in scope and intent to one initiated by President Truman in 1951. Called "Site R," that effort involved construction of an Alternate Joint Communications Center in Raven Rock Mountain, Pennsylvania, to be used in case existing centers in Washington, DC were destroyed by an attack. Like his predecessor, Eisenhower believed it was vital for the government to ensure continuity of operations following an attack on the homeland. The West Virginia bunker was built under the five-star Greenbrier resort and was only placed on full alert once, during the Cuban Missile Crisis in 1962. The public remained completely unaware of the operation until 1992 when the Washington Post broke the story.

Kennedy Administration (1961-1963)

During the first year of his presidency, John F. Kennedy made civil defense more of a priority than at any previous time in U.S. history. He was also the first President to discuss

civil defense publicly, issuing an appeal in the September 7, 1961 issue of LIFE magazine to all Americans to protect themselves "and in doing so strengthen [the] nation." Kennedy continued the approach of his predecessors of including civil defense in deterrence calculations, and he believed that the only effective deterrent was a strong retaliatory capability. However, he also believed that deterrence could fail in the event one faced an irrational enemy, and thus a strong and coordinated approach to civil defense was required. As he stated to Congress on May 25, 1961: "[Civil defense] can be readily justifiable...as insurance for the civilian population in case of an

President John F. Kennedy in his historic "Moon" message to a joint session of Congress on May 25, 1961 also addresses the equally important topic of Civil Defense. Photo credit: NASA.

enemy miscalculation. It is insurance we trust will never be needed – but insurance which we could never forgive ourselves for foregoing in the event of catastrophe."

He concluded by proposing "a nationwide long-range program of identifying present fallout shelter capacity and providing shelter in new and existing structures." To accomplish these goals, Kennedy issued Executive Order 10952 on July 20, 1961, which divided the Office of Civil Defense and Mobilization into two new organizations: the Office of Emergency

Planning (OEP) and the Office of Civil Defense. OEP was part of the President's Executive Office and tasked with advising and assisting the President in determining policy for all nonmilitary emergency preparedness, including civil defense. OCD was part of the Office of the Secretary of Defense, and was tasked with overseeing the nation's civil defense program. The responsibility for carrying out the fallout shelter program was among the program operations assigned to Secretary of Defense Robert McNamara.

The 1961 Berlin crisis gave Kennedy renewed urgency to improve US civil defense. The President emphasized the importance of fallout shelters as a means to save lives.

He stressed that identifying and stocking existing shelters with food and medicine should be made a priority. McNamara explained that this approach was not a major departure from the Eisenhower shelter program; however, the scope was larger and thus required more money. The goal was to provide maximum protection through cost effective means by utilizing existing buildings. Some members of Congress, notably the ranking Republican of the House Appropriations Committee, John Taber, worked hard to limit funding to the shelter project. However, most underscored the importance of the shelter program as a rational response to the growing threat of a nuclear attack. Congress ultimately approved more than $200 million that Kennedy asked for the project, which was twice as much as Eisenhower had ever requested for civil defense.

With the appropriated funds, OCD began a nationwide survey of all existing shelters. In order to be designated a public shelter, a facility had to have enough space for at least 50 people, include one cubic foot of storage space per person, and have a radiation protection factor of at least 100. The materials division of DOD, called the Defense Supply Agency, furnished shelter supplies to local governments, which were then responsible for stocking all shelters in their regions. By 1963, 104 million individual shelter spaces had been identified; and of those 47 million had been licensed, 46 million marked, and 9 million individual spaces had been stocked with supplies.

The President also decided to distribute booklets to the populace that would outline the purpose of the shelter program and the steps that every American should take during an attack. The booklet, created by a team of Madison Avenue writers, was to be sent to every household in the nation. In an unintended twist, the booklets themselves created new controversy. Some presidential aides felt that the pictures used were too graphic, while others felt that they indicated the booklet was meant only for the upper class. Ultimately the Kennedy Administration decided to tone down the content, so as not to cause unnecessary alarm. The booklets were then sent to post offices throughout the nation, so people could pick up copies.

The means of communicating the Administration's civil defense message to the public was not the only target of controversy during this time. Reviving a long-standing debate, some prominent members of Congress, including Albert Thomas, the Chairman of the House Appropriations Subcommittee in charge of civil defense, felt that the Federal government should not be undertaking such a massive sheltering project when civil defense responsibility belonged to State and local governments. Kennedy convened a meeting with eighteen of his top advisors at Hyannis Port, Massachusetts, on the day after Thanksgiving in 1961 to discuss the appropriate next steps for civil defense. There, consensus evolved that the Federal government's primary role was to provide community shelters.

Johnson Administration (1963-1969)

Kennedy's assassination in November 1963 marked the beginning of a drastic cutback in funding of the Nation's civil defense program. The topic began to fall slowly off the public radar, and President Lyndon B. Johnson allowed it to slip further by not pressuring Congress to pass the Shelter Incentive Program bill, which proposed to give every non-profit institution financial compensation for each shelter it built.

Earlier in the decade, Secretary McNamara had begun to describe the concept of "mutual assured destruction" (MAD), which essentially meant that the Soviet Union and the United States had the capacity to effectively annihilate one another with the weapons in their arsenals, such that this constituted an effective deterrent to offensive action. Congress and the public began to accept the doctrine of MAD. As a result, a growing percentage of the population began to wonder if civil defense programs could adequately

Secretary of Defense Robert McNamara in discussion with President Lyndon Johnson, Oval Office of the White House, November 27, 1967. Photo credit: Yoichi Okamoto, courtesy of Lyndon Johnson Library.

protect citizens from a large scale nuclear attack. However, when the U.S. military began expanding its ABM defense system, McNamara re-emphasized the importance of a shelter system because he questioned the wisdom of relying solely on an ABM defense. He argued that "the effectiveness of an ABM defense system in saving lives depends in large part upon the availability of adequate fallout shelters for the population." The belief was that the ABM defense system could be beaten by detonating nuclear weapons upwind of large metropolitan areas and outside the range of the defensive missiles. The result would be radioactive fallout spreading across America's cities. Large numbers of people would die from the exposure to the fallout, unless there were a sufficient number of shelters. Congress opposed financing a shelter system, and McNamara continued to be pessimistic about an ABM defense system saying, "Whether we will ever be able to advance the art of defense as rapidly as the art of offensive developments...I don't know. At the moment it doesn't look at all likely."

In an ironic twist, attention to civil defense was also undermined by a series of major natural disasters that rattled the Nation. Hurricanes Hilda and Betsy devastated the Southeast, an Alaskan earthquake caused a damaging tidal wave in California, and a lethal tornado swept through Indiana on Palm Sunday in 1965. Senator Birch Bayh of Indiana sponsored legislation that granted emergency Federal loan assistance to disaster victims. The bill passed in 1966, and Bayh urged Congress over the next few years to provide even more disaster assistance to citizens. The concept of all-hazards assistance was gaining adherents, at the expense of civil preparedness for attack.

The Vietnam War struck a further blow to civil defense during the Johnson years. As the war progressed, it required increasing amounts of time, money, and resources. Although civil defense efforts continued to receive modest funding, and would for the next twelve years, no major steps were taken to enhance overall capabilities. A transformation in the way the Federal government viewed the task of protecting the public had begun.

Nixon Administration (1969-1974)

By the time President Nixon entered office, public and government interest in civil defense had fallen precipitously from its peak in the early 1960s. According to the New York Times Index, in 1968, only four articles on civil defense appeared in that publication compared to 72 in 1963. However, the new administration did make a major contribution to civil defense by redefining civil defense policy to include preparedness for natural disasters. In no small measure, the President's thinking resulted from the Federal government's lack of preparedness to handle the horrific damage wrought by Hurricane Camille (see discussion below). Upon entering office, Nixon immediately tasked the OEP to complete a broad review of the Nation's civil defense programs.

In June 1970, the OEP released the results of its comprehensive assessment in National Security Study Memorandum 57. The study concluded that the Nation's preparedness for natural disasters was minimal to nonexistent. The Administration responded by introducing two of its most significant domestic policy changes in National Security Decision Memorandum (NSDM) 184. NSDM 184 recommended the establishment of a "dual-use approach" to Federal citizen preparedness programs and the replacement of the Office of Civil Defense with the Defense Civil Preparedness Agency (DCPA). President Nixon would later implement these recommendations, placing the new DCPA under the umbrella of the Department of Defense.

For the first time in the history of civil defense, Federal funds previously allocated for the exclusive purpose of preparing for military attacks could be shared with State and local governments for natural disaster preparedness. This dual-use initiative subscribed to the philosophy that preparations for evacuation, communications, and survival are common to both natural disasters and enemy military strikes on the homeland. From a practical perspective, the dual-use approach allowed more efficient utilization of limited resources, so planners could address a larger number of scenarios. Given that civil defense funding during Nixon's first term barely exceeded the low $80 million per year level of the Eisenhower

Administration (when adjusted for inflation), scarce resources likely played a part in the decision to adopt the new approach.

A series of natural disasters during Nixon's tenure also increased the pressure to expand civil defense to include preparation and response to natural disasters. Several major hurricanes and earthquakes exposed significant flaws in natural disaster preparedness at a time when no centralized system for disaster relief existed. Perhaps most significantly, in August 1969 Hurricane Camille wreaked havoc in the greater Gulf Coast region, highlighting major problems with disaster response. In response, Congress passed the Disaster Relief Act of 1969,

Hurricane Camille caused 256 deaths and $1.421 billion in damages in August 1969. Photo credit: National Oceanic and Atmospheric Administration.

which created the concept of a Federal Coordinating Officer (FCO). The FCO was an individual appointed by the President, who would manage federal disaster assistance on-the-spot at a given disaster area.

The President's decision to increase focus on natural disaster preparedness also aligned with U.S. foreign policy considerations. In order to reinforce the doctrine of MAD, Nixon was deeply involved in negotiations with the Soviet Union to limit defensive weapon capabilities. The first Strategic Arms Limitation Talks treaty (SALT I), signed on May 26, 1972, froze the number of strategic ballistic missile launchers and allowed the addition of new submarine ballistic missile launchers only as replacements for dismantled older launchers. Perhaps most significantly, SALT I limited the superpowers to only two ABM defense deployment sites. Advocates of SALT argued that such agreements were necessary because any increase in defense capabilities would spur another arms race for improved offensive capabilities. The Nixon Administration felt that the SALT I advances would be jeopardized if either side continued to build up nuclear attack-related civil defense programs. This concern helped justify the decision to turn more attention toward civil preparedness for natural disasters.

The dual use approach was attractive to State and local authorities. While in the past State and local officials had been reluctant to participate in nuclear attack planning, the ability to deal with attack preparedness in the context of a particular hazard in a specific area (e.g. floods in coastal or riverine areas, hurricanes in coastal areas, tornadoes in the Midwest and

Plains States, and civil unrest in urban areas) encouraged new coordination and participation.

The change of focus also garnered public support. The interest of the American public in attack planning had waned considerably. There was little enthusiasm for ambitious shelter building projects or evacuation drills. A number of historians attribute this lack of interest to a diminished perception of risk, psychological numbing to the destruction of nuclear weapons, and a growing belief that civil defense measures would not ultimately be effective in the event of nuclear war. Planning for natural disasters was perceived to be more effective, less resource intensive, and able to deliver tangible benefits at the State and local level.

Nixon's broad policy changes were accompanied by equally sweeping organizational changes. Following the replacement of the OCD with the DCPA, another major reorganization took place. In 1970 and 1973, Reorganization Plans 1 and 2 abolished the Office of Emergency Planning and delegated its functions to various agencies. Executive Order 11725 of 1973 solidified the new organizational structure by distributing preparedness tasks to a wide variety of new agencies including the Department of Housing and Urban Development (HUD), the General Services Administration, and the Departments of the Treasury and Commerce. In total, the new bureaucratic structure placed responsibility for disaster relief with more than 100 federal agencies. Not surprisingly, this reorganization is perhaps best known for its ineffectiveness.

Despite the suggestion of great activity, real progress on civil defense, both in the traditional sense and its new dual-use direction, was limited during the Nixon Administration. One illustrative example is the signing into law of the Disaster Relief Act of 1974 (Public Law 93-288). While the Disaster Relief Act sought to remedy bureaucratic inefficiencies and provide direct assistance to individuals and families following a disaster, funding remained low, with levels comparable to spending in the pre-Kennedy years. The Act did succeed in involving State and local governments in all hazards preparedness activities and provided matching funds for their programs. However, soon the federal government's emphasis on all-hazards preparedness would lessen.

Ford Administration (1974-1977)

At first, the Ford Administration supported its predecessor's approach to dual-use preparedness. In March 1975 President Ford strongly endorsed the policy, stating: "I am particularly pleased that civil defense planning today emphasizes the dual use of resources...we are improving our ability to respond...to national disasters..." However, less than a year later, the Office of Management and Budget (OMB) rescinded DOD's use of civil defense funding for natural disaster mitigation and preparedness. Civil defense was returned to the original orientation of nuclear attack preparedness, as seen during the Truman and Eisenhower years.

There were several motivations for this policy change. Perhaps most importantly, the United States had just resumed its intelligence observations of Soviet civil defense after a five year break. Reports from these operations detailed significant Soviet progress in civil defense, compared to relatively small U.S. efforts. Massive Soviet expenditures (estimated at $1 billion per year in 1977) on preparedness initiatives, such as evacuation plans, contributed to a growing concern that the United States was falling behind. Whereas in the United States, civil defense was considered "an insurance policy," the Soviets considered it a "factor of great strategic significance." The most alarmist American commentators concluded that the entire U.S. nuclear arsenal could not inflict significant damage on the Soviet Union, due in large part to its increased civil preparedness.

Developments in Cold War diplomacy likely also contributed to the temporary end of all-hazards planning. Gradually the doctrine of MAD was replaced with new ideas, such as limited nuclear strikes against strategically important military and industrial targets, rather

than population centers. As early as January 10, 1974 Secretary of Defense James Schlesinger stated during a press conference that "the old policy [of MAD]...was no longer adequate for deterrence" and should be replaced by "a set of selective options against different sets of targets." Over the next decade, these ideas of flexible targeting and limited retaliation developed into the policy of "flexible response." Flexible response was based on the idea that both the Soviet Union and the United States had the capability for small-scale nuclear attacks that could be answered by similarly-sized acts of

Secretary of Defense James Schlesinger conducts a Press Briefing in the Pentagon.   October 2, 1975. Photo credit: Office of the Secretary of Defense.

retaliation by the other side. Theoretically, instead of massive retaliation against population centers, targets would be specific, highly-strategic sites. Since some of these sites could be civilian in nature, some level of civil defense and nuclear attack preparedness was deemed necessary. Thus, U.S. policy makers renewed their attention on civil defense, as a means of protecting against targeted highly-strategic attacks.

One result was a new initiative called the Crisis Relocation Plan (CRP). Begun in 1974 by Secretary of Defense James Schlesinger, the CRP favored a strategy of evacuation rather than sheltering. Directed by the DCPA, CRP evacuation planning was conducted at the State level with Federal funds and encompassed all of the necessary support for relocation, food distribution, and medical care. Under the CRP, urban residents would be relocated to rural host counties, with a target ratio of "5 immigrants for every native." The focus on preparedness through the CRP was continued throughout the Ford Administration by incoming Secretary of Defense Donald Rumsfeld, who strongly opposed the dual-use approach. Rumsfeld believed that the Federal government should address only attack preparedness, while peacetime disasters were a State and local responsibility.

Though Administration officials and policymakers defended the CRP as a set of simple and highly effective procedures, the program suffered widespread criticism. The Plan's reliance on a relatively long warning time (1 to 2 days), compared to the shorter notice necessary for sheltering, meant it could only be effective in a situation of rising tensions in which the launch of missiles against the country could be predicted. Additionally, vocal critics from Congress and the public doubted the feasibility of such large-scale evacuations through bottlenecked transportation routes.

Organizationally, the fragmentation of civil defense responsibilities begun under Nixon became increasingly apparent. Nixon's reorganization plans prescribed that the bulk of the responsibility for civil defense fall to three different agencies: the OEP would advise the President, HUD's Federal Disaster Assistance Agency would manage disaster relief, and the DCPA would coordinate State and local preparedness efforts Though these bureaucratic changes were not complete until the Carter Administration, some Congressional committees were already beginning to investigate the problem of disjointed civil defense. In 1976, the House Armed Services Committee recommended that an office within the Executive Office of the President (EOP) be tasked to manage civil defense, while the Joint Committee on Defense Production recommended combining the three agencies into one body. These recommendations, coming during the final months of the Ford Administration, were evaluated in the subsequent Carter Administration.

Overall civil defense funding during Ford's tenure did not change significantly from the Nixon years. With the implementation of the CRP, Secretary of Defense Schlesinger made modest increases in the 1975 budget to develop city evacuation plans and implement population defenses. However, as in previous Administrations, civil defense still competed for funding against more traditional military expenditures, and the 1975 increases were nullified the following year in favor of spending on offensive military capabilities.

In sum, despite ambitious claims of progress by the Ford Administration, civil defense programs within the United States remained less than effective. U.S. nuclear deterrence plans still emphasized offensive capabilities. In its evaluation of the state of civil defense in 1976, the Congressional Research Service unconditionally labeled the efforts "a charade." It would be another five years before significant progress was made.

Carter Administration (1977-1981)

Upon taking office, President Carter immediately began a review of the disjointed system of bureaucracies that managed civil defense. An interagency study led to Presidential Review Memorandum 32 in September of 1977. The study concurred with the 1976 recommendations of the House Armed Services Committee and Joint Committee on Defense Production that the various civil defense agencies must be combined into one coherent agency in direct contact with the White House. In response, Carter issued Presidential Directive (PD) 41 in September of 1978, which sought to clarify the Administration's view of civil defense. However, it did not offer any particular plan for implementation. According to PD 41, civil defense was an element in the strategy to "enhance deterrence and stability". Civil defense still did not become a priority for the

Administration, which concluded that it was not necessary to pursue "equivalent survivability" with the Soviet Union.

Meanwhile, in the midst of a lengthy debate regarding the creation of a single disaster preparedness agency, an unprecedented civilian nuclear accident unfolded on March 28, 1979 at the nuclear energy plant on Three Mile Island, near Harrisburg, Pennsylvania. By highlighting the slow response, poor local-Federal coordination, and miscommunications that occurred; the accident dramatically demonstrated the need for more effective disaster coordination and planning. Partially in response to the near nuclear disaster, on July 20, 1979 the Administration issued Executive Order 12148, which established the Federal Emergency Management Agency (FEMA) as the lead agency for coordinating Federal disaster relief efforts. FEMA absorbed the Federal Insurance Administration, the National Fire Prevention and Control Administration, the National Weather Service Community Preparedness Program, the Federal Preparedness Agency of the General Services Administration, and the Federal Disaster Assistance Administration activities from HUD, and combined them into a single independent agency. At the time, the creation of FEMA represented the single largest consolidation of civil defense efforts in U.S. history.

Despite the reorganization and move toward greater mission clarity, civil defense planning on the ground did not change dramatically. Practical plans continued to reflect traditional civil defense programs and did not adopt the dual-use approach, though Carter did urge FEMA to direct more of its efforts to coping with peacetime disasters. Evacuation continued to be the focus of Federal planners, and Secretary of Defense Harold Brown reaffirmed his predecessor's crisis relocation strategies. When FEMA assumed responsibility for citizen preparedness, the agency called on civil defense planners nationwide to create area-specific CRPs.

The decision to continue to pursue evacuation as the primary civil defense policy was influenced by several factors. Well-funded and extensive Soviet evacuation programs continued to worry key U.S. decision makers, including Brown. Evacuation also made sense in the context of continued resource limitations. According to a 1979 FEMA report, since effective and cost-efficient sheltering in large cities had proven difficult, "the U.S. nuclear civil defense program developed into an evacuation program...as a low-cost survival alternative."

It is likely that the Carter Administration's focus on evacuation was also affected by Cold War diplomacy. The continuing SALT negotiations created a conflict between the desire to advance U.S. civil defense, and the desire to avoid upsetting the delicate strategic balance required for successful threat reduction negotiations. With this balance in mind, maintaining the status quo by continuing to support evacuation policies may have been deemed the best option.

Though the creation of FEMA and the goals of PD 41 signaled renewed interest in civil defense, funding throughout the Carter Administration remained historically low. The 1980 request for $108 million was less than adequate for implementing the new plans. In the following year, Congress did not meet a higher request for funding, instead choosing to allocate funds to other priorities. As had been the case many times before, funding levels did not match the ambitious plans for program improvement.

In keeping civil defense funding low, Congressional leaders had little public opposition to fear. In contrast to generally widespread public participation and acceptance in the peak years of civil defense during the early stages of the Cold War, most people by this time had little faith that any government civil defense planning could lessen the impact of nuclear war. Some local communities refused outright to cooperate with Federal civil defense mandates because they did not believe the CRPs would be effective if a nuclear attack were to occur. This public attitude would continue throughout the remainder of the Cold War period.

Reagan Administration (1981-1989)

It would appear that Ronald Reagan entered office with the intention of building upon the civil defense foundations set by his predecessors. In December 1981, Congress acted dramatically in favor of the dual-use approach by amending the 1950 Civil Defense Act. In this milestone decision, all future civil defense funds would be allotted for natural disasters, as well as attacks on the homeland. The amendment did stipulate that funding and planning for peacetime disasters could not overtly detract from attack preparedness programs. Nevertheless, dual-use preparedness was promoted with much of the same language and reasoning as it was during the Nixon Administration.

Though Reagan was in favor of the dual-use approach, his civil defense strategy was largely a continuation of Carter's. In the midst of deliberations regarding the 1982 budget, the National Security Council (NSC) compiled National Security Division Directive (NSDD) 26, which spelled out the objectives of Carter's Presidential Directive 41 and was designed to promote deterrence, improve natural disaster preparedness, and reduce the possibility of coercion by enemy forces. The unclassified version of NSDD 26 states: "it is a matter of national priority that the United States have a Civil Defense program which provides for the survival of the U.S. population." However, NSDD 26 went further than PD 41 by stipulating a concrete deadline in 1989 for plans to protect the population, and it mandated that civil defense leaders investigate and enhance protection measures for critical industries in case of attack. Furthermore, NSDD 26 for the first time supported research into the development of strategies to ensure economic survival in the event of a nuclear attack. However, drawing upon the CRPs of his predecessors, Reagan continued to promote evacuation as the primary strategy for civil defense. During this period nuclear preparedness became a top priority for FEMA.

Congress and the Administration came into conflict in February 1982, when the President requested $4.2 billion for a seven-year plan to massively boost civil defense programs. Congress did not react positively to this request, particularly because it seemed to be part of Reagan's hawkish stance on Cold War diplomacy. For example, the House Committee on Appropriations criticized FEMA's dependence on evacuation planning at the expense of other preparedness programs and suggested that more attention be paid to peacetime disaster preparation. Expressing their disagreement with FEMA's plans, Congress allocated only $147.9 million to cover FEMA's 1983 budget, about 58% of what the agency had requested. In 1984 and 1985, Congress again blocked requests for funding increases.

In 1983, FEMA responded to the Congressional push for more peacetime disaster preparation with plans for an Integrated Emergency Management System (IEMS) to develop full all-hazard preparedness plans at the Federal level. Under the IEMS, State civil defense planners would facilitate the development of multi-hazard preparedness plans based on threats faced by specific localities. According to the IEMS, this all-hazards approach included "direction, control and warning systems which are common to the full range of emergencies from small isolated events to the ultimate emergency – war." Despite this innovative attempt to integrate civil defense and disaster preparedness concerns, Congress was not sufficiently convinced that the IEMS would effectively address the

---

Strategic Defense Initiative – Star Wars
Missile Defense Agency, Department of Defense
Missile Defense: The First Sixty Years
2004, Excerpts

President Ronald W. Reagan desired a strategic alternative to the national security policy of nuclear deterrence and mutual assured destruction that left America defenseless against Soviet missile attacks. At the same time, U.S. land-based ICBMs were growing more vulnerable to a Soviet first strike, and the United States was unable to satisfactorily field the MX (renamed "Peacekeeper") missile. These factors influenced the Joint Chiefs of Staff in February 1983 to unanimously recommend that the president begin pursuing a national security strategy with an increased emphasis on strategic defenses. In concert with the Joint Chief's recommendation, several prominent missile defense advocates had been persuading the president to embrace strategic defense; these included physicist Edward Teller, known as the "Father of the Hydrogen Bomb," and retired U.S. Army Lieutenant General Daniel O. Graham, who headed High Frontier, a citizen's organization dedicated to leading the U.S. toward a secure future in space. Consequently, on March 23, 1983, President Reagan announced his decision in a nationally televised speech to launch a major new program, the Strategic Defense Initiative (SDI), to determine whether or not missile defenses were technically feasible.
An unexpected consequence of President Reagan's SDI speech occurred the following day when the *Washington Post* quoted a critical comment from Senator Edward M. Kennedy of Massachusetts, who labeled the speech as "reckless Star Wars schemes." The term "Star Wars" derived from the science fiction film of the same name and had been used previously in references to various exotic Pentagon space weaponry projects. Senator Kennedy's remark, however, gave the term new meaning and SDI became widely identified thereafter as "Star Wars."

---

management of all-hazard preparedness, and therefore never met requested FEMA funding levels.

Cold War diplomacy continued to play a role in civil defense decisions under Reagan. President Reagan supported neither the doctrine of mutual assured destruction nor the détente that had been a centerpiece of the Carter Administration. On March 23, 1983 Reagan openly rejected mutual assured destruction with his speech proposing the Strategic Defense Initiative (SDI). SDI focused on using ground-based and space-based systems to protect the United States from attack by strategic nuclear ballistic missiles. SDI flew in the face of the 1972 SALT I agreement banning strategic defenses, and it demonstrated a shift towards more proactive and aggressive defensive measures.

The final years of the Reagan Administration saw a number of actions intended to allay concerns regarding non-attack preparedness. The Meese Memorandum (Executive Order 12656), signed in 1986, delegated lead response roles to certain Federal agencies, depending on the type of disaster. On November 23, 1988 the Disaster Relief Act of 1974 was amended to become what is now known as the Stafford Act, resulting in a clearer definition of FEMA's role in emergency management. The Act defined the disaster declaration process and provided the statutory authority for Federal assistance during a disaster. The agency's role in disaster response would be tested and debated in the years to come.

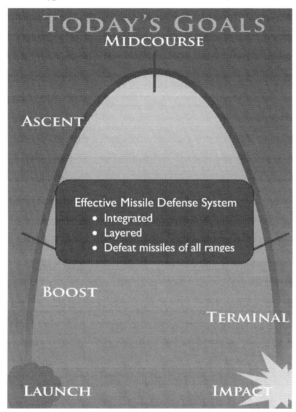

Illustration of US Missile Defense Strategy. Illustration credit: Missile Defense Agency.

Bush Administration (1989-1993)

In the year after George H.W. Bush took office, several natural disasters challenged the Nation's nascent approach to all-hazards preparedness. On March 24, 1989, 11 million gallons of crude oil spilled into Prince William Sound in the Gulf of Alaska from the Exxon Valdez oil tanker. It was the largest oil spill in U.S. history, and the Administration was ill-prepared to manage an environmental crisis of such large scale. Instead of using FEMA through the Stafford Act to coordinate the response, Bush invoked the Federal Water Pollution Control Act, under which the Environmental Protection Agency and Coast Guard managed the event. The Administration drew much criticism for the poor response.

On September 13, 1989, Hurricane Hugo struck the Virgin Islands, Puerto Rico, and South Carolina, inflicting significant damage. This time Bush chose to send Manuel Lujan, Secretary of the Interior, to assess the damage and provide additional executive oversight. FEMA's participation in the response was plagued by shortages of properly trained personnel, communication problems, and a lack of coordination. Within a month of Hurricane Hugo, the Loma Prieta earthquake struck northern California causing an estimated $6 billion in damage. Already stretched thin from dealing with the Hurricane Hugo recovery, FEMA's response continued to be hindered by coordination and staffing problems. Again, President Bush appointed a Cabinet-level representative, Secretary of

Transportation Samuel Skinner, to oversee recovery operations, and again FEMA's contribution to response and recovery was judged inadequate.

The dissatisfaction with FEMA's response to the Exxon Valdez Oil Spill, Hurricane Hugo, and the Loma Prieta Earthquake led FEMA to begin developing the Federal Response Plan (FRP) in November 1990. Drawing from the Incident Command System and Incident Management System framework, the FRP defined how 27 Federal agencies and the American Red Cross would respond to the needs of State and local governments when they were overwhelmed by a disaster. The plan used a functional approach to define the types of assistance (such as food, communications, and transportation) that would be provided by the Federal government to address the consequences of disaster.

By the second year of the Bush administration, significant political changes were occurring. The Berlin Wall fell in 1989, followed shortly by the collapse of the Soviet Union and the fall of communist governments across Eastern Europe. The Cold War had come to a rapid and unanticipated end, and the threat of a strategic nuclear attack on the United States diminished significantly almost overnight. As a result, civil

> **U.S. Executive Office of the President**
> National Security Directive 66
> March 1992, Excerpts
>
> The United States will have a civil defense capability as an element of our overall national security posture. The objective of the civil defense program is to develop the required capabilities common to all catastrophic emergencies and those unique to attack emergencies in order to protect the population and vital infrastructure. Civil defense can contribute to deterrence by denying an enemy any confidence that he could prevent a concerted national response to attack. The civil defense program will support all-hazard integrated emergency management at State and local levels. Disaster-specific programs such as hurricane or flood relief programs which may be incorporated into the civil defense program and which are currently funded within domestic discretionary accounts will continue to be budgeted in this manner. In addition, any equipment or programs not needed for the consequence management of national security emergencies will be funded within the domestic discretionary accounts. The program will be under the direction of the Federal Emergency Management Agency with the support of heads of the Federal Departments and agencies, and under the general policy guidance of the National Security Council. The Department of Defense will support civil authorities in civil defense, to include facilitating the use of the National Guard in each state for response in both peacetime disasters and national security emergencies. Subject to the direction of the President and the Secretary of Defense, readiness of the armed forces for military contingencies will have precedence and civil authorities should not rely exclusively on military support.

defense in the traditional sense was no longer a major priority for emergency planners or Congress. With the recent onslaught of natural and man-made disasters top-of-mind, FEMA planners began to adopt the idea of a true all-hazards approach to disaster preparedness. In March of 1992, President Bush signed National Security Directive 66 instructing FEMA to develop a multi-hazard approach to emergency management, combining civil defense preparedness with natural and man-made disaster preparedness.

Testifying before the Armed Services Subcommittee Hearing on Civil Defense on May 6, 1992, Grant Peterson, Associate Director for State and Local Programs at FEMA, reported that: "[T]he President has approved a new civil defense policy...The new policy acknowledges significant changes in the range of threats, and eliminates the heavy emphasis on nuclear attack. The policy recognizes the need for civil defense to address all forms of catastrophic emergencies, all hazards, and the consequences of those hazards. The new policy increases the emphasis on preparedness to respond to the consequences of all emergencies regardless of their cause. All-hazards consequence management recognizes that regardless of the cause of an emergency situation, certain very basic capabilities are necessary to respond and that planning efforts and resources should be focused on developing the capabilities necessary to respond to all the common effects of all hazards."In August 1992, Hurricane Andrew hit south Florida and the central Louisiana coast. President Bush once again appointed a Cabinet-level representative, Secretary of Transportation Andrew Card, to coordinate Federal relief efforts. Unfortunately, this additional oversight did not result in improved performance as "government at all levels was slow to comprehend the scope of the disaster." And despite the presence of the FRP, FEMA and the other agencies involved in the response and recovery faced the same kinds of coordination and logistical problems they had three years prior. FEMA was strongly criticized by Congress for its poor performance.

As a result of this criticism, FEMA was instructed by Congress to contract with the National Academy of Public Administration (NAPA) to conduct a study of the Federal, State, and local level capacity to respond to major natural disasters. Issued in February 1993, NAPA's assessment, *Coping With Catastrophe*, detailed the obstacles facing emergency management at all levels of government and made recommendations to improve FEMA's ability to prepare and respond to disasters. NAPA concluded that, "a small independent agency could coordinate the federal response to major natural disasters...but only if the White House and Congress take significant steps to make it a viable institution." Because of the timing of the report, it was left to the Clinton Administration to evaluate the findings and implement changes to make FEMA more effective.

Clinton Administration (1993-2001)

Upon taking office, President Bill Clinton appointed James Lee Witt director of FEMA. Witt, the former Director of Emergency Management for the State of Arkansas, immediately reorganized FEMA. He created three functional directorates corresponding to the major phases of emergency management: Mitigation; Preparedness; Training and Exercise; and Response and Recovery. In February of 1996, Clinton elevated the FEMA directorship to Cabinet-level status, improving the line of communication between the Director and the President.

The shift in emergency preparedness towards an all-hazards approach allowed FEMA to focus on addressing natural disasters without having to fear negative political reactions from advocates of civil defense. The Agency's Mitigation Directorate, for example, focused many of its early programs on hazards such as flooding and earthquakes. At the same time, however, recognition of the threat of terrorist attacks inside the United States was beginning to emerge. In 1993, Congress included a joint resolution in the National Defense Authorization Act (NDAA) that called for FEMA to develop "a capability for early detection and warning of and response to: potential terrorist use of chemical or biological agents or weapons; and emergencies or natural disasters involving industrial chemicals or the widespread outbreak of disease."

As evidenced by this resolution, Congress was becoming increasingly concerned about the threat posed by terrorist organizations and technological disasters. Much of this concern resulted from the World Trade Center bombing earlier that year, in which 6 people were killed and 1,042 were wounded. The blast left a five story deep crater and caused $500 million in damages.

In November 1994, the Federal Civil Defense Act of 1950 was repealed and all remnants of civil defense authority were transferred to Title VI of the Stafford Act. This completed the evolution of civil defense into an all-hazards approach to preparedness. FEMA now had the statutory responsibility for coordinating a comprehensive emergency preparedness system to deal with all types of disasters. Title VI also ended all Armed Services Committee oversight over FEMA and significantly reduced the priority of national security programs within FEMA. Money authorized by the Civil Defense Act was reallocated to natural disaster and all-hazards programs, and more than 100 defense and security staff members were reassigned.

Portrait of James Lee Witt, FEMA Director from April 1993 through January 2001. Photo credit: FEMA News Photo.

The period between 1995 and 1996 saw a series of major terrorist attacks launched domestically and abroad, which further influenced U.S. preparedness policies. In March 1995, the Japanese religious cult Aum Shinrikyo released sarin nerve gas on five separate cars of three different subway lines in Tokyo. Twelve people were killed and thousands were injured. One month later, Timothy McVeigh and Terry Nichols detonated a truck bomb at the Alfred P. Murrah Federal Building in Oklahoma City, killing 169 people. On June 25, 1996 the Khobar Towers, a U.S. military facility in Dhahran, Saudi Arabia was bombed, killing 19 Americans.

These events had a profound effect on U.S. lawmakers and the Administration. Two days after the bombing of the Khobar Towers, the Senate adopted an amendment aimed at preventing terrorists from using nuclear, chemical, or biological weapons in the United States. In September Congress passed the NDAA for fiscal year 1997, which included the

Defense Against Weapons of Mass Destruction Act commonly known as the Nunn-Lugar-Domenici Act. This Act required DOD to provide civilian agencies at all levels of government training and expert advice on appropriate responses to the use of a weapon of mass destruction (WMD) against the American public. Lawmakers originally planned to have FEMA lead the training and provide equipment; however, FEMA officials had testified that only DOD had the necessary knowledge and assets.

As a result of the Nunn-Lugar-Domenici legislation, Metropolitan Medical Strike Force Teams were created, as well as a domestic terrorism rapid response team, whose purpose was to aid State and local officials in WMD response. Three years later, WMD preparedness was transferred from DOD to the Office of Domestic Preparedness (ODP) within the Department of Justice (DOJ). In 1999, DOD also established 10 National Guard Rapid Assessment and Initial Detection (RAID) teams, which served to provide technical expertise and equipment to deal with a WMD attack. The unanticipated result of these actions was a new fragmentation of responsibility for civilian preparedness programs. Despite its overtures toward all-hazards preparedness, many of FEMA's efforts remained focused on natural disasters. Meanwhile, DOD through its RAID teams, and DOJ through ODP, became increasingly involved in preparations for and responses to WMD threats.

Apart from these efforts, as the century came to a close, a new concept of homeland security began to emerge. Presidential Decision Directive (PDD) 62, signed in May 1998, created the Office of the National Coordinator for Security, Infrastructure Protection, and Counter-Terrorism within the Executive Office of the President. This office was designed to coordinate counterterrorism policy, preparedness, and consequence management. Later that same year, President Clinton issued PDD 63 on Critical Infrastructure Protection. PDD 63 established principles for protecting the nation by minimizing the threat of smaller-scale terrorist attacks against information technology and geographically-distributed supply chains that could cascade and disrupt entire sectors of the economy. In the absence of a centralized authority for homeland security, Federal agencies were designated as lead agencies in their sector of expertise. The lead agencies were directed to develop sector-specific Information Sharing and Analysis Centers to coordinate efforts with the private sector. PDD 63 also required the creation of a National Infrastructure Assurance Plan.

At the same time, the U.S. Commission on National Security in the 21st Century, chartered by DOD, and known as the Hart-Rudman Commission, began to reexamine U.S. national security policies. One of the Commission's recommendations was the creation of a Cabinet-level National Homeland Security Agency responsible for planning, coordinating, and integrating various U.S. government activities involved in "homeland security". The commission defined homeland security as "the protection of the territory, critical infrastructures, and citizens of the United States by Federal, State, and local government entities from the threat or use of chemical, biological, radiological, nuclear, cyber, or conventional weapons by military or other means." Legislation toward this end was introduced on March 29, 2001, but hearings continued through April of 2001 without passage of the legislation.

Another influential commission formed during the latter stages of the Clinton Administration was the Gilmore Commission, chaired by Virginia Governor Jim Gilmore. The Commission, officially known as the Advisory Panel to Assess Domestic Response Capabilities for Terrorism Involving Weapons of Mass Destruction, developed and delivered a series of five reports to the President and Congress between 1999 and 2003. Of the Gilmore Commission's 164 recommendations, 146 were adopted in whole or in part, including creation of a fusion center to integrate and analyze all intelligence pertaining to terrorism and counterterrorism and the creation of a civil liberties oversight board. However, the impetus to implement many of these recommendations only occurred following the series of devastating attacks on the U.S. homeland that occurred during the initial months of the next administration.

Bush Administration (2001)

The initial months of George W. Bush's presidency saw a general continuation of existing homeland security policies. Prior to the terrorist attacks of September 11, 2001, OMB summarized homeland security as focused on three objectives: counterterrorism, defense against WMD, and the protection of critical infrastructure.

The new Administration did implement changes that affected how national security and homeland security policies would be generated. The Administration abolished the system of ad hoc interagency working groups used by Clinton to address homeland security issues and replaced them with Policy Coordination Committees within the National Security Council. A Counterterrorism and National Preparedness Policy Coordinating Committee was established that was composed of four working groups: Continuity of Federal Operations, Counterterrorism and Security, Preparedness and WMD, and Information Infrastructure Protection and Assurance. The goal of this reorganization was to create a more formalized structure to deal with threats to the homeland.

Then came the September 11, 2001 terrorist attacks. In their wake, there was near-universal agreement within the Federal government that homeland security required a major reassessment, increased funding, and administrative reorganization.

Editor's Comments

Indeed, the theory of "homeland security" has evolved over the decades since World War II. The immediate aftermath of that war brought significant changes to the political landscape of the world. New governments, new policies, and a new balance of world power had been established. With that, a harsh new reality was born - a new and formidable enemy with equal or superior weaponry, larger armies, limitless capabilities, and an aggressive leader. The Soviet Union had emerged as a serious and imminent threat to the United States.

Throughout most of the post World War II presidential administrations, the idea of protecting our homeland centered around the concept of "civil defense". Preparing citizens for nuclear war drew heated debate with sharp contrasting opinions. Whether it was shelter-in-place through fallout bunkers and air raid facilities, or evacuation plans for the major-targeted cities, early political debate focused mostly on reactionary methodologies. It was this singular and narrow approach that hindered the development of true homeland security efforts and placed the United States at a far greater risk for almost half a century.

As the 20th century edged forward, new theories began to emerge. Strict civil defense mindsets gave way to early "emergency management" thinking. Simply instructing citizens - how to survive a devastating enemy attack - was no longer acceptable. Recovery processes were deemed as equally important. These recovery models led to discussions in continuity of operations, threat and vulnerability assessment, and risk mitigation. The true seeds of homeland security had been sewn.

Soon after the fall of the great Soviet empire in the late 1980's, the paramount threat facing the United States would be shifted from nuclear war to a new type of threat – at least new to the continental United States. As evidenced by the horrific events of September 11, 2001, the threat of acts of international terrorism on the United States' infrastructure should be considered real, forthcoming, and significant.

Further Discussion

1. Discuss the **Office of Civilian Defense**, in particular, its successes, failures, and importance.

2. Discuss the **Bull Report** and its impact on the federal government's responsibility for civil defense.

3. Discuss the concept of **Mutual Assured Destruction (MAD)**, the pros and cons.

4. Discuss the contributions of the **Carter Administration** with regard to civil defense planning.

5. Discuss the significance of the **Witt appointment** by the Clinton administration.

Chapter 02

The History of the Department of Homeland Security

"This is a day when all Americans from every walk of life unite in our resolve for justice and peace. America has stood down enemies before, and we will do so this time. None of us will ever forget this day. Yet, we go forward to defend freedom and all that is good and just in our world."

President George W. Bush, September 11, 2001

United States Department of Homeland Security
Brief Documentary History of the Department of
Homeland Security, 2001 – 2008
2008, (Excerpts)

Before the establishment of the Department of Homeland Security, homeland security activities were spread across more than 40 federal agencies and an estimated 2,000 separate Congressional appropriations accounts.

In February 2001, the U.S. Commission on National Security/21st Century (Hart-Rudman Commission) issued its Phase III Report, recommending significant and comprehensive institutional and procedural changes throughout the executive and legislative branches in order to meet future national security challenges. Among these recommendations was the creation of a new National Homeland Security Agency to consolidate and refine the missions of the different departments and agencies that had a role in U.S. homeland security.

In March 2001, Representative Mac Thornberry (R-TX) proposed a bill to create a National Homeland Security Agency, following the recommendations of the U.S. Commission on National Security/21st Century (Hart-Rudman Commission). The bill combined FEMA, Customs, the Border Patrol, and several infrastructure offices into one agency responsible for homeland security-related activities. Hearings were held, but Congress took no further action on the bill.

The Office of Homeland Security

Eleven days after the September 11, 2001, terrorist attacks, President George W. Bush announced that he would create an Office of Homeland Security in the White House and

appoint Pennsylvania Governor Tom Ridge as the director. The office would oversee and coordinate a comprehensive national strategy to safeguard the country against terrorism, and respond to any future attacks.

Executive Order 13228, issued on October 8, 2001, established two entities within the White House to determine homeland security policy: the Office of Homeland Security (OHS) within the Executive Office of the President,

Former Pennsylvania Governor Tom Ridge is selected as the first Assistant to the President for Homeland Security. White House Photo by Eric Draper.

tasked to develop and implement a national strategy to coordinate federal, state, and local counter-terrorism efforts to secure the country from and respond to terrorist threats or attacks, and the Homeland Security Council

The Department of Homeland Security Seal

Overview

The Department of Homeland Security seal was created in June 2003 and is symbolic of the Department's mission - to prevent attacks and protect Americans - on the land, in the sea and in the air.

Description

In the center of the seal, a graphically styled white American eagle appears in a circular blue field. The eagle's outstretched wings break through an inner red ring into an outer white ring that contains the words "U.S. DEPARTMENT OF" in the top half and "HOMELAND SECURITY" in the bottom half in a circular placement.

The eagle's wings break through the inner circle into the outer ring to suggest that the Department of Homeland Security will break through traditional bureaucracy and perform government functions differently. In the tradition of the Great Seal of the United States, the eagle's talon on the left holds an olive branch with 13 leaves and 13 seeds while the eagle's talon on the right grasps 13 arrows.

Centered on the eagle's breast is a shield divided into three sections containing elements that represent the American homeland - air, land, and sea. The top element, a dark blue sky, contains 22 stars representing the original 22 entities that have come together to form the department. The left shield element contains white mountains behind a green plain underneath a light blue sky. The right shield element contains four wave shapes representing the oceans alternating light and dark blue separated by white lines.

Source: http://www.dhs.gov/department-homeland-security-seal

(HSC), composed of Cabinet members responsible for homeland security-related activities, was to advise the President on homeland security matters, mirroring the role the National Security Council (NSC) plays in national security.

The first Homeland Security Presidential Directive (HSPD-1) further delineated the organization and mission of the Homeland Security Council. Future HSPDs recorded and communicated presidential policy with regard to homeland security.

On March 21, 2002, President Bush issued Executive Order 13260, establishing the President's Homeland Security Advisory Council (PHSAC). Members of the PHSAC served as advisors to the president on homeland security matters and represented the private sector, academia, professional service associations, federally funded research and development centers, nongovernmental organizations, state and local governments, and other related professions and communities. The PHSAC held its first meeting on June 12, 2002.

EO 13260 requires the PHSAC to renew its charter every two years. After the creation of DHS, the Council re-chartered itself as the Homeland Security Advisory Council (HSAC) and became an advisory committee to the Secretary of Homeland Security. The Secretary's HSAC held its first meeting on June 30, 2003.

Creating the Department of Homeland Security

One month after the September 11 attacks, Senator Joseph Lieberman (D-CT) introduced S. 1534, a bill to establish a Department of National Homeland Security, co-sponsored by Senator Arlen Specter (R-PA). Following the recommendations of the Hart-Rudman Commission, the bill intended to unite the Federal Emergency Management Agency, the Customs Service, the Border Patrol, the Coast Guard, and agencies responsible for critical infrastructure protection in a Cabinet-level department. The language was similar to H.R 1158 introduced in the House by Mac Thornberry (R-TX) on March 21, 2001. Although hearings were held on the Lieberman bill, there was no further action taken.

In February 2002, President George W. Bush released the FY2003 Budget, the federal government's first post-September 11 budget. The proposed FY 2003 Budget directed $37.7 billion (up from $19.5 billion in 2002) to homeland security efforts, including support for first responders, bioterrorism prevention efforts, border security, and technology, reflecting an increased focus on homeland security.

On June 6, 2002, President Bush addressed the nation and proposed the creation of a permanent Cabinet-level Department of Homeland Security to unite essential agencies charged with protecting the homeland. He outlined four essential missions that corresponded to the four proposed divisions in the department:

1. Border and Transportation Security - Control the borders and prevent terrorists and explosives from entering the country.

2. Emergency Preparedness and Response - Work with state and local authorities to respond quickly and effectively to emergencies.

3. Chemical, Biological, Radiological, and Nuclear Countermeasures - Bring together the country's best scientists to develop technologies that detect biological, chemical, and nuclear weapons to best protect citizens.

4. Information Analysis and Infrastructure Protection - Review intelligence and law enforcement information from all agencies of government, and produce a single daily picture of threats against the homeland.

After his speech, the White House released a document outlining the proposed Department of Homeland Security. The proposal included organization charts of the department, a chart of major government departments and agencies responsible for homeland security activities, congressional committees responsible for homeland security activities, appropriations requested for the new department in the FY2003 budget, and a timeline of administration activities after the 9/11 terrorist attacks.

Although the President of the United States may propose legislation, only Congress can sponsor and pass the legislation necessary to create a new Cabinet-level department. On June 18, 2002, President Bush formally submitted to Congress his proposal for the Department of Homeland Security, including his proposed text for the Homeland Security Act of 2002. The language of the proposal is almost identical to that in the June 6, 2002, document. An analysis of the bill is at the end of the proposal.

After proposing legislation to form the Department of Homeland Security, President Bush issued an executive order that created a Transition Planning Office (TPO) to coordinate, guide, and conduct transition related planning throughout the executive branch of the federal government in preparation for establishment of the proposed Department of Homeland

Security. Bush appointed Assistant to the President for Homeland Security Tom Ridge as the Transition Planning Office Director.

The divisions of the Transition Planning Office aligned with the planned directorates and functions of the future department, including Border and Transportation Security, Information Analysis and Information Protection, Science and Technology, Emergency Preparedness and Response, Communications, etc.

The Transition Planning Office drew its staff from the Office of Homeland Security (OHS), government entities identified for transfer to the Department, such as the Coast Guard, the Transportation Security Administration, and FEMA, as well as from departments and agencies expected to work with the Department, such as the Department of Energy, the Department of Transportation, and the Department of Justice. Although the staffs often overlapped, the TPO was located within the Office of Management and Budget (OMB), not the Office of Homeland Security. OHS employees working in the TPO were required to maintain separate files, email addresses, and funds.

mission

In July 2002, the White House released the first National Strategy for Homeland Security. Developed by the Office of Homeland Security, the National Strategy identified three objectives:

which one shnd fcs been?

1. Prevent terrorist attacks within the United States;

2. Reduce America's vulnerability to terrorism; and *- shnd the joint effut*

3. Minimize the damage and recover from attacks that do occur.

In addition to providing one of the first post 9/11 definitions of "homeland security," the National Strategy also provided direction to federal government departments and agencies homeland security functions and suggested steps that state and local governments, private companies and organizations, and individual Americans could take to improve security.

On June 24, 2002, Representative Dick Armey (R-TX) introduced the President's proposed legislation for the Department to the House of Representatives as H.R. 5005. After amendments in Committee, the bill passed the House by recorded vote (295 to 132) on July 26, 2002. The Senate passed the bill with amendments on November 19, 2002, by a vote of 90 to 9.

President George W. Bush signed the Homeland Security Act of 2002 into law on November 25, 2002.

Section 1502 of the Homeland Security Act of 2002 stipulates that the President could submit a reorganization plan to Congress no later than 60 days after the enactment of the Act. On November 25, 2002, the same day he signed the bill into law, President Bush submitted a reorganization plan in accordance with Section 1502. The plan outlined the time frame for the organization of the new department, setting January 24, 2003, as the effective date of establishment for the Department of Homeland Security. In addition to his own office, the new Secretary was to begin establishing the directorates and offices newly created by the Homeland Security Act and appointing Under Secretaries and Assistant Secretaries. The plan established March 1, 2003, as the date on which the majority of the previously existing agencies, such as the Federal Emergency Management Agency (FEMA), the Transportation Security Administration (TSA), the Coast Guard, the Customs Service, and the United States Secret Service would be transferred to the new department.

The plan also includes a letters from Bush and Mitchell Daniels, Director of the Office of Management and Budget, outlining the plan.

The Department of Homeland Security became operational on January 24, 2003, sixty days after the Homeland Security Act was passed. On that same day, Tom Ridge was sworn in as the first Secretary of Homeland Security. An early DHS organization chart was posted on the DHS web site on January 24, 2003. Along the bottom are the original five directorates: Border and Transportation Security, Emergency Preparedness and Response, Information Analysis and Infrastructure Protection, Management, and Science and Technology. The list of direct reports to the Secretary is incomplete. The chart lists the positions of Assistant Secretary for Border

Security and the Commissioner of Customs under the Under Secretary for Border and Transportation Security. These positions were renamed as the Assistant Secretary for Immigration and Customs Enforcement and the Commissioner of Customs and Border Protection in the Reorganization Plan of January 30, 2003.

Just as the Homeland Security Act of 2002 altered statutes to account for the creation of the Department of Homeland Security, some executive orders required alteration. On January 23, 2003, President George W. Bush issued Executive Order 13284, which outlined changes related to the establishment of the Office of the Secretary on January 24. Later, on February 28, 2003, the President issued Executive Order 13286, which outlined changes that pertained to the transfer of most of the new components to the Department on March 1, 2003. This executive order also outlined the order of succession for the Department.

On January 30, 2003, President Bush submitted a modification to the November 2002 reorganization plan that established and described new organizational units in the Border and Transportation Security Directorate.

Although Section 442 of the Homeland Security Act established a Bureau of Border Security within the Border and Transportation Security Directorate, it did not fully delineate its responsibilities, nor did the November 25, 2002, reorganization plan. The January 2003 plan renamed the Bureau of Border Security as the Bureau of Immigration and Customs Enforcement (now known as U.S. Immigration and Customs Enforcement, or ICE), incorporating parts of the Immigration and Naturalization Service (INS), the Customs Service, and the Federal Protective Service (FPS) and outlined its functions: to enforce immigration and customs laws within the interior of the United States and to protect specified federal buildings.

The January 2003 plan also renamed the U.S. Customs Service as the Bureau of Customs and Border Protection (now known as U.S. Customs and Border Protection, or CBP). The new Bureau incorporated the border and ports of entry functions of the Customs Service, inspection responsibilities and the Border Patrol from INS, and agricultural inspection functions from the Department of Agriculture.

March 1, 2003 marks the official inception date of the Department of Homeland Security. On that date, the majority of the previously existing agencies, such as the Federal Emergency Management Agency (FEMA), the Transportation Security Administration (TSA), the Coast Guard, the Customs Service, and the United States Secret Service transferred to the new department.

Editor's Comments

Original Federal Agencies of the Department of Homeland Security

1. The U.S. Customs Service (Treasury)
2. The Immigration and Naturalization Service (Justice)
3. The Federal Protective Service
4. The Transportation Security Administration (Transportation)
5. Federal Law Enforcement Training Center (Treasury)
6. Animal and Plant Health Inspection Service (part)(Agriculture)
7. Office for Domestic Preparedness (Justice)
8. The Federal Emergency Management Agency (FEMA)
9. Strategic National Stockpile and the National Disaster Medical System (HHS)
10. Nuclear Incident Response Team (Energy)
11. Domestic Emergency Support Teams (Justice)
12. National Domestic Preparedness Office (FBI)
13. CBRN Countermeasures Programs (Energy)
14. Environmental Measurements Laboratory (Energy)
15. National BW Defense Analysis Center (Defense)
16. Plum Island Animal Disease Center (Agriculture)
17. Federal Computer Incident Response Center (GSA)
18. National Communications System (Defense)
19. National Infrastructure Protection Center (FBI)
20. Energy Security and Assurance Program (Energy)
21. U.S. Coast Guard
22. U.S. Secret Service

Current Federal Agencies and Offices of the Department of Homeland Security

1. U.S. Customs and Border Protection
2. U.S. Immigration and Customs Enforcement
3. U.S. Citizenship and Immigration Services
4. Transportation Security Administration
5. Federal Law Enforcement Training Center
6. Federal Emergency Management Agency
7. Science & Technology Directorate
8. US-CERT
9. Office of Cyber Security and Communications
10. Office of Operations Coordination
11. Office of Infrastructure Protection
12. U.S. Coast Guard
13. U.S. Secret Service

Historical Spotlight

The Office of the President of the United States
The Department of Homeland Security
June 2002, (Excerpts)

Homeland Security – The First Nine Months

Sep 11	America attacked.
Sep 11	Department of Defense begins combat air patrols over U.S. cities.
Sep 11	Department of Transportation grounds all U.S. private aircraft.
Sep 11	FEMA activates Federal Response Plan.
Sep 11	U.S. Customs goes to Level 1 alert at all border ports of entry.
Sep 11	HHS activates (for the first time ever) the National Disaster Medical System, dispatching more than 300 medical and mortuary personnel to the New York and Washington, D.C. areas, dispatching one of eight 12-hour emergency "push packages" of medical supplies, and putting 80 Disaster Medical Assistance Teams nationwide and 7,000 private sector medical professionals on deployment alert.
Sep 11	Nuclear Regulatory Commission advises all nuclear power plants, non-power reactors, nuclear fuel facilities and gaseous diffusion plants go to the highest level of security. All complied.
Sep 11	President orders federal disaster funding for New York.
Sep 11	FEMA deploys National Urban Search and Rescue Response team.
Sep 11	FEMA deploys US Army Corp of Engineers to assist debris removal.
Sep 12	FEMA deploys emergency medical and mortuary teams to NY and Washington.
Sep 12	FAA allows limited reopening of the nation's commercial airspace system to allow flights that were diverted on September 11 to continue to their original destinations.
Sep 13	President orders federal aid for Virginia.
Sep 13	Departments of Justice and Treasury deploy Marshals, Border Patrol, and Customs officials to provide a larger police presence at airports as they reopen.
Sep 14	President proclaims a national emergency (Proc. 7463).
Sep 14	President orders ready reserves of armed forces to active duty.
Sep 14	FBI Releases List of Nineteen Suspected Terrorists.
Sep 17	Attorney General directs the establishment of 94 Anti-Terrorism Task Forces, one for each United States Attorney Office.
Sep 18	President signs authorization for Use of Military Force bill.
Sep 18	President authorizes additional disaster funding for New York.
Sep 20	President addresses Congress, announces creation of the Office of Homeland Security and appointment of Governor Tom Ridge as Director.
Sep 21	HHS announces that more than $126 million (part of $5 billion the President released for disaster relief) is being provided immediately to support health services provided in the wake of the attacks.

Sep 22   President signs airline transportation legislation, providing tools to assure the safety and immediate stability of our Nation's commercial airline system, and establish a process for compensating victims of the terrorist attacks.

Sep 25   The first of approximately 7,200 National Guard troops begin augmenting security at 444 airports.

Sep 27   The FBI releases photographs of 19 individuals believed to be the 9/11 hijackers.

Sep 27   Coast Guard mobilized more than 2,000 Reservists in the largest homeland defense and port security operation since World War II.

Oct 1   FEMA declares over $344 million committed to New York recovery so far.

Oct 4   Robert Stevens dies of anthrax in Florida – first known victim of biological terrorism.

Oct 8   President swears-in Governor Ridge as Assistant to the President for Homeland Security, and issues Executive Order creating OHS.

Oct 9   President swears-in General (Retired) Wayne Downing as Director of the Office of Combating Terrorism, and issues Executive order creating OCT.

Oct 10   President unveils "most wanted" terrorists.

Oct 12   FAA restores general aviation in 15 major metropolitan areas.

Oct 16   President issues Executive Order establishing the President's Critical Infrastructure Protection Board to coordinate and have cognizance of Federal efforts and programs that relate to protection of information systems.

Oct 21   FAA restores general aviation in 12 more major metropolitan areas.

Oct 22   President issues Executive Order for HHS to exercise certain contracting authority in connection with national defense functions.

Oct 23   U.S. Customs Service creates new Office of Anti-Terrorism.

Oct 25   Department of Treasury launches Operation Greenquest, a new multi-agency financial enforcement initiative bringing the full scope of the government's financial expertise to bear against sources of terrorist funding.

Oct 26   President signs the USA Patriot Act.

Oct 29   President chairs first meeting of the Homeland Security Council and issues Homeland Security Presidential Directive-1, establishing the organization and operation of the HSC, and HSPD-2, establishing the Foreign Terrorist Tracking Task Force and increasing immigration vigilance.

Oct 30   FAA restricts all private aircraft flying over nuclear facilities.

Nov 8   President announces that the Corporation for National and Community Service (CNCS) will support homeland security, mobilizing more than 20,000 Senior Corps and AmeriCorps participants.

Nov 8   President Bush creates the Presidential Task Force on Citizen Preparedness in the War Against Terrorism to help prepare Americans in their homes, neighborhoods, schools, workplaces, places of worship and public places from the potential consequences of terrorist attacks.

Nov 15   FEMA announces Individual and Family Grant program for disaster assistance.

Nov 28   HHS awards contract to produce 155 million doses of smallpox vaccine by the end of 2002 to bring the total of doses in the nation's stockpile to 286 million, enough to protect every United States citizen.

Nov 29   Attorney General Ashcroft announces Responsible Cooperators Program, which will provide immigration benefits to non-citizens who furnish information to help apprehend terrorists or to stop terrorist attacks.

Dec 3	FBI implements first phase of headquarters reorganization.
Dec 10	U.S. Customs launches "Operation Shield America" to prevent international terrorist organizations from obtaining sensitive U.S. technology, weapons, and other equipment.
Dec 12	Governor Ridge and Canadian Foreign Minister John Manley sign a "smart border" declaration and action plan to improve security and efficiency of the Northern border.
Dec 19	FAA restores general aviation in 30 major metropolitan areas.
Dec 28	President issues Executive Orders on succession in federal agencies.
Jan 10	President signs $2.9 billion bioterrorism appropriations bill.
Jan 11	FAA publishes new standards to protect cockpits from intrusion and small arms fire or fragmentation devices, such as grenades, requiring operators of more than 6,000 airplanes to install reinforced doors by April 9, 2003.
Jan 17	President issues Executive Order authorizing the Secretary of Transportation to increase the number of Coast Guard service members on active duty.
Jan 17	U.S. Customs announces Container Security Initiative.
Jan 17	U.S. Border Patrol officials and other representatives of the INS begin to meet with Native American leaders and law enforcement officials jointly strengthen security along the Southwest and Northern borders.
Jan 17	FBI releases information, photographs, and FBI laboratory photographic retouches on six suspected terrorists.
Jan 18	Department of Transportation meets mandate to submit plans for training security screeners and flight crews.
Jan 23	FBI announces new hiring initiative for FBI Special Agents.
Jan 28	Congress confirms appointment of John W. Magaw as Under Secretary of Transportation for Security.
Jan 30	President issues Executive Order establishing the USA Freedom Corps, encouraging all Americans to serve their country for the equivalent of at least 2 years (4,000 hours) over their lifetimes.
Jan 31	HHS announces state allotments of $1.1 billion to help strengthen their capacity to respond to bioterrorism and other public health emergencies resulting from terrorism.
Feb 3	United States Secret Service ensures security of Super Bowl XXXVI, a National Special Security Event.
Feb 4	President submits the President's Budget for FY 2003 to the Congress, directing $37.7 billion to homeland security, up from $19.5 billion in FY 2002.
Feb 6	Attorney General Ashcroft announces rule change to Board of Immigration Appeals to eliminate backlog, prevent unwarranted delays and improve the quality of board decision-making while ensuring that those in our immigration court system enjoy the full protections of due process.
Feb 8-24	United States Secret Service ensures security of the 2002 Winter Olympics, a National Special Security Event.
Feb 25	Soldiers of the U.S. Army National Guard begin to deploy to augment border security.
Feb 26	Nuclear Regulatory Commission orders all 104 commercial nuclear power plants to implement interim compensatory security measures, formalizing measures taken in response to NRC advisories since September 11, and imposing additional security enhancements as a result of on-going comprehensive security review.

Mar 1	U.S. Customs Service announces action plan to ensure international air carrier compliance with regulations requiring passenger and crew information prior to arrival in the U.S. on flights from foreign locations.
Mar 5	Attorney General Ashcroft announces National Security Coordination Council to ensure seamless coordination of all functions of the Department of Justice relating to national security, particularly efforts to combat terrorism.
Mar 8	To date, the U.S. Coast Guard has conducted over 35,000 port security patrols and 3,500 air patrols; boarded over 10,000 vessels including over 2,000 "high interest vessels;" escorted 6,000 vessels in and out of ports including 2,000 escorted by Sea Marshalls; maintained over 124 security zones; and recalled 2,900 Reservists to active duty.
Mar 12	President establishes the Homeland Security Advisory System (HSPD-3).
Mar 19	President issues Executive Order establishing the President's Homeland Security Advisory Council.
Mar 22	Secretary of State Powell and Mexico Interior Minister Santiago Creel sign a "smart border" declaration and action plan to improve security and efficiency of the Southern border.
Mar 25	U.S. Customs officers begin partnership with Canadian Customs officers to inspect U.S.-bound cargo upon its first arrival in the ports of Montreal, Halifax, and Vancouver.
Mar 25	Nuclear Regulatory Commission orders Honeywell International, Inc., a uranium conversion facility in Illinois, to immediately implement interim compensatory security measures.
Mar 29	HHS announces it will obtain more than 75 million additional doses of smallpox vaccine from Aventis Pasteur Inc., provided the supply, stored in a secure location since 1972, is proven safe and effective.
Apr 5	NRC forms Office of Security to streamline security, safeguards and incident response activities.
Apr 8	INS implements rule changes governing an alien's ability to begin a course of study the period of time visitors are permitted to remain in the United States.
Apr 16	U.S. Customs launches the Customs-Trade Partnership Against Terrorism.
Apr 22	FBI Director Mueller announces key management positions in the counterterrorism division.
Apr 30	Transportation Security Administration announces successful implementation of Federal passenger screeners at Baltimore-Washington airport.
May 14	President Signs Border Security and Visa Entry Reform Act.
May 19	TSA issues 180 day progress report to Congress.
May 22	CIA creates new position of Associate Director of Central Intelligence for Homeland Security, effective May 28.
May 24	Nuclear Regulatory Commission orders decommissioning of commercial nuclear power plants with spent fuel stored in water-filled pools and a spent nuclear fuel storage facility using pool storage to implement interim compensatory security measures for the current threat environment.
May 29	Attorney General Ashcroft and FBI Director Mueller announce reorganization of the FBI to achieve top priority of counter-terrorism and better coordination with the CIA.

Editor's Comments

One of the basic tenets of a protective system, whether it is a corporate security department, a law enforcement agency, or the Department of Homeland Security, is **adaptability**. The ability to adjust allows for a flexible response to an unanticipated risk event. As many security experts would agree, even the best prepared plans do not consider every single possibility or facet of a risk event. It is prudent, therefore, to view all protective systems as works-in-progress. Continuous evaluation, modification, and reapplication are essential for any legitimate anticipatory system.

The Department of Homeland Security is a fluid entity. Federal agencies flow in and out of the Department's immediate jurisdiction. As the terrorist threat evolves, so should the federal entity charged with its opposition. The Department of Homeland Security is not in its finalized form. As new and previously unanticipated risk events become apparent, the Department will conform and respond appropriately. Failure to conform will render protection systems outdated and vulnerable.

In general, protective schemes which are focused on unsupported or isolated solutions will be most vulnerable. For a program to become effective, the objectives of the individual operation must fit seamlessly into the goals of the overall mission. Rogue programs or federal entities that work outside of the mission of the Department of Homeland Security are prone for disconnection. A "disconnect" with the overall protective mission can lead to gaps or fields of vulnerability - any formidable adversary will look for and exploit these types of weaknesses. In contrast, an objective which is fully integrated with the overall mission will reduce areas of exploitation and thus eliminate or mitigate the effect of a negative event.

Further Discussion

1. Discuss the contributions of the **Hart-Rudman Commission**.

2. Discuss **Executive Order 13228**.

3. Discuss President Bush's original **mission of homeland security**, as stated in his June 6, 2002 speech.

4. Discuss the differences between the **"Office"** of Homeland Security and the **"Department"** of Homeland Security.

5. Discuss the **actions of the Federal Government** on September 11, 2001 and the days immediately following.

Chapter 03

Defining Homeland Security

"Security can only be achieved through constant change, through discarding old ideas that have outlived their usefulness and adapting others to current facts."

U.S. Supreme Court Justice William O. Douglas (1898 – 1980)

Congressional Research Service
Defining Homeland Security:
Analysis and Congressional Considerations
April 2012, (Excerpts)

Introduction and Issue

Ten years after the 9/11 terrorist attacks, policymakers continue to grapple with the definition of homeland security. Prior to 9/11, the United States addressed crises through the separate prisms of national defense, law enforcement, and emergency management. 9/11 prompted a strategic process that included a debate over and the development of homeland security policy. Today, this debate and development has resulted in numerous federal entities with homeland security responsibilities. For example, there are 30 federal entities that receive annual homeland security funding excluding the Department of Homeland Security (DHS). The Office of Management and Budget (OMB) estimates that 48% of annual homeland security funding is appropriated to these federal entities, with the Department of Defense (DOD) receiving approximately 26% of total federal homeland security funding. DHS receives approximately 52%.

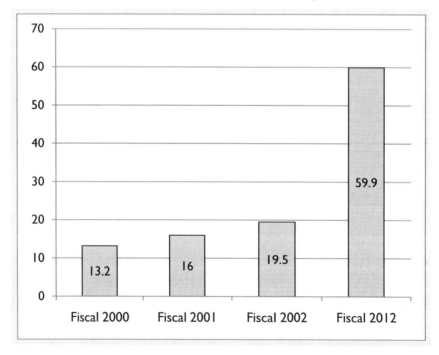

Homeland Security Funding

In billions of dollars

Congress and policymakers are responsible for funding homeland security priorities. These priorities need to exist, to be clear and cogent, in order for funding to be most effective.

Presently, homeland security is not funded on clearly defined priorities. In an ideal scenario, there would be a clear definition of homeland security, and a consensus about it; as well as prioritized missions, goals, and activities. Policymakers could then use a process to incorporate feedback and respond to new facts and situations as they develop. This report examines how varied, and evolving, homeland security definitions and strategic missions may affect the prioritization of national homeland security policy and how it may affect the funding of homeland security. To address this issue, this report first discusses and analyzes examples of strategic documents, their differing homeland security definitions, and their varying homeland security missions.

Evolution of the Homeland Security Concept

The concept of homeland security has evolved over the last decade. Homeland security as a concept was precipitated by the terrorist attacks of 9/11. However, prior to 9/11 such entities as the Gilmore Commission and the United States Commission on National Security discussed the need to evolve the way national security policy was conceptualized due to the end of the Cold War and the rise of radicalized terrorism. After 9/11, policymakers concluded that a new approach was needed to address the large-scale terrorist attacks. A presidential council and department were established, and a series of presidential directives were issued in the name of "homeland security." These developments established that homeland security was a distinct, but undefined concept. Later, the federal, state, and local government responses to disasters such as Hurricane Katrina expanded the concept of homeland security to include significant disasters, major public health emergencies, and other events that threaten the United States, its economy, the

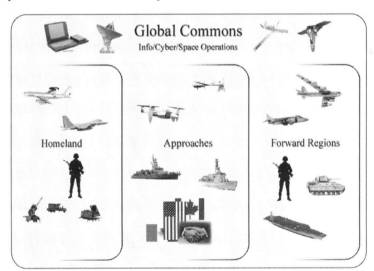

Active layered homeland defense strategy.   Illustration credit: Department of Defense, 2005.

rule of law, and government operations. This later expansion of the concept of homeland security solidified it as something distinct from other federal government security operations such as homeland defense.

Homeland security as a concept suggested a different approach to security, and differed from homeland defense. Homeland defense is primarily a Department of Defense (DOD) activity and is defined as "... the protection of US sovereignty, territory, domestic population, and critical defense infrastructure against external threats and aggression, or other threats as directed by the President." Homeland security, regardless of the definition or strategic document, is a combination of law enforcement, disaster, immigration, and terrorism issues. It is primarily the responsibility of civilian agencies at all levels. It is a coordination of efforts at all levels of government. The differences between homeland security and homeland defense, however, are not completely distinct. A international terrorist organization attack on and within the United States would result in a combined homeland security and homeland defense response, such as on 9/11 when civilian agencies were responding to the attacks while the U.S. military established a combat air patrol over New York and Washington, DC. This distinction between homeland security and homeland defense, and the evolution of homeland security as a concept, was reflected in the strategic documents developed and issued following 9/11.

Evolution of the Homeland Security Definitions and Missions

Prior to 9/11, federal, state, and local governments responded to domestic terrorist attacks in an ad hoc manner. These terrorist attacks, and the governments' responses, however, did not significantly affect how policymakers perceived, defined, and prioritized security as related to the homeland. Two examples of these domestic terrorist attacks are the 1993 World Trade Center (WTC) and the 1995 Alfred Murrah Federal Building bombings.

On February 26, 1993, radicalized Islamic terrorists detonated a bomb beneath the WTC. In response, President Clinton ordered his National Security Council to coordinate the bombings' response and investigation. The CIA's Counterterrorist Center and the National

Security Agency, along with the FBI, were among the numerous federal agencies that participated in the investigation. This use of the National Security Council was an ad-hoc response specifically to this event, and it did not result in the development of strategic documents. On April 19, 1995, Timothy McVeigh exploded a bomb-laden truck in front of the Alfred P. Murrah Federal Building in Oklahoma City. Following this bombing, President Clinton directed the Department of Justice

Timothy McVeigh, (center) one of three people convicted of the Oklahoma City Bombing which killed 168 people, was executed on June 11, 2001. Photo credit: FBI.

(DOJ) to assess the vulnerability of federal facilities to terrorist attacks or violence and to develop recommendations for minimum security standards. These standards, however, were not a wide-ranging strategy for U.S. homeland security strategy. It was the 9/11 terrorist attacks that initiated the debate and development of a broader homeland security strategy.

The 9/11 terrorist attacks on New York City, Pennsylvania, and Washington, DC, were a watershed event. As with the 1993 WTC and 1995 Oklahoma City bombings, the federal, state, and local government's response to the 9/11 terrorists attacks was ad hoc. In New York City, first responders included such entities as the New York police and fire departments, and Port Authority and WTC employees. Following the attack, federal entities such as the FBI, DOD, and elements of the intelligence community (IC) coordinated their efforts in investigating and tracking down the responsible terrorists. However, following the 9/11 initial response and subsequent investigations, it was determined that there was a need to reorganize the government to prepare for, mitigate against, respond to, and recover from future attacks. This decision to reorganize the government resulted in an evolution of homeland security definitions and missions.

The debate over and development of homeland security definitions persists as the federal government continues to issue and implement homeland security strategy.

Definitions

The 2010 *National Security Strategy* states that homeland security is "a seamless coordination among federal, state, and local governments to prevent, protect against, and respond to threats and natural disasters." Homeland security requires coordination because numerous federal, state, and local entities have responsibility for various homeland security activities. The proliferation of responsibilities entitled "homeland security activities" is due to a couple of factors. One factor is that homeland security developed from the pre-9/11 concept of law enforcement and emergency management. Another factor is the continuously evolving definition of "homeland security." Some degree of evolution of the homeland security concept is expected. Policymakers respond to events and crises like terrorist attacks and natural disasters by using and adjusting strategies, plans, and operations. These strategies, plans, and operations also evolve to reflect changing priorities. The definition of homeland security evolves in accordance with the evolution of these strategies, plans, and operations.

Summary of Homeland Security Definitions

- **2007 National Strategy for Homeland Security** (White House)
  A concerted national effort to prevent terrorist attacks within the United States, reduce America's vulnerability to terrorism, and minimize the damage and recover from attacks that do occur.

- **2008 U.S. Department of Homeland Security Strategic Plan** (DHS)
  A unified national effort to prevent and deter terrorist attacks, protect and respond to hazards, and to secure the national borders.

- **2010 National Security Strategy** (White House)
  A seamless coordination among federal, state, and local governments to prevent, protect against and respond to threats and natural disasters.

- **2010 Quadrennial Homeland Security Review** (DHS)
  A concerted national effort to ensure a homeland that is safe, secure, and resilient against terrorism and other hazards where American interests, aspirations, and ways of life can thrive.

- **2010 Bottom-Up Review** (DHS)
  Preventing terrorism, responding to and recovering from natural disasters, customs enforcement and collection of customs revenue, administration of legal immigration services, safety and stewardship of the Nation's waterways and marine transportation system, as well as other legacy missions of the various components of DHS.

- **2011 National Strategy For Counterterrorism** (White House)
  Defensive efforts to counter terrorist threats.

- **2012 Strategic Plan** (DHS)
  Efforts to ensure a homeland that is safe, secure, and resilient against terrorism and other hazards.

Some common themes among these definitions are:

- The homeland security enterprise encompasses a federal, state, local, and tribal government and private sector approach that requires coordination;

- homeland security can involve securing against and responding to both hazard specific and all-hazards threats; and

- homeland security activities do not imply total protection or complete threat reduction.

Each of these documents highlight the importance of coordinating homeland security missions and activities. However, individual federal, state, local, and tribal government efforts are not identified in the documents. Homeland security—according to these documents—is preventing, responding to, and recovering from terrorist attacks, which is consistent with evolving homeland security policy after 9/11.

The focus of the definition of homeland security communicated in these strategy documents differs in regard to two areas that may be considered substantive. Natural disasters are specifically identified as an integral part of homeland security in only four of the six documents, but are not mentioned in the 2007 *National Strategy for Homeland Security* and the 2011 *National Strategy for Counterterrorism.* Only one document—the *Bottom-Up Review*—specifically includes border and maritime security, and immigration in their homeland security definition. The 2012 *Strategic Plan* uses the encompassing terms "other hazards" to define any threat other than terrorism. These issues are significant and call for substantial funding. An absence of consensus about the inclusion of these policy areas may result in unintended consequences for national homeland security operations. For example, not including maritime security in the homeland security definition may result in policymakers, Congress, and stakeholders not adequately addressing maritime homeland security threats, or

[handwritten marginal note: Good that definition changes / it means we are continuing to adapt]

more specifically being able to prioritize federal investments in border versus intelligence activities.

The competing and varied definitions in these documents may indicate that there is no succinct homeland security concept. Without a succinct homeland security concept, policymakers and entities with homeland security responsibilities may not successfully coordinate or focus on the highest prioritized or most necessary activities. Coordination is especially essential to homeland security because of the multiple federal agencies and the state and local partners with whom they interact. Coordination may be difficult if these entities do not operate with the same understanding of the homeland security concept. For example, definitions that don't specifically include immigration or natural disaster response and recovery may result in homeland security stakeholders and federal entities not adequately resourcing and focusing on these activities. Additionally, an absence of a consensus definition may result in Congress funding a homeland security activity that DHS does not consider a priority. For example, Congress may appropriate funding for a counterterrorism program such as the State Homeland Security Grant Program when DHS may have identified an all-hazards grant program, such as Emergency Management Performance Grant Program, as a priority.

It is, however, possible that a consensus definition and overall concept exists among policy makers and federal entities, but that it isn't communicated in the strategic documents.

Finally, DHS Deputy Secretary Jane Lute recently stated that homeland security "... is operation, it's transactional, it's decentralized, it's bottom-driven," and influenced by law enforcement, emergency management, and the political environment. Conversely, DHS Deputy Secretary Lute stated that national security "... is strategic, it's centralized, it's top-driven," and influenced by the military and the intelligence community. Some see in these comments as a reflection of a DHS attempt to establish a homeland security definition that is more operational than strategic and an illustration of the complexity of a common understanding of homeland security and its associated missions.

United States Department of Homeland Security
Quadrennial Homeland Security Review Report:
A Strategic Framework for a Secure Homeland
February 2010, (Excerpts)

Because the term is in such widespread use, it may be easy today to overlook the fact that *homeland security* is a relatively new concept. Yet it is one that can trace its roots to traditional functions such as civil defense, emergency response, law enforcement, customs, border control, and immigration. Homeland security captures the effort to adapt these traditional functions to confront new threats and evolving hazards.

While homeland security is still relatively new, it may be useful to recall that the concept of *national security* was also little known until the 1930s, and was only formally established as an organizing principle after World War II. The *National Security Act of 1947* brought together the Department of War and the Department of the Navy into a single integrated entity that became the Department of Defense. The act also created the National Security Council and a position on the President's staff that would later become the National Security Advisor. The innovation was to bring together under one overall concept the consideration of foreign affairs and military policy, which had been, up until that time, two largely separate governmental domains. Over the decades, aspects of economic policy, trade policy, energy policy, and countering transnational threats were also drawn into the ambit of national security.

In 2002, the *Homeland Security Act* sought to integrate the various elements of homeland security in a similar manner, creating both the Department of Homeland Security and the Homeland Security Council. In effect, the 2002 *Homeland Security Act* added a third concept to the military and foreign affairs pillars of national security by associating domestic security concerns with national security. Homeland security describes the intersection of evolving threats and hazards with the traditional governmental and civic responsibilities of civil defense, emergency response, law enforcement, customs, border control, and immigration. In combining these responsibilities under one overarching concept, homeland security breaks down longstanding stovepipes of activity that could be exploited by those seeking to harm America. Homeland security also creates a greater emphasis on and need for joint actions and efforts across previously discrete elements of government and society.

The Enterprise of Homeland Security

Given this historical context, the question "What is homeland security?" recognizes that, in fact, securing the United States and its people represents an overarching national objective. Equally important, and aside from obviously identifying a Cabinet-level department of the Federal Government, homeland security is a widely distributed and diverse—but unmistakable—national enterprise.

The term "enterprise" refers to the collective efforts and shared responsibilities of Federal, State, local, tribal, territorial, nongovernmental, and private-sector partners—as well as individuals, families, and communities—to maintain critical homeland security capabilities. It connotes a broad-based community with a common interest in the public safety

> ...the question "What is homeland security?" recognizes that, in fact, securing the United States and its people represents an overarching national objective.

and well-being of America and American society and is composed of multiple partners and stakeholders whose roles and responsibilities are distributed and shared. Yet it is important to remember that these partners and stakeholders face diverse risks, needs, and priorities. The

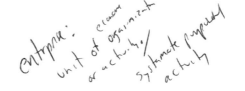

challenge for the enterprise, then, is to balance these diverse needs and priorities, while focusing on our shared interests and responsibilities to collectively secure our homeland.

As the Commander-in-Chief and the leader of the Executive Branch, the President of the United States is uniquely responsible for the safety, security, and resilience of the Nation. The White House leads overall homeland security policy direction and coordination. Individual Federal agencies, in turn, are empowered by law and policy to fulfill various aspects of the homeland security mission. The Secretary of Homeland Security leads the Federal agency as defined by statute charged with homeland security: preventing terrorism and managing risks to critical infrastructure; securing and managing the border; enforcing and administering immigration laws; safeguarding and securing cyberspace; and ensuring resilience to disasters. In some areas, like securing our borders or managing our immigration system, the Department of Homeland Security possesses unique capabilities and, hence, responsibilities. In other areas, such as critical infrastructure protection or emergency management, the Department's role is largely one of leadership and stewardship on behalf of those who have the capabilities to get the job done. In still other areas, such as counterterrorism, defense, and diplomacy, other Federal departments and agencies have critical leadership roles and responsibilities, including the Departments of Justice, Defense, and State, the Federal Bureau of Investigation, and the National Counterterrorism Center. State, local, tribal, and territorial governments all play vital roles in protecting the homeland. Homeland security will only be successful when we fully leverage the distributed and decentralized nature of the entire enterprise in the pursuit of our common goals.

Therefore, key leadership responsibilities to achieve our homeland security missions are discharged through engagement and collaboration with the vast array of homeland security enterprise partners and stakeholders. As a distributed system, no single entity is responsible for or directly manages all aspects of the enterprise. Different agencies and offices direct and lead specific homeland security activities at the Federal, State, local, tribal, and territorial levels, as well as within the private sector—and between and among all of these entities—for the full range of homeland security purposes. And because responsibilities are distributed, entities that provide direction and leadership in one instance may play supporting roles in another.

With the establishment of homeland security, and the linking of domestic security concerns to broader national security interests and institutions, there is a temptation to view homeland security so broadly as to encompass all national security and domestic policy activities. This is not the case. Homeland security is deeply rooted in the security and resilience of the Nation, and facilitating lawful interchange with the world. As such, it intersects with many other functions of government. Homeland security is built upon critical law enforcement functions, but is not about preventing all crimes or administering our Nation's judicial system. It is deeply embedded in trade activities, but is neither trade nor economic policy. It requires international engagement, but is not responsible for foreign affairs. Rather, homeland security is meant to connote a concerted, shared effort to ensure a homeland that is safe, secure, and resilient against terrorism and other hazards where American interests, aspirations, and way of life can thrive.

The Evolution of Homeland Security

As noted earlier, although the integrated concept of homeland security arose at the turn of the 21st century, homeland security traces its roots to concepts that originated with the founding of the Republic. Homeland security describes the intersection of new threats and evolving hazards with traditional governmental and civic responsibilities for civil defense, emergency response, customs, border control, law enforcement, and immigration. Homeland security draws on the rich history, proud traditions, and lessons learned from these historical functions to fulfill new responsibilities that require the engagement of the entire homeland security enterprise and multiple Federal departments and agencies.

The Key Concepts of Homeland Security

For the past 7 years, homeland security has rested on four key activities—prevention, protection, response, and recovery—oriented principally against the threat of terrorism. Preventing a terrorist attack in the United States remains the cornerstone of homeland security. It is clear, however, that this emphasis on terrorism does not capture the full range of interconnected threats and challenges that characterize today's world. A robust notion of homeland security must take account of our essential need to safely, securely, and intensively engage the rest of the world—through trade, travel, and other exchanges. In other words, a place where the American way of life can thrive.

Three key concepts form the general foundation for a comprehensive approach to homeland security going forward: **Security**, **Resilience**, and **Customs and Exchange**.

Security: Protect the United States and its people, vital interests, and way of life. Homeland security relies on our shared efforts to prevent and deter attacks by identifying and interdicting threats, denying hostile actors

> Three key concepts form the general foundation for a comprehensive approach to homeland security going forward: **Security**, **Resilience**, and **Customs and Exchange**.

the ability to operate within our borders, and protecting the Nation's critical infrastructure and key resources. Initiatives that strengthen our protections, increase our vigilance, and reduce our vulnerabilities remain important components of our security. This is not to say, however, that security is a static undertaking. We know that the global systems that carry people, goods, and data around the globe also facilitate the movement of *dangerous* people, goods, and data, and that within these systems of transportation and transaction, there are key nodes—for example, points of origin and transfer, or border crossings—that represent opportunities for interdiction. Thus, we must work to confront threats at every point along their supply chain—supply chains that often begin abroad. To ensure our homeland security then, we must engage our international allies, and employ the full breadth of our national capacity—from the Federal

Government, to State, local, tribal, and territorial police, other law enforcement entities, the Intelligence Community, and the private sector—and appropriately enlist the abilities of millions of American citizens.

Resilience: Foster individual, community, and system robustness, adaptability, and capacity for rapid recovery. Our country and the world are underpinned by interdependent networks along which the essential elements of economic prosperity—people, goods and resources, money, and information—all flow. While these networks reflect progress and increased efficiency, they are also sources of vulnerability. The consequences of events are no longer confined to a single point; a disruption in one place can ripple through the system and have immediate, catastrophic, and multiplying consequences across the country and around the world.

Despite our best efforts, some attacks, accidents, and disasters will occur. Therefore, the challenge is to foster a society that is robust, adaptable, and has the capacity for rapid recovery. In this context, individuals, families, and communities—and the systems that sustain them—must be informed, trained, and materially and psychologically prepared to withstand disruption, absorb or tolerate disturbance, know their role in a crisis, adapt to changing conditions, and grow stronger over time.

This concept is not new, and different eras in our history reflect an unwavering focus on building national resilience. The history of civil defense in the United States, for example, is marked by sweeping national debates about concepts that, if not by name, were nevertheless entirely about resilience. Notable among these was the debate spanning the Truman and Eisenhower administrations about whether to expend resources on sheltering individuals in the face of nuclear attack or to focus investments in a national highway system to facilitate mass evacuation of urban populations. These issues were beset with the same challenges that confront us today, including how to foster a decentralized approach to security, and how to best meet the challenge of helping our citizens prepare psychologically and materially for attacks and disasters that do occur. The rapid evolution of national security threats and the arrival of the information age have increased the urgency of building up—and reemphasizing—our historically resilient posture.

Customs and Exchange: Expedite and enforce lawful trade, travel, and immigration. The partners and stakeholders of the homeland security enterprise are responsible for facilitating and expediting the lawful movement of people and goods into and out of the United States. This responsibility intersects with and is deeply linked to the enterprise's security function. We need a smarter, more holistic approach that embeds security and resilience directly into global movement systems. Strengthening our economy and promoting lawful trade, travel, and immigration must include security and resilience, just as security and resilience must include promoting a strong and competitive U.S. economy, welcoming lawful immigrants, and protecting civil liberties and the rule of law. We view security along with customs and exchange as mutually reinforcing and inextricably intertwined through actions such as screening, authenticating, and maintaining awareness of the flow of people, goods, and information around the world and across our borders.

Customs in Historical Context

After declaring independence, the United States found itself on the brink of bankruptcy. To raise revenue, the second act of Congress—the *Tariff Act of 1789*—authorized the first Secretary of the Treasury, Alexander Hamilton, to collect duties on imported goods. A month later, in its fifth act, Congress established 59 customs collection districts around the country and designated ports of entry under the jurisdiction of the Department of the Treasury's Collectors of Customs.

From inception, the Collectors of Customs were given numerous responsibilities designed to support the collection of customs revenue. Recognizing that revenue would increase if more ships could make it to port safely and quickly, Congress immediately created the Lighthouse Service, which eventually came under Collectors of Customs authority, to construct and maintain all navigational aids. To assist in the collection of duties and tonnage taxes, and to combat smuggling by privateers, which negatively impacted revenue collection, a maritime law enforcement arm was added a year later—the U.S. Revenue Marine. As the Nation's land borders expanded, the U.S. Customs Border Patrol was created to address smuggling between ports of entry.

The Collectors of Customs were assigned other tasks that were inherently intertwined with their customs responsibilities. Because their ships already patrolled the coastline, the Revenue Marine assumed responsibility for maritime security and, in the 1840s with its acquisition of the Life Saving Service, maritime safety. The Collectors of Customs were also charged with implementing immigration policy and enforcing immigration law, because they were representatives of the Federal Government at ports of entry. By 1853, the Collectors of Customs had authority over customs and immigration law enforcement, maritime safety and security, and border security.

Customs and Border Protection officers take a moment to discuss strategies for searching arriving cargo. Photo credit: James R. Tourtellotte, Courtesy U.S. Customs and Border Protection.

Beginning in the late 1800s, however, the Collectors of Customs structure was reorganized. In 1871, the Revenue Marine (which had been renamed the Revenue Cutter Service) and Life Saving Service were removed from Collectors of Customs authority. The two organizations combined in 1915 to form the U.S. Coast Guard. In 1891, Congress moved the Collectors' immigration functions to the Office of the

Superintendent of Immigration, which later evolved into the Immigration and Naturalization Service. By the turn of the century, the Collectors of Customs (eventually renamed the U.S. Customs Service) had become an organization focused solely on customs enforcement and anti-smuggling. Around the same time, growing income from excise taxes and, in 1913, an income tax meant that customs duties were no longer the primary source of Federal Government revenue.* The facilitation of commerce and immigration in support of overall economic growth became a substantial priority alongside the collection of customs revenue. For the next 100 years, customs and immigration enforcement, border security, and maritime safety and security functions remained distributed across multiple agencies within three cabinet departments—the Department of the Treasury (customs), the Department of Justice (immigration enforcement and border security), and the Department of Transportation (maritime safety and security). The creation of the Department of Homeland Security (DHS) in 2003 reunited these long interrelated and mutually supportive functions. Every day as part of DHS, the U.S. Coast Guard, U.S. Customs and Border Protection, Transportation Security Administration, U.S. Citizenship and Immigration Services, and U.S. Immigration and Customs Enforcement undertake countless activities to expedite and facilitate the flow of goods and people across U.S. borders. As these agencies have previously done—in some cases for hundreds of years—they ensure seamless integration of these responsibilities with the task of upholding and promoting the security of the country.

Editor's Comments

What is homeland security? This question is the subject of much debate among academicians, security experts, and the security industry in general. On the surface, homeland security is about terrorism. Specifically, homeland security deals with the prevention, mitigation, and recovery from serious acts of terrorism. Through risk and vulnerability assessment, risk management, and continuity of operations, homeland security seeks to neutralize terrorist threats before they occur, lessen the effects of a successful attack, and to resume or continue the functioning output after such an attack.

Homeland security is not a law enforcement (or criminal justice) function. Although both governmental functions use similar tools, methods, equipment, and/or training, their likenesses stop there. Homeland security is concerned with the protection of the national critical infrastructure, key resources and assets, and the citizens of the United States from acts of terrorism, whether foreign or domestic-based. There may be some traditional law enforcement-type actions used during homeland security operations - such as surveillances, wiretaps, and arrests - however the protection-oriented theme greatly overshadows any contributions to the law enforcement process. On the other hand, law enforcement is about upholding the criminal laws of the United States. Critical infrastructure protection, although a minor consideration, does not rank very high in traditional law enforcement objectives. Crime, punishment, corrections, probation, parole, and juvenile justice are all key concerns within the law enforcement or criminal justice realm.

Homeland security is an enterprise-wide program which requires numerous non-traditional partnerships and key working relationships. The United States has adopted a "collaborative" approach to protecting the homeland, thus distributing the load proportionately. This is a prudent course of action since it is unrealistic, or even negligent, for the federal government to assume the entire burden of homeland security. The government lacks the necessary resources, expertise, protective systems, and training to be solely responsible. Working with the private sector, the government hopes to achieve its goals. For example, under the "collaborative" system, the government recognizes the need to align itself with key sector specific security professionals who have been protecting private organizational assets long before terrorism was a legitimate concern. These security specialists bring years of industry-specific expertise, knowledge of relevant operations, and leveraged partnerships of their own.

Expanding the responsibility of infrastructure protection to all federal, state, and local agencies operates under the same "collaborative" system as with the private sector. Developing relationships with nontraditional "protection" entities serves only to expand the government's resource capabilities.

Further Discussion

1. What is the **homeland security** concept?

2. Discuss the **evolution** of the homeland security concept.

3. Discuss the main **differences** among the standing definitions of homeland security.

4. Discuss the **commonalities** among the standing definitions of homeland security.

5. Discuss the concept of "**enterprise-wide**" and its impact on the concept of homeland security.

Chapter 04

Statutory Authority of Homeland Security

"By tearing down the wall between law enforcement and the intelligence community, we have been able to share information in a way that was virtually impossible before the Patriot Act."

United States Attorney General John Ashcroft, July 2004

United States Department of Homeland Security
Laws and Regulations
Website, (Excerpts)

- **National Security Act of 1947 (Public Law 253)**

    An Act to promote the national security by providing for a secretary of
    Defense; for a national Military Establishment; for a Department of the Army,
    a Department of the navy, and a Department of the Air Force; and for the
    coordination of the activities of the National Military Establishment with
    other departments and agencies of the Government concerned with the
    national security.

- **Central Intelligence Agency Act of 1949 (Public Law 110)**

    An Act to provide for the administration of the Central Intelligence Agency,
    established pursuant to section 102, National Security Act of 1947, and for
    other purposes."

- **Federal Civil Defense Act, 1950 (Public Law 920)**

    An Act to authorize a Federal civil defense program, and for other
    purposes"..."It is the policy and intent of Congress to provide a plan of civil
    defense for the protection of life and property in the United States from
    attack. It is further declared to be the policy and intent of Congress that this
    responsibility for civil defense shall be vested primarily in the several States
    and their political subdivisions. The Federal Government shall provide
    necessary coordination and guidance; shall be responsible for the operations
    of the Federal Civil Defense Administration as set forth in this Act; and shall
    provide necessary assistance as hereinafter authorized.

    [handwritten margin note: Says civil defense is a State issue.]

- **National Security Agency Act of 1959 (Public Law 86-36)**

    The Secretary of Defense (or his designee) is authorized to establish such
    positions, and to appoint thereto, without regard to the civil service laws, such
    officers and employees, in the National Security Agency, as may be necessary
    to carry out the functions of such agency. The rates of basic pay for such
    positions shall be fixed by the Secretary of Defense (or his designee for this
    purpose) in relation to the rates of basic pay provided for in subpart D of part
    III of title 5, United States Code, for positions subject to such title which have
    corresponding levels of duties and responsibilities. Except as otherwise
    provided by law, no officer or employee of the National Security Agency shall
    be paid basic pay at a rate in excess of the maximum rate payable under
    section 5376 of such title and not more than 70 such officers and employees
    shall be paid within the range of rates authorized in section 5376 of such title.

- Homeland Security Presidential Directive 39: U.S. Policy on Counterterrorism (1995)

  Presidential Directive 39 explains the U.S. policy on terrorism. "It is the policy of the United States to deter, defeat and respond vigorously to all terrorist attacks on our territory and against our citizens, or facilities, whether they occur domestically, in international waters or airspace or on foreign territory. The United States regards all such terrorism as a potential threat to national security as well as a criminal act and will apply all appropriate means to combat it."

- Antiterrorism and Effective Death Penalty Act of 1996 (Public Law 104-132)

  An Act to deter terrorism, provide justice for victims, provide for an effective death penalty, and for other purposes." Includes the following subsections relevant to homeland security: the "Mandatory Victims Restitution Act of 1996"; and the "Justice for Victims of Terrorism Act of 1996."

- Presidential Directive 63: Protecting Critical Infrastructure (1998)

  This Presidential Directive builds on the recommendations of the President's Commission on Critical Infrastructure Protection. In October 1997 the Commission issued its report, calling for a national effort to assure the security of the United States' increasingly vulnerable and interconnected infrastructures, such as telecommunications, banking and finance, energy, transportation, and essential government services.

- Executive Order 13228: Establishing the Office of Homeland Security and the Homeland Security Council

  Executive Order 13228 establishes the Office of Homeland Security (the "Office"). The mission of the Office shall be to develop and coordinate the implementation of a comprehensive national strategy to secure the United States from terrorist threats or attacks. The order further details the functions (National Strategy, Detection, Preparedness, Prevention, Protection, Response and Recovery, Incident Management, Continuity of Government, Public Affairs, Cooperation with State and Local Governments and Private Entities, Review of Legal Authorities and Development of Legislative Proposals, and Budget Review), administration, the establishment of the Homeland Security Council, Classification Authority (Top Secret), Continuing Authorities, and General Provisions. Section 9 includes details to Amendments to Executive Order 12656.

Patriot Act

- Uniting and Strengthening America by Providing Appropriate Tools Required to Intercept and Obstruct Terrorism (USA PATRIOT ACT) Act of 2001 (Public Law 107-56)

    An Act to deter and punish terrorist acts in the United States and around the world, to enhance law enforcement investigatory tools, and for other purposes." The following Titles aim to increase and enhance domestic security: Title I-Enhancing Domestic Security Against Terrorism, TITLE II-Enhanced Surveillance Procedures, Title III-International Money Laundering Abatement and Antiterrorist Financing Act of 2001, Title IV-Protecting the Border, Title V-Removing Obstacles to Investigating Terrorism, Title VI-Providing for Victims of Terrorism, Public Safety Officers, and Their Families, Title VII-Increased Information Sharing for Critical Infrastructure Protection, Title VIII-Strengthening the Criminal Laws Against Terrorism, Title IX-Improved Intelligence, and so forth. Section 101 of Title I-Enhancing Domestic Security Against Terrorism addresses the Counterterrorism Fund. It states, "there is hereby established in the Treasury of the United States a separate fund to be known as the "Counterterrorism Fund.

- **Homeland Security Presidential Directive 2: Combating Terrorism Through Immigration Policies (2001)**

    19 hijackers

    Homeland Security Presidential Directive (HSPD) 2 implements policy to work aggressively to prevent aliens who engage in or support terrorist activity from entering the United States and to detain, prosecute, or deport any such aliens who are within the United States.

- **Homeland Security Act of 2002**

    Biggest Fed. Gov't. Re-organization in U.S. History

    The Homeland Security Act of 2002 was signed into law on November 25,

President George W. Bush at the signing of the Homeland Security Act, November 25, 2002. White House Photo.

2002 (Pub. L. 107-296) in response to the September 11, 2001 terrorist attacks. The Act brought together approximately 22 separate federal agencies to establish the Department of Homeland Security and sets forth the primary missions of the Department. The Act has been amended over 30 times since its original passage.

- **Homeland Security Presidential Directive 5: Management of Domestic Incidents 2003**

  Issued on February 28, 2003 by President Bush, Homeland Security Presidential Directive (HSPD) 5 serves the purpose to enhance the ability of the United States to manage domestic incidents by establishing a single, comprehensive national incident management system. This management system would cover the prevention, preparation, response, and recovery of terrorist attacks, major disasters, and other emergencies. The implementation of such a system would allow all levels of government throughout the nation to work efficiently and effectively together. The directive gives further detail on which government officials oversee and have authority for various parts of the national incident management system.

- **Intelligence Reform and Terrorism Prevention Act of 2004 (Public Law 108-458)**

  To reform the intelligence community and the intelligence-related activities of the United States Government, and for other purposes.

- **Implementing Recommendations of the 9-11 Commission Act of 2007 (Public Law 110-53)**

  An Act to provide for the implementation of the recommendations of the National Commission on Terrorist Attacks Upon the United States.

- **Protect America Act of 2007 (Public Law 110-55)**

  An Act to amend the Foreign Intelligence Surveillance Act of 1978 to provide additional procedures for authorizing certain acquisitions of foreign intelligence information and for other purposes.

Statutory Spotlight

Presidential Decision Directive 63
The Clinton Administration's Policy on
Critical Infrastructure Protection
May 22, 1998, (Excerpts)

I. A Growing Potential Vulnerability

The United States possesses both the world's strongest military and its largest national economy. Those two aspects of our power are mutually reinforcing and dependent. They are also increasingly reliant upon certain critical infrastructures and upon cyber-based information systems.

Critical infrastructures are those physical and cyber-based systems essential to the minimum operations of the economy and government. They include, but are not limited to, telecommunications, energy, banking and finance, transportation, water systems and emergency services, both governmental and private. Many of the nation's critical infrastructures have historically been physically and logically separate systems that had little interdependence. As a result of advances in information technology and the necessity of improved efficiency, however, these infrastructures have become increasingly automated and interlinked. These same advances have created new vulnerabilities to equipment failures, human error, weather and other natural causes, and physical and cyber attacks. Addressing these vulnerabilities will necessarily require flexible, evolutionary approaches that span both the public and private sectors, and protect both domestic and international security.

Because of our military strength, future enemies, whether nations, groups or individuals, may seek to harm us in non-traditional ways including attacks within the United States. Our economy is increasingly reliant upon interdependent and cyber-supported infrastructures and non-traditional attacks on our infrastructure and information systems may be capable of significantly harming both our military power and our economy.

II. President's Intent

It has long been the policy of the United States to assure the continuity and viability of critical infrastructures. President Clinton intends that the United States will take all necessary measures to swiftly eliminate any significant vulnerability to both physical and cyber attacks on our critical infrastructures, including especially our cyber systems.

III. A National Goal

No later than the year 2000, the United States shall have achieved an initial operating capability and no later than five years from the day the President signed Presidential Decision Directive 63 the United States shall have achieved and shall maintain the ability to protect our nation's critical infrastructures from intentional acts that would significantly diminish the abilities of:

- The Federal Government to perform essential national security missions and to ensure the general public health and safety;

- State and local governments to maintain order and to deliver minimum essential public services;

- The private sector to ensure the orderly functioning of the economy and the delivery of essential telecommunications, energy, financial and transportation services.

Any interruptions or manipulations of these critical functions must be brief, infrequent, manageable, geographically isolated and minimally detrimental to the welfare of the United States.

IV. A Public-Private Partnership to Reduce Vulnerability

Since the targets of attacks on our critical infrastructure would likely include both facilities in the economy and those in the government, the elimination of our potential vulnerability requires a closely coordinated effort of both the public and the private sector. To succeed, this partnership must be genuine, mutual and cooperative. In seeking to meet our national goal to eliminate the vulnerabilities of our critical infrastructure, therefore, the U.S. government should, to the extent feasible, seek to avoid outcomes that increase government regulation or expand unfunded government mandates to the private sector.

> To succeed, this partnership must be **genuine, mutual** and **cooperative**.

For each of the major sectors of our economy that are vulnerable to infrastructure attack, the Federal Government will appoint from a designated Lead Agency a senior officer of that agency as the Sector Liaison Official to work with the private sector. Sector Liaison Officials, after discussions and coordination with private sector entities of their infrastructure sector, will identify a private sector counterpart (Sector Coordinator) to represent their sector.

Together these two individuals and the departments and corporations they represent shall contribute to a sectoral National Infrastructure Assurance Plan by:

- Assessing the vulnerabilities of the sector to cyber or physical attacks;

- Recommending a plan to eliminate significant vulnerabilities;

- Proposing a system for identifying and preventing attempted major attacks;

- Developing a plan for alerting, containing and rebuffing an attack in progress and then, in coordination with FEMA as appropriate, rapidly reconstituting minimum essential capabilities in the aftermath of an attack.

During the preparation of the sectoral plans, the National Coordinator (see section VI), in conjunction with the Lead Agency Sector Liaison Officials and a representative from the National Economic Council, shall ensure their overall coordination and the integration of the various sectoral plans, with a particular focus on interdependencies.

V. Guidelines

In addressing this potential vulnerability and the means of eliminating it, President Clinton wants those involved to be mindful of the following general principles and concerns.

We shall consult with, and seek input from, the Congress on approaches and programs to meet the objectives set forth in this directive.

The protection of our critical infrastructures is necessarily a shared responsibility and partnership between owners, operators and the government. Furthermore, the Federal Government shall encourage international cooperation to help manage this increasingly global problem.

Frequent assessments shall be made of our critical infrastructures' existing reliability, vulnerability and threat environment because, as technology and the nature of the threats to our critical infrastructures will continue to change rapidly, so must our protective measures and responses be robustly adaptive.

> **The Federal Government shall serve as a model to the private sector on how infrastructure assurance is best achieved and shall, to the extent feasible, distribute the results of its endeavors.**

The incentives that the market provides are the first choice for addressing the problem of critical infrastructure protection; regulation will be used only in the face of a material failure of the market to protect the health, safety or well-being of the American people. In such cases, agencies shall identify and assess available alternatives to direct regulation, including providing economic incentives to encourage the desired behavior, or providing information upon which choices can be made by the private sector. These incentives, along with other actions, shall be designed to help harness the latest technologies, bring about global solutions to international problems, and enable private sector owners and operators to achieve and maintain the maximum feasible security.

The full authorities, capabilities and resources of the government, including law enforcement, regulation, foreign intelligence and defense preparedness shall be available, as appropriate, to ensure that critical infrastructure protection is achieved and maintained. Care must be taken to respect privacy rights. Consumers and operators must have confidence that information will be handled accurately, confidentially and reliably. The Federal Government shall, through its research, development and procurement, encourage the introduction of increasingly capable methods of infrastructure protection.

The Federal Government shall serve as a model to the private sector on how infrastructure assurance is best achieved and shall, to the extent feasible, distribute the results of its endeavors.

We must focus on preventative measures as well as threat and crisis management. To that end, private sector owners and operators should be encouraged to provide maximum feasible security for the infrastructures they control and to provide the government necessary information to assist them in that task. In order to engage the private sector fully, it is preferred that participation by owners and operators in a national infrastructure protection system be voluntary.

Close cooperation and coordination with state and local governments and first responders is essential for a robust and flexible infrastructure protection program. All critical infrastructure protection plans and actions shall take into consideration the needs, activities and responsibilities of state and local governments and first responders.

VI. Structure and Organization

The Federal Government will be organized for the purposes of this endeavor around four components:

Lead Agencies for Sector Liaison

For each infrastructure sector that could be a target for significant cyber or physical attacks, there will be a single U.S. Government department which will serve as the lead agency for liaison. Each Lead Agency will designate one individual of Assistant Secretary rank or higher to be the Sector Liaison Official for that area and to cooperate with the private sector representatives (Sector Coordinators) in addressing problems related to critical infrastructure protection and, in particular, in recommending components of the National Infrastructure Assurance Plan. Together, the Lead Agency and the private sector counterparts will develop and implement a Vulnerability Awareness and Education Program for their sector.

Lead Agencies for Special Functions

There are, in addition, certain functions related to critical infrastructure protection that must be chiefly performed by the Federal Government (national defense, foreign affairs, intelligence, law enforcement). For each of those special functions, there shall be a Lead Agency which will be responsible for coordinating all of the activities of the United States Government in that area. Each lead agency will appoint a senior officer of Assistant Secretary rank or higher to serve as the Functional Coordinator for that function for the Federal Government.

Interagency Coordination

The Sector Liaison Officials and Functional Coordinators of the Lead Agencies, as well as representatives from other relevant departments and agencies, including the National Economic Council, will meet to coordinate the implementation of this directive under the auspices of a Critical Infrastructure Coordination Group (CICG), chaired by the National Coordinator for Security, Infrastructure Protection and Counter-Terrorism. The National Coordinator will be appointed by and report to the President through the Assistant to the President for National Security Affairs, who shall assure appropriate coordination with the Assistant to the President for Economic Affairs. Agency representatives to the CICG should be at a senior policy level (Assistant Secretary or higher). Where appropriate, the

CICG will be assisted by extant policy structures, such as the Security Policy Board, Security Policy Forum and the National Security and Telecommunications and Information System Security Committee.

National Infrastructure Assurance Council

On the recommendation of the Lead Agencies, the National Economic Council and the National Coordinator, the President will appoint a panel of major infrastructure providers and state and local government officials to serve as the National Infrastructure Assurance Council. The President will appoint the Chairman. The National Coordinator will serve as the Council's Executive Director. The National Infrastructure Assurance Council will meet periodically to enhance the partnership of the public and private sectors in protecting our critical infrastructures and will provide reports to the President as appropriate. Senior Federal Government officials will participate in the meetings of the National Infrastructure Assurance Council as appropriate.

VII. Protecting Federal Government Critical Infrastructures

Every department and agency of the Federal Government shall be responsible for protecting its own critical infrastructure, especially its cyber-based systems. Every department and agency Chief Information Officer (CIO) shall be responsible for information assurance. Every department and agency shall appoint a Chief Infrastructure Assurance Officer (CIAO) who shall be responsible for the protection of all of the other aspects of that department's critical infrastructure. The CIO may be double-hatted as the CIAO at the discretion of the individual department. These officials shall establish procedures for obtaining expedient and valid authorizations to allow vulnerability assessments to be performed on government computer and physical systems. The Department of Justice shall establish legal guidelines for providing for such authorizations.

No later than 180 days from issuance of this directive, every department and agency shall develop a plan for protecting its own critical infrastructure,

> # Vulnerability Assessment
> A Department of Defense, command, or unit-level evaluation (assessment) to determine the vulnerability of a terrorist attack against an installation, unit, exercise, port, ship, residence, facility, or other site. Identifies areas of improvement to withstand, mitigate, or deter acts of violence or terrorism.
> Department of Defense Joint Publication 3-07.2

including but not limited to its cyber-based systems. The National Coordinator shall be responsible for coordinating analyses required by the departments and agencies of inter-governmental dependencies and the mitigation of those dependencies. The Critical Infrastructure Coordination Group (CICG) shall sponsor an expert review process for those plans. No later than two years from today, those plans shall have been implemented and shall be updated every two years. In meeting this schedule, the Federal Government shall present a model to the private sector on how best to protect critical infrastructure.

VIII. Tasks

Within 180 days, the Principals Committee should submit to the President a schedule for completion of a National Infrastructure Assurance Plan with milestones for accomplishing the following subordinate and related tasks.

- **Vulnerability Analyses**

  For each sector of the economy and each sector of the government that might be a target of infrastructure attack intended to significantly damage the United States, there shall be an initial vulnerability assessment, followed by periodic updates. As appropriate, these assessments shall also include the determination of the minimum essential infrastructure in each sector.

- **Remedial Plan**

  Based upon the vulnerability assessment, there shall be a recommended remedial plan. The plan shall identify time lines for implementation, responsibilities and funding.

- **Warning**

  A national center to warn of significant infrastructure attacks will be established immediately (see Annex A). As soon thereafter as possible, we will put in place an enhanced system for detecting and analyzing such attacks, with maximum possible participation of the private sector.

- **Response**

  A system for responding to a significant infrastructure attack while it is underway, with the goal of isolating and minimizing damage.

- **Reconstitution**

  For varying levels of successful infrastructure attacks, we shall have a system to reconstitute minimum required capabilities rapidly.

- **Education and Awareness**

  There shall be Vulnerability Awareness and Education Programs within both the government and the private sector to sensitize people regarding the importance of security and to train them in security standards, particularly regarding cyber systems.

- **Research and Development**

  Federally-sponsored research and development in support of infrastructure protection shall be coordinated, be subject to multi-year planning, take into account private sector research, and be adequately funded to minimize our vulnerabilities on a rapid but achievable timetable.

- **Intelligence**

  The Intelligence Community shall develop and implement a plan for enhancing collection and analysis of the foreign threat to our national infrastructure, to include but not be limited to the foreign cyber/information warfare threat.

- **International Cooperation**

  There shall be a plan to expand cooperation on critical infrastructure protection with like-minded and friendly nations, international organizations and multinational corporations.

- **Legislative and Budgetary Requirements**

  There shall be an evaluation of the executive branch's legislative authorities and budgetary priorities regarding critical infrastructure, and ameliorative recommendations shall be made to the President as necessary. The evaluations and recommendations, if any, shall be coordinated with the Director of OMB.

IX. Implementation

In addition to the 180-day report, the National Coordinator, working with the National Economic Council, shall provide an annual report on the implementation of this directive to the President and the heads of departments and agencies, through the Assistant to the President for National Security Affairs. The report should include an updated threat assessment, a status report on achieving the milestones identified for the National Plan and additional policy, legislative and budgetary recommendations. The evaluations and recommendations, if any, shall be coordinated with the Director of OMB. In addition, following the establishment of an initial operating capability in the year 2000, the National Coordinator shall conduct a zero-based review.

Annex A: Structure and Organization

Lead Agencies: Clear accountability within the U.S. Government must be designated for specific sectors and functions. The following assignments of responsibility will apply:

Lead Agencies for Sector Liaison:

- Commerce Information and communications
- Treasury Banking and finance
- EPA Water supply
- Transportation Aviation
- Highways (including trucking and intelligent transportation systems)
- Mass transit
- Pipelines
- Rail
- Waterborne commerce
- Justice/FBI Emergency law enforcement services
- FEMA Emergency fire service
- Continuity of government services
- HHS Public health services, including prevention, surveillance, laboratory services and personal health services
- Energy Electric power
- Oil and gas production and storage

Lead Agencies for Special Functions:

- Justice/FBI Law enforcement and internal security
- CIA Foreign intelligence
- State Foreign affairs
- Defense National defense

In addition, OSTP shall be responsible for coordinating research and development agendas and programs for the government through the National Science and Technology Council. Furthermore, while Commerce is the lead agency for information and communication, the Department of Defense will retain its Executive Agent responsibilities for the National Communications System and support of the President's National Security Telecommunications Advisory Committee.

National Coordinator

The National Coordinator for Security, Infrastructure Protection and Counter-Terrorism shall be responsible for coordinating the implementation of this directive. The National Coordinator will report to the President through the Assistant to the President for National Security Affairs. The National Coordinator will also participate as a full member of Deputies or Principals Committee meetings when they meet to consider infrastructure issues. Although the National Coordinator will not direct Departments and Agencies, he or she will ensure interagency coordination for policy development and implementation, and will review crisis activities concerning infrastructure events with significant foreign involvement. The National Coordinator will provide advice, in the context of the established annual budget process, regarding agency budgets for critical infrastructure protection. The National Coordinator will chair the Critical Infrastructure Coordination Group (CICG), reporting to the Deputies Committee (or, at the call of its chair, the Principals Committee). The Sector Liaison Officials and Special Function Coordinators shall attend the CICG's meetings. Departments and agencies shall each appoint to the CICG a senior official (Assistant Secretary level or higher) who will regularly attend its meetings. The National Security Advisor shall appoint a Senior Director for Infrastructure Protection on the NSC staff.

A National Plan Coordination (NPC) staff will be contributed on a non-reimbursable basis by the departments and agencies, consistent with law. The NPC staff will integrate the various sector plans into a National Infrastructure Assurance Plan and coordinate analyses of the U.S. Government's own dependencies on critical infrastructures. The NPC staff will also help coordinate a national education and awareness program, and legislative and public affairs.

The Defense Department shall continue to serve as Executive Agent for the Commission Transition Office, which will form the basis of the NPC, during the remainder of FY98. Beginning in FY99, the NPC shall be an office of the Commerce Department. The Office of Personnel Management shall provide the necessary assistance in facilitating the NPC's operations. The NPC will terminate at the end of FY01, unless extended by Presidential directive.

Warning and Information Centers

As part of a national warning and information sharing system, the President immediately authorizes the FBI to expand its current organization to a full scale National Infrastructure Protection Center (NIPC). This organization shall serve as a national critical infrastructure threat assessment, warning, vulnerability, and law enforcement investigation and response entity. During the initial period of six to twelve months, the President also directs the National Coordinator and the Sector Liaison Officials, working together with the Sector Coordinators, the Special Function Coordinators and representatives from the National Economic Council, as appropriate, to consult with owners and operators of the critical infrastructures to encourage the creation of a private sector sharing and analysis center, as described below.

National Infrastructure Protection Center (NIPC)

The NIPC will include FBI, USSS, and other investigators experienced in computer crimes and infrastructure protection, as well as representatives detailed from the Department of Defense, the Intelligence Community and Lead Agencies. It will be linked electronically to the rest of the Federal Government, including other warning and operations centers, as well as any private sector sharing and analysis centers. Its mission will include providing timely warnings of intentional threats, comprehensive analyses and law enforcement investigation and response. All executive departments and agencies shall cooperate with the NIPC and provide

The NIPC was transferred to DHS in March 2003 and was dispersed throughout the Department, including the Office of Operations Coordination and the Office of Infrastructure Protection.

such assistance, information and advice that the NIPC may request, to the extent permitted by law.

All executive departments shall also share with the NIPC information about threats and warning of attacks and about actual attacks on critical government and private sector infrastructures, to the extent permitted by law. The NIPC will include elements responsible for warning, analysis, computer investigation, coordinating emergency response, training, outreach and development and application of technical tools. In addition, it will establish its own relations directly with others in the private sector and with any information sharing and analysis entity that the private sector may create, such as the Information Sharing and Analysis Center described below.

The NIPC, in conjunction with the information originating agency, will sanitize law enforcement and intelligence information for inclusion into analyses and reports that it will provide, in appropriate form, to relevant federal, state and local agencies; the relevant owners and operators of critical infrastructures; and to any private sector information sharing and analysis entity. Before disseminating national security or other information that originated from the intelligence community, the NIPC will coordinate fully with the intelligence community through existing procedures. Whether as sanitized or un-sanitized reports, the NIPC will issue attack warnings or alerts to increases in threat condition to any private sector information sharing and analysis entity and to the owners and operators. These warnings may also include guidance regarding additional protection measures to be taken by owners and operators. Except in extreme emergencies, the NIPC shall coordinate with the National Coordinator before issuing public warnings of imminent attacks by international terrorists, foreign states or other malevolent foreign powers.

The NIPC will provide a national focal point for gathering information on threats to the infrastructures. Additionally, the NIPC will provide the principal means of facilitating and coordinating the Federal Government's response to an incident, mitigating attacks, investigating threats and monitoring reconstitution efforts. Depending on the nature and level of a foreign threat/attack, protocols established between special function agencies (DOJ/DOD/CIA), and the ultimate decision of the President, the NIPC may be placed in a direct support role to either DOD or the Intelligence Community.

Information Sharing and Analysis Center (ISAC)

The National Coordinator, working with Sector Coordinators, Sector Liaison Officials and the National Economic Council, shall consult with owners and operators of the critical infrastructures to strongly encourage the creation of a private sector information sharing and analysis center. The actual design and functions of the center and its relation to the NIPC will be determined by the private sector, in consultation with and with assistance from the Federal Government. Within 180 days of this directive, the National Coordinator, with the assistance of the CICG including the National Economic Council, shall identify possible methods of providing federal assistance to facilitate the startup of an ISAC.

Such a center could serve as the mechanism for gathering, analyzing, appropriately sanitizing and disseminating private sector information to both industry and the NIPC. The center could also gather, analyze and disseminate information from the NIPC for further distribution to the private sector. While crucial to a successful government-industry partnership, this mechanism for sharing important information about vulnerabilities, threats, intrusions and anomalies is not to interfere with direct information exchanges between companies and the government. As ultimately designed by private sector representatives, the ISAC may emulate particular aspects of such institutions as the Centers for Disease Control and Prevention that have proved highly effective, particularly its extensive interchanges with the private and non-federal sectors. Under such a model, the ISAC would possess a large degree of technical focus and expertise and non-regulatory and non-law enforcement missions. It would establish baseline statistics and patterns on the various infrastructures, become a clearinghouse for information within and among the various sectors, and provide a library for historical data to be used by the private sector and, as deemed appropriate by the ISAC, by the government. Critical to the success of such an institution would be its timeliness, accessibility, coordination, flexibility, utility and acceptability.

Annex B: Additional Taskings

The National Coordinator shall commission studies on the following subjects:

- Liability issues arising from participation by private sector companies in the information sharing process.

- The necessity of document and information classification and the impact of such classification on useful dissemination, as well as the methods and information systems by which threat and vulnerability information can be shared securely while avoiding disclosure or unacceptable risk of disclosure to those who will misuse it.

- The improved protection, including secure dissemination and information handling systems, of industry trade secrets and other confidential business data, law enforcement information and evidentiary material, classified national security information, unclassified material disclosing vulnerabilities of privately owned infrastructures and apparently innocuous information that, in the aggregate, it is unwise to disclose.

- The implications of sharing information with foreign entities where such sharing is deemed necessary to the security of United States infrastructures. The potential benefit to security standards of mandating, subsidizing, or otherwise assisting in the provision of insurance for selected critical infrastructure providers and requiring insurance tie-ins for foreign critical infrastructure providers hoping to do business with the United States.

Public Outreach

In order to foster a climate of enhanced public sensitivity to the problem of infrastructure protection, the following actions shall order the oversight of the National Coordinator, together with the relevant Cabinet agencies shall consider a series of conferences: (1) that will bring together national leaders in the public and private sectors to propose programs to increase the commitment to information security; (2) that convoke academic leaders from engineering, computer science, business and law schools to review the status of education in information security and will identify changes in the curricula and resources necessary to meet the national demand for professionals in this field; (3) on the issues around computer ethics as these relate to the K through 12 and general university populations.

The National Academy of Sciences and the National Academy of Engineering shall consider a round table bringing together federal, state and local officials with industry and academic leaders to develop national strategies for enhancing infrastructure security.

The intelligence community and law enforcement shall expand existing programs for briefing infrastructure owners and operators and senior government officials.

The National Coordinator shall (1) establish a program for infrastructure assurance simulations involving senior public and private officials, the reports of which might be distributed as part of an awareness campaign; and (2) in coordination with the private sector, launch a continuing national awareness campaign, emphasizing improving infrastructure security.

Internal Federal Government Actions

In order for the Federal Government to improve its infrastructure security, these immediate steps shall be taken:

The Department of Commerce, the General Services Administration, and the Department of Defense shall assist federal agencies in the implementation of best practices for information assurance within their individual agencies.

The National Coordinator shall coordinate a review of existing federal, state and local bodies charged with information assurance tasks, and provide recommendations on how these institutions can cooperate most effectively.

All federal agencies shall make clear designations regarding who may authorize access to their computer systems.

The Intelligence Community shall elevate and formalize the priority for enhanced collection and analysis of information on the foreign cyber/information warfare threat to our critical infrastructure.

The Federal Bureau of Investigation, the Secret Service and other appropriate agencies shall: (1) vigorously recruit undergraduate and graduate students with the relevant computer-related technical skills for full-time employment as well as for part-time work with regional computer crime squads; and (2) facilitate the hiring and retention of qualified personnel for technical analysis and investigation involving cyber attacks.

The Department of Transportation, in consultation with the Department of Defense, shall undertake a thorough evaluation of the vulnerability of the national transportation infrastructure that relies on the Global Positioning System. This evaluation shall include sponsoring an independent, integrated assessment of risks to civilian users of GPS-based systems, with a view to basing decisions on the ultimate architecture of the modernized NAS on these evaluations.

The Federal Aviation Administration shall develop and implement a comprehensive National Airspace System Security Program to protect the modernized NAS from information-based and other disruptions and attacks.

GSA shall identify large procurements (such as the new Federal Telecommunications System, FTS 2000) related to infrastructure assurance, study whether the procurement process reflects the importance of infrastructure protection and propose, if necessary, revisions to the overall procurement process to do so.

OMB shall direct federal agencies to include assigned infrastructure assurance functions within their Government Performance and Results Act strategic planning and performance measurement framework.

The NSA, in accordance with its National Manager responsibilities in NSD-42, shall provide assessments encompassing examinations of U.S. Government systems to interception and exploitation; disseminate threat and vulnerability information;

establish standards; conduct research and development; and conduct issue security product evaluations.

Assisting the Private Sector

In order to assist the private sector in achieving and maintaining infrastructure security:

The National Coordinator and the National Infrastructure Assurance Council shall propose and develop ways to encourage private industry to perform periodic risk assessments of critical processes, including information and telecommunications systems.

The Department of Commerce and the Department of Defense shall work together, in coordination with the private sector, to offer their expertise to private owners and operators of critical infrastructure to develop security-related best practice standards.

The Department of Justice and Department of the Treasury shall sponsor a comprehensive study compiling demographics of computer crime, comparing state approaches to computer crime and developing ways of deterring and responding to computer crime by juveniles.

Statutory Spotlight

Presidential Executive Order 13228
Establishing the Office of Homeland Security
and the Homeland Security Council
October 8, 2001, (Excerpts)

By the authority vested in me as President by the Constitution and the laws of the United States of America, it is hereby ordered as follows:

Section 1. Establishment. I hereby establish within the Executive Office of the President an Office of Homeland Security (the "Office") to be headed by the Assistant to the President for Homeland Security.

Section 2. Mission. The mission of the Office shall be to develop and coordinate the implementation of a comprehensive national strategy to secure the United States from terrorist threats or attacks. The Office shall perform the functions necessary to carry out this mission, including the functions specified in section 3 of this order.

Sections 3. Functions. The functions of the Office shall be to coordinate the executive branch's efforts to detect, prepare for, prevent, protect against, respond to, and recover from terrorist attacks within the United States.

(a) **National Strategy**. The Office shall work with executive departments and agencies, State and local governments, and private entities to ensure the adequacy of the national strategy for detecting, preparing for, preventing, protecting against, responding to, and recovering from terrorist threats or attacks within the United States and shall periodically review and coordinate revisions to that strategy as necessary.

(b) **Detection**. The Office shall identify priorities and coordinate efforts for collection and analysis of information within the United States regarding threats of terrorism against the United States and activities of terrorists or terrorist groups within the United States. The Office also shall identify, in coordination with the Assistant to the President for National Security Affairs, priorities for collection of intelligence outside the United States regarding threats of terrorism within the United States.

(i) In performing these functions, the Office shall work with Federal, State, and local agencies, as appropriate, to:

(A) Facilitate collection from State and local governments and private entities of information pertaining to terrorist threats or activities within the United States;

(B) Coordinate and prioritize the requirements for foreign intelligence relating to terrorism within the United States of executive departments and agencies responsible for homeland security and provide these requirements and priorities to the Director of Central Intelligence and other agencies responsible for collection of foreign intelligence;

(C) Coordinate efforts to ensure that all executive departments and agencies that have intelligence collection responsibilities have sufficient technological capabilities and resources to collect intelligence and data relating to terrorist activities or possible terrorist acts within the United States, working with the Assistant to the President for National Security Affairs, as appropriate;

(D) Coordinate development of monitoring protocols and equipment for use in detecting the release of biological, chemical, and radiological hazards; and

(E) Ensure that, to the extent permitted by law, all appropriate and necessary intelligence and law enforcement information relating to homeland security is disseminated to and exchanged among appropriate executive departments and agencies responsible for homeland security and, where appropriate for reasons of homeland security, promote exchange of such information with and among State and local governments and private entities.

(ii) Executive departments and agencies shall, to the extent permitted by law, make available to the Office all information relating to terrorist threats and activities within the United States.

(c) **Preparedness**. The Office of Homeland Security shall coordinate national efforts to prepare for and mitigate the consequences of terrorist threats or attacks within the United States. In performing this function, the Office shall work with Federal, State, and local agencies, and private entities, as appropriate, to:

(i) Review and assess the adequacy of the portions of all Federal emergency response plans that pertain to terrorist threats or attacks within the United States;

(ii) Coordinate domestic exercises and simulations designed to assess and practice systems that would be called upon to respond to a terrorist threat or attack within the United States and coordinate programs and activities for training Federal, State, and local employees who would be called upon to respond to such a threat or attack;

(iii) Coordinate national efforts to ensure public health preparedness for a terrorist attack, including reviewing vaccination policies and reviewing the adequacy of and, if necessary, increasing vaccine and pharmaceutical stockpiles and hospital capacity;

(iv) Coordinate Federal assistance to State and local authorities and nongovernmental organizations to prepare for and respond to terrorist threats or attacks within the United States;

(v) Ensure that national preparedness programs and activities for terrorist threats or attacks are developed and are regularly evaluated under appropriate standards and that resources are allocated to improving and sustaining preparedness based on such evaluations; and

(vi) Ensure the readiness and coordinated deployment of Federal response teams to respond to terrorist threats or attacks, working with the Assistant to the President for National Security Affairs, when appropriate.

(d) **Prevention**. The Office shall coordinate efforts to prevent terrorist attacks within the United States. In performing this function, the Office shall work with Federal, State, and local agencies, and private entities, as appropriate, to:

(i) Facilitate the exchange of information among such agencies relating to immigration and visa matters and shipments of cargo; and, working with the Assistant to the President for National Security Affairs, ensure coordination among such agencies to prevent the entry of terrorists and terrorist materials and supplies into the United States and facilitate removal of such terrorists from the United States, when appropriate;

(ii) Coordinate efforts to investigate terrorist threats and attacks within the United States; and

(iii) Coordinate efforts to improve the security of United States borders, territorial waters, and airspace in order to prevent acts of terrorism within the United States, working with the Assistant to the President for National Security Affairs, when appropriate.

(e) **Protection.** The Office shall coordinate efforts to protect the United States and its critical infrastructure from the consequences of terrorist attacks. In performing this function, the Office shall work with Federal, State, and local agencies, and private entities, as appropriate, to:

(i) Strengthen measures for protecting energy production, transmission, and distribution services and critical facilities; other utilities; telecommunications; facilities that produce, use, store, or dispose of nuclear material; and other critical infrastructure services and critical facilities within the United States from terrorist attack;

(ii) Coordinate efforts to protect critical public and privately owned information systems within the United States from terrorist attack;

(iii) Develop criteria for reviewing whether appropriate security measures are in place at major public and privately owned facilities within the United States;

(iv) Coordinate domestic efforts to ensure that special events determined by appropriate senior officials to have national significance are protected from terrorist attack;

(v) Coordinate efforts to protect transportation systems within the United States, including railways, highways, shipping, ports and waterways, and airports and civilian aircraft, from terrorist attack;

(vi) Coordinate efforts to protect United States livestock, agriculture, and systems for the provision of water and food for human use and consumption from terrorist attack; and

(vii) Coordinate efforts to prevent unauthorized access to, development of, and unlawful importation into the United States of, chemical, biological, radiological, nuclear, explosive, or other related materials that have the potential to be used in terrorist attacks.

(f) **Response and Recovery**. The Office shall coordinate efforts to respond to and promote recovery from terrorist threats or attacks within the United States. In performing this function, the Office shall work with Federal, State, and local agencies, and private entities, as appropriate, to:

(i) Coordinate efforts to ensure rapid restoration of transportation systems, energy production, transmission, and distribution systems; telecommunications; other utilities; and other critical infrastructure facilities after disruption by a terrorist threat or attack;

(ii) Coordinate efforts to ensure rapid restoration of public and private critical information systems after disruption by a terrorist threat or attack;

(iii) Work with the National Economic Council to coordinate efforts to stabilize United States financial markets after a terrorist threat or attack and manage the immediate economic and financial consequences of the incident;

(iv) Coordinate Federal plans and programs to provide medical, financial, and other assistance to victims of terrorist attacks and their families; and

(v) Coordinate containment and removal of biological, chemical, radiological, explosive, or other hazardous materials in the event of a terrorist threat or attack involving such hazards and coordinate efforts to mitigate the effects of such an attack.

(g) **Incident Management**. The Assistant to the President for Homeland Security shall be the individual primarily responsible for coordinating the domestic response efforts of all departments and agencies in the event of an imminent terrorist threat and during and in the immediate aftermath of a terrorist attack within the United States and shall be the principal point of contact for and to the President with respect to coordination of such efforts. The Assistant to the President for Homeland Security shall coordinate with the Assistant to the President for National Security Affairs, as appropriate.

(h) **Continuity of Government**. The Assistant to the President for Homeland Security, in coordination with the Assistant to the President for National Security Affairs, shall review plans and preparations for ensuring the continuity of the Federal Government in the event of a terrorist attack that threatens the safety and security of the United States Government or its leadership. Office of Communications, shall coordinate the strategy of the executive branch for communicating with the public in the event of a terrorist threat or attack within the United States. The Office also shall coordinate the development of programs for educating the public about the nature of terrorist threats and appropriate precautions and responses.

(j) **Cooperation with State and Local Governments and Private Entities**. The Office shall encourage and invite the participation of State and local governments and private entities, as appropriate, in carrying out the Office's functions.

(k) **Review of Legal Authorities and Development of Legislative Proposals**. The Office shall coordinate a periodic review and assessment of the legal authorities available to executive departments and agencies to permit them to perform the functions described in this order. When the Office determines that such legal authorities are inadequate, the Office shall develop, in consultation with executive departments and agencies, proposals for presidential action and legislative proposals for submission to the Office of Management and Budget to enhance the ability of executive departments and agencies to perform those functions. The Office shall work with State and local governments in assessing the adequacy of their legal authorities to permit them to detect, prepare for, prevent, protect against, and recover from terrorist threats and attacks.

(l) **Budget Review**. The Assistant to the President for Homeland Security, in consultation with the Director of the Office of Management and Budget (the "Director") and the heads of executive departments and agencies, shall identify programs that contribute to the Administration's strategy for homeland security and, in the development of the President's annual budget submission, shall review and provide advice to the heads of departments and agencies for such programs. The Assistant to the President for Homeland Security shall provide advice to the Director on the level and use of funding in departments and agencies for homeland security-related activities and, prior to the Director's forwarding of the proposed annual budget submission to the President for transmittal to the Congress, shall certify to the Director the funding levels that the Assistant to the President for Homeland Security believes are necessary and appropriate for the homeland security-related activities of the executive branch.

Section 4. Administration.

(a) The Office of Homeland Security shall be directed by the Assistant to the President for Homeland Security.

(b) The Office of Administration within the Executive Office of the President shall provide the Office of Homeland Security with such personnel, funding, and administrative support, to the extent permitted by law and subject to the availability of appropriations, as directed by the Chief of Staff to carry out the provisions of this order.

(c) Heads of executive departments and agencies are authorized, to the extent permitted by law, to detail or assign personnel of such departments and agencies to the Office of Homeland Security upon request of the Assistant to the President for Homeland Security, subject to the approval of the Chief of Staff.

Section 5. Establishment of Homeland Security Council.

(a) I hereby establish a Homeland Security Council (the "Council"), which shall be responsible for advising and assisting the President with respect to all aspects of homeland security. The Council shall serve as the mechanism for ensuring coordination of homeland security-related activities of executive departments and agencies and development and implementation of homeland security policies.

Members of the Homeland Security Advisory Council – 2012

- William "Bill" Webster (Chair), Retired Partner, Milbank, Tweed, Hadley & McCloy, LLP
- Chief William "Bill" Bratton (Vice Chair), Chairman of Kroll, Altegrity Security Consulting
- Norman "Norm" Augustine, Former Chairman and Chief Executive Officer, Lockheed Martin Corp.
- Leroy "Lee" Baca, Sheriff, Los Angeles County
- Richard "Dick" Cañas, Security Consultant
- Kenneth "Chuck" Canterbury, President, Fraternal Order of Police
- Jared "Jerry" Cohon, President, Carnegie Mellon University
- Ruth David, President and CEO, ANSER (Analytic Services, Inc.)
- Manny Diaz, Senior Partner, Lydecker Diaz
- Mohamed Elibiary, Foundation, Founder, Lone Star Intelligence, LLC
- Clark Kent Ervin, Director, Homeland Security Program, The Aspen Institute
- Ellen Gordon, Associate Director, Naval Postgraduate School, CHDS
- Lee H. Hamilton, Director, the Center on Congress at Indiana University
- Raymond Kelly, Police Commissioner, City of New York
- John Magaw, Self-employed, Domestic and International Security Consultant
- Bonnie Michelman, Director of Police, Security and Outside Services at Massachusetts General Hospital and instructor at Northeastern University's College of Criminal Justice
- Jeff Moss, Chief Security Officer, Internet Corporation for Assigned Names and Numbers (ICANN)
- Martin O'Malley, Governor, State of Maryland
- Sonny Perdue, Former Governor, State of Georgia
- Harold Schaitberger, General President, International Association of Firefighters
- Joe Shirley Jr., Former President, The Navajo Nation
- Lydia W. Thomas, Trustee, Noblis, Inc.
- Frances Fragos Townsend, Senior Vice President - Worldwide Government, Legal and Business Affairs, MacAndrews & Forbes Holdings Inc.
- Chuck Wexler, Executive Director, Police Executive Research Forum
- John "Skip" Williams, Provost and Vice President for Health, The George Washington University

(b) The Council shall have as its members the President, the Vice President, the Secretary of the Treasury, the Secretary of Defense, the Attorney General, the Secretary of Health and Human Services, the Secretary of Transportation, the Director of the Federal Emergency Management Agency, the Director of the Federal Bureau of Investigation, the Director of Central Intelligence, the Assistant to the President for Homeland Security, and such other officers of the executive branch as the President may from time to time designate. The Chief of Staff, the Chief of Staff to the Vice President, the Assistant to the President for National Security Affairs, the Counsel to the President, and the Director of the Office of Management and Budget also are invited to attend any Council meeting. The Secretary of State, the Secretary of Agriculture, the Secretary of the Interior, the Secretary of Energy, the Secretary of Labor, the Secretary of Commerce, the Secretary of Veterans Affairs, the Administrator of the Environmental Protection Agency, the Assistant to the President for Economic Policy, and the Assistant to the President for Domestic Policy shall be invited to attend meetings pertaining to their responsibilities. The heads of other executive departments and agencies and other senior officials shall be invited to attend Council meetings when appropriate.

(c) The Council shall meet at the President's direction. When the President is absent from a meeting of the Council, at the President's direction the Vice President may preside. The Assistant to the President for Homeland Security shall be responsible for determining the agenda, ensuring that necessary papers are prepared, and recording Council actions and Presidential decisions.

Statutory Spotlight

United States Department of Justice
Highlights of the USA Patriot Act
Website, (Excerpts)

Congress enacted the Patriot Act by overwhelming, bipartisan margins, arming law enforcement with new tools to detect and prevent terrorism: The USA Patriot Act was passed nearly unanimously by the Senate 98-1, and 357-66 in the House, with the support of members from across the political spectrum.

The Act Improves Counter-Terrorism Efforts in Several Significant Ways:

1. **The Patriot Act allows investigators to use the tools that were already available to investigate organized crime and drug trafficking.**

    Many of the tools the Act provides to law enforcement to fight terrorism have been used for decades to fight organized crime and drug dealers, and have been reviewed and approved by the courts. As Sen. Joe Biden (D-DE) explained during the floor debate about the Act, "the FBI could get a wiretap to investigate the mafia, but they could not get one to investigate terrorists. To put it bluntly, that was crazy! What's good for the mob should be good for terrorists." (Cong. Rec., 10/25/01)

- **Allows law enforcement to use surveillance against more crimes of terror.**

   Before the Patriot Act, courts could permit law enforcement to conduct electronic surveillance to investigate many ordinary, non-terrorism crimes, such as drug crimes, mail fraud, and passport fraud. Agents also could obtain wiretaps to investigate some, but not all, of the crimes that terrorists often commit. The Act enabled investigators to gather information when looking into the full range of terrorism-related crimes, including: chemical-weapons offenses, the use of weapons of mass destruction, killing Americans abroad, and terrorism financing.

- **Allows federal agents to follow sophisticated terrorists trained to evade detection.**

   For years, law enforcement has been able to use "roving wiretaps" to investigate ordinary crimes, including drug offenses and racketeering. A roving wiretap can be authorized by a federal judge to apply to a particular suspect, rather than a particular phone or communications device. Because international terrorists are sophisticated and trained to thwart surveillance by rapidly changing locations and communication devices such as cell phones, the Act authorized agents to seek court permission to use the same techniques in national security investigations to track terrorists.

- **Allows law enforcement to conduct investigations without tipping off terrorists.**

   In some cases if criminals are tipped off too early to an investigation, they might flee, destroy evidence, intimidate or kill witnesses, cut off contact with associates, or take other action to evade arrest. Therefore, federal courts in narrow circumstances long have allowed law enforcement to delay for a limited time when the subject is told that a judicially-approved search warrant has been executed. Notice is always provided, but the reasonable delay gives law enforcement time to identify the criminal's associates, eliminate immediate threats to our communities, and coordinate the arrests of multiple individuals without tipping them off beforehand. These delayed notification search warrants have been used for decades, have proven crucial in drug and organized crime cases, and have been upheld by courts as fully constitutional.

- **Allows federal agents to ask a court for an order to obtain business records in national security terrorism cases.**

Examining business records often provides the key that investigators are looking for to solve a wide range of crimes. Investigators might seek select records from hardware stores or chemical plants, for example, to find out who bought materials to make a bomb, or bank records to see who is sending money to terrorists. Law enforcement authorities have always been able to obtain business records in criminal cases through grand jury subpoenas, and continue to do so in national security cases where appropriate. These records were sought in criminal cases such as the investigation of the Zodiac gunman, where police suspected the gunman was inspired by a Scottish occult poet, and wanted to learn who had checked the poet's books out of the library. In national security cases where use of the grand jury process was not appropriate, investigators previously had limited tools at their disposal to obtain certain business records. Under the Patriot Act, the government can now ask a federal court (the Foreign Intelligence Surveillance Court), if needed to aid an investigation, to order production of the same type of records available through grand jury subpoenas. This federal court, however, can issue these orders only after the government demonstrates the records concerned are sought for an authorized investigation to obtain foreign intelligence information not concerning a U.S. person or to protect against international terrorism or clandestine intelligence activities, provided that such investigation of a U.S. person is not conducted solely on the basis of activities protected by the First Amendment.

2. **The Patriot Act facilitated information sharing and cooperation among government agencies so that they can better "connect the dots."**

The Act removed the major legal barriers that prevented the law enforcement, intelligence, and national defense communities from talking and coordinating their work to protect the American people and our national security. The government's prevention efforts should not be restricted by boxes on an organizational chart. Now

> # The Patriot Act allows law enforcement officials to obtain a search warrant anywhere a terrorist-related activity occurred.

police officers, FBI agents, federal prosecutors and intelligence officials can protect our communities by "connecting the dots" to uncover terrorist plots before they are completed. As Sen. John Edwards (D-N.C.) said about the Patriot Act, "we simply cannot prevail in the battle against terrorism if the right hand of our government has no idea what the left hand is doing" (Press release, 10/26/01)

•   Prosecutors and investigators used information shared pursuant to section 218 in investigating the defendants in the so-called "Virginia Jihad" case. This prosecution involved members of the Dar al-Arqam Islamic Center, who trained for jihad in Northern Virginia by participating in paintball and paramilitary training, including eight individuals who traveled to terrorist training camps in Pakistan or Afghanistan between 1999 and 2001. These individuals are associates of a violent Islamic extremist group known as Lashkar-e-Taiba (LET), which operates in Pakistan and Kashmir, and that has ties to the al Qaeda terrorist network. As the result of an investigation that included the use of information obtained through FISA, prosecutors were able to bring charges against these individuals. Six of the defendants have pleaded guilty, and three were convicted in March 2004 of charges including conspiracy to levy war against the United States and conspiracy to provide material support to the Taliban. These nine defendants received sentences ranging from a prison term of four years to life imprisonment.

3.   **The Patriot Act updated the law to reflect new technologies and new threats.**

The Act brought the law up to date with current technology, so we no longer have to fight a digital-age battle with antique weapons-legal authorities leftover from the era of rotary telephones. When investigating the murder of *Wall Street Journal* reporter Daniel Pearl, for example, law enforcement used one of the Act's new authorities to use high-tech means to identify and locate some of the killers.

- **Allows law enforcement officials to obtain a search warrant anywhere a terrorist-related activity occurred.**

    Before the Patriot Act, law enforcement personnel were required to obtain a search warrant in the district where they intended to conduct a search. However, modern terrorism investigations often span a number of districts, and officers therefore had to obtain multiple warrants in multiple jurisdictions, creating unnecessary delays. The Act provides that warrants can be obtained in any district in which terrorism-related activities occurred, regardless of where they will be executed. This provision does not change the standards governing the availability of a search warrant, but streamlines the search-warrant process.

- **Allows victims of computer hacking to request law enforcement assistance in monitoring the "trespassers" on their computers.**

    This change made the law technology-neutral; it placed electronic trespassers on the same footing as physical trespassers. Now, hacking victims can seek law enforcement assistance to combat hackers, just as burglary victims have been able to invite officers into their homes to catch burglars.

4.   **The Patriot Act increased the penalties for those who commit terrorist crimes.**

Americans are threatened as much by the terrorist who pays for a bomb as by the one who pushes the button. That's why the Patriot Act imposed tough new penalties on those who commit and support terrorist operations, both at home and abroad. In particular, the Act:

- **Prohibits the harboring of terrorists.**

  The Act created a new offense that prohibits knowingly harboring persons who have committed or are about to commit a variety of terrorist offenses, such as: destruction of aircraft; use of nuclear, chemical, or biological weapons; use of weapons of mass destruction; bombing of government property; sabotage of nuclear facilities; and aircraft piracy.

- **Enhanced the inadequate maximum penalties for various crimes likely to be committed by terrorists:**

  Including arson, destruction of energy facilities, material support to terrorists and terrorist organizations, and destruction of national-defense materials.

- **Enhanced a number of conspiracy penalties:**

  Including for arson, killings in federal facilities, attacking communications systems, material support to terrorists, sabotage of nuclear facilities, and interference with flight crew members. Under previous law, many terrorism statutes did not specifically prohibit engaging in conspiracies to commit the underlying offenses. In such cases, the government could only bring prosecutions under the general federal conspiracy provision, which carries a maximum penalty of only five years in prison.

- **Punishes terrorist attacks on mass transit systems.**

- **Punishes bioterrorists.**

- **Eliminates the statutes of limitations for certain terrorism crimes and lengthens them for other terrorist crimes.**

The government's success in preventing another catastrophic attack on the American homeland since September 11, 2001, would have been much more difficult, if not impossible, without the USA Patriot Act. The authorities Congress provided have substantially enhanced our ability to prevent, investigate, and prosecute acts of terror.

Editor's Comments

Perhaps the two most significant pieces of legislation since the Civil Rights movement of the 1960's are the USA PATRIOT ACT of 2001 and the Homeland Security Act of 2002.

The Patriot Act conferred new powers to U.S. law enforcement officials with respect to terrorism investigations. Typically reserved for organized crime and drug trafficking investigations, these enhanced tools included "roving wiretaps", a delay in the need for judicially-approved search warrants during electronic surveillances, and access to business records with court approval (a departure from the traditional requirements of a grand jury subpoena). The Patriot Act also updated existing law to reflect new technologies and new threats and increased penalties for terrorist crimes. Despite this apparent need, lawmakers were concerned with expanding police powers and installed "sunset" provisions (an expiration date for the use of these powers - usually represented in a block of years) within most of these entitlements.

The Homeland Security Act initiated the single largest federal government reorganization in the history of the United States. Seemingly in an instant, 22 federal agencies, including a branch of the United States Armed Forces (Coast Guard), and hundreds of thousands of federal employees were transferred from their existing organizational structures. The recipient of these vital resources was the newly restructured "Department" of Homeland Security. Initially configured as an "Office" of the White House, the Homeland Security Act promoted this organization to the ranks of a legitimate federal department. Also promoted was its organizational head. Special Assistant to the President Tom Ridge assumed the title of "Secretary" and immediately occupied a seat on the President's Cabinet.

With its new resources and elevated status in place, the Department of Homeland Security shifted its primary focus to mission refinement and internalized restructuring.

Further Discussion

1. Discuss the significance of the **Antiterrorism and Effective Death Penalty Act of 1996**.

2. Discuss **Presidential Decision Directive 63** and its role in post 9/11 homeland security.

3. Discuss both the benefits and detriments associated with the **USA Patriot Act of 2001**.

4. Discuss the impact of the **National Security Act of 1947** and the **Central Intelligence Agency Act of 1949** on homeland security.

5. Discuss the need/areas for **future legislation** in the homeland security discipline.

Chapter 05

Organizational Structure

"Everyone in the homeland must play a part. I ask the American people for their patience, their awareness and their resolve. This job calls for a national effort. We've seen it before, whether it was building the transcontinental railroad, fighting World War II or putting a man on the moon; there are some things we can do immediately and we will. Others will take more time, but we will find something for every American to do".

Tom Ridge, Director of the Office of Homeland Security, October 2001

United States Department of Homeland Security
Department Structure
Website, (Excerpts)

Components of the Department of Homeland Security

Office of the Secretary

— Janet Napolitano [handwritten]

The Office of the Secretary oversees Department of Homeland Security (DHS) efforts to counter terrorism and enhance security, secure and manage our borders while facilitating trade and travel, enforce and administer our immigration laws, safeguard and secure cyberspace, build resilience to disasters, and provide essential support for national and economic security - in coordination with federal, state, local, international and private sector partners. The Office of the Secretary is comprised of 11 sections:

- **The Privacy Office**

    [handwritten: open this intro?] The Department of Homeland Security Privacy Office is the first statutorily required privacy office in any federal agency, responsible for evaluating Department programs, systems, and initiatives for potential privacy impacts, and providing mitigation strategies to reduce the privacy impact. The mission of the Privacy Office is to preserve and enhance privacy protections for all individuals, to promote transparency of Department operations, and to serve as a leader in the federal privacy community.

- **The Office for Civil Rights and Civil Liberties**

    The Department of Homeland Security Office for Civil Rights and Civil Liberties (CRCL) supports the Department's mission to secure the nation while preserving individual liberty, fairness, and equality under the law.

    CRCL integrates civil rights and civil liberties into all of the Department activities:

    o Promoting respect for civil rights and civil liberties in policy creation and implementation by advising Department leadership and personnel, and state and local partners.

    o Communicating with individuals and communities whose civil rights and civil liberties may be affected by Department activities, informing them about policies and avenues of redress, and promoting appropriate attention within the Department to their experiences and concerns.

    o Investigating and resolving civil rights and civil liberties complaints filed by the public regarding Department policies or activities, or actions taken by Department personnel.

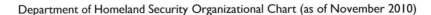

Department of Homeland Security Organizational Chart (as of November 2010)

    o   Leading the Department's equal employment opportunity programs and promoting workforce diversity and merit system principles.

- **The Office of the Inspector General**

    The OIG serves as an independent and objective inspection, audit, and investigative body to promote effectiveness, efficiency, and economy in the Department of Homeland Security's programs and operations, and to prevent and detect fraud, abuse, mismanagement, and waste in such programs and operations.

- **The Citizenship and Immigration Services Ombudsman**

    The Ombudsman's Office was created by Congress in the Homeland Security Act of 2002 to help individuals and employers who need to resolve a problem with U.S. Citizenship and Immigration Services (USCIS) and to make recommendations to fix systemic problems and improve the quality of services provided by USCIS.

- **The Office of Legislative Affairs**

    The Office of Legislative Affairs serves as primary liaison to members of Congress and their staffs. The office responds to inquiries from Congress; notifies Congress about Department initiatives, policies, and programs; and keeps other governmental bodies informed concerning Homeland Security measures that affect their operations and Department actions in jointly undertaken security endeavors.

    The Office of Legislative Affairs enhances the ability of the Department to prevent, protect against and respond to threats and hazards to the nation, as well as to ensure safe and secure borders, by providing timely information about Homeland Security and national security issues to members of Congress, the White House and Executive Branch, and to other federal agencies and governmental entities.

    Assistant Secretary, Office of Legislative Affairs Nelson Peacock. Photo credit: Department of Homeland Security.

- **The Office of the General Council**

    The Office of the General Counsel comprises all lawyers within the Department of Homeland Security—over 1,750 dedicated attorneys at headquarters and at operating components.

The Homeland Security Act defines the general counsel as the "chief legal officer of the Department." In this role, he is ultimately responsible for all of the Department's legal determinations and for overseeing all of its attorneys. The general counsel is also the Department's regulatory policy officer, managing the rulemaking program and ensuring that all Department of Homeland Security regulatory actions comply with relevant statutes and executive orders.

The Office of the General Counsel's central tasks include:

- o Providing complete, accurate, and timely legal advice on possible courses of action for the Department;

- o Ensuring that Homeland Security policies are implemented lawfully, quickly, and efficiently;

- o Protecting the rights and liberties of any Americans who come into contact with the Department;

- o Facilitating quick responses to congressional requests for information;

- o Representing the Department in venues across the country, including in the immigration courts of the United States.

- **The Office of Public Affairs**

    The Office of Public Affairs coordinates the public affairs activities of all of the Department's components and offices, and serves as the federal government's lead public information office during a national emergency or disaster.

    The Office of Public Affairs is the primary point of contact for news media, organizations and the general public seeking information about Department of Homeland Security's programs, policies, procedures, statistics, and services. The Office assists the Secretary on all public affairs, as well as strategic and internal communications matters.

- **The Office of Counternarcotics Enforcement**

    The Office of Counternarcotics Enforcement (CNE) coordinates policy and operations to stop the entry of illegal drugs into the United States, and works to track and sever the connections between illegal drug trafficking and terrorism.

    The responsibilities of the Director of CNE include:

    - o Coordinating policy and operations within the Department, between the Department and other federal departments and agencies, and between the Department and state and local agencies with respect to stopping the entry of illegal drugs into the United States;

- o Ensuring the adequacy of resources within the Department for stopping the entry of illegal drugs into the United States;

- o Recommending the appropriate financial and personnel resources necessary to help the Department better fulfill its responsibility to stop the entry of illegal drugs into the United States;

- o Tracking and severing connections between illegal drug trafficking and terrorism within the Joint Terrorism Task Force construct; and

- o Representing the Department on all task forces, committees, or other entities whose purpose is to coordinate the counternarcotics enforcement activities of the Department and other federal, state or local agencies.

- **The Office of the Executive Secretariat**

  The Office of the Executive Secretariat (ESEC) provides all manner of direct support to the Secretary and Deputy Secretary, as well as related support to leadership and management across the Department. This support takes many forms, the most well known being accurate and timely dissemination of information and written communications from throughout the Department and homeland security partners to the Secretary and Deputy Secretary.

- **The Office of the Military Advisor to the Secretary**

  The Military Advisor's Office advises on facilitating, coordinating and executing policy, procedures, preparedness activities and operations between the Department and the Department of Defense.

- **The Office of Intergovernmental Affairs**

  The Office of Intergovernmental Affairs (IGA) promotes an integrated national approach to homeland security by coordinating and advancing federal interaction with state, local, tribal, and territorial (SLTT) governments. IGA is responsible for opening the homeland security dialogue with executive-level partners at the SLTT levels, along with the national associations that represent them.

  IGA is focused on four major areas, each of which is served by a "Desk" dedicated to serving its stakeholders. The State, Local, Tribal, and Public Engagement

Assistant Secretary for Office of Intergovernmental Affairs: Betsy Markey. Photo credit: Department of Homeland Security.

Desks are each served by a Director, who is charged with overseeing outreach and developing lasting partnerships with state, local, tribal, and territorial (SLTT) stakeholders on a variety of issues and policy agendas.

o **State Desk**

The State Desk is the designated lead for state relations and consultation at the Department. Governors, State Homeland Security Advisors (HSA), and state agencies constitute a large amount of the Department's outreach and collaboration. IGA State Coordinators are tasked with maintaining relationships and situational awareness of events and issues in all 56 states and territories, as well as communicating with numerous associations that address homeland security-related issues.

State Coordinators are also responsible for maintaining an up-to-date awareness and continuous communication with all Department of Homeland Security components, and facilitating direct communication and flow of information on all Department issues with our SLTT stakeholders.

o **Local and Urban Affairs Desk**

The Local and Urban Affairs Desk is the designated lead for local and urban relations and consultation at the Department. Through the Local and Urban Affairs Desk at IGA, the Department emphasizes direct relationships with cities and localities across the country in order to understand the needs of one of our key stakeholders and to incorporate local and urban views into the policy formation process.

o **Tribal Desk**

IGA is the designated lead for tribal relations and consultation at the Department. IGA has identified a number of near- and medium-term actions the Department should take to implement the policies and directives of E.O. 13175 and the November 5, 2009 Presidential Memorandum.

o **Public Engagement Desk**

The Public Engagement Desk at IGA extends beyond Intergovernmental Affairs, to include special projects, policy, and outreach initiatives. The Public Engagement Desk serves as the primary coordinator between IGA, the Office of Legislative Affairs (OLA), and the Private Sector Office (PSO) to streamline communication and coordination efforts with intergovernmental partners throughout the Department. Additionally, the Public Engagement Desk is responsible for strategic communication and announcements from the Department's Office of Public Affairs to IGA stakeholders during steady-state as well as crisis communications.

Department Spotlight

The Office of the General Council

- **Transportation Security Administration (TSA)**

    The responsibilities of the TSA chief counsel include providing legal advice to the commissioner and other senior TSA leaders on legal issues associated with the TSA mission, as well as overseeing both criminal and civil enforcement of federal laws relating to transportation security; conducting or managing litigation before courts or administrative tribunals; assisting in the development of TSA's legislative and regulatory programs; interpreting applicable statutory or regulatory authority; helping to shape TSA's legal posture in international matters, and advising TSA on implementing TSA security directives and necessary adjustments to operating procedures.

General Counsel: Ivan K. Fong. Photo credit: Department of Homeland Security.

- **Customs and Border Protection (CBP)**

    The responsibilities of the CBP chief counsel include providing legal advice to the commissioner and other senior CBP leaders on legal issues associated with the CBP mission, as well as providing legal advice and support to all components of CBP; representing CBP in administrative hearings; providing litigation support to the Department of Justice; completing the administrative collection of civil fines and penalties; providing comprehensive legal services to all components of CBP; reviewing legislative and regulatory proposals; and providing legal training to operational staff.

- **U.S. Citizenship and Immigration Services (USCIS)**

    The responsibilities of the USCIS chief counsel include providing legal advice to the director and other senior USCIS leaders on legal issues associated with the USCIS mission, as well as providing legal support to USCIS components and the DOJ Office of Immigration Litigation; providing legal advice on the adjudication of applicants for temporary visa status, permanent residence, citizenship and asylum; offering legal education and training to USCIS personnel; reviewing legislative and regulatory proposals; representing USCIS in visa petition appeals and in administrative proceedings.

- **Immigration and Customs Enforcement (ICE)**

    The responsibilities of the principal legal advisor include providing legal advice to the assistant secretary and other senior ICE leaders on legal issues associated with the ICE mission, as well as representing the Department in all exclusion, deportation, and removal proceedings; prosecuting removal court cases; handling Board of Immigration Appeal cases; providing litigation support to U.S. Attorney Offices; assisting with removal order reinstatements, administrative removal orders, and expedited removals; reviewing legislative and regulatory proposals; providing legal training and ethics guidance to all ICE personnel; and representing ICE in court and administrative proceedings.

- **U.S. Secret Service (USSS)**

    The responsibilities of the USSS chief counsel include providing legal advice to the director and other senior Secret Service leaders on legal issues associated with the Secret Service protective and investigative missions, and its administrative responsibilities, as well as providing support to the DOJ in their defense of claims against the Secret Service and its employees; preparing comments on proposed legislation, draft testimony, and policy; directing the agency's ethics program; reviewing documents related to assets forfeiture; making determinations concerning the release of information under the FOIA, the Privacy Act, civil/criminal discovery, subpoena or other request; and representing the Secret Service in administrative hearings.

- **Federal Emergency Management Agency (FEMA)**

    The responsibilities of the FEMA chief counsel include providing legal advice to the administrator and other senior FEMA leaders on legal issues associated with the FEMA mission, as well as interpreting applicable statutory or regulatory authority with respect to disaster and emergency assistance, national preparedness, National Continuity Programs, the National Flood Insurance Program and the National Response Framework; conducting or managing litigation before courts and administrative tribunals; providing legal advice on fiscal law issues, procurement actions, FOIA and Privacy Act; reviewing legislative and regulatory proposals; and providing training and counseling through the Alternative Dispute Resolution Program to reduce complaints against the agency and improve workplace communication and coordination.

- **U.S. Coast Guard (USCG)**

    The responsibilities of the judge advocate general include delivering legal services throughout the Coast Guard to support mission execution, managing the Coast Guard Legal Program, and providing legal advice to the commandant and other senior leaders in areas including international and maritime law, including drug and alien migrant interdiction, counterterrorism and defense operations, marine safety and facilitating maritime commerce, and protecting living marine resources and the environment; military justice; litigation and claims; legislation and rulemaking; environmental law; legal assistance; and major systems acquisition.

- **Federal Law Enforcement Training Center (FLETC)**

  The responsibilities of the FLETC chief counsel include providing legal advice to the Director and other senior FLETC leaders on legal issues associated with the FLETC mission, as well as representing FLETC in Equal Employment Opportunity and employment disciplinary cases; representing FLETC in administrative hearings; providing legal advice and assistance in procurement related matters and representing FLETC in bid protest and contract disputes; processing and adjudicating claims under the Military and Civilian Employees Compensation Act and the Federal Tort Claims Act; providing legal advice and assistance on fiscal law issues and legislative matters; providing legal advice on information/intellectual law matters to include copyright, the Freedom of Information Act (FOIA) and the Privacy Act; and providing legal training for federal, state, local and international law enforcement officers attending basic and advanced training at FLETC's four domestic and two international training sites.

National Protection and Programs Directorate

The goal of the National Protection and Programs Directorate is to advance the Department's risk-reduction mission. Reducing risk requires an integrated approach that encompasses both physical and virtual threats and their associated human elements.

- **The Federal Protective Service**

The Federal Protective Service is a federal law enforcement agency that provides integrated security and law enforcement services to federally owned and leased buildings, facilities, properties and other assets.

The FPS mission is to render federal properties safe and secure for federal employees, officials and visitors in a professional and cost effective manner by

Photo credit: Department of Homeland Security.

deploying a highly trained and multi-disciplined police force. As the federal agency charged with protecting and delivering integrated law enforcement and security services to facilities owned or leased by the General Services Administration (GSA), FPS employs 1,225 federal staff (including 900 law enforcement security officers, criminal investigators, police officers, and support personnel) and 15,000 contract guard staff to secure over 9,000 buildings and safeguard their occupants.

Primary Protective Services

- Conducting Facility Security Assessments
- Designing countermeasures for tenant agencies
- Maintaining uniformed law enforcement presence
- Maintaining armed contract security guards
- Performing background suitability checks for contract employees
- Monitoring security alarms via centralized communication centers

Additional Protective Services

- Conducting criminal investigations
- Sharing intelligence among local/state/federal
- Protecting special events
- Working with FEMA to respond to natural disasters
- Offering special operations including K-9 explosive detection
- Training federal tenants in crime prevention and Occupant Emergency Planning

- **Office of Cybersecurity and Communications**

   The Office of Cybersecurity and Communications is responsible for enhancing the security, resiliency, and reliability of the nation's cyber and communications

manfunct

The NCCIC is organized into six functional branches:

- **Operations** - coordinates incident response efforts internally, with public and private sector partners, and with existing NCCIC operational elements.
- **Watch & Warning** - fuses information, analysis, requests, and data from DHS and outside sources, and develops recommendations for mitigating emerging threats.
- **Analysis** - examines data from a wide spectrum of public and private sector partner sources, to inform and enrich the knowledge of existing and emerging threats.
- **Planning** - develops strategic plans for the NCCIC, writes action plans used to respond to and manage real-world emergencies, and documents incidents as they evolve.
- **Assist & Assess** - coordinates the deployment of appropriate personnel from existing operational units to the site of an incident to analyze, contain, and mitigate the effects of a cyber or communications emergency.
- **Liaison** - ensures information sharing between the NCCIC and its partners is seamless and constant, and that activities are coordinated and collaborative.

infrastructure. CS&C actively engages the public and private sectors as well as international partners to prepare for, prevent, and respond to catastrophic incidents that could degrade or overwhelm these strategic assets.

CS&C works to prevent or minimize disruptions to our critical information infrastructure in order to protect the public, economy, government services, and the overall security of the United States. It does this by supporting a series of continuous efforts designed to further safeguard federal government systems by reducing potential vulnerabilities, protecting against cyber intrusions, and anticipating future threats.

As the Sector-Specific Agency for the Communications and Information Technology (IT) sectors, CS&C coordinates national level reporting that is consistent with the National Response Framework (NRF).

- **Office of Infrastructure Protection**

Critical Infrastructure

Systems and assets, whether physical or virtual, so vital that the incapacity or destruction of such may have a debilitating impact on the security, economy, public health or safety, environment, or any combination of these matters, across any Federal, State, regional, territorial, or local jurisdiction.

National Infrastructure Protection Plan

The Office of Infrastructure Protection is a component within the National Protection and Programs Directorate. IP leads the coordinated national program to reduce risks to the nation's critical infrastructure posed by acts of terrorism, and to strengthen national preparedness, timely response, and rapid recovery in the event of an attack, natural disaster, or other emergency.

Protecting the nation's critical infrastructure is a key Department of Homeland Security mission established in 2002 by the National Strategy for Homeland Security and the Homeland Security Act.

This is a complex mission. Critical infrastructure ranges from the nation's electric power, food and drinking water to its national monuments, telecommunications and transportation systems, chemical facilities, and much more. The vast majority of critical infrastructure in the United States is privately owned and operated, making public-private partnerships essential to protect and boost the resilience of critical infrastructure and respond to events.

IP manages mission complexity by breaking it down into three broad areas:

- Identify and analyze threats and vulnerabilities.
- Coordinate nationally and locally through partnerships with both government and private sector entities that share information and resources.
- Mitigate risk and effects (encompasses both readiness and incident response).

IP's vision is a safe, secure, and resilient critical infrastructure based on and sustained through strong public and private partnerships. The IP mission is to lead the national effort to mitigate terrorism risk to, strengthen the protection of, and enhance the all-hazard resilience of the nation's critical infrastructure.

To fulfill its mission, IP understands that critical infrastructure owners and operators, planners, and responders need to know:

- What the specific risks are in their locations and to their industries.
- How to coordinate with others within and across sectors and share vital information.
- How to prepare, protect, and respond.

IP addresses these needs through the **National Infrastructure Protection Plan (NIPP)** and a robust set of programs and activities to support critical infrastructure partners in the field. The NIPP establishes both a partnership structure for coordination across 18 critical infrastructure sectors, and a risk management framework to identify assets, systems, networks, and functions whose loss or compromise pose the greatest risk. IP is building on this foundation through expanded mission collaboration with partners, to strengthen not only the protection of critical infrastructure, but also its resilience.

The NIPP structure provides a foundation for strengthening disaster response and recovery. The Critical Infrastructure and Key Resources Support Annex to the National Response Framework (NRF) provides a bridge between the NIPP "steady-state" processes for infrastructure protection and the NRF unified approach to domestic incident management. These documents provide the overarching doctrine that ensures full integration of the two vital homeland security mission areas – critical infrastructure protection and domestic incident management.

Within the sector framework, IP works with public and private partners coordinating efforts to protect critical infrastructure and strengthen incident response. IP initiatives fall into six programmatic areas:

- Partnerships, Outreach, and Training
- Contingency Planning and Incident Management
- Chemical Facility Security and Compliance
- Critical Infrastructure Protective Security and Field Operations
- Infrastructure Analysis, Research, and Development
- Infrastructure Information Collection and Protection

- **Office of Risk Management and Analysis**

  The Office of Risk Management and Analysis (RMA) works to ensure that risk information and analysis are provided to inform a full range of homeland security decisions, including strategy formulation, preparedness priorities, and resource allocations.

  Provides Risk Analysis

  Combining cutting-edge risk analytic techniques with an understanding of the complex nature of homeland security hazards and systems, RMA provides risk and decision analysis to inform a range of prioritization, strategy and policy decisions.

  - **The Strategic National Risk Assessment (SNRA):** Part of the Administration's effort to develop a National Preparedness System and identify core capabilities, in support of Presidential Policy Directive 8 (PPD-8).

  - **Risk Assessment Process for Informed Decision-making (RAPID):** An all-hazards assessment of risk designed to provide information to Department leadership on homeland security risks, and the risk reduced by homeland security programs in support of policy and resource allocation decisions.

  - **Special Events Risk Methodology:** An objective framework for determining the risk associated with Special Events used to inform decisions on the provision of federal support.

  - **National Level Risk Assessments:** High-level assessments of the risks to national interests that will inform strategic-level homeland security decisions.

  Enhances Risk Management Capabilities of Partners

  As a thought leader for the Department on risk management, RMA advances the practice of risk management and its application to homeland security by providing tools, training and technical assistance to a variety of partners across the homeland security enterprise.

- **Technical Assistance:** Tailored analysis, methodological review, guidance and other technical assistance to support the ability of homeland security partners to analyze and manage risk in a consistent and defensible manner.

- **Risk Management Training:** A comprehensive learning and development plan designed to advance and integrate risk management training at the Department.

- **Establishment and Fostering of Partnerships:** Professional relationships with organizations and agencies across the homeland security enterprise, including international bodies, to promote collaboration and integration.

- **Risk Knowledge Management System:** A centralized information-sharing service to support risk analysis and risk management activities across the homeland security enterprise by archiving, curating, and sharing risk-related information, data and models.

Integrates Homeland Security Risk Management Approaches

RMA is leading the effort to establish a common framework for homeland security risk management, including developing policy, doctrine, guidance and governance.

- **Integrated Risk Management Framework:** The governance, doctrine, policy and processes for integrating risk management at the Department; includes the Integrated Risk Management Policy and Directive, the DHS Risk Lexicon, Risk Management Guidelines, and the Fundamentals for Risk Management.

- **Risk Steering Committee Leadership and Support:** The Department's primary body for risk governance, providing a forum for all components and offices to discuss and advance the integration of risk management.

- **Doctrine and Guidance:** Risk Management Fundamentals is the first in a series of publications that will provide a structured approach for the distribution and employment of risk information and analysis efforts across the Department.

- **US-VISIT**

US-VISIT supports the Department of Homeland Security's responsibility to protect the nation by providing biometric identification services that help federal, state, and local government decision makers accurately identify the people they encounter and determine whether those people pose a risk to the United States. US-VISIT supplies the technology for collecting and storing biometric data, provides analysis, updates its watch-list, and ensures the integrity of the data.

Science and Technology Directorate

The Science and Technology (S&T) Directorate manages science and technology research to protect the homeland, from development through transition for Department components and first responders.

The Directorate is comprised of four groups that address basic research through advanced technology development and transition - spanning six primary divisions that address critical homeland security needs. The Directorate captures the technical requirements of Department components through the Capstone Integrated Product Team (IPT) process.

Lead Groups

- **The Homeland Security Enterprise and First Responders Group (FRG)**

  Identifies, validates, and facilitates the fulfillment of First Responder requirements through the use of existing and emerging technologies, knowledge products, and the acceleration of standards. This organization manages working groups, teams, and stakeholder outreach efforts to better understand the requirements of first responders. FRG manages the following offices:

  - Office of Interoperability and Compatibility
  - Technology Clearinghouse/R-Tech
  - National Urban Security Technology Laboratory (NUSTL)

- **The Homeland Security Advanced Research Projects Agency**

  Manages a portfolio of highly innovative programs that are transforming the future mission space for Homeland Security. HSARPA projects push scientific limits to address customer-identified needs. HSARPA manages the following technical divisions:

  - **Borders & Maritime Security Division** develops and transitions tools and technologies that improve the security of our nation's borders and waterways, without impeding the flow of commerce and travel.

  - **Chemical/Biological Defense Division** works to increase the nation's preparedness against chemical and biological threats through improved threat awareness, advanced surveillance and detection, and protective countermeasures.

- **Cyber Security Division** develops the technical capabilities of protecting computer systems and networks

- **Explosives Division** develops the technical capabilities to detect, interdict, and lessen the impacts of non-nuclear explosives used in terrorist attacks against mass transit, civil aviation, and critical infrastructure.

- **Human Factors/Behavioral Sciences Division** develops the technical capabilities to detect, interdict, and lessen the impacts of non-nuclear explosives used in terrorist attacks against mass transit, civil aviation, and critical infrastructure.

- **Infrastructure Protection & Disaster Management Division** focuses on identifying and mitigating the vulnerabilities of the 18 critical infrastructure and key assets that keep our society and economy functioning.

- **The Director of Acquisition Support and Operations Analysis (ASOA)**

  Serves as a conduit for Department components seeking support on a range of technical and analytical requirements and document development throughout the acquisition life cycle. ASOA is made up of three primary components including:

  - Office of Systems Engineering (SYS)

  - Capstone Analysis & Requirements Office (CAR)

  - Test & Evaluation and Standards Office (TES)

- **The Director of Research and Development Partnerships (RDP)**

  Conducts effective outreach and engagement through close partnerships with Department operating components and science and technology groups across the national laboratories, interagency and intelligence communities, academic institutions and the private sector, both domestic and abroad.

  The RDP Group includes:

  - Interagency Office

  - International Cooperative Programs Office

  - Office of National Laboratories
    - Plum Island Animal Disease Center

- ▪ National Bio-defense Analysis and Countermeasures Center
- ▪ National Bio and Agro-Defense Facility
- ▪ Chemical Security Analysis Center

- o Office of Public-Private Partnerships
  - ▪ Small Business Innovative Research Office
  - ▪ Long Range Broad Agency Announcement Office
  - ▪ Office of SAFETY Act Implementation
  - ▪ Commercialization Office

- o Office of University Programs

- o Homeland Security Science & Technology Advisory Committee

- o Executive Director & National Science and Technology Council Liaison

- o Special Projects Office

The Directorate for Management

The Directorate for Management is responsible for Department budgets and appropriations, expenditure of funds, accounting and finance, procurement; human resources, information technology systems, facilities and equipment, and the identification and tracking of performance measurements.

The Office of Policy

The Office of Policy strengthens homeland security by developing and integrating Department-wide policies, planning, and programs in order to better coordinate the Department's prevention, protection, response and recovery missions.

The Office of Policy:

- Leads coordination of Department-wide policies, programs, and planning, which will ensure consistency and integration of missions throughout the entire Department.

- Provides a central office to develop and communicate policies across multiple components of the homeland security network and strengthens the Department's ability to maintain policy and operational readiness needed to protect the homeland.

- Provides the foundation and direction for Department-wide strategic planning and budget priorities.

- Bridges multiple headquarters' components and operating agencies to improve communication among departmental entities, eliminate duplication of effort, and translate policies into timely action.

- Creates a single point of contact for internal and external stakeholders that will allow for streamlined policy management across the Department.

The Office of Health Affairs

The Office of Health Affairs (OHA) serves as the Department of Homeland Security's principal authority for all medical and health issues. OHA provides medical, public health, and scientific expertise in support of the Department of Homeland Security mission to prepare for, respond to, and recover from all threats. OHA serves as the principal advisor to the Secretary and the Federal Emergency Management Agency (FEMA) Administrator on medical and public health issues. OHA leads the Department's workforce health protection and medical oversight activities. The office also leads and coordinates the Department's biological and chemical defense activities and provides medical and scientific expertise to support the Department's preparedness and response efforts.

Office of Heath Affairs Goals

- Provide expert health and medical advice to Department leadership
- Build national resilience against health incidents
- Enhance national and Department medical first responder capabilities
- Protect the Department workforce against health threats

OHA comprises the following divisions:

- **The Health Threats Resilience Division** strengthens national capabilities to prepare and secure the nation against the health impacts of CBRN incidents and other intentional and naturally occurring events.

- **The Workforce Health and Medical Support Division** leads the Department's workforce health protection and medical oversight activities.

The Office of Intelligence and Analysis

The I&A mission is to equip the Homeland Security Enterprise with the intelligence and information it needs to keep the homeland safe, secure, and resilient. I&A's mission is supported by four strategic goals:

Analysis

Our analysis is guided by our Program of Analysis (POA), an assessment of key analytic issues, framed as key intelligence questions (KIQ). These KIQs are shaped by customer needs, Administration and Departmental leadership priorities, and resources. Our KIQs are organized by time frame.

- **Immediate and Ongoing Threat KIQs** focus on short term or operational issues such as imminent terrorist threats to the homeland. Production that addresses these threats provides the Administration and DHS leadership with the intelligence analysis to better inform near-term operational decision to increase the nation's security.

- **Strategic Context KIQs** focus on providing context, trend, or pattern analysis. Production that addresses these KIQs helps our customers understand recent threats in a broader, global, or historical perspective and they shape strategies to combat the threats or address gaps in homeland security. These would include, for example, how the evolving cartel-related violence in Mexico compares to past cartel wars or how threats to our national infrastructure are changing.

- **Opportunity KIQs** focus on emerging issues or topics for which reporting streams are new or fragmentary; for example, these KIQs may describe the kinds of polices or activities that have been effective in combating newly emerging threats.

As might be expected of an intelligence element supporting a Cabinet-level Department, about half of our KIQs in the POA focus on providing intelligence to respond to the strategic needs of our customers. This is followed by our focus on immediate and ongoing threat. About 10 percent of our focus is on identifying new topics and issues that could impact the Department and its customers.

Collection

Our Homeland Security Standing Information Needs (HSEC SINs) form the foundation for information collection activities within the Department and provide other Intelligence Community (IC) and Homeland Security Enterprise members the ability to focus their collection, analytic, and reporting assets in support of the homeland security mission. The HSEC SINs are updated and published annually to ensure the information needs of the Homeland Security Enterprise are continuously collected, identified, and documented. The institutionalized use of HSEC SINs within collection, production, and dissemination practices enhances the ability of Homeland Security Enterprise members to effectively identify and share information with their stakeholders and partners.

Information Sharing

The Office of Intelligence and Analysis (I&A) has a unique mandate within the Intelligence Community and is the federal government lead for sharing information and intelligence with state, local, tribal and territorial governments and the private sector. It is these non-federal partners who now lead the Homeland Security Enterprise in preventing and responding to evolving threats to the homeland. I&A serves as the information conduit and intelligence advocate for state, local, tribal, and territorial governments. I&A supports state and major urban area fusion centers with deployed personnel and systems, training, and collaboration. This National Network of Fusion

Centers is the hub of much of the two-way intelligence and information flow between the federal government and our state, local, tribal and territorial partners. The fusion centers represent a shared commitment between the federal government and the state and local governments who own and operate them. Individually, each represents a vital resource for merging information from national and local sources to prevent and respond to all threats and hazards. Collectively, their collaboration with the federal government, one another (state-to-state and state-to-locality), and with the private sector represents the new paradigm through which we view homeland security. Fusion centers have contributed and will continue to contribute to improvements in information sharing and collaboration that will enhance the nation's overall preparedness.

I&A assumes the program management role for the Department's engagement with the Nationwide Suspicious Activity Reporting (SAR) Initiative (NSI) Program Management Office (PMO). As part of that role, I&A is a direct liaison with the NSI PMO and facilitates the efforts of DHS components and fusion centers in becoming active NSI participants. Additionally, I&A leverages SAR data to create analytical products that assist federal, state, local and tribal partners in their respective homeland security missions.

DHS Intelligence Enterprise

The DHS Intelligence Enterprise consists of diverse components with distinct mission sets: Customs and Border Protection, Immigration and Customs Enforcement, U.S. Citizenship and Immigration Services, U.S. Coast Guard, Transportation Security Administration, U.S. Secret Service, and the Federal Emergency Management Administration. The U/SIA serves as the Chief Intelligence Officer (CINT) for the DHS Intelligence Enterprise. I&A works with, oversees, and advocates for the DHS Intelligence Enterprise members. The CINT leverages the strength of the entire Enterprise in support of individual and collective missions, with I&A acting as a catalyst for promoting enterprise-wide solutions and projects that are designed to capitalize on the individual strengths of the Department and make them mutually reinforcing. I&A also seeks to leverage the capabilities of the IC in support of these important homeland security missions.

Most recently, I&A has initiated the Homeland Security Intelligence Priorities Framework and the Intelligence Enterprise Management Catalogue. The two activities are important tools that will allow DHS to strategically assess all Departmental intelligence and intelligence-related activities. The Intelligence Enterprise Management Catalogue will be a central database that serves as a repository of data on the intelligence functions, capabilities, activities and assets of the DHS Intelligence Enterprise.

The Office of Operations Coordination and Planning

The Office of Operations Coordination and Planning works to deter, detect, and prevent terrorist acts by coordinating the work of federal, state, territorial, tribal, local, and private sector partners and by collecting and fusing information from a variety of sources.

The Office is responsible for:

- Conducting joint operations across all organizational elements.
- Coordinating activities related to incident management.
- Employing all Department resources to translate intelligence and policy into action.
- Overseeing the National Operations Center (NOC) which collects and fuses information from more than 35 Federal, State, territorial, tribal, local, and private sector agencies.

Information is shared and fused on a daily basis by the two halves of the Office that are referred to as the "Intelligence Side" and the "Law Enforcement Side." Each half is identical and functions in tandem with the other but requires a different level of clearance to access information. The Intelligence Side focuses on pieces of highly classified intelligence and how the information contributes to the current threat picture for any given area. The Law Enforcement Side is dedicated to tracking the different enforcement activities across the country that may have a terrorist nexus. The two pieces fused together create a real-time snap shot of the nation's threat environment at any moment.

Through the National Operations Center, the Office provides real-time situational awareness and monitoring of the homeland, coordinates incidents and response activities, and, in conjunction with the Office of Intelligence and Analysis, issues advisories and bulletins concerning threats to homeland security, as well as specific protective measures. The NOC – which operates 24 hours a day, seven days a week, 365 days a year – coordinates information sharing to help deter, detect, and prevent terrorist acts and to manage domestic incidents. Information on domestic incident management is shared with Emergency Operations Centers at all levels through the Homeland Security Information Network (HSIN).

Federal Law Enforcement Training Center

The FLETC serves as an interagency law enforcement training organization for 90 Federal agencies. The FLETC also provides services to state, local, tribal, and international law enforcement agencies. The FLETC is headquartered at Glynco, Ga., near the port city of Brunswick, halfway between Savannah, Ga., and Jacksonville, Fla.

In addition to Glynco, the FLETC operates two other residential training sites in Artesia, N.M., and Charleston, S.C. The FLETC also operates a non-residential in-service re-qualification and advanced training facility in Cheltenham, Md., for use by agencies with large concentrations of personnel in the Washington, D.C., area.

The FLETC has oversight and program management responsibilities at the International Law Enforcement Academies (ILEA) in Gaborone, Botswana, and Bangkok, Thailand. The FLETC also supports training at other ILEAs in Hungary and El Salvador.

DHS Agency Spotlight

Federal Law Enforcement Training Center

For many years, Federal law enforcement organizations in the metropolitan Washington, D.C. area found it difficult to maintain perishable shooting and vehicle operations skills due to a severe shortage of adequate training facilities. In 2000, Congress enacted Public Law 106-346 directing the FLETC "to establish and operate a metropolitan area law enforcement training center for the Department of the Treasury, other Federal agencies, the United States Capitol Police, and the Washington D.C. Metropolitan Police Department," as well as "training for other State and local law enforcement agencies on a space-available basis." The principal function of the center is for firearms and vehicle operations re-qualifications and other continuing professional training.

Since 1970, FLETC has served as the Federal Government's leader in, and provider of, world-class law enforcement training. The Cheltenham training facility continues the FLETC tradition of excellence by providing experienced law enforcement officers relevant, value-added, world-class training with top-rated instructors, course materials, and facilities.

Secretary of Homeland Security Tom Ridge addresses students at the FLETC's Glynco Headquarters, March 25, 2004. Photo credit: Department of Homeland Security.

The 372-acre Cheltenham, Maryland facility is located 15 miles from downtown Washington, D.C., and offers over 24,500 law enforcement officers, from over 76 agencies in the metropolitan Washington, D.C. area, the opportunity to maintain their firearms and vehicle operations skills, as well as, broaden and formalize their knowledge and skills associated with contemporary law enforcement responsibilities.

During 2000, Congress directed the Federal Law Enforcement Training Center (FLETC) to locate suitable properties within the metropolitan Washington, D.C. area to be used for firearms requalification and pursuit driver training programs for area law enforcement officers. Subsequently, the former U.S. Naval Communications Detachment at Cheltenham, Maryland was located for this purpose and on May 10, 2001, GSA transferred the site to the Department of the Treasury, FLETC.

While serving as a U.S. Navy communications station from 1938 to 1998, the Naval Communications Detachment at Cheltenham, Maryland was a critical participant in several important events in US history, including the attack on Pearl Harbor, Hawaii and the 1962 Cuban missile crisis. FLETC Cheltenham carries on this rich tradition of serving our nation.

History

During 2000, Congress directed the Federal Law Enforcement Training Center (FLETC) to locate suitable properties within the metropolitan Washington, D.C. area to be used for firearms requalification and pursuit driver training programs for area law enforcement officers. Subsequently, the former U.S. Naval Communications Detachment at Cheltenham, Maryland was located for this purpose and on May 10, 2001, GSA transferred the site to the Department of the Treasury, FLETC.

While serving as a U.S. Navy communications station from 1938 to 1998, the Naval Communications Detachment at Cheltenham, Maryland was a critical participant in several important events in US history, including the attack on Pearl Harbor, Hawaii and the 1962 Cuban missile crisis. FLETC Cheltenham carries on this rich tradition of serving our nation.

Facilities

- Large indoor firing range (151,605 square feet, 108 firing points, four 25-yard ranges, two 50-yard ranges & one 100-yard range).
- 2.2 mile driver training ranges, including skid control, NEVO, highway response and urban grid.
- Multi-purpose classrooms for leadership and management training.
- Partner agencies office space.
- Video teleconferencing.
- Computer laboratories.
- Firearms simulators.
- Driver training simulators.
- Over 400 acres available for scenario-based exercises, crowd control drills, canine operations, etc.

The Domestic Nuclear Detection Office

The Domestic Nuclear Detection Office (DNDO) is a jointly staffed agency within the Department of Homeland Security. DNDO is the primary entity in the U.S. government for implementing domestic nuclear detection efforts for a managed and coordinated response to radiological and nuclear threats, as well as integration of federal nuclear forensics programs. Additionally, DNDO is charged with coordinating the development of the global nuclear detection and reporting architecture, with partners from federal, state, local, and international governments and the private sector.

Strategic Objectives

- Develop the global nuclear detection and reporting architecture.
- Develop, acquire, and support the domestic nuclear detection/reporting system.
- Characterize detector system performance before deployment.
- Facilitate situational awareness through information sharing and analysis.
- Establish operational protocols to ensure detection leads to effective response.
- Conduct a transformational research and development program.
- Provide centralized planning, integration, and advancement of U.S. government nuclear forensics programs.

Directorates of DNDO

- **Architecture Directorate** determines gaps and vulnerabilities in the existing global nuclear detection architecture, then formulates recommendations and plans to develop an enhanced architecture.

- **Mission Management Directorate** manages DNDO programs in key mission areas, including: Ports of Entry, general aviation, maritime, and the domestic interior.

- **Product Acquisition & Deployment Directorate** carries out the engineering development, production, developmental logistics, procurement and deployment of current and next-generation nuclear detection systems.

- **Transformational & Applied Research Directorate** conducts, supports, coordinates, and encourages an aggressive, long-term research and development program to address significant architectural and technical challenges unresolved by R&D efforts on the near horizon.

- **Operations Support Directorate** develops the information sharing and analytical tools necessary to create a fully integrated operating environment. Residing in the Operations Support Directorate is the Joint Analysis Center, which is an interagency coordination and reporting mechanism and central monitoring point for the GNDA.

- **Systems Engineering & Evaluation Directorate** ensures that DNDO proposes sound technical solutions and thoroughly understands systems performance and potential vulnerabilities prior to deploying those technologies.

- **Red Team & Net Assessments** independently assesses the operational performance of planned and deployed capabilities, including technologies, procedures, and protocols.

- **National Technical Nuclear Forensics Center** provides national-level stewardship, centralized planning and integration for an enduring national technical nuclear forensics capability.

The Transportation Security Administration

The Transportation Security Administration protects the Nation's transportation systems to ensure freedom of movement for people and commerce.

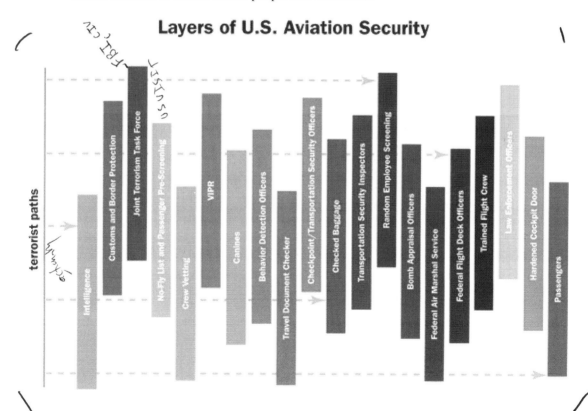

The Transportation Security Administration (TSA) was created in the wake of 9/11 to strengthen the security of the nation's transportation systems while ensuring the freedom of movement for people and commerce. Within a year, TSA assumed responsibility for security at the nation's airports and deployed a federal workforce to screen all commercial airline passengers and baggage. In March 2003, TSA transitioned from the Department of Transportation to the Department of Homeland Security.

TSA employs a risk-based strategy to secure U.S. transportation systems, working closely with stakeholders in aviation, rail, transit, highway, and pipeline sectors, as well as the partners in the law enforcement and intelligence community. The agency continuously sets the standard for excellence in transportation security through its people, processes, technologies and use of intelligence to drive operations.

A TSA official conducts an identification check. Photo credit: Brigitte Dittberner / Department of Homeland Security.

- TSA's nearly 50,000 Transportation Security Officers screen more than 1.7 million passengers each day at more than 450 airports nationwide.

- TSA deploys approximately 2,800 Behavior Detection Officers at airports across the country, leading to more than 2,200 arrests to date.

- TSA utilizes more than 400 TSA explosives specialists in aviation and multimodal environments.

- Thousands of Federal Air Marshals are deployed every day on domestic and international flights.

- TSA has trained and deployed approximately 800 explosives detection canine teams to airports and mass transit systems nationwide.

- TSA screens approximately more than 1.7 million passengers a day and has detected more than 1,000 firearms during airport security screening this year.

- TSA conducts daily background checks on over 15 million transportation-related employees working in or seeking access to the Nation's transportation system.

- To date, approximately 500 advanced imaging technology machines are deployed at airports nationwide, leading to the detection of prohibited, illegal or dangerous items. To further enhance privacy protections, TSA has installed new software on millimeter wave units that automatically detect potential threats using a generic outline of a person for all passengers.

TSA uses layers of security to ensure the security of the traveling public and the Nation's airport checkpoints that their Transportation Security Officers operate. These checkpoints, however, constitute only one security layer of the many in place to protect aviation. Others include intelligence gathering and analysis, checking passenger manifests against watch lists, random canine team searches at airports, federal air marshals, federal flight deck officers and more security measures both visible and invisible to the public.

Each one of these layers alone is capable of stopping a terrorist attack. In combination their security value is multiplied, creating a much stronger, formidable system. A terrorist who has to overcome multiple security layers in order to carry out an attack is more likely to be pre-empted, deterred, or to fail during the attempt.

Program Spotlight

Air Cargo Security Program

When most people use shipping companies, they assume that their next day or two-day package is rushed to the airport immediately to hop onto the next flight. Only a small percent of packages actually make it onto an airplane. An even smaller amount is placed on a passenger-carrying plane. Of the hundreds of thousands of tons of cargo shipped from coast to coast every day, only about 50,000 tons are classified as air cargo. Of that amount, about one quarter is shipped by domestic passenger air carriers.

The Transportation Security Administration (TSA) is responsible for ensuring the security of all modes of transportation, including cargo placed aboard airplanes and particularly focuses on passenger-carrying planes.

TSA worked closely with Congress for more than six months to significantly strengthen security in air cargo through the 9/11 Bill, which was signed into law on August 3, 2007. TSA has met the mandates of the law to date and currently 50 percent of air cargo on passenger carrying aircraft is screened. One hundred percent of the cargo on 96 percent of the flights originating in the United States is now screened. Eighty-five percent of the passengers flying each day from U.S. airports are on planes where all of the cargo has been fully screened.

TSI-C Headcounts

TSA has significantly increased the number of **Transportation Security Inspectors** (Cargo) since FY 2006

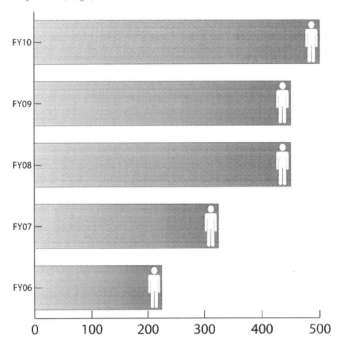

One step in achieving 100 percent screening is the requirement for all airlines operating narrow body passenger aircraft from U.S. airports to screen 100 percent of cargo transported on them.

By working with air carriers and members of the air cargo community, we began screening 100 percent of cargo transported on narrow-body (single-aisle) aircraft. TSA achieved this milestone in October 2008 – a full 22 months before the deadline.

The passenger security impact of this screening is significant: although these aircraft carry only 25 percent of domestic air cargo on passenger aircraft, they account for the majority - approximately 95 percent - of domestic passenger flights. More importantly, these flights carry more than 80 percent of all passengers on flights originating in the United States. Even at the statutory deadline for screening 50 percent of air cargo aboard passenger aircraft, TSA is effectively protecting the vast majority of the flying public.

TSA already has in place a multi-layered, high-tech, industry-cooperative approach, utilizing surprise cargo security inspections called "strikes," covert testing, security directives and 100 percent screening at 250 smaller airports. In 2008, TSA eliminated all exemptions to screening of air cargo for the first time and increased the amount of cargo which is subject to mandatory screening.

With TSA's new air cargo regulation, TSA will be doing 100,000 more background checks, specifically on cargo employees who screen cargo and/or have knowledge of how it is going to be transported or actually transport the cargo. The rule requires more robust checks and more visibility on the shipping companies and their employees. Additionally, TSA has extended security areas at the airport to include air cargo areas.

TSA's more than 460 canine teams each spend at least 25 percent of their work day in the cargo environment. TSA currently has 120 canine teams specifically assigned to the screening of air cargo at our nation's highest cargo volume airports. This presence has significantly increased the amount of cargo screening we are able to conduct.

Program Spotlight

Covert Testing Program

Covert testing in aviation security dates back to the 1970s when airport security checkpoints were first created. What started as rudimentary mock bombs and guns being snuck through the airport has evolved to highly sophisticated systems, used by expert testers with insider knowledge. These experts not only know the system better than anyone, they have the distinct advantage of not being subjected to TSA's 18 other layers of security in addition to the checkpoint. Today's covert testers are the best in the history of aviation in the U.S. and are testing security with items as small as a pen cap.

Many people think the purpose of covert testing is to catch an officer missing an object. While this makes surprising headlines in newspapers and scares the public, the reality is that covert testing is a tool to identify vulnerabilities in the system and uncover weaknesses of training, procedures or technology. It is not designed to test an individual officer or airport but to act as a measure of system-wide effectiveness and drive improvement through training.

"Shoe Bomber" Richard Reid, an al Qaeda-trained terrorist, hid explosives in his black hiking boots hoping to blow up a packed American Airlines flight over the Atlantic Ocean in December 2001. Photo credit: FBI.

It would be simple to make covert testing nothing more than a rubber stamp of security, reverting back to pre-9/11 test kits and touting success rates in the high 90 percentages but that wouldn't provide the critical feedback and adaptive training input required to counter today's terrorist.

The 9/11 hijackers exploited a static system, one that was easy to navigate around and worked inflexibly. Today's covert testers are one of the best assets we have to continually raise the bar on security. In fact, as security officers adapt and begin to consistently discover covert testing methods, testers start all over again, creating more difficult and harder-to-detect tests. This years' long game of cat and mouse more closely simulates real terrorist probing and operations and keeps officers alert and informed of the latest techniques and improvements.

Testing of officers takes many forms, some of these include:

- **Threat Image Projection (TIP)**

  This electronic system randomly superimposes images of bombs and bomb parts into real carry-on bags. Officers can encounter a TIP image in any of the millions of carry-on bags at checkpoints across the country any time of day or night. There are tens of thousands of TIP images and the system is updated with the latest intelligence-driven threats added on a regular basis. Officers are evaluated on the images they detect and training is tailored to drive improvement in detection of threats across the system.

- **Aviation Screening Assessment Program (ASAP)**

  These locally generated assessments use inert bombs, bomb parts and other threat items from checkpoint bomb kits to identify weaknesses in our screening process in order to strengthen screening performance through training, procedures, or technology. These items are placed on TSA or local, state and federal employees or in carry-on or checked bags; passengers are NEVER asked to conduct these assessments or any other TSA covert tests. Recently TSA completed over 4,500 assessments from coast to coast under this program.

- **TSA's Office of Inspection (TSA OI)**

  TSA's Office of Inspection conducts covert tests around the nation with no notice to local or headquarters officials. These expert testers are trained in the latest methods of smuggling bombs, bomb parts and weapons through checkpoints using techniques acquired by national and international intelligence partners and gathered through years of experience. Airports are selected based on a number of factors, including intelligence, threats to aviation and the airport environment. All airports are subject to no-notice testing by TSA-OI. For safety purposes local police are notified the morning that testing begins. Only after testing starts is local TSA management made aware and officers are subjected to no-notice testing. After testing is complete, agents unveil the tests and discuss results with officers and local officials so that training may be improved.

  TSA-OI also works closely with the Office of Security Operations to tailor training to address covert testing results on a national level, raising the bar on security and adapting to the latest threats and techniques.

- **Department of Homeland Security Office of Inspector General (DHS IG)**

  The DHS IG conducts hundreds of covert tests at airports from coast to coast and acts completely independently from TSA. DHS IG agents measure the effectiveness of screening protocols and communicate these results to TSA and the Department of Homeland Security in order to increase effectiveness of screening and security. TSA uses these independent results to validate and improve training.

- **Government Accountability Office (GAO)**

  With over 3,000 employees in offices from Atlanta to Seattle, the GAO, Congress' investigative arm, also conducts independent tests of airport security. They report their findings to Congress and share results with TSA. GAO results have led to increases of security through enhanced training and use of technology.

Covert testing is a critical element of the aviation security system. It measures effectiveness, identifies vulnerabilities, constantly adapts to challenge officers while incorporating intelligence in a useable way. Simply put, without difficult, adapting covert testing, the aviation security system would not be as effective as it is.

Some best practices developed as a result of covert testing include; placing testing bomb kits at every checkpoint in the nation to help officers familiarize themselves with bombs and components, enhanced scrutiny of shoes and other bulky clothing and many other significant enhancements.

United States Customs and Border Protection

United States Customs and Border Protection (CBP) is one of the Department of Homeland Security's largest and most complex components, with a priority mission of keeping terrorists and their weapons out of the U.S. It also has a responsibility for securing and facilitating trade and travel while enforcing hundreds of U.S. regulations, including immigration and drug laws.

U.S. Customs and Border Protection is responsible for guarding nearly 7,000 miles of land border the United States shares with Canada and Mexico and 2,000 miles of coastal waters surrounding the Florida peninsula and off the coast of Southern California. The agency also protects 95,000 miles of maritime border in partnership with the United States Coast Guard.

To secure this vast terrain, CBP's U.S. Border Patrol agents, Air and Marine agents, and CBP officers and agriculture specialists, together with the nation's largest law enforcement canine program, stand guard along America's front line.

- CBP officers protect America's borders at official ports of entry, while Border Patrol agents prevent illegal entry into the United States of people and contraband between the ports of entry.

- CBP's Office of Air and Marine, which manages the largest law enforcement air force in the world, patrols the nation's land and sea borders to stop terrorists and drug smugglers before they enter the United States.

- CBP agriculture specialists prevent the entry of harmful plant pests and exotic foreign animal diseases and confront emerging threats in agro- and bioterrorism.

Each year, more than 11 million maritime containers arrive at our seaports. At land borders, another 11 million arrive by truck and 2.7 million by rail. We are responsible for knowing what is inside, whether it poses a risk to the American people, and ensuring that all proper revenues are collected.

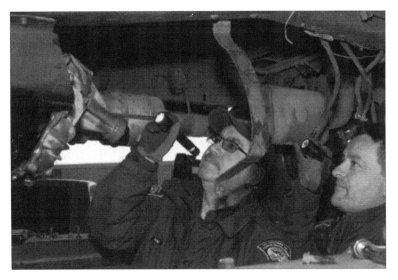

Two U.S. Customs & Border Protection Officers inspecting the remains of a pickup truck that was found to have 5.4 pounds of heroin concealed in the transfer case. The vehicle was trying to bring the heroin in from Mexico. The vehicle was searched at the Paso Del Norte Port of Entry. Photo credit: Steven Green / Department of Homeland Security

Fostering legitimate and safe travel is also a key goal of CBP, which increases passenger security through effective risk assessment. The Secure Electronic Network for Rapid Inspection program, or SENTRI, and the NEXUS U.S.-Canada are trusted traveler programs that expedite entry into the United States, Advance Passenger Information System and the Rice-Chertoff Initiative have aided in accomplishing CBP's travel goals. The Electronic System for Travel Authorization, which is an automated system to pre-approve visitors from Visa Waiver countries; and Global Entry, a trusted traveler program for U.S. citizens, U.S. Nationals, U.S. Lawful Permanent Residents and or citizens of other participating countries.

Effective Targeting

CBP assess all people and cargo entering the U.S. from abroad for terrorist risk. We are able to better identify people who may pose a risk through initiatives such as: the Advance Passenger Information System, United States Visitor and Immigrant Status Indication Technology (known as US-VISIT), and the Student and Exchange Visitor System. CBP regularly refuses entry to people who may pose a threat to U.S. security.

In addition, CBP uses advance information from the Automated Targeting System, Automated Export System, and the Trade Act of 2002 Advance Electronic Information Regulations to identify cargo that may pose a threat. CBP's Office of Intelligence and Operations Coordination's National Targeting Centers enhance these initiatives by

One of many U.S. ports of entry. Photo credit: United States Customs and Border Protection.

synthesizing information to provide tactical targeting. Using risk management techniques, the centers identify suspicious individuals or containers before arrival.

The Automated Commercial Environment has made electronic risk management far more effective. The ACE Secure Data Portal provides a single, centralized on-line access point to connect CBP and the trade community. CBP's modernization efforts enhance border security while optimizing the ever-increasing flow of legitimate trade.

CBP also screens high-risk imported food shipments in order to prevent bio-terrorism/agro-terrorism. For the first time, U.S. Food and Drug Administration and CBP personnel are working side by side at the NTC to protect the U.S. food supply by taking action, implementing provisions of the Bioterrorism Act of 2002. CBP and FDA are able to react quickly to threats of bio-terrorist attacks on the U.S. food supply or to other food related emergencies.

Partnering With Other Countries

CBP has created smarter borders by extending our zone of security beyond our borders.

The Container Security Initiative was announced in January 2002 as a strategy to secure and protect the United States against terrorism and acts of terror involving the international maritime supply chain. CBP stations teams of U.S. officers in 58 operational foreign seaports to work together with host country counterparts to identify and inspect potentially high-risk shipments before they reach the U.S. More than 80 percent of maritime containerized cargo destined to the U.S. originates in or transits through a CSI port and is screened prior to being laden aboard a U.S.-bound vessel.

CBP has implemented joint initiatives with our bordering countries, Canada and Mexico: The Smart Border Declaration and associated 30-Point Action Plan with Canada and The Smart Border Accord with Mexico. The Secure Electronic Network for Travelers' Rapid Inspection (SENTRI) allows pre-screened, low-risk travelers from Mexico to be processed in an expeditious manner through dedicated lanes. Similarly, on our northern border with Canada, we are engaging in NEXUS to identify and facilitate low-risk travelers. Along both borders, CBP has implemented the Free and Secure Trade program. The FAST program utilizes transponder technology and pre-arrival shipment information to process participating trucks as they arrive at the border, expediting trade

On April 23, 2009 CBP launched the International Expedited Travel arrangement with the government of the Netherlands and formed an arrangement called FLUX. As a result of this arrangement, U.S. Citizens approved for Global Entry may apply for and participate in Privium, the government of the Netherlands' trusted traveler program. Reciprocally, citizens of the Netherlands approved for Privium may apply for and participate in Global Entry.

In addition, an agreement with Canada allows CBP to target, screen, and examine rail shipments headed to the U.S. CBP has attachés in Mexico and Canada to coordinate border security issues. CBP Border Patrol agents, the Royal Canadian Mounted Police, and the Drug Enforcement Administration, as well as state and local law enforcement agencies from Canada and the U.S. have joined together to form 14 Integrated Border Enforcement Teams. Covering our entire mutual border with Canada, these teams are used to target cross-border smuggling between Canada and the United States. The teams focus on criminal activity such as smuggling of drugs, humans, and contraband as well as cross-border terrorist movements.

Partnering With the Private Sector

Processing the sheer volume of trade entering the U.S. each year requires help from the private sector. The Customs-Trade Partnership Against Terrorism is a joint government-business initiative designed to strengthen overall supply chain and border security while facilitating legitimate, compliant trade. To date, more than 9,800 companies are partnering with CBP. C-TPAT is the largest, most successful government-private sector partnership to arise out of 9/11.

In addition CBP is piloting the Advanced Trade Data Initiative. This program works with the trade community to obtain information on U.S. bound goods at the earliest possible point in the supply chain. Partnering with carriers, importers, shippers and terminal operators, we are gathering supply chain data and feeding it into our systems to validate container shipments during the supply process. This information increases CBP's existing ability to zero in on suspect movements and perform any necessary security inspections at the earliest point possible in the supply chain.

Inspection Technology and Equipment

Given the magnitude of CBP's responsibility the development and deployment of sophisticated detection technology is essential. Deployment of Non-Intrusive Inspection technology is increasing and viewed as "force multipliers" that enable CBP officers to screen or examine a larger portion of the stream of commercial traffic.

CBP does not rely on any single technology or inspection process. Instead, officers and agents use various technologies in different combinations to substantially increase the likelihood that terrorist weapons including a nuclear or radiological weapon will be detected and interdicted.

Technologies deployed to our nation's land, sea, and airports of entry include large-scale x-ray and gamma-imaging systems. CBP has deployed radiation detection technology including Personal Radiation Detectors, radiation isotope identifiers, and radiation portal monitors. CBP uses trained explosive detector dogs. CBP's Laboratories and Scientific Services Fast Response Team reacts to calls on suspicious containers. The Laboratories and Scientific Services also operates a 24 hours a day, seven days a week, 365 days a year hotline at its Chemical, Biological, Radiation, and Nuclear Technical Data Assessment and Teleforensic Center.

Outbound Inspections – Keeping Weapons and Money from Falling into Terrorist Hands

CBP has the authority to search outbound, as well as in-bound shipments, and uses targeting to carry out its mission in this area. Targeting of outbound shipments and people is a multi-dimensional effort that is enhanced by inter-agency cooperation.

CBP in conjunction with the Department of State and the Bureau of the Census has put in place regulations that require submission of electronic export information on U.S. Munitions List and for technology for the Commerce Control List. This information flows via the Automated Export System. CBP is also working with the Departments of State and Defense to improve procedures on exported shipments of foreign military sales commodities. CBP also works with Immigration and Customs Enforcement and the Bureau of Alcohol, Tobacco, Firearms, and Explosives to seize outbound illicit cash/monetary instruments and illegal exports of firearms /ammunition.

Protecting Border Areas Between Official Ports of Entry

Border Patrol agents and Office of Air and Marine personnel are securing areas between the ports of entry by implementing a comprehensive border enforcement strategy, expanding, integrating, and coordinating the use of technology and communications through.

- **Integrated Surveillance Intelligence System** is a system that uses remotely monitored night-day camera and sensing systems to better detect, monitor, and respond to illegal crossings.

- **Unmanned Aerial Systems** – CBP's remotely piloted surveillance aircraft – are equipped with sophisticated on-board sensors. UASs provide long-range surveillance and are useful for monitoring remote land border areas where patrols cannot easily travel and infrastructure is difficult or impossible to build.

- **Remote Video Surveillance Systems** provide coverage 24-hours-a-day, 7-days-a-week to detect illegal crossings on both the northern and southern borders.

- **Geographic Information System**, a CBP Border Patrol southwest border initiative to track illegal migration patterns.

U.S. Citizenship and Immigration Services

U.S. Citizenship and Immigration Services (USCIS) is the federal agency that oversees lawful immigration to the United States. We are a component of the Department of Homeland Security.

Some of the services they provide include:

- **Citizenship (Includes the Related Naturalization Process)**

    Individuals who wish to become U.S. citizens through naturalization submit their applications to USCIS. They determine eligibility, process the applications and, if approved, schedule the applicant for a ceremony to take the Oath of Allegiance. They also determine

USCIS Chief of Staff Rebecca Carson stands with child during an adopted children's naturalization ceremony as Ambassador Susan Jacobs congratulates child. Photo credit: Andrea Sanchez / Department of Homeland Security.

eligibility and provide documentation of U.S. citizenship for people who acquired or derived U.S. citizenship through their parents.

- **Immigration of Family Members**

  They manage the process that allows current permanent residents and U.S. citizens to bring close relatives to live and work in the United States.

- **Working in the U.S.**

  They manage the process that allows individuals from other countries to work in the United States. Some of the opportunities are temporary, and some provide a path to a green card (permanent residence).

- **Verifying an Individual's Legal Right to Work in the United States (E-Verify)**

  They manage the system that allows participating employers to electronically verify the employment eligibility of their newly hired employees.

- **Humanitarian Programs**

  They administer humanitarian programs that provide protection to individuals inside and outside the United States who are displaced by war, famine and civil and political unrest, and those who are forced to flee their countries to escape the risk of death and torture at the hands of persecutors.

- **Adoptions**

  They manage the first step in the process for U.S. citizens to adopt children from other countries. Approximately 20,000 adoptions take place each year.

- **Civic Integration**

  They promote instruction and training on citizenship rights and responsibilities and provide immigrants with the information and tools necessary to successfully integrate into American civic culture.

- **Genealogy**

  The USCIS Genealogy Program provides family historians and other researchers with timely access to historical immigration and naturalization records of deceased immigrants.

U.S. Immigration and Customs Enforcement

U.S. Immigration and Customs Enforcement is the principal investigative arm of the U.S. Department of Homeland Security (DHS) and the second largest investigative agency in the federal government. Created in 2003 through a merger of the investigative and enforcement elements of the U.S. Customs Service and the Immigration and Naturalization Service, ICE now has more than 20,000 employees in offices in all 50 states and 47 foreign countries.

ICE's primary mission is to promote homeland security and public safety through the criminal and civil enforcement of federal laws governing border control, customs, trade, and immigration. The agency has an annual budget of more than $5.7 billion dollars, primarily devoted to its two principal operating components - Homeland Security Investigations (HSI) and Enforcement and Removal Operations (ERO).

ICE Homeland Security Investigations (HSI) special agents participate in a rigorous training exercise utilizing armored vehicles designated for Special Response Teams. Exercises like this one prepare special agents for national security events. Photo credit: U.S. Immigration and Customs Enforcement.

In June 2010, ICE issued its strategic plan for Fiscal Years 2010-2014. This comprehensive plan lays out how ICE will most effectively meet its responsibilities for criminal investigation and civil immigration enforcement over the next five years. Moreover, ICE is taking steps to streamline and improve its management structure to give the agency a clearer sense of identity and focus.

The plan details four key priorities for the agency's future:

- Prevent terrorism and enhance security
- Protect the borders against illicit trade, travel and finance
- Protect the borders through smart and tough interior immigration enforcement
- Construct an efficient, effective agency

Prevent Terrorism and Enhance Security

ICE seeks to prevent terrorist attacks against the United States and to dismantle threats to homeland security before they materialize. This includes preventing the entry of people and materials that pose a threat to national security; investigating and removing suspected terrorists or their supporters; and preventing the export of weapons and sensitive technologies that could be used to harm the United States, its people, and its allies. Recognizing that preventing terrorism and enhancing our nation's security is a shared responsibility, ICE will work closely and collaboratively with its partners in the intelligence community and in federal, state, local and tribal law enforcement.

> **ICE will continue to target aliens who pose a threat to national security for apprehension and removal from the United States.**

- **Prevent Terrorist Entry into the United States**

    ICE will expand its efforts to identify and prevent the entry of terrorists or their associates into the United States. ICE will do this in two ways. First, ICE will expand its Visa Security Program to those U.S. Embassies and Consulates identified by the Departments of State and Homeland Security as having the highest risk from a terrorism perspective. This expansion will proceed in order of risk, subject to appropriations and departmental approval. Second, ICE will use its broad criminal authorities to investigate, disrupt and dismantle criminal activities that facilitate terrorist travel to, financing in, or employment in the United States. These criminal activities include alien smuggling with a terrorism nexus; international passport, visa and identity fraud; illicit financing schemes designed to support terrorists or their associates; and employment authorization fraud at sensitive government, transportation and industrial facilities in the United States.

- **Remove Individuals Posing a Security Threat**

    ICE will continue to target aliens who pose a threat to national security for apprehension and removal from the United States. ICE will do this through a combined use of intelligence, investigative, detention and attorney personnel. Principal responsibility in this regard will fall to ICE personnel in ICE's Compliance Enforcement Unit (CEU), the Joint Terrorism Task Force (JTTF) and ICE's National Security Law Division.

- **Support Direct Investigation of Terrorists through the JTTF**

    ICE will continue to support and participate in the direct investigation of suspected terrorists through the FBI-led Joint Terrorism Task Forces. ICE holds the position of the Deputy Director of the National JTTF and is the second largest federal investigative contributor to the JTTF. Funding permitting, ICE will seek to join all 106 local JTTFs in the country by 2011.

- **Protect the United States and Its Allies through Counter-proliferation Investigations**

   ICE will expand its counter-proliferation program, placing the strongest emphasis on the most serious threats, namely state-sponsored attempts to obtain nuclear materials, advanced weaponry and sensitive technology. ICE will open a Center for Excellence, collect and share intelligence to identify networks that facilitate the trafficking of sensitive technologies and weaponry, and continue initiatives such as Project Shield America to investigate domestic exporters and brokers who illegally export U.S. munitions, dual-use commodities, and other items that could harm our nation's security and the security of our allies. ICE will use cyber crime expertise to advance investigations of vendors, buyers and traders who violate export control laws and transfer technology over the Internet.

Protect the Borders Against Illicit Trade, Travel and Finance

Transnational criminal and terrorist organizations attempt to exploit lawful movement and transportation systems and to create alternative, illicit pathways through which people and illegal goods—narcotics, funds and weaponry—can cross the border. ICE plays a critical role in the department's layered approach to border security. As DHS's largest investigative agency, ICE responds to investigate criminal activity if U.S. Customs and Border Protection (CBP) interdicts contraband at the border. ICE then investigates the criminals, criminal enterprises and networks behind the illicit activity. Protecting and securing the borders involves ICE action overseas, at the border and ports of entry and inside the United States. Border security includes the ability to control unlawful movement across the border in either direction of people, goods and contraband, and protecting the movement of lawful commerce. Within that framework, ICE will focus on the following key objectives: (1) dismantling organized alien smuggling; (2) targeting drug trafficking organizations; (3) pursuing international money laundering and bulk cash smuggling; (4) countering international weapons trafficking; (5) targeting human trafficking and trans-national sexual exploitation; and (6) invigorating intellectual property rights investigations to protect lawful commerce.

- **Dismantle Cross-border Criminal Networks through Border Enforcement Security Task Forces**

   Securing the border against transnational crime and criminal organizations requires innovation as found in ICE's Border Enforcement Security Task Forces (BESTs). Over the next five years, ICE will expand BESTs beyond the existing 17 task forces and the 83 foreign, federal, state and local law enforcement agencies that actively participate in joint investigations today. ICE will continue to expand cooperation with our foreign law enforcement partners and place vetted members in our BESTs to help ICE better protect its land borders and seaports. ICE will co-locate with our foreign and domestic law enforcement partners to advance immediate and enhanced information sharing and expedite our response to strategic intelligence. ICE will rely heavily on and expand the BEST as a further tool to prevent the smuggling of contraband and aliens at the borders and through our seaports.

- **Dismantle Organized Alien Smuggling**

  To improve enforcement efforts against organized alien smugglers, ICE will reorient and increase its anti-smuggling activities over the next five fiscal years. First, ICE will pursue intelligence-driven investigations to target large scale smuggling organizations regardless of where they operate. Particular emphasis will be placed on those smuggling rings that pose a national security risk, jeopardize lives, or engage in violence, abuse, hostage taking, or extortion. Second, ICE will coordinate with CBP to ensure aggressive investigation and prosecution of individual smuggling cases that arise along the border. Third, ICE will target all links in the smuggling chain, not just the immediate smugglers. For example, ICE will target the overseas recruiters and organizers, the fraudulent document vendors, and the transportation and employment networks within the United States. Finally, ICE will pursue legislation to increase penalties against organized smugglers and provide additional criminal offenses to better address spotters who assist criminals who smuggle aliens and contraband.

- **Target Transnational Sexual Exploitation of Children, Child Sexual Exploitation and Human Trafficking of Children**

  A substantial number of children each year fall prey to sexual predators who use international, computer-based networks, or cross borders as they target children for pornography and sexual exploitation. To enhance our work in this area, ICE will use undercover operations and innovative approaches to identify child sex tourists and those who traffic minors and other victims. Essential to our success is coordinating with our national and international partners, both governmental and non-governmental. To increase leads and disrupt activity, ICE will educate those in the travel and hospitality industry so they can identify indicia of sexual exploitation and trafficking. In addition, ICE will identify and apprehend any removable alien convicted of offenses against minors and, when possible, present such aliens for criminal prosecution. ICE will continue outreach to increase the number of child sex tourism and human trafficking cases identified, investigated and resolved.

- **Target Drug Trafficking Organizations**

  Securing the border includes reducing the flow of narcotics and combating the violence that flows from drug trafficking. To make the most effective use of our resources, ICE will increasingly prioritize investigations against the

The San Diego Tunnel Task Force arrested six individuals and seized more than 32 tons of marijuana after discovering one of the most sophisticated smuggling tunnels along the U.S.-Mexico border in recent years. Photo credit: U.S. Immigration and Customs Enforcement

highest-level members of violent drug trafficking organizations, along with investigations of narco-terrorists and importers of precursor materials. To do this, ICE will expand the use of electronic surveillance and cooperation with international law enforcement partners, particularly in Mexico, Colombia and Canada. This cooperation will include intelligence sharing, training and participation on task forces. Acknowledging that our narcotics investigations must relate to transnational drug trafficking, leads about domestic drug trafficking will be referred to the Drug Enforcement Agency (DEA) and other law enforcement agencies. ICE will strengthen relationships and collaboration with CBP and the DEA.

- **Pursue Money Laundering and Bulk Cash Smuggling Investigations**

  Transnational criminal organizations are driven by greed and require money and capital to further their illicit activity. Attacking their proceeds is an effective and important tool to weaken and dismantle criminal organizations. To that end, ICE will direct its expertise in financial investigations toward the investigation of transnational criminal organizations, including terrorists and alien and narcotics smugglers. ICE will use a risk-based approach to prioritize among possible cases against terrorist and criminal organizations. ICE will expand trade-based money laundering enforcement and the Bulk Cash Smuggling Center, which promotes partnerships with other law enforcement agencies and increases opportunities for joint enforcement operations domestically and internationally. To promote heightened information sharing and identify important trends, ICE will strengthen relationships with financial institutions, trade organizations and other law enforcement agencies.

- **Invigorate Intellectual Property Investigations**

    As an important aspect of the department's mission to protect lawful trade and commerce, ICE will increasingly leverage our partnerships with private industry to address and prevent the smuggling of falsely labeled commodities, particularly those that could harm public safety. The Intellectual Property Rights Center will serve as a platform for producing actionable intelligence and coordinating multi-district, multi-agency investigations and seizures. ICE will more aggressively work to protect intellectual property rights, prevent export violations, confront theft via the Internet, and address commercial fraud in collaboration with domestic and foreign law enforcement partners and private industry.

Protect the Borders through Smart and Tough Interior Immigration Enforcement

Enforcement and Removal Operations officers, with assistance from federal, state and local counterparts, arrested more than 3,100 convicted criminal aliens and immigration fugitives during a six-day nationwide "Cross Check" enforcement operation. Photo credit: U.S. Immigration and Customs Enforcement.

Protecting and securing the borders involves action overseas, at the border and ports of entry, and inside the United States. ICE will engage in effective enforcement at the border and ports of entry by supporting the apprehension, detention and removal of newly arriving aliens seeking to enter illegally. Within the United States, ICE will pursue an effective worksite enforcement program to reduce the incentive for aliens to come to, enter and remain unlawfully. ICE also will prioritize the removal of convicted criminal aliens and gang members who undermine public security and reduce the quality of life in our communities. ICE will protect the integrity of the immigration system by enforcing final orders of removal and targeting fraud and abuse that undermine the sound administration of the nation's immigration laws. Finally, a critical part of immigration enforcement is reforming the immigration detention system.

- **Detaining and Removing Aliens Seeking Illegal Entry**

  The Department of Homeland Security has worked diligently to phase out a practice known as "catch and release." Now, newly arriving aliens who do not successfully evade detection are apprehended, detained and removed as appropriate by law. ICE will continue to commit detention and removal resources to support effective border controls.

- **Create a Culture of Employer Compliance**

  The opportunity to work in the United States motivates many to seek illegal entry. Therefore, enforcing the immigration-related employment laws is a critical component of border security. To create a culture of compliance among employers, ICE will use the following two-pronged strategy: (1) aggressive criminal and civil enforcement against those employers who knowingly violate the law; and (2) continued implementation of programs, such as E-Verify and ICE's IMAGE program, to help employers comply. Criminal investigations will increasingly focus on employers who abuse and exploit workers or otherwise engage in egregious conduct. To support a meaningful civil audit program, ICE will hire additional auditors and centralize some auditing functions. Through the "I E-Verify" campaign, ICE will work with U.S. Citizenship and Immigration Services (USCIS) to increase public support for companies that use compliance tools. Finally, ICE will seek better statutory tools to address illegal employment.

- **Prosecute and Remove Criminals and Gang Members**

  To best protect our communities and public safety, ICE will investigate and remove aliens who present a risk to national security or public safety, including terrorists, gang members and convicted criminals. To do this most efficiently, ICE will devise a strategy that incorporates all ICE programs with some responsibility in this area. In addition to targeting convicted criminal aliens, ICE will focus on removing transnational gang members and, when possible, charging them and their conspirators with criminal offenses, whether related to violent crime or immigration offenses. Interviewing members and associates in immigration custody is an important tool to collecting intelligence about transnational gangs and their leaders. Involving foreign law enforcement officials and information sharing will advance investigations and efforts to dismantle transnational gangs.

- **Protect the Integrity of the Immigration System**

  Multiple agencies in the executive branch, along with the legislative branch, invest significant resources adjudicating applications for admission and benefits, litigating and deciding immigration cases and enforcing final orders of removal. To best protect the system, ICE will work closely with USCIS and the Department of State to identify, address and prevent the many large-scale, organized frauds perpetrated on the government each year. In addition, ICE will pursue criminal cases against individuals who lie on applications, engage in fraud and pose a threat to national security or public safety. As ICE attorneys have great insight into possible fraud, they will actively refer cases to ICE agents and, as possible, serve as Special Assistant United States Attorneys to assist with prosecutions. ICE will expand the number of document and benefit fraud task forces to every Special Agent in Charge office. Following criminal cases, ICE will work closely with USCIS to address lingering administrative fraud. Also to protect the integrity of the immigration system, ICE will remove aliens who receive final orders, with a focus on convicted criminals and those who have most recently received orders. Similarly, ICE will begin to invest more resources to identify and remove aliens soon after they overstay non-immigrant visas.

- **Achieve Efficiency in the Removal Process**

    To expend government resources wisely, ICE will work to increase efficiency in every step of the removal process—from apprehension through removal—using the institutional removal program and other programs to reduce the duration of an alien's stay in ICE custody and increase compliance with final orders. Reducing transportation and removal costs is a critical aspect of efficiency. For the same reason, ICE will work closely with the Department of State to improve the process for securing travel documents and country clearances. Also for efficiency, ICE will coordinate budget requests, staffing needs and facility and court locations with the Executive Office for Immigration Review (EOIR).

- **Reform the Detention System to Meet the Needs of ICE**

    ICE is reforming the immigration detention system to reduce reliance on excess capacity in state and local penal facilities and improve detention conditions and medical care. Within the next five fiscal years, ICE will apply new detention standards to existing facilities and solicit proposals for no less than four regional facilities designed and located to suit the needs of ICE and allow ready access to legal services, visitation, recreation, medical services, emergency rooms and transportation hubs. A major pillar of detention reform is improving medical, mental health and dental care, and ensuring more uniform care. With a new classification instrument, ICE will be able to detain aliens in conditions commensurate with their risk and any specialized needs. To ensure proper federal oversight, ICE will more directly and aggressively monitor the conditions of detention. Recognizing the value of enforcing removal orders without detaining people, ICE will develop a cost effective Alternatives to Detention program that results in high rates of compliance.

Construct an Efficient, Effective Agency

The management and organization of ICE must help to propel the success of ICE's employees, improve employee morale, and the overall mission of ICE. The management functions within ICE will support and soundly advise the operational functions. The development of a well-trained, diverse and talented workforce is essential to solidifying the agency's success and reputation as a premier law enforcement agency. Fiscal discipline, sound budgeting, modern information systems and transparency to the public will continue to guide ICE.

- **Realign the Organization's Responsibilities**

    ICE's organization falls intuitively into the following four major areas: criminal investigations; civil immigration enforcement; management; and legal. ICE will begin to more clearly align programs within those major areas to achieve efficiency, promote collaboration and avoid duplication.

    With respect to the legal program, the Office of the Principal Legal Advisor (OPLA) will provide high quality, thorough and timely guidance to other ICE programs, including to our criminal investigators. OPLA will exercise sound discretion and promote efficiency and the agency's priorities as it exercises the Assistant Secretary's removal authority in immigration hearings.

- **Build and Retain a Stellar Workforce and Management Team**

    To promote a well-balanced workforce, reduce reliance on contractors and detailees, and build a core of employees and managers who understand congressional relations, the media, the department and the full range of ICE's mission, ICE will identify and institute a career path for agents, officers, attorneys and other professionals. To succeed in building and retaining a stellar workforce, ICE will expand recruitment efforts, streamline the hiring process, focus on diversity and training, and consider quality of life issues such as joint duty locations for married employees. To ensure sound practices, training will emphasize ethics, integrity, the handling of informants and criminal law and procedure, and the agency will develop new anti-corruption initiatives, increase awareness of workforce integrity issues, and quickly adjudicate any alleged violations. To aid employees, ICE will gather and standardize all policies and procedures and make current versions readily available.

- **Promote the Mission and Success of ICE**

    Recognizing that the mission of ICE is not broadly understood, ICE will better define itself and promote its mission and success to the department, public, media, Congress, community groups and other law enforcement entities. ICE is a premier investigative federal law enforcement agency—the second largest in the United States—and over the next five fiscal years, young people interested in law enforcement careers will increasingly understand the unique and exciting mission of ICE. As ICE is better understood through increased outreach and branding, employees will feel increasingly proud of the hours they dedicate to the work of ICE.

- **Use Resources Wisely**

  ICE will effectively manage its resources, assets, technology and information and spend its money wisely, with a full understanding of what its mission costs and how policy decisions influence resource needs. Through thoughtful alignment of strategic goals and objectives, budget requests will accurately reflect ICE's resource requirements. ICE will incorporate performance elements to measure the outcomes of its resource allocation decisions, budget execution and capital management efforts. ICE will invest in its infrastructure to eliminate waste, become more energy-efficient and make optimal use of space, systems and assets. ICE will proactively identify and correct financial and operational risks and continually strengthen internal controls to safeguard the public's resources and trust.

United States Coast Guard

The U.S. Coast Guard is one of the five armed forces of the United States and the only military organization within the Department of Homeland Security. Since 1790 the Coast Guard has safeguarded our Nation's maritime interests and environment around the world. The Coast Guard is an adaptable, responsive military force of maritime professionals whose broad legal authorities, capable assets, geographic diversity and expansive partnerships provide a persistent presence along our rivers, in the ports, littoral regions and on the high seas. Coast Guard presence and impact is local, regional, national and international. These attributes make the Coast Guard a unique instrument of maritime safety, security and environmental stewardship.

For over two centuries the U.S. Coast Guard has safeguarded our Nation's maritime interests in the heartland, in the ports, at sea, and around the globe. We protect the maritime economy and the environment, we defend our maritime borders, and we save those in peril. This history has forged our character and purpose as America's Maritime Guardian — *Always Ready* for all hazards and all threats.

Today's U.S. Coast Guard, with nearly 42,000 men and women on active duty, is a unique force that carries out an array of civil and military responsibilities touching almost every facet of the U.S. maritime environment.

By law, the Coast Guard has 11 missions:

1. Ports, waterways, and coastal security
2. Drug interdiction

3.   Aids to navigation
4.   Search and rescue
5.   Living marine resources
6.   Marine safety
7.   Defense readiness
8.   Migrant interdiction
9.   Environmental protection
10. Ice operations
11. Other law enforcement

Ports, Waterways, and Coastal Security

The Homeland Security Act of 2002 divided the Coast Guard's eleven statutory missions between homeland security and non-homeland security. Reflecting the Coast Guard's historical role in defending our nation, the Act delineated Ports, Waterways and Coastal Security (PWCS) as the first homeland security mission. The Commandant of the Coast Guard designated PWCS as the service's primary focus alongside search and rescue.

Coast Guard rescue operations. Photo credit: United States Coast Guard.

The PWCS mission entails the protection of the U.S. Maritime Domain and the U.S. Marine Transportation System (MTS) and those who live, work or recreate near them; the prevention and disruption of terrorist attacks, sabotage, espionage, or subversive acts; and response to and recovery from those that do occur. Conducting PWCS deters terrorists from using or exploiting the MTS as a means for attacks on U.S. territory, population centers, vessels, critical infrastructure, and key resources. PWCS includes the employment of awareness activities; counterterrorism, antiterrorism, preparedness and response operations; and the establishment and oversight of a maritime security regime. PWCS also includes the national defense role of protecting military outload operations.

The definitive source for information regarding the Coast Guard's port security history remains Coast Guard Pub 1 and the Coast Guard's historian. PWCS is a new name for the Coast Guard's mission previously called Port and Environmental Security (PES). PES included port security, container inspection, and marine firefighting.

In 2003, the Coast Guard addressed its PWCS responsibilities and functions by initiating Operation Neptune Shield (ONS). The Coast Guard supplemented ONS with tactical and strategic documents: the 2005 publication of Chapter 10 to the Maritime Law Enforcement Manual, the 2006 Coast Guard Strategic Plan for Combating Maritime Terrorism, and the 2008 Combating Maritime Terrorism Strategic and Performance Plan.

The July 2005 terrorist bombings in London highlighted the need to protect U.S. mass transit systems, including ferries. Later, the effects of hurricanes Katrina and Rita highlighted the criticality of preparedness for recovery of the MTS following a large-scale disaster. The 2008 terrorist attack via the maritime domain against Mumbai, India, highlighted the tie between border security and PWCS. After each event, the Coast Guard reviewed its PWCS strategy and made adjustments where appropriate.

The Coast Guard's systematic, maritime governance model for PWCS employs a triad consisting of domain awareness, maritime security regimes, and maritime security and response operations carried out in a unified effort by international, governmental, and private stakeholders.

Maritime domain awareness means the effective understanding of anything associated with the maritime domain that could impact the security, safety, economy, or environment of the U.S. Attaining and sustaining an effective understanding and awareness of the maritime domain requires the collection, fusion, analysis, and dissemination of prioritized categories of data, information, and intelligence. These are collected during the conduct of all Coast Guard missions. Awareness inputs come from Field Intelligence Support Teams, Maritime Intelligence Fusion Centers, Nationwide Automatic Identification System and other vessel tracking systems, and public reporting of suspicious incidents through America's Waterway Watch.

Maritime security regimes comprise a system of rules that shape acceptable activities in the maritime domain. Regimes include domestic and international protocols and/or frameworks that coordinate partnerships, establish maritime security standards, collectively engage shared maritime security interests, and facilitate the sharing of information. Domestically, the Coast Guard-led Area Maritime Security Committees carry out much of the maritime security regimes effort. Abroad, the Coast Guard works with individual countries and through the International Maritime Organization, a specialized agency of the United Nations. Together, regimes and domain awareness inform decision makers and allow them to identify trends, anomalies, and activities that threaten or endanger U.S. interests.

Defeating terrorism requires integrated, comprehensive operations that maximize effectiveness without duplicating efforts. Security and response operations consist of counterterrorism and antiterrorism activities.

Counterterrorism activities are offensive in nature. The Maritime Security Response Team (MSRT) is a highly specialized resource with advanced counterterrorism skills and tactics. The MSRT is trained to be a first responder to potential terrorist situations; deny terrorist acts; perform security actions against non-compliant actors; perform tactical facility entry and enforcement; participate in port level counterterrorism exercises; and educate other forces on Coast Guard counterterrorism procedures.

Antiterrorism activities are defensive in nature. As a maritime security agency, the Coast Guard uses its unique authorities, competencies, capacities, operational capabilities and partnerships to board suspect vessels, escort ships deemed to present or be at significant risk, enforce fixed security zones at maritime critical infrastructure and key resources, and patrol the maritime approaches, coasts, ports, and rivers of America. Coast Guard cutters, boats, helicopters, and shoreside patrols are appropriately armed and trained. Many current and planned antiterrorism activities support the Department of Homeland Security Small Vessel Security Strategy. Twelve Maritime Safety and Security Teams (MSSTs) enforce security zones, conduct port state control boardings, protect military outloads, ensure maritime security during major marine events, augment shoreside security at waterfront facilities, detect Weapons of Mass Destruction, and participate in port level antiterrorism exercises in their homeports and other ports to which elements of an MSST may be assigned for operations.

Viewing maritime initiatives and policies as part of a larger system enables a better understanding of their relationships and effectiveness. A well designed system of regimes, awareness, and operational capabilities creates overlapping domestic and international safety nets, layers of security, and effective stewardship making it that much harder for terrorists to succeed.

Drug interdiction

COSTA RICO, Central America (Feb. 12, 2002) -- Warning shots are fired in front of a drug go-fast boat from a Coast Guard MH-68A helicopter off the coast of Costa Rico. Photo credit: U.S. Coast Guard.

The Coast Guard is the lead federal agency for maritime drug interdiction and shares lead responsibility for air interdiction with the U.S. Customs Service. As such, it is a key player in combating the flow of illegal drugs to the United States. The Coast Guard's mission is to reduce the supply of drugs from the source by denying smugglers the use of air and maritime routes in the Transit Zone, a six million square mile area, including the Caribbean, Gulf of Mexico and Eastern Pacific. In meeting the challenge of patrolling this vast area, the Coast Guard coordinates closely with other federal agencies and countries within the region to disrupt and deter the flow of illegal drugs.

The Coast Guard is the lead federal agency for maritime drug interdiction and shares lead responsibility for air interdiction with the U.S. Customs Service. As such, it is a key player in combating the flow of illegal drugs to the United States. The Coast Guard's mission is to reduce the supply of drugs from the source by denying smugglers the use of air and maritime routes in the Transit Zone, a six million square mile area, including the Caribbean, Gulf of Mexico and Eastern Pacific. In meeting the challenge of patrolling this vast area, the Coast Guard coordinates closely with other federal agencies and countries within the region to disrupt and deter the flow of illegal drugs. In addition to deterrence, Coast Guard drug interdiction accounts for nearly 52% of all U.S. government seizures of cocaine each year. For Fiscal Year 2002 the rate of Coast Guard cocaine seizures alone had an estimated import value of approximately $3.9 billion.

- **Counter-drug smuggling mission background**

    In 1870, Chinese immigrants became the first known drug smugglers when they began smuggling opium in merchant ship cargoes and baggage. Since then, drug smuggling by maritime routes has grown in size, scope and sophistication as demand skyrocketed. For example, around the turn of the century, when cocaine use was first in vogue, a relatively limited amount of the population was directly affected by the problems of cocaine abuse. But in later years, as the drugs of choice shifted from cocaine to heroin and opium, then later to marijuana and back to cocaine, drug smugglers began utilizing maritime sea and air routes to transport larger shipments of drugs to the U.S. For nearly a century, the maritime drug smuggling business slowly evolved while the Coast Guard focused its attention on the major events of the day, including World War I, Prohibition, World War II, the Korean and Vietnam wars.

    During the 1920's Congress tasked the Coast Guard with enforcing the 18th Amendment, necessitating a dramatic increase in resources and funding for the Coast Guard. The massive effort needed to curtail the substantial level of alcohol smuggling required the single largest appropriation for personnel and new ship construction in its history. In addition, the Navy transferred more than 20 WWI-era destroyers and minesweepers for conversion to the Coast Guard's battle with rum-runners, which ended with the 21st Amendment repealing Prohibition. The Coast Guard's unique expertise in countering smuggling operations also came into play during the Vietnam War, when the Navy asked for our expertise to support "Operation Market Time," an intensive multi-year campaign to stop the Communist flow of arms and supplies by sea. The Coast Guard utilized its expertise in stopping smuggling while facilitating legitimate commerce. Our patrol boats and cutters patrolled 1,200 miles of coastline and had to contend with more than 60,000 junks and sampans. The Coast Guard and Navy's success in "Operation Market Time," substantially reduced the amount of at- sea smuggling, forcing the Viet Cong to use the longer and more difficult land route of the infamous Ho Chi Minh Trail.

Shortly after the war in Vietnam ended, the Coast Guard found itself fighting another war~a war that is still going on today with a determined, well-financed opposition. In the early 1970's maritime drug smuggling became a much more significant problem for the Coast Guard and we began making seizures while engaged in other operations, like Search and Rescue and Fisheries Law Enforcement. 1973 saw a dramatic increase in smuggling attempts and the Coast Guard conducted its first Coast Guard-controlled seizure on March 8, 1973, when the USCGC Dauntless boarded a 38-foot sports fisherman, the Big L and arrested its master and crew, with more than a ton of marijuana on board. Since then, the Coast Guard has seized countless tons of marijuana and cocaine. Since Fiscal Year 1997 to present, the Coast Guard has seized 806,469 pounds of cocaine and 333,285 pounds of marijuana.

Aids to Navigation

The Coast Guard Navigation Center provides maritime navigation and information services that enhance the safety, security, and efficiency of U.S. waterways.

- Providing nationwide GPS augmentation signals
- Tracking vessel movements for enhanced situational awareness
- Publishing maritime advisories and related navigation information
- Managing the Coast Guard's electronic chart portfolio
- Receiving and coordinating investigation of GPS outage reports

Search and Rescue

Search and Rescue (SAR) is one of the Coast Guard's oldest missions. Minimizing the loss of life, injury, property damage or loss by rendering aid to persons in distress and property in the maritime environment has always been a Coast Guard priority. Coast

Guard SAR response involves multi-mission stations, cutters, aircraft and boats linked by communications networks. The National SAR Plan divides the U.S. area of SAR responsibility into internationally recognized inland and maritime SAR regions. The Coast Guard is the Maritime SAR Coordinator. To meet this responsibility, the Coast

Guard maintains SAR facilities on the East, West and Gulf coasts; in Alaska, Hawaii, Guam, and Puerto Rico, as well as on the Great Lakes and inland U.S. waterways. The Coast Guard is recognized worldwide as a leader in the field of search and rescue.

Living Marine Resources

The Coast Guard enforces fisheries laws at sea, as tasked by the Magnuson-Stevens Fisheries Conservation and Management Act (MSFCMA). Their fisheries priorities are, in order of importance:

- **Protecting the U.S. Exclusive Economic Zone from foreign encroachment**

    The MSFCMA of 1976 extended U.S. fisheries management authority out to the full 200 miles authorized by international law. The U.S. EEZ is the largest in the world, containing 3.4 million square miles of ocean and 90,000 miles of coastline. Foreign fishers operating illegally in this area are, effectively, stealing resources from the U.S., and our fisheries managers have no way of measuring or accounting for this loss.

- **Enforcing domestic fisheries law**

    U.S. Domestic Fisheries support a $24 billion dollar industry. Fisheries Management Plans (FMPs), to ensure the sustainability of these fisheries are developed by regional Fisheries Management Councils, each of which have a non-voting Coast Guard member. The Coast Guard is responsible for enforcing these FMPs at sea, in conjunction with NOAA Fisheries enforcement ashore. In addition to FMP enforcement, we enforce laws to protect marine mammals and endangered species.

- **International fisheries agreements**

    Realizing that fish do not recognize national boundaries, the Coast Guard works closely with the Department of State to develop and enforce international fisheries agreements. Most notably, the Coast Guard enforces the United Nations High Seas Driftnet Moratorium in the North Pacific, where illegal drift netters may catch U.S. origin salmon.

Marine Safety

The Coast Guard is in the midst of implementing the Marine Safety Enhancement Plan (MSEP). The MSEP is a multi-layered, several-year comprehensive program to enhance Marine Safety systems, knowledge, and processes in order to be more effective and efficient in promoting safe, secure, and environmentally sound maritime commerce. Specific tasks include bolstering inspector and investigator capacity, improving technical competencies, reinvigorating industry partnerships, improving mariner credentialing services, and expanding rulemaking capability to meet current and future needs of the maritime public and industry.

Actions to implement the MSEP have included reprogramming and adding over 400 positions to the Marine Safety workforce, broadening its experience base by increasing civilian marine inspection and investigations positions, designating Feeder Ports and building the infrastructure to train entry-level marine inspectors, establishing seven National Centers of Expertise (each focusing on specific maritime industry sectors), and increasing responsiveness (shortening cycle times) to merchant mariners, maritime industry, and the American public. The MSEP was developed in late 2007, based on the Coast Guard's Marine Safety statutory requirements at that time. Since then, the Coast Guard Authorization Act of 2010 was enacted, increasing Marine Safety requirements.

Defense Readiness

For more than 210 years, the Coast Guard has served the nation as one of the five armed forces. Throughout its distinguished history, the Coast Guard has enjoyed a unique relationship with the Navy. By statute, the Coast Guard is an armed force, operating in the joint arena at any time and functioning as a specialized service under the Navy in time of war or when directed by the President. It also has command responsibilities for the U.S. Maritime Defense Zone, countering potential threats to American's coasts, ports, and inland waterways through numerous port-security, harbor-defense, and coastal-warfare operations and exercises.

Today, U.S. national security interests can no longer be defined solely in terms of direct military threats to America and its allies. With the terrorist attacks on September 11, 2001, the U.S. has fully realized the threat faced on the home front from highly sophisticated and covert adversarial groups. The Coast Guard has assumed one of the lead roles in responding to these unscrupulous attacks upon our nation by providing homeland security in our nation's harbors, ports and along our coastlines. Commercial, tanker, passenger, and merchant vessels have all been subject to increased security measures enforced by the Coast Guard.

The Coast Guard's national defense role to support U.S. military commanders-in-chiefs (CINCs) is more explicitly outlined in a memorandum of agreement signed by the Secretaries of Defense and Transportation in 1995. Four major national-defense missions were assigned to the Coast Guard. These missions–**maritime intercept operations, deployed port operations/security and defense, peacetime engagement,** and **environmental defense operations**–are essential military tasks assigned to the Coast Guard as a component of joint and combined forces in peacetime, crisis, and war.

Outside of U.S. coastal waters, the Coast Guard assists foreign naval and maritime forces through training and joint operations. Many of the world's maritime nations have forces that operate principally in the littoral seas and conduct missions that resemble those of the Coast Guard. And, because it has such a varied mix of assets and missions, the Coast Guard is a powerful role model that is in ever-increasing demand abroad. The service's close working relations with these nations not only improve mutual cooperation during specific joint operations in which the Coast Guard is involved but also support U.S. diplomatic efforts in general: promoting democracy, economic prosperity, and trust between nations.

Migrant Interdiction

As the United States' primary maritime law enforcement agency, the Coast Guard is tasked with enforcing immigration law at sea. The Coast Guard conducts patrols and coordinates with other federal agencies and foreign countries to interdict undocumented migrants at sea, denying them entry via maritime routes to the United States, its territories and possessions. Thousands of people try to enter this country illegally every year using maritime routes, many via smuggling operations. Interdicting migrants at sea means they can be quickly returned to their countries of origin without the costly processes required if they successfully enter the United States.

When successful, illegal immigration can potentially cost U.S. taxpayers billions of dollars each year in social services. In addition to relieving this financial burden on our citizens, the Coast Guard's efforts help to support legal migration systems. Primarily, the Coast Guard maintains its humanitarian responsibility to prevent the loss of life at sea, since the majority of migrant vessels are dangerously overloaded, unseaworthy or otherwise unsafe.

As the primary maritime law enforcement agency, the Coast Guard is tasked with enforcing immigration law at sea. The Coast Guard conducts patrols and coordinates with other federal agencies and foreign countries to interdict undocumented migrants at sea, denying them entry via maritime routes to the U.S., its territories and possessions. Interdicting migrants at sea means they can be quickly returned to their countries of origin without the costly processes required if they successfully enter the United States. The Coast Guard supports the National Policy to promote safe, legal, and orderly migration.

Illegal immigration can cost U.S. taxpayers billions of dollars each year in social services. In addition to relieving this financial burden on our citizens, the Coast Guard's efforts help to support the use of legal migration systems. Primarily, the Coast Guard maintains its humanitarian responsibility to prevent the loss of life at sea, since the majority of migrant vessels are dangerously overloaded, unseaworthy or otherwise unsafe.

Protection from political persecution and torture are important concerns for the U.S. During the course of migrant interdictions, Coast Guard crews may encounter migrants requesting protection. The Department of State (Bureau of Population, Refugees, and Migration) and the Bureau of Citizenship and Immigration Services establish the policies in this area and handle all potential asylum cases on our cutters.

The Coast Guard's role in migrant interdiction has been a part of our history since the service's inception (see History of Coast Guard in Illegal Immigration). The mission gained high visibility during the first mass migration emergency the United States faced between April 21 and September 28, 1980. Fidel Castro permitted any person who wanted to leave Cuba free access to depart from the port of Mariel, Cuba. Known as the Mariel Boatlift, approximately 124,000 undocumented Cuban migrants entered the United States by a flotilla of mostly U.S. vessels in violation of U.S. law. The Coast Guard interdicted vessels en route to Mariel Harbor, as well as provided search and rescue assistance to vessels bound for the United States. The Coast Guard also provided assistance to other federal agencies in the processing, investigation and prosecution of boat owners suspected of violating U.S. law.

The hazards of illegal maritime migration was highlighted in 1981, when the bodies of 30 Haitian migrants washed ashore on Hillsboro Beach, FL. In response to 1980 mass migration from Cuba and the increasing number of Haitian migrants landing in the U.S., on September 29, 1981, President Reagan issued Presidential Proclamation 4865, which suspended the entry of undocumented migrants to the U.S. from the high seas.

Between 1991 and 1995, there was a dramatic increase in the number of undocumented migrants interdicted by the Coast Guard. During this period, over 120,000 migrants from 23 countries were interdicted. Haitian migrants began increased departures after a 1991 coup in Haiti. These migrants were processed for asylum claims first on ships, then at Guantanamo Bay, Cuba (GTMO). Those that were identified as leaving for economic reasons were returned to Haiti. The camp eventually became a magnet for those departing seeking food, shelter, and a chance to get into the U.S. During this time, the camp at GTMO contained over 12,000 migrants.

In 1992, President Bush issued Executive Order 12807 directing the Coast Guard to enforce the suspension of the entry of undocumented migrants by interdicting them at sea, and return them to their country of origin or departure.

In 1993, Operation ABLE MANNER commenced. This operation concentrated Coast Guard patrols in the Windward Passage (the body of water between Haiti and Cuba) to interdict Haitian migrants. Operation ABLE MANNER continued until a new government was in place in Haiti in 1994. Today, Haitian migrants still leave Haiti attempting to reach the U.S. Many travel to the Bahamas and enter on smaller boats, while some attempt direct entry to the U.S. in large boat loads. There is a Coast Guard Liaison Officer at the U.S. Embassy in Port au Prince, Haiti, who handles various migration, counterdrug, and international engagement issues with Haiti.

In 1994, the Coast Guard was involved in its largest peacetime operation since the Vietnam war, responding to two mass migrations at the same time-first from Haiti, then from Cuba. Over 63,000 migrants were rescued and prevented from illegally entering the U.S. in Operations ABLE MANNER and ABLE VIGIL. At its height, Operation ABLE MANNER involved 17 U.S. Coast Guard vessels, patrolling the coast of Haiti while Operation ABLE VIGIL involved 38 Coast Guard cutters patrolling the Straits of Florida. Migration from Cuba continues.

There has been a shift from migrants taking to sea in rafts to employing smugglers. The dangers of this are no less than rafting as illustrated by the deaths of numerous migrants in 1998-2000, when overloaded vessels capsized.

The Dominican Republic has historically been a major source country for undocumented migrants attempting to enter the U.S. Crossing the Mona Passage (the body of water between the Dominican Republic and Puerto Rico) to enter Puerto Rico, thousands of people have taken to sea in a variety of vessels, the most common is a homemade fishing vessel known as a Yola. Most of these migrants are smuggled by highly organized gangs. From April 1, 1995 through October 1, 1997, the Coast Guard conducted Operation ABLE RESPONSE, with enhanced operations dedicated to interdicting Dominican migrants. Over 9,500 migrants were interdicted or forced to turn back.

In addition to the migrant threat from these Caribbean countries, there has been an alarming increase in the number of migrants from Asia, most of whom are from the People's Republic of China. Very often Chinese migrants rely on well-organized, extremely violent, alien smugglers to gain entry into the United States. The living conditions on the vessels used to smuggle migrants are appalling, with overcrowded holds and unsafe sanitary conditions. In many cases, migrants are transferred to smaller pick up vessels offshore for the final ride to the U.S., or they're taken to Central American countries and smuggled across the U.S. land border. Beginning in 1998, more Chinese migrants began making trips from China attempting to enter Guam, which continues to be a significant problem. The International Information Programs has additional information on Chinese Alien Smuggling.

In 1999 and 2000, Coast Guard cutters on Counterdrug patrol in the Eastern Pacific have encountered increasing numbers of migrants being smuggled from Ecuador to points in Central America and Mexico. While this may not have a direct connection to the U.S., the Coast Guard acts for humanitarian reasons. Most of these vessels do not have the proper conditions to transport these migrants and lack the safety equipment in the event of an emergency. The Coast Guard works with the flag state of the vessels and other countries to escort the vessels to the closest safe port.

Undocumented migrants continue to pose a threat to the U.S. today. While the primary threat comes from Haiti, the Dominican Republic, the People's Republic of China, and Cuba, the Coast Guard has interdicted migrants of various nationalities throughout the world.

Marine Environmental Protection

The Marine Environmental Protection program develops and enforces regulations to avert the introduction of invasive species into the maritime environment, stop unauthorized ocean dumping, and prevent oil and chemical spills. This program is complemented by the Marine Safety program's pollution prevention activities.

In 2008, the Coast Guard refined its planning to support implementation of the National Response Framework, the national all hazards, incident management, and emergency response architecture. The Coast Guard also incorporated lessons learned from the motor vessel (M/V) COSCO BUSAN Incident Specific Preparedness Report into an improved policy that better aligns response planning at local, state, and Federal levels

Ice Operations

The Coast Guard conducts icebreaking services to assist vessels and communities in emergency situations and facilitate essential commercial maritime activities in the Great Lakes and Northeast regions. In 2008, the Coast Guard, in concert with the Government of Canada and the commercial icebreaking industry, sustained navigable waterways for commercial traffic and assisted with 680 ice transits, representing the transport of over $2B (U.S.) of cargo.

The Coast Guard conducting icebreaking services in the Great Lakes and Northeast regions. Photo credit: United States Coast Guard.

Beyond domestic operations, the Coast Guard operates the only U.S.-flagged heavy icebreakers capable of providing year-round access to the Polar regions. In 2008, the busiest iceberg season in a decade, the International Ice Patrol facilitated commerce by broadcasting position information on 1,029 icebergs crossing south of 48 degrees north latitude.

Other Law Enforcement

Preventing illegal foreign fishing vessel encroachment in the EEZ is a primary Coast Guard role vital to protecting the integrity of the Nation's maritime borders and ensuring the health of U.S. fisheries. The Coast Guard also enforces international agreements to suppress damaging illegal, unreported, and unregulated (IUU) fishing activity on the high seas.

In 2008, the Coast Guard detected 81 incursions by foreign fishing vessels into the U.S. EEZ. The Coast Guard also participated in the 2008 multi-national high seas drift net (HSDN) enforcement campaign, Operation North Pacific Watch. Through this campaign, the Coast Guard interdicted two Chinese-flagged HSDN vessels, facilitating their seizure by Chinese officials.

The U.S. Coast Guard uses a variety of platforms to conduct its daily business. Cutters and small boats are used on the water and fixed and rotary wing (helicopters) aircraft are used in the air.

Aircraft

The Jayhawk's state-of-the-art radar, radio, and navigation equipment enables the helicopter to carry out the Coast Guard's search and rescue, law enforcement, military readiness, and marine environmental protection missions efficiently and effectively. Photo credit: United States Coast Guard.

There are a total of 211 aircraft in CG inventory. This figure fluctuates operationally due to maintenance schedules. Major Missions: Search/Rescue, Law Enforcement, Environmental Response, Ice Operations, and Air Interdiction. Fixed-wing aircraft (C-130 Hercules turboprops and HU-25 Falcon jets) operate from large and small Air Stations. Rotary wing aircraft (H-65 Dolphin and HH-60 Jayhawk helicopters) operate from flight-deck equipped Cutters, Air Stations and Air Facilities.

Boats

All vessels under 65 feet in length are classified as boats and usually operate near shore and on inland waterways. Craft include: Motor Lifeboats; Motor Surf Boats; Large Utility Boats; Surf Rescue Boats; Port Security Boats; Aids to Navigation Boats; and a variety of smaller, non-standard boats including Rigid Inflatable Boats. Sizes range from 64 feet in length down to 12 feet.

MAKO is the 3rd Hull of the of Coast Guard patrol boat (WPB), called the "Marine Protector" class and named for marine animals. MAKO was built at Bollinger Shipyard in Lockport, Louisiana and entered service in September 1998 in Cape May, New Jersey. Photo credit: United States Coast Guard.

Cutters

A "Cutter" is basically any CG vessel 65 feet in length or greater, having adequate accommodations for crew to live on board. Larger cutters (over 179 feet in length) are under control of Area Commands (Atlantic Area or Pacific Area).

Cutters at or under 175 feet in length come under control of District Commands. Cutters, usually have a motor surf boat and/or a rigid hull inflatable boat on board. Polar Class icebreakers also carry an Arctic Survey Boat (ASB) and Landing Craft.

Federal Emergency Management Agency

The Federal Emergency Management Agency coordinates the federal government's role in preparing for, preventing, mitigating the effects of, responding to, and recovering from all

One of several FEMA National Response Coordination Centers. Photo credit: FEMA.

domestic disasters, whether natural or man-made, including acts of terror. FEMA can trace its beginnings to the Congressional Act of 1803. This act, generally considered the first piece of disaster legislation, provided assistance to a New Hampshire town following an extensive fire. In the century that followed, ad hoc legislation was passed more than 100 times in response to hurricanes, earthquakes, floods and other natural disasters.

By the 1930s, when the federal approach to problems became popular, the Reconstruction Finance Corporation was given authority to make disaster loans for repair and reconstruction of certain public facilities following an earthquake, and later, other types of disasters. In 1934, the Bureau of Public Roads was given authority to provide funding for highways and bridges damaged by natural disasters. The Flood Control Act, which gave the U.S. Army Corps of Engineers greater authority to implement flood control projects, was also passed. This piecemeal approach to disaster assistance was problematic and it prompted legislation that required greater cooperation between federal agencies and authorized the President to coordinate these activities.

The 1960s and early 1970s brought massive disasters requiring major federal response and recovery operations by the Federal Disaster Assistance Administration, established within the Department of Housing and Urban Development (HUD). Hurricane Carla struck in 1962, Hurricane Betsy in 1965, Hurricane Camille in 1969 and Hurricane Agnes in 1972. The Alaskan Earthquake hit in 1964 and the San Fernando Earthquake rocked Southern California in 1971. These events served to focus attention on the issue of natural disasters and brought about increased

> **The Federal Emergency Management Agency coordinates the federal government's role in preparing for, preventing, mitigating the effects of, responding to, and recovering from all domestic disasters, whether natural or man-made, including acts of terror.**

legislation. In 1968, the National Flood Insurance Act offered new flood protection to homeowners, and in 1974 the Disaster Relief Act firmly established the process of Presidential disaster declarations.

However, emergency and disaster activities were still fragmented. When hazards associated with nuclear power plants and the transportation of hazardous substances were added to natural disasters, more than 100 federal agencies were involved in some aspect of disasters, hazards and emergencies. Many parallel programs and policies existed at the state and local level, compounding the complexity of federal disaster relief efforts. The National Governor's Association sought to decrease the many agencies with which state and local governments were forced work. They asked President Jimmy Carter to centralize federal emergency functions.

Executive Order 12127

President Carter's 1979 executive order merged many of the separate disaster-related responsibilities into the Federal Emergency Management Agency (FEMA). Among other agencies, FEMA absorbed: the Federal Insurance Administration, the National Fire Prevention and Control Administration, the National Weather Service Community Preparedness Program, the Federal Preparedness Agency of the General Services Administration and the Federal Disaster Assistance Administration activities from HUD. Civil defense responsibilities were also transferred to the new agency from the Defense Department's Defense Civil Preparedness Agency.

John Macy was named as FEMA's first director. Macy emphasized the similarities between natural hazards preparedness and the civil defense activities. FEMA began development of an Integrated Emergency Management System with an all-hazards approach that included "direction, control and warning systems which are common to the full range of emergencies from small isolated events to the ultimate emergency - war."

The new agency was faced with many unusual challenges in its first few years that emphasized how complex emergency management can be. Early disasters and emergencies included the contamination of Love Canal, the Cuban refugee crisis and the accident at the Three Mile Island nuclear power plant. Later, the Loma Prieta Earthquake in 1989 and Hurricane Andrew in 1992 focused major national attention on FEMA. In 1993, President Clinton nominated James L. Witt as the new FEMA director. Witt became the first agency director with experience as a state emergency manager. He initiated sweeping reforms that streamlined disaster relief and recovery operations, insisted on a new emphasis regarding preparedness and mitigation, and focused agency employees on customer service. The end of the Cold War also allowed Witt to redirect more of FEMA's limited resources from civil defense into disaster relief, recovery and mitigation programs.

In 2001, President George W. Bush appointed Joe M. Allbaugh as the director of FEMA. Within months, the terrorist attacks of Sept. 11th focused the agency on issues of national preparedness and homeland security, and tested the agency in unprecedented ways. The agency coordinated its activities with the newly formed Office of Homeland Security, and FEMA's Office of National Preparedness was given responsibility for helping to ensure that the nation's first responders were trained and equipped to deal with weapons of mass destruction.

A New Mission: Homeland Security

Billions of dollars of new funding were directed to FEMA to help communities face the threat of terrorism. Just a few years past its 20th anniversary, FEMA was actively directing its "all-hazards" approach to disasters toward homeland security issues. In March 2003, FEMA joined 22 other federal agencies, programs and offices in becoming the Department of Homeland Security. The new department, headed by Secretary Tom Ridge, brought a coordinated approach to national security from emergencies and disasters - both natural and man-made.

On October 4, 2006, President George W. Bush signed into law the Post-Katrina Emergency Reform Act. The act significantly reorganized FEMA, provided it substantial new authority to remedy gaps that became apparent in the response to Hurricane Katrina in August 2005, the most devastating natural disaster in U.S. history, and included a more robust preparedness mission for FEMA.

United States Secret Service

The United States Secret Service (USSS) safeguards the nation's financial infrastructure and payment systems to preserve the integrity of the economy, and protects national leaders, visiting heads of state and government, designated sites, and National Special Security Events

Investigations

In April 1865, President Lincoln authorized the establishment of the Secret Service under the U.S. Department of the Treasury for the purpose of suppressing counterfeit currency. As the original guardian of the nation's financial payment systems, the Secret Service has established a long history of protecting American consumers and industries from financial fraud. Today, the Secret Service continues this core mission by investigating violations of U.S. laws relating to currency, financial crimes, financial payment systems, computer crimes and electronic crimes. The Secret Service utilizes investigative expertise, science and technology, and partnerships to detect, prevent and investigate attacks on the U.S. financial infrastructure.

The United States Secret Service investigates many types of financial fraud. Photo credit: United States Secret Service.

- **Protect the nation's financial infrastructure by reducing losses due to counterfeit currency, financial and electronic crimes and identity theft.**

  o Reduce the proportion of counterfeit currency relative to the amount of genuine U.S. currency in circulation at home and abroad.

  o Reduce the amount of financial losses resulting from electronic crimes, financial crimes, computer crimes, compromised payment systems, identity theft and other types of financial crimes.

Protection

Following the assassination of President McKinley in 1901, the Secret Service began protecting the President of the United States. Throughout the 20th century, the protective mission expanded to include the protection of additional national leaders, including presidential candidates, visiting heads of state and government, designated sites and events of national significance. Protection includes all activities related to identifying threats, mitigating vulnerabilities and creating secure environments wherever protectees work, reside and travel and where specially designated events take place.

President Barack Obama arrives at Port Columbus International Airport. Columbus, Ohio with Sen. Sherrod Brown, Rep. Mary Jo Kilroy, and the Secret Service. Photo credit: U.S. Secret Service.

- **Protect national leaders, visiting heads of state and government, designated sites and NSSEs.**

  o   Ensure the safety and security of national leaders, visiting heads of state and government, major candidates for President and Vice President and other designated protectees.

  o   Safeguard the White House complex, the Vice President's Residence, foreign missions and other high-profile sites.

  o   Effectively lead and manage the planning, coordination and implementation of operational security plans at designated NSSEs.

Infrastructure

For the past century, the Secret Service's internal infrastructure has supported and sustained operational success. The solid foundation of progressive scientific tools, technologies, systems, policies, training programs and support services has enabled Secret Service personnel to achieve the operational mission efficiently and effectively.

- **Enhance the administrative, professional and technical infrastructure as well as the management systems and processes that sustain the investigative and protective mission.**

  o   Foster development, acquisition and deployment of cutting-edge advances in science and technology.

o   Strengthen the agency's ability to recruit, develop and retain a highly-specialized and dedicated workforce to fulfill mission-critical requirements.

o   Implement innovative techniques and business strategies to assess and improve organizational practices, policies and procedures for increased effectiveness.

o   Uphold the Secret Service's reputation of personal integrity and professional responsibility.

o   Enhance stewardship of resources and management best practices to ensure long-term fiscal viability.

o   Foster an environment of open communication within the Secret Service and with key partners.

Editor's Comments

Interestingly, one federal agency not absorbed by the Department of Homeland Security is the Federal Bureau of Investigation (FBI). At first glance, it seems strange to leave out the largest and most acclaimed federal law enforcement entity. It is even more interesting since "terrorism" has been integrated into the Bureau's core mission. The FBI mission states:

> As an intelligence-driven and a threat-focused national security and law enforcement organization, the mission of the FBI is to protect and defend the United States against terrorist and foreign intelligence threats, to uphold and enforce the criminal laws of the United States, and to provide leadership and criminal justice services to federal, state, municipal, and international agencies and partners.

The priorities of the FBI reveal:

> The FBI focuses on threats that challenge the foundations of American society or involve dangers too large or complex for any local or state authority to handle alone. In executing the following priorities, we will produce and use intelligence to protect the nation from threats and to bring to justice those who violate the law.

These priorities include:

1.   Protect the United States from terrorist attack
2.   Protect the United States against foreign intelligence operations and espionage
3.   Protect the United States against cyber-based attacks and high-technology crimes
4.   Combat public corruption at all levels
5.   Protect civil rights
6.   Combat transnational/national criminal organizations and enterprises

7. Combat major white-collar crime
8. Combat significant violent crime
9. Support federal, state, local and international partners
10. Upgrade technology to successfully perform the FBI's mission

Although terrorism is listed as the number one priority of the FBI, it is the additional responsibilities of the Bureau which drive its exclusion from a purely homeland security operation. These non-terrorism investigations (or programs) are considerable and drain a majority of FBI resources.

These investigations and programs include:

- Cyber Crime
- Public Corruption
- Environmental Crime
- Civil Rights
- Organized Crime
- Violent Gangs
- White-Collar Crime
- Significant Violent Crime
- FBI Ten Most Wanted Fugitives
- Crimes Against Children
- Art Crime
- Indian Country
- Background Investigations

————————————

Further Discussion

1. Discuss the importance of the **Office for Civil Rights and Civil Liberties**.

2. Discuss the role of the **Transportation Security Administration** in anti-terrorism measures.

3. Discuss the role of the **United States Coast Guard** in anti-terrorism measures.

4. Discuss the justifications for transferring the **United States Secret Service** into the Department of Homeland Security.

5. Discuss the significance of leaving the **Federal Bureau of Investigation** outside the control of the Department of Homeland Security (from both perspectives).

Chapter 06

Partners in Homeland Security

"Let us strive for more partnerships; a bigger team; and an even greater willingness from our citizens to share responsibility for our collective security".

Secretary Janet Napolitano, January 2011

United States Department of Homeland Security
Critical Infrastructure Sector Partnerships
Department Website, (Excerpts)

Critical Infrastructure Sector Partnerships

The protection of the nation's critical infrastructure requires an effective partnership framework that fosters integrated, collaborative engagement and interaction among public- and private-sector partners.

The Department of Homeland Security Office of Infrastructure Protection (IP), in close coordination with public and private-sector critical infrastructure partners, leads the coordinated national effort to mitigate risk to the nation's critical infrastructure through the development and implementation of an effective critical infrastructure protection program.

Partnership between the public and private sectors is essential, in part because the private sector owns and operates approximately 85% of the nation's critical infrastructure, government agencies have access to critical threat information, and each controls security programs, research and development, and other resources that may be more effective if discussed and shared, as appropriate, in a partnership setting.

United States Department of Justice
Office of Justice Programs
Engaging the Private Sector to Promote Homeland Security:
Law Enforcement-Private Security Partnerships
September 2005, (Excerpts)

Law Enforcement-Private Security Partnerships

With the push in local policing throughout the 1990s toward a new model of service delivery that focused on problem solving and partnerships (called community policing), sheriffs' offices and police departments engaged community organizations, neighborhood residents, other government agencies, and the private sector in collaborative partnerships to reduce crime and disorder. Law enforcement tapped into resources and expertise previously unavailable to them, with a focus on a shared vision, shared responsibility, and shared success. These partnerships reduced crime and encouraged a public trust that had been dormant in some communities for decades.

Since the attacks of September 11, 2001, law enforcement-private security partnerships have been viewed as critical to preventing terrorism. Local law enforcement and private security organizations working together is vitally important to homeland security; the private sector owns or protects the overwhelming majority of the country's infrastructure, but local law enforcement tends to possess any threat information regarding that infrastructure. In short, because neither law enforcement nor private security can protect the nation's infrastructure alone, law enforcement-private security partnerships are essential to bridging the gap. Even though existing partnerships may need improvement, we can build on the lessons learned from community policing.

Law enforcement-private security partnerships are not new. The International Association of Chiefs of Police's (IACP's) Private Sector Liaison Committee has been in place for almost 20 years. ASIS (formerly the American Society for Industrial Security) International established a Law Enforcement Liaison Council to promote understanding and cooperation between private security and law enforcement. Recognizing a gap in homeland security, IACP called a national policy summit on the issue. Prior to September 11, IACP, the National Sheriffs' Association, and ASIS joined together, with funding from the U.S. Department of Justice, Office of Justice Programs' Bureau of Justice Assistance (BJA), to launch "Operation Cooperation," a national effort to increase collaboration between the private sector, particularly private security, and state and local law enforcement agencies. The document that emerged from that work, *Operation Cooperation: Guidelines for Partnerships Between Law Enforcement and Private Security Organizations*, is as relevant today as when it was published in 2000. The document focused on how the public and private sector could pool their resources to reduce crime and public disorder. The principles it elucidated are particularly important to our nation's focus on homeland security since September 11. With chemical, biological, nuclear, and traditional terror threats a reality, the need for collaborative partnerships between local law enforcement and private security is as great today as it ever has been.

The record shows that neither public law enforcement nor firefighters were the first to respond to the attack on the Twin Towers in 2001; private security personnel stationed in the two buildings and nearby facilities rapidly and selflessly became the first responders. Since September 11—and as a component of the national and world focus on preventing terrorist acts—the discourse on private security and its relationship to law enforcement has assumed a more complex dimension and reached new heights.

The 9/11 Commission estimated that 85 percent of the nation's infrastructure is privately owned. Infrastructure includes not only physical assets, such as buildings, but also energy production facilities and assets, utilities (e.g., water and waste management), and transportation and communication networks. The number of people employed by private security, moreover, is at least three times larger than the number employed by public law enforcement. The amount of money spent on private security is many times greater than state, county, and local law enforcement expenditures combined. The growth in private protective forces ranges from mobile community patrols to executive protection personnel.

Two further considerations attest to the urgency of public-private security partnerships: the sheer size of the United States and terrorists' expressed interest in inflicting mass casualties on its people.

Because partnerships are a core component of community policing, the Office of Community Oriented Policing Services (COPS) supported a national policy summit on partnerships in 2004. More than 140 representatives, ranging from chiefs of police to private security executives, concluded that law enforcement partnerships with private security have not evolved to the same degree as they have with community organizations. Law

The DHS for a Day program provides private sector stakeholders a glimpse into how various Department of Homeland Security (DHS) Components make the Nation safer on a day-to-day basis. The program also builds and strengthens connections between DHS and the private sector, ensuring that all partners across the country can participate fully in the Homeland Security Enterprise. Photo credit: Department of Homeland Security.

enforcement officials who meet regularly with neighborhood leaders, representatives of the faith community, and others do not routinely meet with corporate security directors or others in the security industry. Enormous strides were made in reducing crime and disorder through community partnerships in the 1990s. Further successes in public-private security partnerships will depend on leadership, planning, and relationship building.

This document provides important background information on law enforcement-private security partnerships; discusses why these partnerships are important to homeland security and supplies information that enables police chiefs and sheriffs to make partnerships successful; and profiles a number of law enforcement-private security partnerships that local and state agencies might consider replicating.

Private and Public: Definitions and Background

While some overlap in the missions of public law enforcement and private security exists, the two groups are not the same. To explain how local law enforcement and private security can better protect the country, this section starts by clarifying the difference between public and private security. "Public policing" consists of services offered by local, state, tribal, and federal agencies, i.e., local and state police, tribal agencies, and sheriffs' offices. These agencies provide the bulk of policing services across the United States. "For the most part, they are not concerned with corporate internal problems; they are concerned primarily with street crimes."

Private security services, on the other hand, fall into two categories: (1) proprietary or corporate security; and (2) contract or private security firms. Corporate security generally refers to the security departments that exist within businesses or corporations. Contract security firms by contrast sell their services to the public, including businesses, homeowners, and banks.

Private security is not a monolithic entity. Just as differences exist between state and local law enforcement, private security performs functions that can differ considerably. IACP's summit report notes that "[a] security practitioner could be an experienced director of security at a major multinational corporation, a manager of contract security officers at a client site, a skilled computer crime investigator, an armed protector at a nuclear power plant, or an entry-level guard at a retail store." For local police chiefs and sheriffs, some or all of these classes of private security might be appropriate to incorporate into their homeland security strategies, depending on the characteristics of their jurisdictions.

Law enforcement and private security have strengths and weaknesses that must be considered to form realistic expectations of what each can bring to partnerships. Private security is often criticized for absent or inadequate pre-employment screening, training, standards, certification, and regulation, and high turnover rates. However, recent findings indicate that private security has made gains in these areas. Private sector security also has significant strengths. The sheer number of private security officers makes it an important force. It often is able to protect small geographic areas with large numbers of officers or guards, something law enforcement cannot afford. Some private security officers, moreover, possess specialized technical capacity, including the knowledge and ability to protect computer networks, chemical plants, financial institutions, health care institutions, and retail establishments. Law enforcement often does not possess this knowledge or only the largest agencies possess it. More generally, the large and growing security industry "is armed with considerable and often sophisticated resources to deter crime and prevent other losses."

The public law enforcement community is substantially smaller in size. Yet it is strong where private security is weak. To begin with, public law enforcement powers are far greater than those of private security. The selection process for becoming a deputy or police officer, moreover, is rigorous and includes a thorough background investigation. Law enforcement officers are well trained, receiving academy, field, and in-service instruction. Officers tend to stay at the same agency for the duration of their careers, and officers in agencies that practice community policing are likely to have established rapport and trust with local citizens and business groups that can share information with them. Trust and information are invaluable for preventing terrorist acts. Law enforcement agencies, however, like private security, have limitations. They sometimes lack the financial resources of private firms because of tight budgets. Law enforcement response time can also lag: In rural jurisdictions it is not unusual for a service call to require a considerable drive; in urban jurisdictions, on the other hand, a considerable delay in response can result from a heavy call load.

The IACP's summit report notes that in some respects, "the line between public law enforcement and private security [can be] blurred." It is not unusual for law enforcement executives at local, state, and federal levels to start a second career in private security. Sheriffs' deputies and police officers work part time in private security to supplement their incomes. Colleges and universities are also much more likely to possess "private sector, sworn law enforcement agencies" than they were 20 years ago.

Benefits of Law Enforcement-Private Security Partnerships

The advent of radical terrorism in the United States has placed great pressure on the law enforcement community. Specifically, agencies have been searching for a way to balance homeland security and traditional crime and disorder responsibilities. Limited and sometimes scarce resources must be allocated based on need, leading some chief executives to acknowledge that they are having considerable difficulty conducting this balancing act. Private security officials are experiencing a similar phenomenon. While their traditional responsibility to protect people, property, and information has continued, they are now also expected to be active participants in the national effort to protect the country's infrastructure.

Clearly, law enforcement and private security have much to gain from each other. **Law enforcement** can:

- Prepare private security to assist in emergencies.
- Coordinate efforts to safeguard the nation's critical infrastructure.
- Obtain free training and services.
- Gain additional personnel and expertise.
- Use the private sector's specialized knowledge and advanced technology.
- Obtain evidence in criminal investigations.
- Gather better information about incidents (through reporting by security staff).
- Reduce the number of calls for service.

Private security can:

- Coordinate plans with the public sector regarding evacuation, transportation, and food services during emergencies.
- Gain information from law enforcement regarding threats and crime trends.
- Develop relationships so that private practitioners know whom to contact when they need help or want to report information.
- Build law enforcement understanding of corporate needs (e.g., confidentiality).
- Boost law enforcement's respect for the security field.

Working together, private security and law enforcement can realize impressive benefits:

- Creative problem solving.
- Increased training opportunities.
- Information, data, and intelligence sharing.
- "Force multiplier" opportunities. (uniformed police in stire)
- Access to the community through private sector communications technology.
- Reduced recovery time following disasters.

Obstacles to Law Enforcement-Private Security Partnerships

While the benefits of law enforcement-private security partnerships are many, a chief executive must know that these partnerships are not without obstacles: barriers to information sharing, lack of trust, and misinformation are the primary problems.

Barriers to Information Sharing

Corporations hire former law enforcement, FBI, and CIA employees as security staff because these individuals typically retain strong information networks. Although these information networks are clearly valuable, information sharing of this type is normally limited and often inefficient. Law enforcement and the private sector must work together to cultivate more effective systems of information sharing.

Barriers to information sharing between law enforcement and private security clearly exist. Starting with private security limitations, law enforcement staff should bear in mind the for-profit nature of businesses. Specifically, because the private sector is in the business of making money, companies often do not want to release, give away, or otherwise share privileged business information that could ultimately hurt profitability. For example, if company representatives speak candidly at a public meeting, business competitors could exploit this information, as it may become publicly available through Freedom of Information Act requests. Law enforcement agencies, by the same token, have their own difficulties: They may be reticent to share information with companies owned by foreign enterprises and may also not be able to do so legally. When it comes to sharing information, however, the two greatest barriers are a lack of trust and misinformation.

> ### Area Police/Private Security Liaison (APPL) — New York
>
> APPL, created in 1986, enhances public-private security cooperation. It aims to protect persons and property, encourage the exchange of information between police and security, and eliminate issues of credibility and misperception. While it started with only 30 private security organizations, it now boasts more than 1,000.
>
> Because New York City is a high-priority target for terrorists, NYPD operates under a heightened state of awareness. The police work with APPL to review police security alertness at member facilities.

Lack of Trust (biggest barrier)

Although there are exceptions, one obstacle to creating effective partnerships may be a lack of trust between law enforcement and private security. Despite considerable discussion about partnerships between the two groups, overlapping missions, and the need to work together, the level of trust is reported to be quite low. The two sectors often view each other as having separate goals and have even viewed each other as competitors.

Both sides must overcome the trust obstacle. Peter Homel, Director of the Crime Prevention Division of the New South Wales Attorney General's Department, asserts that partnerships cannot endure that are not based on mutual trust. If trust does exist, it is often based on the working relationship of top executives seeking to establish a law enforcement-private security partnership. In many cases, these executives have worked together in the past because many security managers and directors serve in local law enforcement agencies prior to joining private industry. But trust at the top among a couple of key players cannot overcome decades of distrust across the professions.

To develop trust, police chiefs, sheriffs, and their staffs must: *explain mission*

- Create a vision and passion that brings workers together.
- Deliver what is promised.
- Ensure consistency. Constant change or change that is not understood destroys credibility.
- Communicate.
- Draw out and address past suspicions and concerns.
- Pay attention to detail.
- Train.
- Ensure equity and equality. Both sides must produce their share of work and be recognized for it.
- Reinforce the importance of the partnership (with an emphasis on sharing the credit for successes).
- Admit mistakes and learn from them. Both sides will make errors.

Misinformation and Misunderstanding

Perception

One of the major causes of lack of trust is misinformation and misunderstanding. Often, neither law enforcement nor private security has an accurate understanding of what the other does or can do. This can be problematic with regard to crime and disorder, but in the area of homeland security and terrorism it can be perilous. Even smaller scale terrorist acts can cause considerable physical, psychological, and economic damage. As noted in *Perspectives on Preparedness*, "the private sector's current lack of integration into domestic preparedness programs is dangerous." Every law enforcement officer needs to know how private security can help with homeland security and he or she must know this *before* an incident occurs, not after. The best way to gain this information is from the source: private security professionals in their community.

If law enforcement-private security partnerships are to be effective, law enforcement executives must work with their private security counterparts to communicate clear and consistent messages not only to each other, but also down through their organizations to the line-level officer or guard. At the national policy summit, joint training was recommended so that each side knows what the other has to offer. Training can also broaden the knowledge of line-level employees (e.g., private security guards could receive training on homeland security, crime prevention, and problem solving).

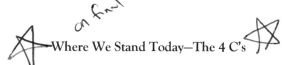

Where We Stand Today—The 4 C's

In the past, lack of trust and knowledge has inhibited the formation of law enforcement-private security partnerships. This is not to say, however, that gains have not been made over the years. As the *Operation Cooperation* guidelines noted, "law enforcement agencies and private security operations (both contract security providers and corporate security departments) have increasingly come together, pooling their strengths to prevent and solve crimes." Today, however, these partnerships must not simply prevent and solve crimes, they must also prevent terrorist acts. And although significant progress has been made in establishing partnerships, some partnerships are more comprehensive and effective than others. Understanding the 4 C's—*communication, cooperation, coordination,* and *collaboration*—is crucial to achieving effective partnerships.

Readers can think of each of the 4 C's as a step on the way to full partnering. **Communication**, the exchange of information and ideas, is the first step in establishing a relationship between two organizations. The second step, **cooperation**, involves partners undertaking a joint project or operation such as the sharing of personnel. **Coordination**, the third step, is achieved when the partners adopt a common goal, for instance, to reduce crime in a certain neighborhood. The final and most comprehensive step, **collaboration**, occurs when partners understand that their missions overlap and adopt policies and projects designed to share resources, achieve common goals, and strengthen the partners. The goal of public-private partnerships, described in greater detail below, is to achieve collaboration.

> ## 4 C's of Partnership
>
> ✓ **Communication**
> ✓ **Cooperation**
> ✓ **Coordination**
> ✓ **Collaboration**

What We Need to Do — The 12 Components of Partnerships

Understanding that law enforcement-private security partnerships are important to the nation's security is only a first step. Defining and operationalizing a partnership are the critical next steps. What do chief executives need to do to engage in these partnerships? First, they must understand what a partnership is. Although this may seem too simple a factor to consider, people often overlook the basics. And agencies seeking to achieve collaboration must understand the components that their partnerships will contain.

 A successful public-private partnership has 12 essential components:

- Common goals.
- Common tasks.
- Knowledge of participating agencies' capabilities and missions.
- Well-defined projected outcomes.
- A timetable.
- Education for all involved.

- A tangible purpose.
- Clearly identified leaders.
- Operational planning.
- Agreement by all partners as to how the partnership will proceed.
- Mutual commitment to providing necessary resources.
- Assessment and reporting

Executives need to agree on these components *before* the partnership moves forward. For the police chief or sheriff, this may include not only working with a corporation's security director but also with the corporation's chief executive or similar designee. Private security professionals at the summit, both executives and others, expressed great interest in collaborating with local law enforcement to protect the nation's infrastructure. They simply need to be asked.

Executives should also be mindful of adopting policies that only partially contribute to successful partnerships. For instance, although the following can be elements in a partnership, in and of themselves they do not constitute a public-private collaboration:

- Executives attending partner meetings.
- Officers attending partner meetings.
- Individual projects undertaken with private security.
- Joint grants undertaken with private security.

Attending meetings and working on projects can be integral *parts* of a partnership. In fact, meetings are often used to share information and plan activities. Likewise, working together on projects or grants is often of value. However, these activities do not add up to the 12 threads that tie groups together in collaborative partnerships.

How We Do It—The Nine Guidelines for Collaboration

DHS Guidelines for Collaboration

While public-private cooperation can take many forms, *collaborative partnerships* are more defined; *collaboration* requires common goals and tasks, clearly identified leaders, and the other components described above. *Cooperation*, as suggested previously, might simply entail government contracting with private security for services traditionally performed by law enforcement agencies, or the employment of off-duty police officers or sheriffs' deputies by private security agencies. However, these activities only scratch the surface of what the two sides can do to foster public safety. Homeland security arrangements between law enforcement and private security require much more than cooperation.

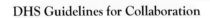
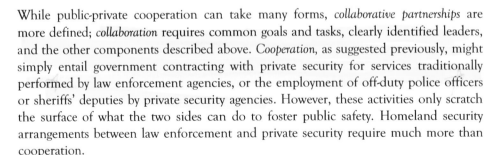

The U.S. Department of Homeland Security (DHS) has issued recommendations for jurisdictions seeking to improve *collaboration* with their private sector counterparts. DHS suggests that agencies:

- Recognize the need for prevention.

- Establish a system, center, or task force to serve as a clearinghouse for all potentially relevant domestically generated terrorism information.

- Ensure timely interpretation and assessment of information.

- Prepare Memorandums of Understanding (MOUs) and formal coordination agreements between public and private agencies. MOUs should describe mechanisms for exchanging information about vulnerabilities and risks, coordination of responses, and processes to facilitate information sharing and multijurisdictional preemption of terrorist acts.

- Use community policing initiatives, strategies, and tactics to identify suspicious activities related to terrorism.

- Explicitly develop "social capital" through collaboration among the private sector, law enforcement, and other partners so that data, information, assistance, and "best practices" may be shared and collaborative processes developed.

- Coordinate federal, state, and local information, plans, and actions for assessments, prevention procedures, infrastructure protection, and funding priorities to address prevention.

- Establish a regional prevention information command center and coordinate the flow of information regarding infrastructure.

- Include prevention and collaboration measures in exercises.

Outreach and Trust

The key to success is implementation. When implemented properly, collaborative partnerships can minimize (and sometimes avoid) duplicative efforts and leverage limited resources. Once a sheriff or police chief has decided to engage a private security entity in a partnership, initial outreach will be necessary. Outreach is easiest when trust levels are high. In these instances, the public sector chief executive will likely have established a relationship with his or her private sector counterpart as trust is normally built over time. For those chief executives who have not engaged their private sector counterparts before, an initial gesture of goodwill, respect, commitment, and purpose can go a long way.

Formalization and Memorandums of Understanding

Once trust has been established, police chiefs and sheriffs should formalize the new relationship by signing an MOU. Formalization shows employees that the partnership is a priority. At the national level, summit participants called on public and private sector leaders to make a formal commitment to partnerships and to endorse "the implementation of sustainable public-private partnerships as a preferred tool to address terrorism, public disorder, and crime." As part of this effort, law enforcement chief executives should expect, measure, and reward efforts.

Formalization helps institutionalize homeland security-driven partnerships. As steps toward achieving this goal, summit participants encouraged:

- The Commission on Accreditation for Law Enforcement Agencies (CALEA) and state accreditation bodies to require public-private partnerships as an accreditation standard.

- Law enforcement agencies and private security organizations to institutionalize communication by sharing personnel directories with each other; to make collaboration an objective in their strategic plans; and to require monthly and annual reporting of progress.

As part of writing an MOU and general startup, partners will need to identify the partnership's goals, establish their expectations, and educate and train personnel and other stakeholders. The goals of partnerships can be quite varied. The *Operation Cooperation* guidelines noted eight areas in which law enforcement and private security can collaborate:

- Networking.
- Information sharing.
- Crime prevention.
- Resource sharing.
- Training.
- Legislation.
- Operations.
- Research and guidelines.

Each of these areas contains a homeland security or terrorism prevention element.

Networking

An example of networking might be breakfast and lunch meetings to discuss the common problems both groups have in

> Lending expertise is an excellent example of resource sharing that can benefit terrorism prevention. As noted earlier, private security companies often have considerable technical knowledge that the local law enforcement community may lack.

protecting critical infrastructure. These meetings could elicit not only a constructive exchange about the pressures, motivations, and constraints on both the public and private sides of the equation, but also possible solutions.

Information sharing

The lifeblood of any policing agency is information; thus, information sharing (and its analyzed counterpart, intelligence sharing) should be a central component of any law enforcement-private security partnership. Information sharing includes planning for critical incident response, protecting infrastructure, enhancing communications, minimizing liability, and strategically deploying resources. Information should flow in both directions between law enforcement and private security.

Crime prevention

Crime prevention *is* terrorism prevention. The links between crime and terrorism are well understood—whether that connection has to do with document fraud or the illegal drug market. Terrorists often commit a number of lesser crimes toward their goal of the actual terrorist act. Based on what is known of terrorist groups and their penchant for "casing" targets (sometimes years in advance), it is not unreasonable to assume that terrorists might trespass on private property for these purposes. While private security may have in the past simply barred such individuals from returning to the property, they might now photograph trespassers and share the photographs with local law enforcement. Even without unlawful activity, private security should share any information about anything that is unusual or suspicious with law enforcement, especially when it involves the photographing of critical infrastructure.

Resource sharing

Lending expertise is an excellent example of resource sharing that can benefit terrorism prevention. As noted earlier, private security companies often have considerable technical knowledge that the local law enforcement community may lack.

Training

Lending expertise has clear connections to training. Another way to include training in a partnership is to host speakers on topics of joint interest, which can be extremely beneficial to law enforcement and private security, broadening the knowledge base of both.

Legislation

Law enforcement and private security can work together to track legislation that is important to both. More importantly, they should help legislators at the local, state, and national levels understand how legislation can affect, impair, or assist homeland security—not the least of which might be related to the sharing of certain types of sensitive information.

Operations

For line-level officers, investigators, and command staffs, the greatest opportunities for collaboration with private security are in the operational areas. Terrorism-related opportunities for collaboration include critical incident planning, the investigation of complex financial fraud or computer crimes (i.e., cybercrime), and joint sting operations (e.g., those targeting cargo theft).

Research and guidelines

The review and distribution of and action on research papers and protocols are areas in which law enforcement and private security can collaborate. Research and guidelines might be related to product tampering, closed-circuit television, security personnel standards, or whatever happens to be the homeland security issue of most importance to a region.

These examples are not intended to exhaustively illustrate the types of collaborative activities in which private security and law enforcement might engage. Many other examples exist for each of the eight areas, some of which will be discussed in the chapter "Local and Regional Programs and Initiatives." Regardless of activity, it is important to keep the 4 C's in mind: *communication, cooperation, coordination,* and *collaboration.* Each "C" represents an increasingly sophisticated component of the partnership. The end goal always is to collaborate.

Choosing Liaison Officers

Once both sides agree to form a partnership and set common goals and objectives through an MOU, selecting the right person as a liaison officer is an important, and often overlooked, responsibility. The success of a partnership often depends on the liaison. No substitute exists for a well-informed officer who is committed to and passionate about a partnership. These officers become invaluable resources, motivating others to accomplish the goals and tasks of the partnership, improving information sharing, and fostering lasting relationships—all-important elements in a successful partnership.

Executives should also bear in mind that selecting the wrong law enforcement officer to represent the department—even for a single meeting—can be devastating. Unfortunately, officers are sometimes thrust into liaison roles without adequate preparation, understanding, or commitment. They are not briefed on how or why the partnership was begun or its goals. Police chiefs and sheriffs should take the following steps to select and support their liaison:

- Involve supervisors in the selection process— supervisors are the closest management rank to officers and most often best know the strengths and weaknesses of the officers under their command. Before the selection is made, supervisors should develop or be given criteria on the type of involvement and time commitment required for the position, and its projected outcomes. Supervisors should take a lead role in the selection process.

- Fit officers to the assignment. "Fit" should be based on a candidate's personal interests, prior experience, and commitment.

- Give as much notice as possible before asking officers to represent the department as liaison. This allows them time to prepare.

- Inform officers of the desired outcomes of the partnership.

- Explain expectations clearly at the start of the process.

- Educate officers on the "who, what, when, where, why, and how" of partnerships. Officers should know how to facilitate a partnership and support its mission.

- Introduce officers to key players.

- Follow up regularly on participation by officers. Follow-up demonstrates a commitment by people other than the liaison and provides additional perspective on the partnership's progress. Additional guidance can be given to the liaison.

Just as selecting the wrong law enforcement officer as liaison can lead to failure, selecting the wrong private security guard or officer can do the same. The problem in selecting private security personnel is perhaps more complicated. As noted above, private security prescreening, standards, and training are often lacking. Law enforcement and private security executives both recognize these deficiencies. Summit participants noted that the "protection of the nation's critical infrastructure depends substantially on the competence of private security officers" and recommended that an advisory council work to improve the selection and training of private security officers.

<hr>

United States Department of Homeland Security
Federal Emergency Management Agency
Building Resilience through Public-Private Partnerships
Progress Report
January 2012, (Excerpts)

Template for Private Sector Integration into Community Preparedness

Introduction and Scope

This document provides a template for integrating the private sector into governmental homeland security and emergency management programs. Over the past decade, government and the private sector have worked together to improve coordination before, during, and after incidents. These efforts have achieved varying degrees of success. Where we see the most success, it is evident that, with government and the private sector working together, there is a mutual benefit that results in a more vigilant, prepared and resilient community. This document provides a template for integrating the private sector into the Whole Community approach to preparedness.

Definitions

The terms "government" and "private sector" have different meanings to different audiences. For clarity in the context of this document, the terms are defined as follows:

- **Government**: The governmental offices at the local, tribal, state and federal level responsible for preventing, protecting against, mitigating, responding to, and recovering from the threats and hazards facing our communities.

- **Private Sector**: Those entities within the local economy, not controlled by the government, that serve as key stakeholders in the community's ability to prevent, protect against, mitigate, respond to, or recover from, threats and hazards that pose the greatest risk to the community. This includes those entities that provide essential services like telecommunications, electricity, natural gas or heating fuels, water, and sewer services, but also includes the broader audience of for-profit and not-for-profit organizations that can serve both as a resource to, and can benefit from, the community's preparedness program. NOT included in this definition are those entities whose business models are based on providing preparedness related services to government. This is not meant to discount the important services they provide but more to recognize that these entities are already closely integrated with government.

Concept

In its simplest form, private sector integration into the community preparedness program is an issue of information exchange before, during, and after an incident. The complexities lie in operationalizing and sustaining an information exchange process that provides a mutual benefit to both government and the private sector. An assessment of current best practices reveals some common components of a successful program that align along the five mission areas of our preparedness system:

Prevention and Protection Mission Areas (the ability to avoid, prevent, or stop terrorist threats, and the ability to safeguard communities from acts of terrorism and manmade or natural disasters): The critical private sector integration tasks in these two mission areas are the sharing of

> In its simplest form, private sector integration into the community preparedness program is an issue of information exchange before, during, and after an incident.

relevant, timely, and actionable information with the private sector, and ensuring access to effective mechanisms for the private sector to report terrorism related information or suspicious activity to law enforcement. Components that support successful integration are:

- **Private Sector Networks:** These are existing or newly established private sector networks that have the means of sharing information between their members and government fusion centers or law enforcement. They are typically comprised of key stakeholders in the Prevention and Protection mission areas. They may be aligned along critical infrastructure/key resource sectors or be existing local trade and professional organizations (for example: the FBI's local InfraGard chapters, Chambers of Commerce, Sector Specific Councils, etc.). Typically no one single network represents the private sector, so it is necessary to establish a network of networks.

- **Private Sector Liaisons:** These are members of the private sector who are trained and credentialed to serve as a communication and coordination link between the government (typically fusion centers) and the private sector for the purposes of intelligence and information sharing.

- **Communications Systems:** These are the technological means by which information is transferred, posted, and maintained. They are as simple as managed email list serve systems, web based portals, or teleconference capabilities that enable the sharing of information between fusion centers or law enforcement and designated private sector networks.

- **Information Requirements and Protocols:** This is the most challenging and important component of a successful information sharing system. There must be a mutual benefit and agreement regarding what information is needed, how it is shared and how it is organized so that it is timely, relevant, and if necessary, actionable by the receiver.

- **Advisory Council:** This is the feedback mechanism to assess and improve information sharing in the prevention and protection mission areas. The council consists of key representatives of government and private sector stakeholder groups (the key senders and receivers of information).

Mitigation Mission Area (the ability to reduce loss of life and property by lessoning the impact of disasters): The critical tasks in this mission area are a common and shared understanding of the threats and hazards that pose the greatest risk to the community, and the operational coordination that appropriately integrates critical private sector stakeholders in the community planning and long term risk and vulnerability reduction process. Local governments play the lead role in facilitating and adopting effective mitigation policies and strategies. The long term resilience of the community's economy depends on a shared approach to community mitigation and the involvement of those key private sector entities that are major contributors to the local economy.

Response Mission Area (the ability to save lives, protect property and the environment, and meet basic human needs after an incident has occurred): This is the most critical mission area for effective private sector integration. Disasters impact the whole community. The ability to rapidly understand the impacts, prioritize and organize response efforts, and mobilize necessary resources requires a whole community approach in which the private sector plays a significant role. Similar to the prevention and protection mission areas, there are several common components to successful private sector integration in the Response mission area:

- **Private Sector Networks**: These may be the same networks leveraged for Prevention and Protection but may involve different representatives that are more focused on the impact to the business or how it can assist in the response. These networks share a common need for information exchange and coordination with government emergency management functions. These networks may be organized based on known impacts of an incident, infrastructure sectors, essential service providers, or the anticipated time phasing of actions for life safety, incident stabilization, and initial recovery actions. Their primary purpose is information exchange for mutual situational awareness and problem solving. Again, typically no one single network represents the private sector, so it is necessary to establish a network of networks. In some cases, specific organizations have been established to serve this purpose but sustainment and acceptance of these organizations is a current issue.

- **Private Sector Liaisons**: These are members of the private sector who are trained and credentialed to serve as a communication and coordination link between the government (typically the EOC or Emergency Manager) and the private sector for the purposes of information sharing and resource coordination. These individuals typically work in the EOC, participate as part of the incident command, and have defined duties involving information exchange, coordination, operations, planning and resource coordination.

- **Communications Systems**: These are the technological means by which information is transferred, posted, and maintained for situational awareness, problem identification and solution, and resource coordination. They are as simple as managed email list serve systems, web based portals, or teleconference capabilities that enable the sharing of information between EOC Emergency Managers and designated private sector networks. In some cases, there are established business emergency operations centers that are either virtual or physical to better facilitate private sector coordination. The challenge with these systems has been in developing and maintaining them so they are timely and effective when incidents occur.

- **Information Requirements and Protocols**: Both government and the private sector have critical information needs during an incident. Traditional media and emerging social media provide important information but not necessarily information that is operationally actionable by either government or the private sector. The identification of mutually beneficial information requirements and protocols prior to the incident is critical in order to provide actionable value to both entities. The EOC uses the Private Sector Liaison to activate communications links with Private Sector Networks via established communications systems and begins following protocols for exchanging information requirements. Those requirements include, but are not limited to, assessment of the situation for current and future threats/hazards, damage assessment to critical infrastructure/essential services, assessment for potential cascading effects, identification of unmet needs, prioritization and coordination of projected future response and resource actions, and future schedule for further information coordination activities.

- **Pre-Identification of Private Sector Resources**: One evolving issue is the need to pre-identify private sector resources that could assist in response and recovery. Some actions are attempting to develop resource typing standards and registry systems to aid in decision making and acquisition of private sector resources. Other systems align private sector entities with Emergency Support Functions and have integrated pre-identified private sector mission support packages or strike teams into the government's response system.

- **Advisory Council**: This is the feedback mechanism to assess and improve information sharing, response actions, and resource coordination during incidents. The council consists of key representatives of government and private sector stakeholder groups in the response mission area.

Recovery Mission Area (the ability of communities to recover from disasters): Like mitigation, local government plays the lead role in facilitating the decisions that drive long term recovery. Operational coordination and planning must include those private sector entities that serve as the main employers and economic contributors to the community. Local government leaders are typically aware of the key private sector entities or representative organizations and the corresponding leaders that must be involved in community recovery. The private sector's involvement in decisions that impact them financially is critical to whether businesses rebuild in a community and more importantly, whether the community recovers economically.

Conclusion

As a nation, we have yet to fully integrate the private sector into our preparedness system. Our government doctrine identifies the necessity for involving the private sector across all preparedness mission areas but the ability to operationally implement that doctrine has had spotty success. That said, there are many successful examples where integration is working and serves a mutual benefit toward whole community preparedness. This appendix has provided a template of the components common to those successful programs. Once established, the key to sustaining these programs is their integration into the community's preparedness cycle, which is the continuous cycle of planning, organizing, training, equipping, exercising, evaluating, and taking corrective action in an effort to ensure effective coordination. With government and the private sector working together as part of a whole community approach, there is a mutual benefit that results in a more vigilant, prepared, and resilient community.

United States Department of Homeland Security National Infrastructure Protection Plan: Partnering to Enhance Protection and Resiliency 2009, (Excerpts)

Primary roles for Critical Infrastructure and Key Resource partners include:

Department of Homeland Security: Coordinates the Nation's overall CIKR protection efforts and oversees NIPP development, implementation, and integration with national preparedness initiatives.

Sector-Specific Agencies: Implement the NIPP framework and guidance as tailored to the specific characteristics and risk landscapes of each of the CIKR sectors.

Other Federal Departments, Agencies, and Offices: Implement specific CIKR protection roles designated in HSPD-7 or other relevant statutes, executive orders, and policy directives.

State, Local, Tribal, and Territorial Governments: Develop and implement a CIKR protection program, in accordance with the NIPP risk management framework, as a component of their overarching homeland security programs.

Regional Partners: Use partnerships that cross jurisdiction-al and sector boundaries to address CIKR protection within a defined geographical area.

Boards, Commissions, Authorities, Councils, and Other Entities: Perform regulatory, advisory, policy, or business oversight functions related to various aspects of CIKR operations and protection within and across sectors and jurisdictions.
Private Sector Owners and Operators: Undertake CIKR protection, restoration, coordination, and cooperation activities, and provide advice, recommendations, and subject matter expertise to all levels of government.

Homeland Security Advisory Councils: Provide advice, recommendations, and expertise to the government regarding protection policy and activities.

Academia and Research Centers: Provide CIKR protection subject matter expertise, independent analysis, research and development (R&D), and educational programs.

United States Department of Homeland Security
Critical Infrastructure Sector Partnerships
Public Website, (Excerpts)

Critical Infrastructure Partnership Advisory Council

The Department of Homeland Security has established the Critical Infrastructure Partnership Advisory Council (CIPAC) to facilitate effective coordination between federal infrastructure protection programs with the infrastructure protection activities of the private sector and of state, local, territorial and tribal governments.

The CIPAC represents a partnership between government and critical infrastructure/key resource (CIKR) owners and operators and provides a forum in which they can engage in a broad spectrum of activities to support and coordinate critical infrastructure protection.

CIPAC membership will encompass CIKR owner/operator institutions and their designated trade or equivalent organizations that are identified as members of existing Sector Coordinating Councils (SCCs). It also includes representatives from federal, state, local and tribal governmental entities identified as members of existing Government Coordinating Councils (GCCs) for each sector.

Sector Coordinating Councils (SCC)

The sector partnership model encourages critical infrastructure owners and operators to create or identify Sector Coordinating Councils as the principal entity for coordinating with the government on a wide range of critical infrastructure protection activities and issues.

The SCCs are self-organized, self-run, and self-governed, with a spokesperson designated by the sector membership. Specific membership will vary from sector to sector, reflecting the unique composition of each sector; however, membership should be representative of a broad base of owners, operators, associations, and other entities—both large and small—within a sector.

> The CIPAC represents a partnership between government and critical infrastructure/key resource (CIKR) owners and operators and provides a forum in which they can engage in a broad spectrum of activities to support and coordinate critical infrastructure protection.

The SCCs enable owners and operators to interact on a wide range of sector-specific strategies, policies, activities, and issues. The SCCs serve as principal sector policy coordination and planning entities.

The primary functions of an SCC include the following:

- Represent a primary point of entry for government into the sector for addressing the entire range of critical infrastructure protection activities and issues for that sector;

- Serve as a strategic communications and coordination mechanism between critical infrastructure owners, operators, and suppliers, and, as appropriate, with the government during emerging threats or response and recovery operations, as determined by the sector;

- Identify, implement, and support the information-sharing capabilities and mechanisms that are most appropriate for the sector;

- Facilitate inclusive organization and coordination of the sector's policy development regarding critical infrastructure protection planning and preparedness, exercises and training, public awareness, and associated plan implementation activities and requirements;

- Advise on the integration of federal, state, local, and regional planning with private-sector initiatives; and

- Provide input to the government on sector research and development efforts and requirements.

The SCCs are encouraged to participate in efforts to develop voluntary consensus standards to ensure that sector perspectives are included in standards that affect critical infrastructure protection.

Sector Coordinating Councils:

- Chemical Sector Council
- Commercial Facilities Sector Council
- Communications Sector Council
- Critical Manufacturing Sector Council
- Dams Sector Council
- Defense Industrial Base Sector Council
- Emergency Services Sector Council
- Energy Sector Council
- Financial Services Sector Council
- Food and Agriculture Sector Council
- Government Facilities Sector Council
- Healthcare and Public Health Sector Council
- Information Technology Sector Council
- National Monuments and Icons Council
- Nuclear Sector Council
- Postal and Shipping Sector Council
- State, Local, Tribal and Territorial Government Coordinating Council
- Transportation Sector Council
- Water Sector Council

Government Coordinating Councils (GCC)

A **Government Coordinating Council** is formed as the government counterpart for each Sector Coordinating Council (SCC) to enable interagency and cross-jurisdictional coordination. The GCC comprises representatives from across various levels of government (federal, state, local, or tribal), as appropriate to the operating landscape of each individual sector.

Each GCC is co-chaired by a representative from the designated Sector-Specific Agency (SSA) with responsibility for ensuring appropriate representation on the GCC and providing cross-sector coordination with State, local, and tribal governments. Each GCC is co-chaired by the Department's Assistant Secretary for Infrastructure Protection or his/her designee. The GCC coordinates strategies, activities, policy, and communications across governmental entities within each sector.

The primary functions of a GCC include the following:

- Provide interagency strategic communications and coordination at the sector level through partnership with DHS, the SSA, and other supporting agencies across various levels of government;

- Participate in planning efforts related to the development, implementation, update, and revision of the National Infrastructure Protection Plan (NIPP) and the Sector-Specific Plans (SSPs);

- Coordinate strategic communications and discussion and resolution of issues among government entities within the sector; and

- Coordinate with and support the efforts of the SCC to plan, implement, and execute the nation's critical infrastructure protection mission.

Critical Infrastructure and Key Resources Cross-Sector Council

Cross-sector issues and interdependencies are addressed among the SCCs through the Critical Infrastructure and Key Resources (CIKR) Cross-Sector Council, which comprises the leadership of each of the SCCs. The Partnership for Critical Infrastructure Security provides this representation with support from the Department's CIKR Executive Secretariat. The partnership coordinates cross-sector initiatives to support critical infrastructure protection by identifying legislative issues that affect such initiatives and by raising awareness of issues in critical infrastructure protection.

The primary activities of the CIKR Cross-Sector Council include:

- Providing senior-level, cross-sector strategic coordination through partnership with DHS and the SSAs;

- Identifying and disseminating critical infrastructure protection best practices across the sectors;

- Participating in coordinated planning efforts related to the development, implementation, and revision of the NIPP and the SSPs or aspects thereof; and coordinating with DHS to support efforts to plan and execute the nation's critical infrastructure protection mission.

Regional Consortium Coordinating Council

Because of the specific challenges and interdependencies facing individual regions and the broad range of public and private sector security partners, regional efforts are often complex and diverse. The Regional Consortium Coordinating Council brings together representatives of regional partnerships, groupings, and governance bodies to enable critical infrastructure protection coordination among partners within and across geographical areas and sectors.

Federal Senior Leadership Council (FSLC)

The objective of the NIPP Federal Senior Leadership Council is to drive enhanced communications and coordination among federal departments and agencies that have a role in implementing the NIPP and Homeland Security Presidential Directive-7, "Critical Infrastructure Identification, Prioritization, and Protection." The members of the FSLC include the Sector-Specific Agencies for each of the critical infrastructure sectors as well as several additional agencies named in HSPD-7.

State, Local, Tribal, and Territorial Government Coordinating Council (SLTTGCC)

The State, Local, Tribal, and Territorial Government Coordinating Council (SLTTGCC) serves as a forum to ensure that State, local, and tribal homeland security partners are fully integrated as active participants in national critical infrastructure protection efforts, and to provide an organizational structure to coordinate across jurisdictions on state and local government-level critical infrastructure protection guidance, strategies, and programs. The SLTTGCC will provide the state, local, tribal, or territorial perspective or feedback on a wide variety of critical infrastructure issues.

The primary functions of the SLTTGCC include the following:

- Providing senior-level, cross-jurisdictional strategic communications and coordination through partnership with the Department, the SSAs, and critical infrastructure owners and operators;

- Participating in planning efforts related to the development, implementation, update, and revision of the NIPP and SSPs or aspects thereof;

- Coordinating strategic issues and issue management resolution among federal departments and agencies, and State, local, tribal, and territorial partners;

- Coordinating with the Department to support efforts to plan, implement, and execute the nation's critical infrastructure protection mission; and

- Providing the Department with information on state, local, tribal, and territorial-level critical infrastructure protection initiatives, activities, and best practices.

Critical Infrastructure Partnership Advisory Council (CIPAC)

The Critical Infrastructure Partnership Advisory Council (CIPAC) provides the operational mechanism for carrying out the sector partnership structure. The CIPAC provides the framework for owner and operator members of Sector Coordinating Councils (SCC) and members of Government Coordinating Councils (GCC) to engage in intra-government and public-private cooperation, information sharing, and engagement across the entire range of critical infrastructure protection activities.

Successful execution of the sector partnership structure requires an environment in which members of the SCCs and GCCs can interact freely and share sensitive information and advice about threats, vulnerabilities, protective measures, and lessons learned. CIPAC, which has been exempted from the requirements of the Federal Advisory Committee Act (FACA), is the mechanism to allow meaningful dialogue on key critical infrastructure protection issues and agreement on mutual action between government and owner/operator entities.

CIPAC is a non-decisional body and includes sector members and government members. Sector members are the members of that sector's SCC that are owners and/or operators and the trade associations that represent them. Government members are the federal, state, local, and tribal government agencies (or their representative bodies) that comprise the GCC for each sector.

Partnership Spotlight

U.S. Communications Sector Coordinating Council
Public Website, (Excerpts)

Communications Sector Coordinating Council (CSCC)

The Mission

The Communications Sector Coordinating Council (CSCC), with its government partners, works to protect the Nation communications critical infrastructure and key resources (CIKR) from harm and to ensure that the Nation's communications networks and systems are secure, resilient, and rapidly restored after a natural or manmade disaster.

The Sector

The Communications Sector assets include multiple fully interconnected telecommunications networks with high-speed fiber optic routes, central office and transmission facilities, optical switches, buildings, mobile switching offices, antenna sites, satellite facilities, and the physical infrastructure which supports cyber space. Protection of these assets ensures the availability of multiple services including traditional voice, VoIP, mobile voice, Internet access, email, Instant Messaging, up/downstream Internet website data transmission, streaming video, high resolution video, digital photographs, etc. The communications infrastructure is a complex system of systems that incorporates multiple technologies and services with diverse ownership. The infrastructure includes wireline, wireless, satellite, cable, and broadcasting technology platforms, and provides the transport networks that support the Internet and other key information systems. With a strong and well-refined focus on risk management, long-established processes and procedures for network security and rapid response and recovery under all hazards assure the continued operation of vital communications services.

Cross Sector Activities:

The CSCC coordinates with the other 17 critical infrastructure sectors through the Partnership for Critical Infrastructure Security (PCIS) to address cross-sector issues and interdependencies. The PCIS provides senior-level cross-sector strategy coordination through partnership with DHS and the sector-specific federal agencies or SSAs.

Communications Sector Coordinating Council Membership:

- Federal Communications Commission (FCC)
- Federal Reserve Board (FRB)
- General Services Administration (GSA)
- National Association of Regulatory Utility Commissioners (NARUC)
- U.S. Department of Agriculture
- U.S. Department of Commerce
- U.S. Department of Defense
- U.S. Department of Homeland Security
- U.S. Department of Justice
- U.S. Department of State
- U.S. Department of the Interior
- 3U Technologies, LLC
- Alcatel-Lucent
- Americom-GS
- Association of Public Television Stations
- AT&T
- The Boeing Company
- Century Link
- CTIA - The Wireless Association
- Cincinnati Bell
- Cisco Systems, Inc.
- Comcast
- Computer Sciences Corporation (CSC)
- Digi International
- DirecTV
- Harris Corporation
- Hughes Network Systems
- Internet Security Alliance (ISA)
- Intrado

- Iridium
- Juniper Networks
- Level 3 Communications
- McLeodUSA
- The MITRE Corporation
- Motorola
- National Association of Broadcasters (NAB)
- National Cable & Telecommunications Association (NCTA)
- NeuStar
- Nortel
- Powerwave
- Research in Motion (RIM)
- Rural Cellular Association
- The Satellite Broadcasting and Communications Association
- Satellite Industry Association
- Savvis, Inc.
- Sprint
- Telcordia
- Telecommunications Industry Association (TIA)
- TeleContinuity, Inc.
- TerreStar Networks, Inc.
- Tyco
- Utilities Telecom Council
- U.S. Internet Services Provider Association (USISPA)
- U.S. Telecom Association (USTelecom)
- VeriSign Authentication Services
- Verizon

Editor's Comments

The key to solving most complex problems rests in the ability to marshal resources and leverage relationships. In fact, it is the propensity to call upon existing partnerships which has defined the "modern" approach to threat mitigation.

Central to the partnership concept is active communication. DHS has incorporated stakehol' communication as a core element in many homeland security programs. An example of this c found within the "fusion center" program. By creating a national network of information "DHS has ensured that front-line law enforcement, public safety, fire service, emergency public health, critical infrastructure protection, and private sector security personnel have resource for the receipt, analysis, gathering, and sharing of threat-related information" (DHS Website). It is this level of communication which fuels the partnership process.

In addition to active communication, the partnership concept necessitates unity of mission. As a significant group effort, the homeland security function requires coordination, fluidity, and balance among its many individual parts. All components need to be mission-oriented - working within the organizational structure – while providing a unique contribution to the global process. Individual efforts must be guided by a common organizational objective.

DHS embraces unity of mission through its sector partnership model. "For each critical infrastructure sector, a Sector Coordinating Council representing the private sector and a Government Coordinating Council have been created to share data, techniques, best practices, and to support systematic risk-based planning. DHS provides guidance, tools, and support to assist these sector-specific groups in working together to carry out their individual responsibilities" (DHS Website).

—————————————

Further Discussion

1. Discuss the **public/private** partnership model.

2. Discuss the **evolution** of the public/private partnership model.

3. Discuss the **problems** associated with the public/private partnership model.

4. Discuss **improvements** and/or **alternatives** to the public/private partnership model.

5. Discuss the significance of the **sector coordinating councils**.

Part II

Functions of Homeland Security

- o The Mission of Homeland Security
- o Risk Management
- o Emergency Management
- o The Terrorist Threat
- o American Jihadists
- o Combating Terrorism

Chapter 07

The Mission of Homeland Security

"The war on terror will not be won on the defensive. We must take the battle to the enemy, disrupt his plans, and confront the worst threats before they emerge. In the world we have entered, the only path to safety is the path of action. And this nation will act."

President George W. Bush, June 1, 2002

United States Department of Homeland Security
Quadrennial Homeland Security Review Report:
A Strategic Framework for a Secure Homeland
February 2010, (Excerpts)

Overview of the Homeland Security Missions

The vision of homeland security is to ensure a homeland that is safe, secure, and resilient against terrorism and other hazards where American interests, aspirations, and way of life can thrive.

As noted earlier, three key concepts form the foundation of our national homeland security strategy designed to achieve this vision: **Security, Resilience,** and **Customs and Exchange.** In turn, these key concepts drive broad areas of activity that the QHSR process defines as homeland security missions. *These missions are enterprise-wide, and not limited to the Department of Homeland Security.* These missions and their associated goals and objectives tell us in detail what it means to prevent, to protect, to respond, and to recover, as well as to build in security, to ensure resilience, and to facilitate customs and exchange. Hundreds of thousands of people from across the Federal Government, State, local, tribal, and territorial governments, the private sector, and other nongovernmental organizations are responsible for executing these missions. These are the people who regularly interact with the public, who are responsible for public safety and security, who own and operate our Nation's critical infrastructures and services, who perform research and develop technology, and who keep watch, prepare for, and respond to emerging threats and disasters. These homeland security professionals must have a clear sense of what it takes to achieve the overarching vision articulated above.

There are five **homeland security missions**. The missions and associated goals are as follows:

Mission 1: Preventing Terrorism and Enhancing Security
Goal 1.1 Prevent Terrorist Attacks
Goal 1.2 Prevent the Unauthorized Acquisition or Use of Chemical, Biological, Radiological, and Nuclear Materials and Capabilities
Goal 1.3 Manage Risks to Critical Infrastructure, Key Leadership, and Events

Mission 2: Securing and Managing Our Borders
Goal 2.1 Effectively Control U.S. Air, Land, and Sea Borders
Goal 2.2 Safeguard Lawful Trade and Travel
Goal 2.3 Disrupt and Dismantle Transnational Criminal Organizations

Mission 3: Enforcing and Administering Our Immigration Laws
Goal 3.1 Strengthen and Effectively Administer the Immigration System
Goal 3.2 Prevent Unlawful Immigration

Mission 4: Safeguarding and Securing Cyberspace
Goal 4.1 Create a Safe, Secure, and Resilient Cyber Environment
Goal 4.2 Promote Cybersecurity Knowledge and Innovation

Mission 5: **Ensuring Resilience to Disasters**
Goal 5.1 Mitigate Hazards
Goal 5.2 Enhance Preparedness
Goal 5.3 Ensure Effective Emergency Response
Goal 5.4 Rapidly Recover

Mission 1: Preventing Terrorism and Enhancing Security

Preventing terrorism in the United States is the cornerstone of homeland security. Ensuring that malicious actors cannot conduct terrorist attacks within the United States, preventing the illicit or hostile use of chemical, biological, radiological, and nuclear (CBRN) materials or capabilities within the Unites States, and managing risks to our critical infrastructure and key resources helps us realize our vision of a secure and resilient Nation.

RQ-1 Predators, like the one shown here, are being deployed from Creech Air Force Base, Nev., to provide intelligence, surveillance and reconnaissance capabilities. Photo credit: Department of Defense.

Key Strategic Outcomes

- Acts of terrorism against transportation systems are thwarted prior to successful execution.

- The manufacture, storage, or transfer of dangerous materials is protected by physical, personnel, and cybersecurity measures commensurate with the risks.

- Any release of high-consequence biological weapons is detected in time to protect populations at risk from the release.

- Critical infrastructure sectors adopt and sector partners meet accepted standards that measurably reduce the risk of disrupting public health and safety, critical government services, and essential economic activities.

- Governmental executive leadership is protected from hostile acts by terrorists and other malicious actors.

Goal 1.1: Prevent Terrorist Attacks

Malicious actors are unable to conduct terrorist attacks within the United States.

Success in achieving this goal rests on our ability to strengthen public- and private-sector activities designed to counter terrorist efforts to plan and conduct attacks. Success also depends on strengthening our ability to investigate and arrest perpetrators of terrorist crimes and to collect intelligence that will help prevent future terrorist activities.

Objectives:

- Understand the threat

    Acquire, analyze, and appropriately share intelligence and other information on current and emerging threats. Homeland security partners require a shared understanding of the current and emerging threats from terrorists and other malicious actors to inform the development of risk management strategies. As has long been recognized, information and intelligence regarding emerging threats must be collected, analyzed, and disseminated appropriately and promptly. Homeland security partners must use compatible information architecture and data standards where possible to maximize the acquisition, access, retention, production, use, management, and appropriate safeguarding of this information.

- Deter and disrupt operations

    Deter, detect, and disrupt surveillance, rehearsals, and execution of operations by terrorists and other malicious actors. We must deter and disrupt malicious actors and dismantle support networks at every step of their operations. This objective also includes identifying and disrupting efforts to corrupt cyber or movement systems, breach confidentiality, or deny authorized access. Prompt and appropriate law enforcement and legal action against perpetrators and dismantling of their support networks will mitigate hostile actions.

- Protect against terrorist capabilities

    Protect potential targets against the capabilities of terrorists, malicious actors, and their support networks to plan and conduct operations. We must be able to protect against the capabilities that malicious actors might use to conduct terrorism against the United States. This objective includes detecting, disrupting, and preventing the ability of malicious actors intent on using terrorism to train, plan, travel, finance their operations, communicate, and acquire weapons—including high-yield explosives. We must protect against the full range of these capabilities in order to reduce the likelihood of a successful attack against the United States.

- Stop the spread of violent extremism

  Prevent and deter violent extremism and radicalization that contributes to it. Reducing violent extremism will frustrate terrorist efforts to recruit operatives, finance activities, and incite violence. In particular, efforts must focus not only at the community level, but also on cyberspace.

- Engage communities

  Increase community participation in efforts to deter terrorists and other malicious actors and mitigate radicalization toward violence. Individual citizens and cohesive communities are key partners in the homeland security enterprise and have an essential role to play in countering terrorism. Mechanisms for identifying and reporting suspicious activities must be made clear and accessible. Moreover, enhanced public preparedness and effective warning systems can empower communities, help minimize fear, and diminish the effectiveness of terrorist tactics.

Goal 1.2: **Prevent the Unauthorized Acquisition or Use of CBRN Materials and Capabilities**

Malicious actors, including terrorists, are unable to acquire or move dangerous chemical, biological, radiological, and nuclear materials or capabilities within the United States.

Although the Nation remains committed to preventing all attacks by terrorists and other malicious actors, certain chemical, biological, radiological, and nuclear attacks pose a far greater potential to cause catastrophic consequences. Consequently, particular attention must be paid to the security of dangerous chemical, biological, radiological, and nuclear materials and technologies.

Objective:

- Anticipate emerging threats

  Identify and understand potentially dangerous actors, technologies, and materials. It is incumbent upon us to identify changing capabilities *before* their first use so that appropriate risk management strategies can be developed and executed. Homeland security partners must identify, characterize, and have timely and appropriate information and analysis on emerging and potentially dangerous technologies and materials. Information and analysis on emerging threats must be appropriately and effectively shared among homeland security partners.

- Control access to CBRN

  Prevent terrorists and other malicious actors from gaining access to dangerous materials and technologies. American industry transforms raw materials and technologies into economic progress, but in the wrong hands, such materials and capabilities pose critical threats to public health and safety. Controlling access to CBRN materials and technologies is an essential step in preventing their illicit use. Access to these materials and technologies must be limited to legitimate users. Industries that manufacture, store, or sell potentially dangerous materials, and experts with knowledge of their use, must maintain awareness of the status of CBRN materials and technologies and assume responsibility for their security and control. Personnel surety programs must be strengthened. Finally, the manufacturing, storage, and transfer of dangerous materials must be protected by physical and cybersecurity measures commensurate with the risks they pose.

- **Control movement of CBRN**

  Prevent the illicit movement of dangerous materials and technologies. Should malicious actors obtain CBRN, attacks can be prevented or deterred if movement of CBRN is more effectively controlled. Differentiating between the licit and illicit movement of dangerous materials and technologies will require the cooperation of public- and private-sector homeland security enterprise partners to ensure such materials and technologies are secure and accounted for, and their movement is known to appropriate authorities. Terrorists and other malicious actors must be impeded in their ability to move dangerous materials, technologies, and expertise into, within, or out of the United States through appropriate screening, detection, and inspection regimes, and through efforts to prevent the financing of their activities.

- **Protect against hostile use of CBRN**

  Identify the presence of and effectively locate, disable, or prevent the hostile use of CBRN. Measures must be in place to discover the presence of CBRN, as well as to rapidly apply the technology and expertise necessary to locate, disable, or otherwise prevent use of CBRN weapons.

Goal 1.3: Manage Risks to Critical Infrastructure, Key Leadership, and Events vulnerability to attack or disruption.

The American way of life depends upon the effective functioning of the Nation's critical infrastructure and key resources, and the protection of key leadership and events. Although considerable advances have been made in identifying critical infrastructure assets and systems, and understanding the current, emerging, and future risks to those infrastructures, the breadth of the infrastructure, its increasing reliance on cyberspace, and its criticality necessitates continued diligence.

Objectives:

- **Understand and prioritize risks to critical infrastructure**

Identify, attribute, and evaluate the most dangerous threats to critical Infrastructure and those categories of critical infrastructure most at risk. Homeland security partners and stakeholders need a shared understanding of the risks to and the interdependencies that connect the Nation's critical infrastructure and key resources. Homeland security partners must provide and receive information and assessments on current and emerging risks in time to carry out their risk management responsibilities, while enjoying access to the data, tools, and expertise to make informed risk management decisions. Acquisition, access, retention, production, use, and management of threat and risk information must be maximized through compatible information architecture and data standards. Risk management decisions made by homeland security partners must account for interdependencies across sectors and jurisdictions.

- **Protect critical infrastructure**

  Prevent high-consequence events by securing critical infrastructure assets, systems, networks, or functions—including linkages through cyberspace—from attacks or disruption. Homeland security partners must be aware of the risk profiles of and risk management strategies for critical infrastructure, to include key governmental sites that have national symbolic importance as well as serve as vital functions to our democratic institutions. Measures to control, and in some cases deny, access to critical infrastructure assets, systems, and networks must be consistently implemented, upgraded, and enforced. These measures must also continuously adapt based on an improved understanding of changing threats and risks. Additionally, business processes and infrastructure operations must be changed or revised and technologies incorporated to reduce the risk of high-consequence events.

- **Make critical infrastructure resilient**

  Enhance the ability of critical infrastructure systems, networks, and functions to withstand and rapidly recover from damage and disruption and adapt to changing conditions. The Nation cannot rely on protection strategies alone to ensure the continuity of critical functions, particularly those necessary for public health and safety. Homeland security partners must develop, promulgate, and update guidelines, codes, rules, regulations, and accepted standards when appropriate, that measurably reduce the risk of damage and disruption to critical functions, networks, and systems, and ensure their resilience. Design of new infrastructure and infrastructure improvements must anticipate change in the risk environment, incorporate lessons from past events and exercises, and consider and build in security and resilience from the start. Finally, a skilled workforce with sufficient capacity and expertise is necessary in order to ensure the functionality of critical infrastructure.

- Protect governmental leaders, facilities, and special events

    Preserve continuity of government and ensure security at events of national significance. Preserving continuity of government is essential to the stability of the Nation. Detecting, disrupting, and responding to crises under any contingency requires collaboration throughout the homeland security enterprise. Identifying, analyzing, and disseminating protective intelligence information pertaining to individuals, groups, and technologies that pose a danger to our Nation's leadership and visiting heads of state and government is imperative to safeguarding our Nation's interests. So too is actual protection of government facilities. In addition, Federal, State, local, tribal, and territorial homeland security partners execute operational security plans that ensure the safety of American citizens at events of national significance. Homeland security stakeholders play a critical role in the execution of layered security measures to address the threat spectrum. Developing and fostering critical coalitions such as task forces, fusion centers, and working groups reinforces strategic investigative alliances, aids in identifying patterns and trends, and allows sharing of emerging technologies, systems, and methodologies.

Mission 2: Securing and Managing Our Borders

A safe and secure homeland requires that we maintain effective control of our air, land, and sea borders; that we safeguard lawful trade and travel; and that we disrupt transnational

A Border Patrol agent monitors the horizon for signs of illegal border crossings.
Photo credit: United States Customs and Border Protection.

organizations that engage in smuggling and trafficking across the U.S. border. This three-pronged approach to securing and managing our borders can only be achieved by working with partners from across the homeland security enterprise to establish secure and resilient global trading, transportation, and transactional systems that facilitate the flow of lawful travel and commerce. This approach also depends on partnerships with Federal, State, local, tribal, territorial, and international law enforcement agencies to share information and conduct coordinated and integrated operations. In working together, we can more effectively achieve our shared vision and preserve our freedoms and way of life.

Key Strategic Outcomes

- The entry or approach of all high-consequence WMD and related materials and technologies is prevented.

- Terrorists and other high-risk individuals are prevented from using commercial or noncommercial transportation destined for the United States.

- The identity of all individuals who are encountered at U.S. borders and in global movement systems entering the United States is verified.

- Individuals with known ties to terrorism or transnational criminal activities are not granted access to secure areas within the global movement system.

- No highly dangerous pathogens or organisms are introduced across U.S. borders.

Goal 2.1: Effectively Control U.S. Air, Land, and Sea Borders Prevent the illegal flow of people and goods across U.S. air, land, and sea borders while expediting the safe flow of lawful travel and commerce.

Key to achieving secure and well-managed borders are the broad legal authorities utilized by trained officers to conduct appropriate searches, seizures, arrests, and other key enforcement activities. These security and enforcement activities are balanced, however, by the need to facilitate the lawful transit of people and goods across our borders. Through the collection, analysis, and proper sharing of information, the use of screening and identification verification techniques, the employment of advanced detection and other technologies, the use of "trusted traveler" or "trusted shipper" approaches, and cooperation with our international partners and the private sector, we can achieve security at our borders, enforce the laws, and ensure our prosperity and freedom by speeding lawful travel and commerce.

Objectives:

- **Prevent illegal entry**

   Prevent the illegal entry of people, weapons, dangerous goods, and contraband, and protect against cross-border threats to health, food, environment, and agriculture, while facilitating the safe flow of lawful travel

and commerce. Central to the mission of controlling our borders is preventing the illegal entry of dangerous persons, contraband, or other illicit goods— whether they are terrorists, highly dangerous weapons, illicit drugs, dangerous pathogens, invasive species, or counterfeit software. Preventing illegal entry must be accomplished both at official ports of entry—in concert with facilitating the safe flow of lawful travel and commerce—and in the long stretches between these points, as well as along our maritime borders and across our air boundaries. We must substantially increase situational awareness at our borders and approaches in order to help detect and classify potential threats and effectively resolve them. We must positively identify individuals encountered to determine their risk to the country, and expedite the collection, sharing, and analysis of all relevant information so that border officers can make accurate security determinations, reduce unknowns in the system, and expedite low-risk individuals and commerce. We must enhance measures aimed at deterring illegal migration and contraband smuggling, thereby reducing "pull" factors that draw unlawful migrants and dangerous goods. Finally, we must build on our existing partnerships with our North American neighbors in order to collaboratively address threats to the continent and approaches and more effectively expedite and secure the lawful flow of travel and commerce within the North American community.

- Prevent illegal export and exit

   Prevent the illegal export of weapons, proceeds of crime, and other dangerous goods, and the exit of malicious actors. Gaining control of the borders also means gaining better control of what leaves our country. Indeed, violent international drug trafficking organizations are fueled by the proceeds of drug sales smuggled out of the United States, and armed by weapons, some of which are obtained in this country and smuggled across our borders. Hostile and criminal actors seek to smuggle weapons, weapons components, bulk cash, and controlled technologies out of the United States, as well as seek U.S.-based financing for their activities. To address these threats, relevant authorities must identify and assess the risk of all commercial cargo exiting the United States through official channels, and known or suspected terrorists or criminals must be prevented from departing the United States. Additionally, outbound smuggling must be reduced through collaboration with international and private-sector partners, both at home and overseas. Finally, authorities throughout the homeland security enterprise must identify, share, and act upon information to prevent all known or suspected terrorists and wanted criminals from leaving the United States or seeking to enter neighboring countries.

Goal 2.2: Safeguard Lawful Trade and Travel

Ensure security and resilience of global movement systems
The global economy is increasingly a seamless economic environment connected by systems and networks that transcend national boundaries. The United States is

deeply linked to other countries through the flow of goods and services, capital and labor, and information and technology into and across our borders. As much as

One of many U.S. ports of entry. Photo credit: United States Customs and Border Protection.

these global systems and networks are critical to the United States and our prosperity, their effectiveness and efficiency also make them attractive targets for exploitation by our adversaries, terrorists, and criminals. Thus, border security cannot begin simply at our borders. The earlier we can identify, understand, interdict, and disrupt plots and illegal operations, the safer we will be at home. In other words, our borders should not be our first line of defense against global threats. This premise demands a focus on using our national leverage to build partnerships to secure key nodes and conveyances in the global trading and transportation networks, as well as to manage the risks posed by people and goods in transit. Moreover, U.S. national interests—in a competitive U.S. economy and a stable global trading system—require us to work with international partners and the private sector to secure global movement systems. These same national interests are also served by ensuring the free, lawful movement of people and commerce through the global economy and across U.S. borders in a manner that does not impair economic vitality, while at the same time safeguarding privacy, civil rights, and civil liberties.

Objectives:

- Secure key nodes

   Promote the security and resilience of key nodes of transaction and exchange within the global supply chain. A variety of actors are involved in the complex process of moving goods and people through the global supply chain from origin to final destination. Each nodal transfer—such as from one international airport or seaport to another, or from one entity to the next—presents adversaries with a new opportunity to introduce a threat into the global supply chain or exploit this system for their own purposes. These key nodes and exchange points must be secured from threats and made able to withstand disruption. In addition, advance information and sophisticated analytic capabilities must be used to reduce unknowns in the system, so that interventions can focus on identified threats or higher risks. Finally, the U.S. Government must work with its international partners and the private sector to build on existing efforts to develop, strengthen, and implement international standards for securing the key systems of the global economy and more effectively facilitating the flow of lawful travel and commerce throughout the world and across U.S. borders.

- **Secure conveyances**

  Promote the security and resilience of conveyances in the key global trading and transportation networks. A key component of global movement systems are the conveyances—the forms of transit used to move people and goods from a point of origin toward a final destination—and the operators in that system, including air carriers, cruise ship operators, exporters, cargo carriers, importers, manufacturers, and longshoremen, among others. Operators and the conveyances used to move people and goods from an origin toward a final destination must be identified and determined not to pose a threat to the United States or the larger global movement system. In addition, operators must ensure against the misuse of equipment or transportation that would allow for the introduction of dangerous or illegal contents into the system. Finally, conveyances or shipments approaching or entering the United States through a port of entry must be assessed to determine if they may legally enter the United States, or whether they should be subject to additional inspection, if deemed a potential threat or if authorities otherwise believe appropriate.

- **Manage the risk posed by people and goods in transit**

  People seeking to come to the United States, as well as goods in transit, must be positively identified and determined not to pose a threat to this country or the larger global movement system as far in advance as possible. For movement of people, this assessment can be performed early through visa processes, online application for travel authorization, and advance provision of passenger biographical information, in order to expedite the flow of international travel. For movement of goods, the assessment is ideally done well before shipment to the United States, or even earlier in the supply chain, in conjunction with private-sector entities and international partners. Identifying people and goods that pose minimal risk as early in the process as possible and securely expediting their travel to and through the United States also facilitates the flow of lawful travel and commerce and reduces friction in the global economy. Supporting networks to share information and analysis regarding people and goods must be robust and effective while protecting privacy and civil liberties. Enhanced global standards for information collection and sharing increase the effectiveness of these risk assessment efforts. These activities are key to ensuring the safe, lawful flow of commerce, reducing processing times for individuals and goods seeking lawful entry to the country, and ensuring that the United States remains open for business to the world and welcoming of international visitors.

Goal 2.3: Disrupt and Dismantle Transnational Criminal Organizations

Disrupt and dismantle transnational organizations that engage in smuggling and trafficking across the U.S. border. We have also learned in the years since 9/11 that it is not enough to simply interdict trouble at the border or enhance the protection of global systems for trade and travel. Criminals, terrorist networks, and other malicious actors will seek to exploit the same interconnected systems and networks of the global economy for nefarious purposes, or create their own illicit pathways for smuggling and trafficking—of illegal drugs, illegal migrants, terrorists, or even highly dangerous weapons. When these organizations or actors are successful, they also may increase corruption and engage in a wide variety of other criminal activities such as money laundering, bulk cash smuggling, and intellectual property crime, which threaten the rule of law, potentially endanger lives, and generate wider destabilization. Thus, our border strategy must also focus on reducing the power and capability of these transnational criminal and terrorist organizations.

Objectives:

- **Identify, disrupt, and dismantle transnational criminal and terrorist organizations**

  Disrupt transnational criminal or terrorist organizations involved in cross-border smuggling, trafficking, or other cross-border crimes, dismantle their infrastructure, and apprehend their leaders. Identifying, disrupting, and dismantling criminal and terrorist organizations transcends any one Federal agency, State, local, tribal, or territorial law enforcement agency, or Intelligence Community partner. Success will require many key activities. First, all relevant information held by authorities concerning known or suspected terrorists, criminals, illicit organizations and networks, and inadmissible foreign nationals must be appropriately shared among agencies so malicious actors are interdicted by authorities. Working together, the operations of the major transnational criminal and terrorist organizations must be disrupted, and supporting organizations, networks, and infrastructure must be substantially dismantled. The leaders of these organizations must be apprehended and brought to justice.

- Disrupt illicit pathways

  Identify, disrupt, and dismantle illicit pathways used by criminal and terrorist organizations. In addition to exploiting lawful systems for global travel and trade, criminal and terrorist organizations create their own illegal pathways for smuggling and trafficking people and goods across international borders. While these routes and conveyances may be used today to transport illicit narcotics or facilitate illegal migration, the same routes may also be used to smuggle terrorists and their tools and finances, or even highly dangerous weapons and materials. Working appropriately with domestic law enforcement partners, the Intelligence Community, and foreign partners, we must identify these illicit pathways, understand their nodes and conveyances, monitor their use, and effectively intervene to stop dangerous people or goods in transit and dismantle the pathways themselves

Mission 3: Enforcing and Administering Our Immigration Laws

A fair and effective immigration system must protect the public while also enriching American society and promoting economic prosperity. At the same time, it must also deter immigration violations, work to eliminate the conditions that foster illegal immigration, and improve the efficiency, fairness, and integrity of our immigration system.

ICE removes Mexican national wanted for murder. Photo credit: United States Immigration and Customs Enforcement.

Key Strategic Outcomes

- The identities of individuals seeking immigration services are verified at first contact and throughout the immigration process.

- All workers are verified as legally authorized to work in the United States.

- Real-time information, data, trends, and intelligence on terrorist or criminal organizations and individuals are accessible to all Federal immigration partners.

- Criminal organizations and individuals are prevented from transporting, housing, or harboring illegal aliens.

- All communities that are home to immigrant populations have programs that effectively integrate immigrants into American civic society.

Goal 3.1: Strengthen and Effectively Administer the Immigration System Promote lawful immigration, expedite administration of immigration services, and promote the integration of lawful immigrants into American society. Effective administration of the immigration system depends on ensuring that immigration decisions are fair, lawful, and sound; that the immigration system is interactive and user friendly; that policy and procedural gaps are systematically identified and corrected; and that vulnerabilities that would allow persons to exploit the system are eliminated. In addition, effectively administering the immigration system includes efforts to integrate lawful immigrants into American society.

Objectives:

- **Promote lawful immigration**

    Clearly communicate with the public about immigration services and procedures. Lawful immigration contributed greatly to the building of America and continues to enrich our society, our economy, and our way of life. Promoting lawful immigration requires transparent procedures and sustained efforts to inform the public about immigration programs and policies. Thus, to promote lawful immigration, all appropriate information regarding immigration programs, eligibility requirements, application instructions, and status updates must be available to external users through multiple user-friendly avenues, including an interactive, Web-based portal. Feedback from stakeholders must be obtained and assessed in an integrated manner, and solutions, current policies, and policy changes must be clearly communicated to stakeholders and to the public.

- **Effectively administer the immigration services system**

    Create a user-friendly system that ensures fair, consistent, and prompt decisions. Applications for immigration services must be efficiently and effectively received and managed. All information needed to make immigration decisions must be available to appropriate agencies electronically and in real-time, including active individual case files and biometric information. In addition, gaps and inconsistencies in policies and procedures must be identified and corrected, while policy guidance must be effectively communicated to the field. Finally, policy implementation must be evaluated to ensure compliance and consistency in the field.

- Promote the integration of lawful immigrants into American society

  Provide leadership, support, and opportunities to lawful immigrants to facilitate their integration into American society and foster community cohesion. Homeland security partners and stakeholders must work collectively to provide strategies that respect newcomers while encouraging and assisting eligible immigrants to naturalize. Communities that are home to lawful immigrants must have the necessary tools to engage lawful immigrants in civic activities and community issues. New lawful immigrant communities should be encouraged to become an integral part of American life. For their part, new lawful immigrants must obey all applicable laws and take affirmative steps to fully join their new society. This includes learning English and the civic principles that form the foundation of responsible citizenship.

Goal 3.2: Prevent Unlawful Immigration

Reduce conditions that encourage foreign nationals to illegally enter and remain in the United States, while identifying and removing those who violate our laws. To prevent illegal immigration, all agencies charged with immigration administration and enforcement activities must address conditions and factors that create incentives for those illegally entering and staying within the United States. This effort includes identifying the conditions and addressing gaps in current laws, policies, and procedures that foster illegal immigration. Enforcement efforts must prioritize the identification and removal of dangerous foreign nationals who threaten our national security or the safety of our communities and must include safe and humane detention conditions and respect for due process and civil rights as accorded by law.

Objectives:

- Reduce demand

  Eliminate the conditions that encourage illegal employment. Reducing demand for unauthorized workers is essential to preventing illegal immigration. An employment eligibility verification system is critical in identifying employers whose business model depends on the abuse of workers without legal status. This verification system must be implemented with appropriate regard to privacy and civil rights. Furthermore, only a strong enforcement program that identifies and punishes employers who knowingly employ unauthorized workers as part of their business model will serve as an effective deterrent. Developing a collaborative, interagency approach to bring the combined authorities and enforcement resources of Federal, State, local, tribal, and territorial partners to target abusive employers will reduce demand for unauthorized workers by increasing the penalties against those who exploit them.

- Eliminate systemic vulnerabilities

  Prevent fraud, abuse, and exploitation, and eliminate other systemic vulnerabilities that threaten the integrity of the immigration system. Systemic vulnerabilities that threaten the integrity of the immigration system must be eliminated by identifying and targeting system deficiencies and the root causes of system misuse. Fraud facilitators, criminal and terrorist organizations, and individuals must be prevented from engaging in immigration fraud and violators must be prosecuted. Targeting systemic vulnerabilities may require changing processes, amending regulations, collaborating with other partner agencies, or working with the Congress to strengthen our laws. Information sharing on fraud schemes, trends, immigration crime subjects, and intelligence among Federal, State, local, tribal, and territorial law enforcement partners helps drive decisions and, thus, is a key component of this approach. Timeliness, clarity, and completeness of information are vital to screening operations, immigration decision-making, and combating fraud.

- Prevent entry or admission

  Prevent entry or admission of criminals, fugitives, other dangerous foreign nationals, and other unauthorized entrants. Homeland security efforts must focus on keeping criminal, fugitive, and other dangerous foreign nationals from entering the United States. The use of technology and information sharing among key Federal partners is essential so that dangerous individuals are detected before they are granted an immigration benefit or visa, or are admitted at a port of entry. Threat screening processes, biometric identification, and timely access to information on trends and fraud must all be strengthened to enhance their effectiveness.

- Arrest, detain, prosecute, and remove

  Arrest, detain, prosecute, and remove criminal, fugitive, dangerous, and other unauthorized foreign nationals consistent with due process and civil rights protections. Dangerous criminal aliens, human rights violators, and other foreign nationals who threaten our national security must be a high priority for law enforcement. This principle also applies when assigning detainees to higher or lower security detention facilities, or when providing alternatives to detention. Arrested individuals must be screened to identify victims of trafficking, refugees, and exploited persons, and they must be provided with access to legal resources.

Mission 4: Safeguarding and Securing Cyberspace

Our security and way of life depend upon a vast array of interdependent and critical networks, systems, services, and resources. To have an infrastructure that is secure and resilient, enables innovation and prosperity, and protects privacy and other civil liberties by design, we must secure cyberspace and manage other risks to its safe use.

Key Strategic Outcomes

- Critical information systems and information and communications services are secure, reliable, and readily available.

- Homeland security partners develop, update, and implement guidelines, regulations, and standards that ensure the confidentiality, integrity, and reliability of systems, networks, and data.

- Cyber disruptions or attacks are detected in real-time, consequences are mitigated, and services are restored rapidly.

- Academic institutions produce and homeland security partners sustain a cybersecurity workforce that meets national needs and enables competitiveness.

- Critical infrastructure sectors adopt and sector partners meet accepted standards that measurably reduce the risk of cyber disruption or exploitation.

Goal 4.1: Create a Safe, Secure, and Resilient Cyber Environment

Ensure malicious actors are unable to effectively exploit cyberspace, impair its safe and secure use, or attack the Nation's information infrastructure. Cyber infrastructure forms the backbone of the Nation's economy and connects every aspect of our way of life. While the cyber environment offers the potential for rapid technological advancement and economic growth, a range of malicious actors may seek to exploit cyberspace for dangerous or harmful purposes, cause mass disruption of communications or other services, and attack the Nation's infrastructure through cyber means. We must secure the system of networks and information upon which our prosperity relies while promoting economic growth, protecting privacy, and sustaining civil liberties. Both public- and private-sector efforts are required to achieve these aims. In addition, a robust law enforcement and counterintelligence capability is essential to the success of our cybersecurity efforts.

Objectives:

- **Understand and prioritize cyber threats**) *Know adversarys*

    Identify and evaluate the most dangerous threats to Federal civilian and private-sector networks and the Nation. The speed of innovation in the cyber realm requires that sharing of information and analysis occur before malicious actors can exploit vulnerabilities. We must continuously sharpen our understanding of risks to our critical information infrastructure. Risk management decisions must incorporate cyber risks based on technological as well as non-technological factors, and must address the differing levels of security required by different activities. Information and intelligence regarding emerging cyber threats and vulnerabilities must be collected, analyzed, and shared appropriately and promptly. Homeland security partners must provide and receive information and assessments on risks to and incidents involving information systems, networks, and data in time to carry out their risk management responsibilities. Finally, homeland security partners must use compatible information architecture and data standards to maximize the appropriate acquisition, access, retention, production, use, management, and safeguarding of risk information.

- **Manage risks to cyberspace**

    Protect and make resilient information systems, networks, and personal and sensitive data. As with other aspects of homeland security, we cannot close every vulnerability and mitigate every risk. Instead, we must develop a risk management approach that accepts certain risks, reduces others, and concentrates on the most consequential. Developing and implementing effective risk management strategies incorporating both protection and resilience for cyber infrastructure will require partnership, coordination, and cooperation across all elements of the homeland security enterprise. Homeland security partners must develop, promulgate, and update guidelines, codes, rules, regulations, and accepted standards when appropriate, that ensure the confidentiality, integrity, and availability of systems, networks, and data without impairing innovation, and while enhancing privacy. Government must focus on and address strategic vulnerabilities in cyberspace. Government must also lead by example, effectively securing its own networks. However, both critical infrastructure sectors and government agencies must meet accepted standards that measurably reduce risk of cyber attack or disruption to public health and safety, critical government services, and essential economic activities. Security controls on information systems, networks, and data must be consistently implemented, monitored, upgraded, and enforced.

- **Prevent cyber crime and other malicious uses of cyberspace**

  Disrupt the criminal organizations and other malicious actors engaged in high-consequence or wide-scale cyber crime. The cyber environment presents the potential for sophisticated cyber threats, cyber espionage, and cyber attacks. We must identify and mitigate cyber threats by coordinating and integrating robust counterintelligence, counterterrorism, intelligence, and law enforcement activities to prevent attacks, disruptions, and exploitations. Through law enforcement efforts, we must identify and locate domestic and international cyber criminals involved in significant cyber intrusions, identity theft, financial crime, and national security-related crimes committed utilizing the Internet. We must ensure that criminal organizations engaged in high-consequence or wide-scale cyber crime are aggressively investigated and disrupted, and their leaders arrested, indicted, and prosecuted. Through counterintelligence efforts, we must identify and thwart hostile intelligence collection activities and other cyber threats directed against the Nation.

- **Develop a robust public-private cyber incident response capability**

  Manage cyber incidents from identification to resolution in a rapid and replicable manner with prompt and appropriate action. The evolving nature of cyber threats necessitates that we recognize and respond to cyber incidents in a comprehensive and coordinated fashion involving both the public and private sectors. Cyber disruptions or attacks must be identified in time for a comprehensive response, and homeland security partners must develop and improve cyber incident contingency plans. Additionally, cyber incidents must be managed in accordance with a commonly understood and integrated response framework, and real-time analysis capabilities and processes must mitigate these incidents with an appropriate response. Finally, critical services must be restored and consequences must be mitigated following cyber incidents.

  > Cybersecurity is a dynamic field, and cyber threats and challenges evolve at breathtaking speed.

Goal 4.2: Promote Cybersecurity Knowledge and Innovation

Ensure that the Nation is prepared for the cyber threats and challenges of tomorrow. Cybersecurity is a dynamic field, and cyber threats and challenges evolve at breathtaking speed. Education, training, awareness, science, technology, and innovation must flourish in order to meet this challenge. While we must protect the Nation from cyber attacks that occur today, we must also prepare now to mitigate the most consequential cybersecurity risks that the United States and its people will face in 5, 10, and 20 years. We must make long-term investments that sustain a safe, secure, and reliable cyber environment, enable prosperity, further social and community uses of the Internet, and facilitate transactions and trade, while safeguarding privacy and civil liberties.

Objectives

- **Enhance public awareness**

    Ensure that the public recognizes cybersecurity challenges and is empowered to address them. As we have seen in other homeland security mission areas, an aware and empowered public is our best defense against threats, and our greatest resource in building resilience and fostering innovation. Each individual, every business enterprise, and each government agency has a vital role to perform if cyberspace is to realize its full potential. For the Nation to remain secure and prosperous, government must not only succeed at its own cybersecurity mission but must also empower others to succeed in theirs. Communications to the public must emphasize their role in cybersecurity. Leaders in the public and private sectors must be more informed of the security implications of their decisions with respect to cyberspace.

- **Foster a dynamic workforce**

    Develop the national knowledge base and human capital capabilities to enable success against current and future threats. A capable workforce must exist to protect cyber infrastructure from current, emerging, and future risks. A knowledgeable cybersecurity workforce must exist across government with sufficient capacity and expertise to manage current and emerging risks. We must better understand our own cyber strengths and weaknesses and those of our adversaries. Through learning, we can adapt and recalibrate our approaches, our areas of emphasis, and our operational objectives.

- **Invest in innovative technologies, techniques, and procedures**

    Create and enhance science, technology, governance mechanisms, and other elements necessary to sustain a safe, secure, and resilient cyber environment. Cyberspace's inherent characteristics demand constant innovation in order to effectively counter threats. Small vulnerabilities can lead to severe challenges in securing the Nation's vast—and vastly critical—information infrastructure. Relatively small investments in adversary attack capabilities can require disproportionately large investments in defense. Technology will assist us, and better ways of using technology and people will allow us to bring capabilities to bear more effectively. There must be continuous emphasis on cyber research, development, innovation, and interoperability, which drives advances in technologies, techniques, and procedures. As part of the homeland security enterprise, government should work creatively and collaboratively with the private sector to identify tailored solutions that both take into account the need to protect public and private interests and take an integrated approach to achieving clear objectives, preventing mass disruptions and exploitations of government systems and critical infrastructure through cyberspace. We must prioritize investment in programs that demonstrate the best opportunity to help mitigate national cyber risk. Innovation in technology, practice, and policy must further protect—not erode—privacy and civil liberties.

Mission 5: Ensuring Resilience To Disasters

The strategic aims and objectives for ensuring resilience to disasters are grounded in the four traditional elements of emergency management: hazard mitigation, enhanced preparedness, effective emergency response, and rapid recovery. Together, these elements will help create a Nation that understands the hazards and risks we face, is prepared for disasters, and can withstand and rapidly and effectively recover from the disruptions they cause.

Key Strategic Outcomes

- A standard for general community hazard mitigation is collaboratively developed and adopted by all communities.

FEMA Mobile Communications Operations Vehicle (MCOV). Photo credit: FEMA.

- Individuals and families understand their responsibilities in the event of a community-disrupting event and have a plan to fulfill these responsibilities.

- Preparedness standards for life safety, law enforcement, mass evacuation and shelter-in-place, public health, mass care, and public works capabilities, including capacity levels for catastrophic incidents, have been developed and are used by all jurisdictions.

- Jurisdictions have agreements in place to participate in local, regional, and interstate mutual aid.

- All organizations with incident management responsibilities utilize the *National Incident Management System*, including the Incident Command System, on a routine basis and for all federally declared disasters and emergencies.

Goal 5.1: Mitigate Hazards

Strengthen capacity at all levels of society to withstand threats and hazards. Though the occurrence of some disasters is inevitable, it is possible to take steps to reduce the impact of damaging events that may occur. The Nation's ability to withstand threats and hazards requires an understanding of risks and robust efforts to reduce vulnerabilities. Mitigation provides a critical foundation to reduce loss of life and property by closing vulnerabilities and avoiding or lessening the impact of a disaster, thereby creating safer communities. Mitigation seeks to break out of the cycle of disaster damage, reconstruction, and repeated damage. Mitigating vulnerabilities reduces both the direct consequences and the response and recovery requirements of disasters.

Objectives:

- **Reduce the vulnerability of individuals and families**

  Improve individual and family capacity to reduce vulnerabilities and withstand disasters. Individuals and families must be a focal point of mitigation efforts, as they are best positioned to reduce their own vulnerabilities. Promoting individual and family mitigation requires identifying the factors that influence the psychological and social resilience of individuals. Government must actively engage to help individuals understand the risks that their communities face, the resources available to them, and the steps they can take to prepare themselves, their homes, and their businesses.

- **Mitigate risks to communities**

  Improve community capacity to withstand disasters by mitigating known and anticipated hazards. Community-level mitigation measures have historically proven successful in reducing the effects of disasters. Standards for general community hazard mitigation, such as building codes and land and water use policies, must be in place and enforced around the country. In addition, measures to reduce the consequences of disasters on critical infrastructure and essential systems and services, including supply chains, health care systems, communications networks, and transportation systems, must be incorporated into development planning. Insurance policies—including those offered or otherwise supported by the Federal Government—should include hazard mitigation incentives.

Goal 5.2: Enhance Preparedness

Engage all levels and segments of society in improving preparedness. Active participation by all segments of society in planning, training, organizing, and heightening awareness is an essential component of national preparedness. While efforts have traditionally focused on the preparedness of government and official first responders, individuals prepared to care for themselves and assist their neighbors in emergencies are important partners in community preparedness efforts. Because neighbor-to-neighbor assistance, when done safely, decreases the burden on first responders, individuals should be seen as force multipliers who may also offer specialized knowledge and skills.

Objectives:

- **Improve individual, family, and community preparedness**

  Ensure individual, family, and community planning, readiness, and capacity-building for disasters. Prepared individuals and families enhance overall community resilience and reduce the burden on government emergency responders. Individuals and families must be prepared to care for themselves for a reasonable period of time after a disaster—some experts have suggested the first 72 hours—and assist their neighbors, reserving scarce public resources to assist those who are injured, incapacitated, or otherwise unable to care for themselves. The public must be engaged in order to build a collective understanding of their risks, the resources available to assist their preparations, and their roles and responsibilities in the event of a disaster. Participation in community disaster response programs such as Community Emergency Response Teams (CERTs), other Citizen Corps programs, and similar volunteer teams maintained by nongovernmental organizations must be enhanced, and community-based training and exercises must be increased, to help individuals gain the skills necessary to respond to disasters safely and in coordination with local authorities. Community organizations, including local NGOs, faith-based groups, and advocacy groups for vulnerable populations—often cornerstones of communities, but not traditionally involved in emergency management—must be integrated into community planning, risk reduction, and preparedness activities.

- Strengthen capabilities

  Enhance and sustain nationwide disaster preparedness capabilities, to include life safety, law enforcement, mass evacuation and shelter-in-place, public health, mass care, and public works. Homeland security partners must be

Oxford Conn. residents attend a meeting on programs available through local, state and federal programs. Photo credit: FEMA.

prepared for the variety of requirements resulting from a disaster. Joint hazard identification and risk analysis can help determine consensus-based, tiered preparedness standards for States, regions, and localities. These preparedness standards will then allow us to develop nationally the capabilities we will need to address the full range of threats and hazards that we face. Because success in day-to-day operations often foreshadows success in larger incidents, critical emergency response capabilities must be enhanced and all organizations with incident management responsibilities must be encouraged to use the Incident Command System (ICS) or a comparable system compliant with the *National Incident Management System* for day-to-day emergencies. In addition, we must evaluate our performance in exercises and learn from our responses to actual incidents to identify and close capability and capacity gaps and improve response and recovery operations.

Goal 5.3: Ensure Effective Emergency Response

Strengthen response capacity nationwide. Because it is impossible to eliminate all risks, a resilient Nation must have a robust capacity to respond when disaster strikes. Such response must be effective and efficient and grounded in the basic elements of incident management. When an incident occurs that is beyond local response capabilities, communities must be able to obtain assistance from neighboring jurisdictions and regional partners quickly, making a robust regional capacity vital to effective emergency response.

Objectives:

- **Provide timely and accurate information to the public**

  Establish and strengthen pathways for clear, reliable, and current emergency information, including effective use of new media. Timely, appropriate, and reliable communication with the public before, during, and immediately after disasters is a key component of societal resilience. In today's environment of speed-of-light communications and pervasive social networking technologies, homeland security partners must take full advantage of cutting-edge tools and capabilities to promote widespread situational awareness. As such, information sharing and public alert and warning must be viewed as mutually supportive efforts in seeking to combine the networked power of new media and "Web 2.0" technologies with existing homeland security information-sharing capabilities such as fusion centers, emergency operations centers, and joint terrorism task forces. Moreover, emergency information must be accessible through as many pathways as possible, to include multiple languages, through social networks in low-income areas, and to those with special needs.

- **Conduct effective disaster response operations**

  Respond to disasters in an effective and unified manner. An effective response requires that incident management organizations at all levels of government embrace common doctrine, undertake joint planning and training, and work to establish interoperable communications and equipment capabilities across jurisdictions, providing the flexibility, adaptability, and scalability necessary to match the complexity of many modern disasters. This cohesion will allow responders to improvise effectively in the face of unforeseen circumstances. First responders must be able to use the on-scene command, resource management, and communications and information management elements of the *National Incident Management System*. Jurisdictions across the Nation must have the ability to accurately characterize incidents and track the status of personnel and resources responding to major disasters and emergencies.

- **Provide timely and appropriate disaster assistance**

  Improve governmental, nongovernmental, and private-sector delivery of disaster assistance. Effectively delivering disaster assistance requires improved coordination and preparedness among governmental, nongovernmental, and private-sector resources, including local businesses and faith-based and community organizations. Humanitarian relief services such as emergency sheltering and individual financial assistance must be efficiently and effectively administered. Effective operations during disasters require integration of nongovernmental assets in planning, training, and exercises

Goal 5.4: Rapidly Recover

Improve the Nation's ability to adapt and rapidly recover. Major disasters and catastrophic events produce changes in habitability, the environment, the economy, and even in geography that can often preclude a return to the way things were. We must anticipate such changes and develop appropriate tools, knowledge, and skills to adapt, improve sustainability, and maintain our way of life in the aftermath of disaster. Recent events have highlighted the challenges we face in dealing with disaster recovery. From sheltering and re-housing displaced survivors to reconstituting critical infrastructure and reestablishing the economic base of devastated areas, the challenges are profound. Individuals, businesses, nonprofit organizations, local, tribal, State, and Federal governments all have responsibilities in disaster recovery, underscoring the need to improve coordination and unity of effort.

Objectives:

- **Enhance recovery capabilities**

  Establish and maintain nationwide capabilities for recovery from major disasters. Nationwide—at all levels of government and in nongovernmental organizations—sufficient capabilities for disaster recovery must be developed and maintained. While no government program can make communities and individuals whole, we must do a better job with the limited resources we have. This requires the development of a national strategic approach for disaster recovery and the use of standards for enhanced recovery capabilities. Federal roles and responsibilities must be clarified, and all jurisdictions must maintain and exercise recovery plans.

- **Ensure continuity of essential services and functions**

  Improve capabilities of families, communities, private-sector organizations, and all levels of government to sustain essential services and functions. Communities, government entities, and private-sector organizations must develop and exercise continuity plans. Business continuity standards and practices must continue to gain acceptance. During a disaster, families and communities, as well as businesses and governmental entities, must be able to sustain critical capabilities and restore essential services in a timely manner.

Editor's Comments

Critical Infrastructure and Key Resources Sectors

1. Agriculture and Food
2. Banking and Finance
3. Chemical
4. Commercial Facilities
5. Communications
6. Critical Manufacturing
7. Dams
8. Defense Industrial Base
9. Emergency Services
10. Energy
11. Government Facilities
12. Healthcare and Public Health
13. Information Technology
14. National Monuments and Icons
15. Nuclear Reactors, Materials, and Waste
16. Postal and Shipping
17. Transportation Systems
18. Water

Sector Spotlight

United States Department of Homeland Security
Agriculture and Food
Critical Infrastructure and Key Resources Sector-Specific Plan
May 2007, (Excerpts)

Executive Summary

Protecting the Nation's agriculture and food critical infrastructure and key resources (CI/KR) is an important responsibility shared by Federal, State, local, and tribal governments and private industry. Because of the open nature of many portions of the Food and Agriculture Sector, attacks against the Nation by using food or agricultural infrastructure or resources as weapons could have a devastating impact on public health and the economy. Traditional physical security practices alone cannot protect the sector. A protection plan for food and agriculture infrastructure and resources must focus on planning and preparedness, as well as early awareness of an attack. Science-based surveillance measures are essential to recognizing a possible attack on the sector so that rapid response and recovery efforts can be implemented to mitigate the impact of an attack. A protection plan must also be coordinated closely with response and recovery plans.

The National Infrastructure Protection Plan (NIPP) provides the unifying structure for the integration of existing and future CI/KR protection efforts into a single national program. The cornerstone of the NIPP is its risk management framework. Risk, in the context of the NIPP, is defined as the potential for loss, damage, or disruption to the Nation's CI/KR resulting from destruction, incapacitation, or exploitation during some future manmade or naturally occurring event. The framework applies to the general threat environment, as well as to specific threats or incident situations.

Sector Profile and Goals

The U.S. Food and Agriculture Sector with its complex production, processing, and delivery systems has the capacity to feed people beyond the boundaries of the Nation. The sector comprises more than 2 million farms, approximately 900,000 firms, and 1.1 million facilities. Almost entirely under private ownership, it operates in highly competitive global markets, strives to operate in harmony with the environment, and provides economic opportunities and improved quality of life for rural and urban Americans. The sector accounts for roughly one-fifth of the Nation's economic activity when measured from inputs to tables of consumers at home and away from home.

The U.S. Department of Agriculture (USDA) has Sector-Specific Agency (SSA) responsibility for production agriculture and shares SSA responsibilities for food safety and defense with the Department of Health and Human Services (HHS) Food and Drug Administration (FDA). Specifically, FDA is responsible for the safety of 80 percent of all food consumed in the United States, including the entire domestic and imported food supply; however, meat; poultry; and frozen, dried, and liquid eggs are under the authority of USDA.

This Sector-Specific Plan (SSP) for CI/KR protection focuses on a portion of the U.S Food and Agriculture Sector as defined in the February 2003 *National Strategy for Phys cal Protect on of Critical Infrastructures and Key Assets (the National Strategy)*. The National Strategy defines the Food and Agriculture Sector as the supply chains for feed, animals, and animal products; crop production and the supply chains of seed, fertilizer, and other necessary related materials; and the post-harvesting components of the food supply chain, from processing, production, and packaging through storage and distribution to retail sales, institutional food services, and restaurant or home consumption.1 In general terms, the sector comprises our agricultural production and food systems from farm to table.

Sector Mission and Vision

The mission of the Food and Agriculture Sector is twofold: (1) to protect against any attack on the food supply, including production agriculture, that would pose a serious threat to public health, safety, welfare, or the national economy; and (2) to provide this steadily evolving sector with a central focus, emphasizing protection and strengthening of the

> ### Vision Statement for the Food and Agriculture Sector
>
> Prevent the contamination of the food supply that would pose a serious threat to public health, safety, and welfare. Provide the central focus for a steadily evolving and complex industry/sector, with particular emphasis on the protection and strengthening of the Nation's capacity to supply safe, nutritious, and affordable food. In doing so, ensure that the industry has incorporated the concepts of HSPD-7 in their own critical asset protection plans, vulnerability/risk-reduction plans, and continuity of operations plans (COOP). The sector will provide leadership on food, agriculture, natural resources, and related issues based on sound public policy, the best available science, and efficient management.

Nation's capacity to supply safe, nutritious, and The Government Coordinating Council (GCC) and the Sector Coordinating Council (SCC) work collaboratively to accomplish the mission and to fulfill the vision. The sector councils are the primary method of coordination for the sector security partners. The GCC, with representation from Federal, State, local, and tribal governments, is the public sector portion of the Food and Agriculture public/private partnership, and the SCC is a self-governing body representing the food and agriculture industries. The GCC will work with the SCC to refine both the sector vision and mission statement for inclusion in the next iteration of the SSP.

Identify Assets, Systems, Networks, and Functions

Each sector must understand its critical components in order to meet the requirements of Homeland Security Presidential Directive 7 (HSPD-7) Critical Infrastructure Identification, Prioritization, and Protection and the NIPP for a strategic approach to infrastructure protection. Only after the sector is aware of each component may it consider threats, assess vulnerabilities, develop and implement protective measures or mitigation strategies, address research and development (R&D) needs, and measure success. A protection plan for this sector must begin with the farm and inputs, move through processing, and end affordable food. Securing the sector presents unique challenges because U.S. agriculture and food systems are extensive, open, interconnected, diverse, and complex structures providing attractive potential targets for terrorist attacks. Attacks on the sector, such as introducing animal or plant disease or food contamination, could result in severe animal, plant, or public health and economic con-sequences because food products rapidly move in commerce to consumers without leaving enough time to detect and identify a causative agent. The members of the government and industry public/private sector have established the following vision for the Food and Agriculture Sector: with the consumer. The protection plan must consider interdependent sectors, including cyber, chemicals, water, energy, communication, banking and finance, and transportation.

The Food and Agriculture Sector comprises systems of individual assets that are closely dependent upon each other. Because of its complexity, the sector has struggled to identify its most critical assets, systems, networks, and functions. While the sector understands its individual systems and basic interrelationships, the challenge has been to understand the complexities and interdependencies across the farm-to-table continuum on national and regional scales.

USDA and sector security partners have initiated the Agriculture and Food Criticality Project to identify the functions per-formed at an aggregate level by the Food and Agriculture Sector.2 Information from this project will be used to define criteria for sector infrastructure, which will facilitate the identification and prioritization of critical assets, systems, networks, and functions within the sector. USDA will incorporate findings from the project regularly into this SSP and share that information with security partners to ensure that, upon the project's completion, the sector will be prepared to identify critical assets, systems, networks, and functions and determine the parameters of information to be collected for each.

Assess Risks (Consequences, Vulnerabilities, and Threats)

While many risk assessment tools are available for use by sector security partners, the GCC and SCC have selected the CARVER + Shock methodology to assess risk to specific commodities and processes within the Food and Agriculture Sector. This approach was selected, in part, because it offers a simplified and standardized means for conducting risk assessments that aid in the identification of attractive targets. This tool, selected by the sector as a whole, will be the focus for the SSP; other tools, which may be in use by individual sector partners, will not be addressed in this plan.

The CARVER + Shock approach provides a consistent means for evaluating the consequences, vulnerability, and threat faced by assets, systems, networks, and functions in the Food and Agriculture Sector. This methodology meets the baseline criteria for assessment methodologies (as required in the NIPP guidelines, appendix 5A) by being complete and consistent and by providing unbiased assessments across the wide range

> **The modified CARVER tool evaluates a seventh attribute, the combined health, economic, and psychological impacts of an attack, or the SHOCK attributes of a target.**

of assets and systems found in the sector; it also encourages careful examination of each point or node in the system. The CARVER + Shock approach is transparent and can be used independently or in concert by industry and government analysts to produce results that are defensible and reproducible.

CARVER is an acronym for the following six attributes used to evaluate the appeal of a target for attack:

- Criticality: Measure of public health and the economic impacts of an attack;
- Accessibility: Ability to physically access and egress from target;
- Recuperability: Ability of system to recover from an attack;
- Vulnerability: Ease of accomplishing attack;
- Effect: Amount of direct loss from an attack as measured by loss in production; and
- Recognizability: Ease of identifying target.

Prioritize Infrastructure

A prioritization of the sector's infrastructure requires a "systems" perspective because many individual pieces have interdependencies within and beyond the sector. The sector must determine what constitutes its assets, systems, networks, and functions and then establish criteria for differentiating between those in each category that are critical and those that are non-critical.

Traditionally, CI/KR protection efforts have focused on physical security for structures, (e.g., installations and equipment). These efforts tailored their approach to physical assets that have well-defined perimeters, such as chemical plants and nuclear power generation facilities. In contrast, the Food and Agriculture Sector has extensive, open, widely dispersed, diverse, and complex interdependent systems; therefore, the physical asset-based approach may not fit the Food and Agriculture Sector. To address the need for a tailored approach and a methodology to help determine what is critical in this sector, the GCC and SCC initiated the Agriculture and Food Criticality Project. The project brings together a multidisciplinary team of subject matter experts and analysts to develop, refine, and apply a methodology to objectively determine the criticality of assets, systems, networks, and functions in the Food and Agriculture Sector.

Develop and Implement Protective Programs

The protection and integrity of America's agricultural production and food supply systems are essential to the health and welfare of both the domestic and global community and the security of the national economy. Protective programs within the sector are based on the findings from risk or vulnerability assessments and on Intelligence Community and law enforcement-related information. The success of the variety of programs that address safeguarding plant and animal production agriculture and food defense depends upon the coordinated work of a broad range of Federal, State, local, tribal, and private sector security partners. USDA and its sector security partners collaborate to develop and implement protective programs that address the prevention, protection, response, and recovery elements of the protective spectrum.

Protecting the systems in this sector requires science-based approaches that enable the sector to rapidly identify when a threat agent is present and to swiftly respond to a threat agent. Science-based approaches should result in a shorter and more effective recovery, thus making the sector a less attractive terrorist target.

Measure Progress

Within USDA, the USDA Results Agenda and the President's Management Agenda provide the guidance used to evaluate pro-gram performance. In addition, the White House Office of Management and Budget (OMB) developed the Program Assessment Rating Tool (PART) to facilitate performance measurement and to assess and improve program performance across the Federal Government.

As part of the preparation for the next version of the SSP, the sector will work to develop sector-specific metrics. In the interim, the GCC and SCC will continue to consider and review security and defense programs, and USDA will rely on the guidance provided by PART. PART emphasizes the relationship between outcome, output, and efficiency measures; each kind of measure provides valuable information about program performance. Collectively, PART measures convey a comprehensive story about an agency's products and services, how effective they are, and their results.

CI/KR Protection Research and Development

Within the sector, Federal funds typically support high-level (sector-wide or industry-wide) R&D at the Federal or State level. The USDA Economic Research Service (ERS), USDA's primary in-house source of economic information and research, supports sector efforts to protect critical assets, systems, networks, and functions. Private industry hosts R&D that is more focused or addresses a gap in protection that the government is not addressing; collaborative public and private efforts are common.

At the Federal level, the Agricultural Research Service (ARS) is the in-house scientific research arm of USDA that conducts research to meet the needs of its stakeholders within USDA, other Federal agencies, State and local governments, and industry. Most R&D activities are prioritized based on risk or similar assessment findings and all are subject to budgetary limitations. Also, the USDA Cooperative State Research, Education, and Extension Service (CSREES) supports extramural sector research. CSREES provides funding and leadership to land grant university-based cooperative extension services, State cooperative extension services, and State agricultural experiment stations, as well as to other research and outreach organizations for critical assets, systems, networks, and functions protection related to food and agriculture.

To track the many R&D activities within the sector and to prioritize R&D needs, the GCC and SCC have established the Food and Agriculture Sector Joint Committee on Research. The mission of this committee is to assess and advise the Food and Agriculture Sector (GCC and SCC) on homeland security researchable needs and goals. The committee will make use of existing vulnerability work, consider threat information, review current R&D projects, make discovery of operational needs in the sector, consult or involve the research community as needed, and refine or update recommendations periodically.

The committee will annually provide to the GCC and SCC a collective and coordinated list of researchable food and agriculture priority needs from both the perspective of those in operations and implementation (the private sector and the States), and the government agencies involved in maintaining homeland security coordination and oversight (the SSAs).

Manage and Coordinate SSA Responsibilities

The SSP reflects the sector's goals and priorities; therefore, it needs to be maintained and updated regularly. Updates to the SSP will undergo a thorough review that includes collaboration with the SCC, GCC, and other sector security partners on a triennial basis.3

The USDA Homeland Security Office (HSO), responsible for version control of the document and the only entity authorized to revise it, will lead the SSP maintenance and triennial review. This process will be coordinated closely with FDA.

HSO will update the document, as warranted, on an ad hoc basis as a result of changes in the sector's security posture, goals, and priorities (developed on an annual basis by the sector). To ensure accuracy and to reinforce the partnership nature of this effort, any revised versions of the SSP will be coordinated with the SCC and GCC prior to release. This process will include reviewing the frequency of issuing updates.

USDA does not have authority over resources and budgets for the entire sector. As a result, USDA has limited information concerning how sector security partners allocate resources related to sector security and has minimal influence over how future resources are allocated. When reporting on budgetary and resource plans, USDA will continue to rely on the coordinated Food and Agriculture Defense Initiative, a collaborative budget process for setting funding levels for security and defense programs across the relevant USDA agencies and offices and across FDA.

United States Department of Homeland Security
National Infrastructure Protection Plan:
Partnering to Enhance Protection and Resiliency
February 2009, (Excerpts)

Protecting and ensuring the continuity of the critical infrastructure and key resources (CIKR) of the United States is essential to the Nation's security, public health and safety, economic vitality, and way of life. CIKR includes systems and assets, whether physical or virtual, so vital to the United States that the incapacitation or destruction of such systems and assets would have a debilitating impact on national security, national economic security, public health or safety, or any combination of those matters. Terrorist attacks on our CIKR, as well as other manmade or natural disasters, could significantly disrupt the functioning of government and business alike and produce cascading effects far beyond the affected CIKR and physical location of the incident. Direct and indirect impacts could result in large-scale human casualties, property destruction, economic disruption, and mission failure, and also significantly damage national morale and public confidence. Terrorist attacks using components of the Nation's CIKR as weapons of mass destruction (WMD) could have even more devastating physical, psychological, and economic consequences.

The CIKR Protection Component of the Homeland Security Mission

The result of this interrelated set of national authorities, strategies, and initiatives is a common, holistic approach to achieving the homeland security mission that includes an emphasis on preparedness across the board and on the protection of America's CIKR as a

> **The NIPP and NRF are complementary plans that span a spectrum of prevention, protection, response, and recovery activities to enable this coordinated approach on a day-to-day basis, as well as during periods of heightened threat.**

steady-state component of routine, day-to-day business operations for government and private sector partners.

The NIPP and NRF are complementary plans that span a spectrum of prevention, protection, response, and recovery activities to enable this coordinated approach on a day-to-day basis, as well as during periods of heightened threat. The NIPP and its associated SSPs establish the Nation's steady-state level of protection by helping to focus resources where investment yields the greatest return in terms of national risk management. The NRF addresses response and short-term recovery in the context of domestic threat and incident management. The National Preparedness Guidelines support implementation of both the NIPP and the NRF by establishing national priorities and guidance for building the requisite capabilities to support both plans at all levels of government.

Each of the guiding elements includes specific requirements for DHS and other Federal departments and agencies to build engaged partnerships and work in cooperation and collaboration with State, local, tribal, and private sector partners. This cooperation and collaboration between government and private sector owners and operators is specifically applicable to the CIKR protection efforts outlined in the NIPP.

The NIPP risk management framework, partnership model, and information-sharing mechanisms are structured to support coordination and cooperation between the public and private sectors while recognizing the differences between and within sectors, acknowledging the need to protect sensitive information, establishing processes for information sharing, and providing for smooth transitions from steady-state operations to incident response.

Relationship of the NIPP and SSPs to Other CIKR Plans and Programs

The NIPP and the SSPs outline the overarching elements of the CIKR protection effort that generally are applicable within and across all sectors. The SSPs are an integral component of the NIPP and exist as independent documents to address the unique perspective, risk landscape, and methodologies and approaches associated with each sector. Homeland security plans and strategies at the State, local, and tribal levels of government address CIKR protection within their respective jurisdictions, as well as mechanisms for coordination with various regional efforts and other external entities. The NIPP also is designed to work with the range of CIKR protection-related plans and programs instituted by the private sector, both through voluntary actions and as a result of various regulatory requirements. These plans and programs include business continuity and resilience measures. NIPP processes are designed to enhance coordination, cooperation, and collaboration among CIKR partners within and across sectors to synchronize related efforts and avoid duplicative or unnecessarily costly security requirements.

Sector-Specific Plans

Based on guidance from DHS, the SSPs were developed jointly by the SSAs in close collaboration with the SCCs, GCCs, and others, including State, local, and tribal CIKR partners with key interests or expertise appropriate to the sector. The SSPs provide the means by which the NIPP is implemented across all sectors, as well as a national framework for each sector that guides the development, implementation, and updating of State and local homeland security strategies and CIKR protection programs. The SSPs for the original 17 sectors were officially released on May 21, 2007, after review and comment by the Homeland Security Council's Critical Infrastructure Protection Policy Coordination Committee. The SSP for the Critical Manufacturing Sector was released in 2009.

The SSPs are tailored to address the unique characteristics and risk landscapes of each sector while also providing consistency for protective programs, public and private protection investments, and resources. The SSPs serve to:

- Define sector partners, authorities, regulatory bases, roles and responsibilities, and interdependencies;

- Establish or institutionalize already existing procedures for sector interaction, information sharing, coordination, and partnership;

- Establish the goals and objectives, developed collaboratively among sector partners, that are required to achieve the desired protective posture for the sector;

- Identify international considerations;

- Identify areas for government action above and beyond an owner/operator or sector risk model; and

- Identify the sector-specific approach or methodology that SSAs use, in coordination with DHS and other sector partners, to conduct the following activities through the NIPP framework:

    o Identify priority CIKR and functions within the sector, including cyber considerations;

    o Assess sector risks, including potential consequences, vulnerabilities, and threats;

    o Assess and, as appropriate, prioritize assets, systems, networks, and functions of national-level significance within the sector;

o   Develop risk-mitigation programs based on detailed knowledge of sector operations and risk landscape;

o   Provide protocols to transition between steady-state CIKR protection and incident response in an all-hazards environment;

o   Use metrics to measure and communicate program effectiveness and risk management progress within the sector;

o   Address R&D requirements and activities relevant to the sector; and

o   Identify the process used to promote cooperation and information sharing within the sector.

The structure for the SSPs facilitates cross-sector comparisons and coordination by DHS and other SSAs.

State, Regional, Local, Tribal, and Territorial CIKR Protection Programs

The National Preparedness Guidelines define the development and implementation of a CIKR protection program as a key component of State, regional, local, tribal, and territorial homeland security programs. Creating and managing a CIKR protection program for a given jurisdiction entails building an organizational structure and mechanisms for coordination between government and private sector entities that can be used to implement the NIPP risk management framework. This includes taking action within the jurisdiction to: set goals and objectives; identify assets, systems, and networks; assess risks; set priorities for CIKR across sectors and jurisdictional levels; implement protective programs and resiliency strategies; measure the effectiveness of risk management efforts; and share information among relevant public and private sector partners. These elements form the basis of focused CIKR protection programs and guide the implementation of the relevant CIKR protection-related goals and objectives outlined in State, local, and tribal homeland security strategies. To assist in the development of such CIKR protection programs, DHS issued a collaboratively developed Guide to Critical Infrastructure and Key Resources Protection at the State, Regional, Local, Tribal, and Territorial Levels (2008).

In a regional context, the NIPP risk management framework and information-sharing processes can be applied through the development of a regional partnership model or the use of existing regional coordinating structures. Effective regional approaches to CIKR protection involve coordinated information sharing, planning, and sharing of costs. Regional approaches also include exercises to bring public and private sector partners together around: a shared understanding of the challenges to regional resilience; analytical tools to inform decision-makers on risk and risk management, with the associated benefits and costs; and forums to enable decision-makers to formulate protective measures and identify funding requirements and resources within and across sectors and jurisdictions.

State, regional, local, tribal, and territorial CIKR protection efforts enhance implementation of the NIPP and the SSPs by providing unique geographical focus and cross-sector coordination potential. To ensure that these efforts are consistent with other CIKR protection planning activities, the basic elements to be incorporated in these efforts are provided in appendix 5A. The recommended elements described in this appendix: recognize the variations in governance models across the States; recognize that not all sectors are represented in each State or geographical region; and are flexible enough to reflect varying authorities, resources, and issues within each State or region.

Other Plans or Programs Related to CIKR Protection

Federal partners should review and revise, as necessary, other plans that address elements of CIKR protection to ensure that they support the NIPP in a manner that avoids duplication and unnecessary layers of CIKR protection guidance. Examples of government plans or programs that may contain relevant prevention, protection, and response protocols or activities that relate to or affect CIKR protection include plans that address: State, local, and tribal hazard mitigation; continuity-of-operations (COOP); continuity-of-government (COG); environmental, health, and safety operations; and integrated contingency operations. Review and revision of State, local, and tribal strategies and plans should be completed in accordance with overall homeland security and grant program guidance.

Private sector owners and operators develop and maintain plans for business risk management that include steady-state security and facility protection, as well as business continuity and emergency management plans. Many of these plans include heightened security requirements for CIKR protection that address the terrorist threat environment. Coordination with these planning efforts is relevant to effective implementation of the NIPP. Private sector partners are encouraged to consider the NIPP when revising these plans and to work with government partners to integrate their efforts with Federal, State, local, and tribal CIKR protection efforts, as appropriate.

CIKR Protection and Incident Management

Together, the NIPP and the NRF provide a comprehensive, integrated approach to addressing key elements of the Nation's homeland security mission to prevent terrorist attacks, reduce vulnerabilities, and respond to incidents in an all-hazards context. The NIPP establishes the overall risk-informed approach that defines the Nation's steady-state posture with respect to CIKR protection and resiliency, while the NRF and NIMS provide the overarching framework, mechanisms, and protocols required for effective and efficient domestic incident management. The NIPP risk management framework, information-sharing network, and partnership model provide vital functions that, in turn, inform and enable incident management decisions and activities.

The National Response Framework

The NRF provides an all-hazards approach that incorporates best practices from a wide variety of disciplines, including fire, rescue, law enforcement, public works, and emergency medical services. The operational and resource coordinating structures described in the NRF are designed to support decision-making during the response to a specific threat or incident and serve to unify and enhance the incident management capabilities and resources of individual agencies and organizations acting under their own authority. The NRF applies to a wide array of natural disasters, terrorist threats and incidents, and other emergencies.

> **The NRF provides an all-hazards approach that incorporates best practices from a wide variety of disciplines, including fire, rescue, law enforcement, public works, and emergency medical services.**

The NRF core document and annexes, including the CIKR Support Annex, describe processes for coordination among: various Federal departments and agencies; State, local, and tribal governments; and private sector partners, both for pre-incident preparedness, and post-incident response and short-term recovery. The NRF specifies incident management roles and responsibilities, including emergency support functions designed to expedite the flow of resources and program support to the incident area. The SSAs and other Federal departments and agencies have roles within the NRF structure that are distinct from, yet complementary to, their responsibilities under the NIPP. Ongoing implementation of the NIPP risk management framework, partnerships, and information-sharing networks sets the stage for CIKR security and restoration activities within the NRF by providing mechanisms to quickly assess the impact of the incident on both local and national CIKR, assist in establishing priorities for CIKR restoration, and augment incident-related information sharing.

Transitioning From NIPP Steady-State to Incident Management

The variety of alert and warning systems that exist for natural hazards, technological or industrial accidents, and terrorist incidents provide the bridge between steady-state operations using the NIPP risk management framework and incident management activities using the NRF concept of operations. These all-hazards alert and warning mechanisms include programs such as National Weather Service hurricane and tornado warnings, and alert and warning systems established around nuclear power plants and chemical stockpiles. In the context of terrorist incidents, HSAS provides a progressive and systematic approach that is used to match protective measures to the Nation's overall threat environment. This link between the current threat environment and the corresponding protective actions related to specific threat scenarios and to each HSAS threat level provides the indicators used to transition from the steady-state processes detailed in the NIPP to the incident management processes described in the NRF.

DHS and CIKR partners develop and implement stepped-up protective actions to match the increased terrorist threat conditions specified by HSAS, and to address various other all-hazards alerts and warning requirements. As warnings or threat levels increase, NRF coordinating structures are activated to enable incident management. DHS and CIKR partners carry out their NRF responsibilities and also use the NIPP risk management framework to provide the CIKR protection dimension of incident operations.

The process for integrating CIKR protection with incident management and transitioning from NIPP steady-state processes to NRF incident management coordination includes the following actions by DHS, SSAs, and other CIKR partners:

- Increasing protection levels to correlate with the specific threat vectors or threat level communicated through HSAS or other relevant all-hazards alert and warning systems, or in accordance with sector-specific warnings using the NIPP information-sharing networks;

- Using the NIPP information-sharing networks and risk management framework to review and establish national priorities for CIKR protection; facilitating communications between CIKR partners; and informing the NRF processes regarding priorities for response and recovery of CIKR within the incident area, as well as on a national scale;

- Working with sector-level information-sharing entities and owners and operators on information-sharing issues during the active response mode. In addition, the DHS Office of Public Affairs has an established communications protocol to facilitate timely information exchange and necessary coordination with the CIKR sectors and their Federal, State, local, and private sector partners during those national-level incidents that involve a coordinated Federal response.

Editor's Comments

The mission of DHS is comprehensive and incorporates five distinct areas:

1. Prevent terrorism and enhancing security
2. Secure and manage our borders
3. Enforce and administer our immigration laws
4. Safeguard and secure cyberspace
5. Ensure resilience to disasters

It is interesting to note that as the mission of DHS has evolved since its inception, so too has its budget. With an initial budget of only 19.5 billion dollars in fiscal year 2002, the Department's annual budget has since tripled making DHS one of the largest funded departments in the federal government.

DHS Annual Budget (in billions of dollars)

2002 $19.5
2003 $32.5
2004 $36.2
2005 $40.2
2006 $41.1
2007 $42.9
2008 $47.3
2009 $52.5
2010 $55.1
2011 $55.3
2012 $59.9

_____

Further Discussion

1.   Discuss the mission of **preventing terrorism and enhancing security**.

2.   Discuss the mission of **securing and managing our borders**.

3.   Discuss the mission of **enforcing and administering our immigration laws**.

4.   Discuss the mission of **safeguarding and securing cyberspace**.

5.   Discuss the mission of **ensuring resilience to disasters**.

Chapter 08

Risk Management

train your organization
for what is needed to be
resilient. (Birk-on-back)

*"**Risk Management** is the process' for identifying, analyzing, and communicating risk and accepting, avoiding, transferring, or controlling it to an acceptable level considering associated costs and benefits of any actions taken"*

DHS Risk Lexicon, 2010 Edition

United States Department of Homeland Security
Risk Management Fundamentals:
Homeland Security Risk Management Doctrine
2011, (Excerpts)

Homeland Security Risks

The United States homeland security environment is complex and filled with competing requirements, interests, and incentives that must be balanced and managed effectively to ensure the achievement of key national objectives. The safety, security, and resilience of the Nation are threatened by an array of hazards, including acts of terrorism, malicious activity in cyberspace, pandemics, manmade accidents, transnational crime, and natural disasters. At the same time, homeland security organizations must manage risks associated with workforce management, acquisitions operations, and project costs. Collectively, these external and internal risks have the potential to cause loss of life, injuries, negative psychosocial impact, environmental degradation, loss of economic activity, reduction of ability to

perform mission essential functions, and loss of confidence in government capabilities.

It is the role of DHS and its partners to understand and manage these myriad homeland security risks. We live in a dynamic and uncertain world where the past does not serve as a complete guide to the future. In addition, the systems that provide the functions essential for a thriving society are increasingly intricate and interconnected. This means that potential disruptions to a system are not fully understood and can have large and unanticipated cascading effects throughout American security. Compounding this complexity is the fact that future trends — such as technological advancements, global climate change, asymmetric threats, and the evolving nature of Nation-states — have the potential to significantly alter the homeland security risk landscape in unexpected ways. Yet such emerging trends hold promise as well as peril and should be understood and managed.

Sound Decision Making

Establishing the capability and capacity to identify, understand, and address such complex challenges and opportunities is the crux of risk management. Risk management is an approach for making and implementing improved homeland security decisions.

To improve decision making, leaders in DHS and their partners in the homeland security enterprise must practice foresight and work to understand known and uncertain risks, as best they can, in order to make sound management decisions. These leaders need to consider the risks facing the homeland to make appropriate resource tradeoffs and align management approaches. Addressing these risks and promoting security is a shared responsibility that depends on unity of effort among Federal, state, local, tribal and territorial governments, the private sector, non-governmental organizations, and the citizenry as a whole.

The Value of Risk Management

The Secretary of Homeland Security has established the requirement for DHS to build and promote an integrated approach to homeland security risk management, working with partners across the homeland security enterprise. The Department's role in establishing integrated risk management is to build security, safety, and resilience across domains by connecting efforts to prevent terrorism and enhance security, secure and manage our borders, enforce and administer our immigration laws, safeguard and secure cyberspace, ensure resilience to disasters, and provide essential support in assuring national and economic security.

> **Improved homeland security depends on connecting information about risks, activities, and capabilities and using this information to guide prevention, protection, response, and recovery efforts.**

Improved homeland security depends on connecting information about risks, activities, and capabilities and using this information to guide prevention, protection, response, and recovery efforts. The establishment of sound risk management practices across DHS and the homeland security enterprise will help protect and enhance national interests, conserve resources, and assist in avoiding or mitigating the effects of emerging or unknown risks. At the organizational level, the application of risk management will complement and augment strategic and operational planning efforts, policy development, budget formulation, performance evaluation and assessments, and reporting processes.

Risk management will not preclude adverse events from occurring; however, it enables national homeland security efforts to focus on those things that are likely to bring the greatest harm, and employ approaches that are likely to mitigate or prevent those incidents. Furthermore, the American people, resources, economy, and way of life are bolstered and made more resilient by anticipating, communicating, and preparing for hazards, both internal and external, through comprehensive and deliberate risk management.

Risk management is not an end in and of itself, but rather part of sound organizational practices that include planning, preparedness, program evaluation, process improvement, and budget priority development. The value of a risk management approach or strategy to decision makers is not in the promotion of a particular course of action, but rather in the ability to distinguish between various choices within the larger context. Establishing the infrastructure and organizational culture to support the execution of homeland security risk management is a critical requirement for achieving the Nation's security goals. Risk management is essential for homeland security leaders in prioritizing competing requirements and enabling comprehensive approaches to measure performance and detail progress.

Risk Management Applications

The practice of risk management allows for a systematic and comprehensive approach to homeland security decision making. Risk management promotes the development and use of risk analysis3to inform homeland security decision making, to better inform selection among alternative strategies and actions, and to evaluate the effectiveness of the activities we undertake. Risk management applications include:

Strategic Planning

Homeland security strategies should be designed to address the risks that a particular organization faces, taking a long-term view to building capabilities that can mitigate risk through prevention, protection, response, and recovery activities. Homeland security strategies should shape how organizations approach building and sustaining capabilities.

Capabilities-based Planning

Risk management allows planners to prioritize which capabilities might have the greatest return on investment in preparedness activities. Risk management can also help identify which capabilities are most relevant to an organization and identify potential capability gaps.

Resource Decisions

Risk management should be a key component of an evidence-driven approach to requesting and allocating resources, including grant funding. By understanding risk, organizations can identify realistic capability requirements, fund projects that bring the greatest return on investment, describe desired outcomes and how they will mitigate risk, and explain the rationale behind those decisions in clear, objective, and transparent terms.

Operational Planning

Through risk management, organizations can better understand which scenarios are more likely to impact them, what the consequences would be, what risks merit special attention, what actions must be planned for, and what resources are likely to be needed, as well as what risks have the ability to negatively impact operations.

Exercise Planning

Risk management can be used to identify realistic scenarios for exercises, zeroing in on special threats and hazards, as well as priority capabilities and applicable assets.

Real-world Events

Risk management can help decision makers weigh potential courses of action within a contextual understanding of the risk of different threats and hazards to critical assets, geographic areas, and population centers during a crisis.

Research and Development

Risk analysis can be used to inform decisions on filling homeland security gaps and identifying opportunities that may be best met with enhanced technologies and/or innovative solutions, thereby establishing priorities for long-term research and development investments.

III Homeland Security Risk Management Tenets and Principles

Risk management enables homeland security leaders to distinguish between and among alternative actions, assess capabilities, and prioritize activities and associated resources by understanding risk and its impact on their decisions.

Standard risk management principles are not designed to promote uniformity or conformity; rather, they offer broad guidance that should be uniquely tailored for the specific needs of each organization. While a "one-size-fits-all" approach for homeland security risk management is neither feasible nor desirable, all DHS risk management programs should be based on two **key tenets**:

> **Standard risk management principles are not designed to promote uniformity or conformity; rather, they offer broad guidance that should be uniquely tailored for the specific needs of each organization.**

- Risk management should enhance an organization's overall decision making process and maximize its ability to achieve its objectives.

- Risk management is used to shape and control risk, but cannot eliminate all risk.

The **key principles** for effective risk management include:

- Unity of Effort

- Transparency
- Adaptability
- Practicality
- Customization

A description of each principle follows:

Unity of Effort: The principal of unity of effort reiterates that homeland security risk management is an enterprise-wide process and should promote integration and synchronization with entities that share responsibility for managing risks.

Risk management efforts should be coordinated and integrated among all partners, with shared or overlapping risk management responsibilities, to include Federal, state, local, tribal, and territorial governments, as well as the private sector, non-governmental organizations, and international partners. Most homeland security measures involve representatives of different organizations, and it is important that there is unity of effort amongst those charged with managing risks to ensure consistent approaches are taken and that there is a shared perspective of security challenges.

Transparency

The principle of transparency establishes that effective homeland security risk management depends on open and direct communications.

Transparency is vitally important in homeland security risk management due to the extent to which the decisions involved affect a broad range of stakeholders. Transparency is important for the analysis that contributes to the decision making. It includes the assumptions that supported that analysis, the uncertainty involved with it, and the communications that follow the decision. Risk management should not be a "black box" exercise where analysis is hidden. Those impacted by a risk management approach should be able to validate the integrity of the approach.

This principle does not countermand the times when there is need for security of sensitive or classified information; however, it does suggest that the processes and methodologies used for homeland security risk management may be shared even if the information is not. In turn, transparency will foster honest and realistic dialogue about opportunities and limitations.

Adaptability

The principle of adaptability includes designing risk management actions, strategies, and processes to remain dynamic and responsive to change.

The homeland security landscape is constantly evolving as priorities, threats, and circumstances change, requiring DHS to adapt to meet the Nation's expectations and requirements. DHS and its homeland security partners must be flexible in their approach to managing risk. This means that homeland security solutions must be dynamic. A changing world, filled with adaptive adversaries, increased interdependencies, and new technologies, necessitates security measures that are equally adaptable.

NEWS & TERRORISM
COMMUNICATING IN A CRISIS
A fact sheet from the National Academies and the U.S. Department of Homeland Security

> "Communication before, during and after a biological attack will be a critical element in effectively responding to the crisis and helping people to protect themselves and recover."
>
> *A Journalist's Guide to Covering Bioterrorism (Radio and Television News Director's Foundation, 2004)*

BIOLOGICAL ATTACK
HUMAN PATHOGENS, BIOTOXINS, AND AGRICULTURAL THREATS

WHAT IS IT?

A **biological attack** is the intentional release of a pathogen (disease-causing agent) or biotoxin (poisonous substance produced by a living organism) against humans, plants, or animals. An attack against people could be used to cause illness, death, fear, societal disruption, and economic damage. An attack on agricultural plants and animals would primarily cause economic damage, loss of confidence in the food supply, and possible loss of life. It is useful to distinguish between two kinds of biological agents:

- Transmissible agents that spread from person to person (e.g., smallpox, Ebola) or animal to animal (e.g., foot and mouth disease).
- Agents that may cause adverse effects in exposed individuals but that do not make those individuals contagious to others (e.g., anthrax, botulinum toxin).

Availability of Agents

The Centers for Disease Control and Prevention (CDC) lists the biothreat agents considered to pose the highest threat (see Table 1). Once obtained, agents must be cultured or grown in quantity and then processed for use in an attack ("weaponized"). Agents can be:

- **Isolated from sources in nature.** The threat agents in Table 1 are either biotoxins or agents that cause zoonotic diseases (that occur in wildlife and are transmissible to humans)—except for smallpox, which is solely a human disease and has been eradicated from nature.
- **Acquired from laboratories or bioweapons stockpile.** Smallpox virus is officially studied in only two laboratories in the world. Anthrax is widely studied in labs. Hemorrhagic fever viruses are studied only in limited high-security locations. Most high threat agents had been studied and stockpiled in bioweapons programs outside the United States until as recently as the 1990s.
- **Synthesized or genetically manipulated in a laboratory.** This would require expertise and access to advanced technology.

How Biological Agents Could Be Disseminated

For an attack on people, biological agents could be disseminated in one or more of the following ways:

- **Aerosol dissemination** is the dispersal of an agent in air from sprayers or other devices. The agent must be cultured and processed to the proper size to maximize human infections, while maintaining the agent's stability and pathogenicity (ability to produce illness). An aerosol attack might take place outdoors in a populated area or

Table 1. Diseases/Agents Listed by the CDC as Potential Bioterror Threats (as of March 2005). The U.S. Department of Agriculture maintains lists of animal and plant agents of concern.

CATEGORY A: Easily disseminated and/or contagious; high mortality rates; might disrupt society; requires special action for public health preparedness.

Bacteria (single-celled organisms):
- Anthrax *(Bacillus anthracis)*
- Plague *(Yersinia pestis)*
- Tularemia *(Francisella tularensis)*

Viruses (DNA or RNA requiring other host cells to replicate):
- Smallpox (Variola major virus)
- Viral Hemorrhagic Fevers: Ebola, Marburg, Lassa, Machupo *(various families of viruses)*

Biotoxins (poisonous substances produced by living organisms):
- Botulism *(Clostridium botulinum toxin)*

CATEGORY B: Moderately easy to disseminate; moderate illness rates, low mortality; requires enhanced diagnostic capacity, surveillance.

Bacteria:
- Brucellosis *(Brucella species)*
- Glanders *(Burkholderia mallei)*
- Melioidosis *(Burkholderia pseudomallei)*
- Psittacosis *(Chlamydia psittaci)*
- Food safety threats *(e.g., Salmonella species, Escherichia coli O157:H7, Shigella)*
- Water safety threats *(e.g., Vibrio cholerae, Cryptosporidium parvum)*

Viruses:
- Viral encephalitis *(Alphaviruses)*

Rickettsia (micro-organisms that live in cells):
- Q fever *(Coxiella burnetii)*
- Typhus fever *(Rickettsia prowazekii)*

Biotoxins:
- Epsilon toxin of Clostridium perfringens
- Ricin toxin from castor beans
- Staphylococcal enterotoxin B

CATEGORY C: Emerging infectious diseases that could be a future threat. (not all-inclusive)

Viruses:
- Examples are Nipah virus and Hantavirus

Practicality

The principle of practicality pertains to the acknowledgement that homeland security risk management cannot eliminate all uncertainty nor is it reasonable to expect to identify all risks and their likelihood and consequences.

The limitations of managing homeland security risk arises from the dynamic nature of homeland security threats, vulnerabilities, and consequences, as well as the uncertainty that is generally associated with assessing risks. This is especially true when facing a threat from an adaptive adversary, such as a terrorist or criminal organization.

Homeland security decisions often are made amidst uncertainty, but that uncertainty does not preclude the need for sound analysis or well thought-out and structured decision making. Risk management is an effective and important management practice that should lead to better-supported decisions and more effective programs and operations.

Customization

The principle of customization emphasizes that risk management programs should be tailored to match the needs and culture of the organization, while being balanced with the specific decision environment they support.

DHS organizations and personnel should tailor the methods for the dissemination of risk information and decision making and communications processes to fit the needs of their mission. The customization principle includes ensuring that the organization's risk management approach is appropriately governed and uses the best available information. This assures that the risk management effort is systematic, timely, and structured based on the values of the organization. However, the principle of customization does not supersede the need to adhere to organizational standards, requirements, and operating procedures for risk management when there is a requirement for working together to analyze risks and promote joint decision making.

IV Comprehensive Approach to Risk Management

DHS decision makers should employ a comprehensive approach to understanding and managing risks so that they can enhance the quality of decisions throughout their organization – thus supporting the DHS Policy for Integrated Risk Management.5 Doing so serves to improve decision making by allowing organizations to attempt to balance internal and external sources of risk to achieve their strategy. This section identifies the types of risks facing DHS organizations, and sets forth some necessary practices for managing these risks in an understandable way.

Internal Sources of Risk

Risks impacting organizational effectiveness arise from both internal and external sources. Examples of internal sources are issues such as financial stewardship, personnel reliability, and systems reliability. Organizations across government and the private sector are all subject to these types of internal risks. These internal risks have the potential to derail effective operations and adversely affect mission accomplishment. A comprehensive approach to risk management serves to identify weaknesses and assists in creating internal systems and processes that minimize the potential for mission failure.

External Sources of Risk

Many organizations have additional risks to manage that are caused by external factors. Examples include global, political, and societal trends, as well as hazards from natural disasters, terrorism, malicious activity in cyberspace, pandemics, transnational crime, and man-made accidents. It is these hazards and threats that caused the Nation to make a significant commitment in homeland security, and it is important that the risks from external threats remain at the forefront of consideration for homeland security organizations.

Organizations should implement comprehensive risk management approaches to ensure all internal and external risks are considered in a holistic way. Organizations must manage risks as a system, while considering the underlying factors that directly impact organizational effectiveness and mission success.

In order to consider the whole of homeland security risks, the categories in the following table help to define the landscape for an organization as it establishes a comprehensive approach to risk management. Identifying and understanding risks and their interactions ensures DHS leaders have a more complete perspective to manage risks and promote organizational effectiveness.

Key Business Practices

Effective management of risk is fostered and executed through a few key requirements. First and foremost, an organization must employ risk management with commitment and active participation by its leadership. If decision makers within an organization fully endorse and prioritize risk management practices, then employees at all levels will strive to understand and adopt risk management principles. Furthermore, risk

> # First and foremost, an organization must employ risk management with commitment and active participation by its leadership.

management is only effective if it is used to inform decision making. This means that for risk management efforts to be successful, leaders must support risk management practices and incorporate risk information into their decision making.

Second, managing risk requires a consistent approach across the organization. Although processes do not need to be identical, they should facilitate the ability to compare risks, as required, across the organization and provide reasonable assurance that risk management can be conducted coherently. Managing risk as a system allows for greater situational awareness of how varied risks and mitigation efforts may impact other activities.

Third, an organization must be able to view risk on a comprehensive, enterprise-wide basis. Most risk information is viewed by the individuals responsible for managing particular risks, who are not necessarily able to see how risks can affect other parts of the organization or to see the cumulative risks the organization faces. Thus, an organization requires some sort of function that allows for information to cascade up, providing its leadership with an organization-wide view of its risks so as to promote better tradeoff decisions and enhance application of foresight.

V. The Homeland Security Risk Management Process

To bolster common, interoperable, and systematic approaches to risk management, DHS organizations should employ a standardized risk management process.

This approach promotes comparability and a shared understanding of information and analysis in the decision process, and facilitates better structured and informed decision making. The homeland security risk management process should be implemented while keeping in mind the previously articulated risk management principles.

The **process is comprised of** the following:

- Defining and framing the context of decisions and related goals and objectives;

- Identifying the risks associated with the goals and objectives;

- Analyzing and assessing the identified risks;

- Developing alternative actions for managing the risks and creating opportunities, and analyzing the costs and benefits of those alternatives;

- Making a decision among alternatives and implementing that decision; and

- Monitoring the implemented decision and comparing observed and expected effects to help influence subsequent risk management alternatives and decisions.

Risk Communications

The foundation for each element of the risk management process is effective communications with stakeholders, partners, and customers. Consistent, two-way communication throughout the process helps ensure that the decision maker, analysts,

Organizational Risk Categories

	Strategic Risks	Operational Risks	Institutional Risks
Definition	Risk that affects an organization's vital interests or execution of a chosen strategy, whether imposed by external threats or arising from flawed or poorly implemented strategy.	Risk that has the potential to impede the successful execution of operations with existing resources, capabilities, and strategies.	Risk associated with an organization's ability to develop and maintain effective management practices, control systems, and flexibility and adaptability to meet organizational requirements.
Description	These risks threaten an organization's ability to achieve its strategy, as well as position itself to recognize, anticipate, and respond to future trends, conditions, and challenges. Strategic risks include those factors that may impact the organization's overall objectives and long-term goals.	Operational risks include those that impact personnel, time, materials, equipment, tactics, techniques, information, technology, and procedures that enable an organization to achieve its mission objectives.	These risks are less obvious and typically come from within an organization. Institutional risks include factors that can threaten an organization's ability to organize, recruit, train, support, and integrate the organization to meet all specified operational and administrative requirements.

and ultimately those charged to implement any decision share a common understanding of what the risk is and what factors may contribute to managing it. The concepts of uncertainty, perception, and tolerance for loss, which are intertwined with the concept of risk, should be accounted for as part of this communication. Effective communication is also an essential element in executing adopted courses of action and in explaining risks and risk management decisions to external parties such as the public. Such external communications may occur throughout the risk management process and should be considered integral to effective risk management.

Risk Management Processes

The homeland security risk management process supports every mission of DHS and partner organizations and is generally compatible with other documented risk management processes. These include other risk management frameworks and standards promulgated by transnational organizations and other governments.7 Although it is influenced by all of those approaches, this process is specifically designed for the totality of the homeland security mission and is intended to be utilized to provide DHS with a standard process for risk management.

Elements of the Homeland Security Risk Management Process

Risk management supports a spectrum of homeland security decisions, including strategic planning, standards and doctrine development, policy formulation, budget and resource allocation, program implementation, program evaluation and assessment, research and development investments, short-term operational activities, and problem-solving. The sections that follow describe all the steps in the application of the risk management process to support such decision making.

However, the realities of an organization's environment dictate that, at times, implementing the six-step risk management process may not be a linear progression. Program managers, operational personnel, analysts, and decision makers may be required to improvise and truncate steps in the process based on time and resource constraints. For example, to support operations such as law enforcement efforts and incident management activities, this risk management process is often executed in a less structured or expedited manner. In a tactical setting, such as law enforcement activities, circumstances may require that the decision cycle be completed in a matter of seconds. This is the reality of the homeland security operating environment and the necessity that comes with reacting swiftly during times of stress.

Note that even when the risk management process is expedited or cannot be sequentially executed, it is still appropriate to continue through the cycle after a decision has been made to allow adjustments in execution and to better evaluate performance.

The homeland security risk management process consists of the following sequence of planning and analysis efforts:

1. Define the Context

To execute risk management, it is critical to define the context for the decision that the risk management effort will support. For complex problem-solving, an organization will typically assemble a risk analysis and management team (which are frequently referred to as a planning team, a task force, or a working group, among other descriptions) to help decision makers go through the risk management process. When establishing the context, analysts must understand and document the associated requirements and constraints that will influence the decision making process, as well as key assumptions. While the analysis and management team members do not have to be risk experts, they must gain an understanding of the environment in which the risks are to be managed, taking into account political and policy concerns, mission needs, stakeholder interests, and risk tolerance. Defining the context will inform and shape successive stages of the risk management cycle.

The considerations for defining the context can be as complex and varied as the decisions they are intended to support. The following is intended to offer some structure in scoping the **variables to be considered** when executing the risk management process, although often times it is not feasible to study all of these factors:

Goals and Objectives

Ensure that the goals and objectives of the risk management effort align with the desired requirements, outcome, or end-state of the decision making process. Clearly defined goals and objectives are essential to identifying, assessing, and managing those areas that may threaten success.

Mission Space and Values

When defining the decision context, consider the mission space and values of the organization and its decision makers.

Policies and Standards

Ensure that risk management efforts complement and take into account any risk management policies, standards, or requirements the organization has in place.

Scope and Criticality of the Decision

Understand the decisions that have to be made, and the range of options available to leaders. The breadth and depth of the decisions' impact must also be considered. The risk analysis and management effort should be commensurate to that criticality.

Decision Makers and Stakeholders

Organizational leaders and their staff must be engaged at the outset of a risk management process so that the approach and presentation of results can be tailored to their preferences. It is also helpful to understand the authorities and responsibilities of leaders, as well as their comfort level with risk management concepts and language.

Similarly, stakeholders — those individuals or groups affected by the decisions — should be appropriately engaged and represented throughout the risk management process to ensure concerns are being addressed. This can be accomplished through direct interaction, such as conferences and public meetings.

Decision Timeframe

The timeframe in which a decision must be made and executed will dictate a number of the attributes of the risk management effort, including how much time is available for conducting formal analysis and decision review. Related to this issue is the frequency of the decision, which can also affect the risk management effort's analytic depth. The time horizon that the decision will impact must also be considered, such as whether the decision will have an influence only in the short-term or over a long period of time.

Risk Management Capabilities and Resources

At the beginning of the risk management process, it is useful to identify the staff, money, skill sets knowledge levels, and other resources available for risk analysis and management efforts. The implemented approach needs to be feasible and aligned with the organization's capabilities, capacity, and processes. Additionally, the resources applied to support the effort should be commensurate with the complexity of the issues involved and the magnitude of the decision. For example, it would be irresponsible to spend significant resources to support a decision with a minimal projected impact.

Risk Tolerance

Determining and understanding the decision makers' general risk tolerance level is helpful before embarking on the risk management process. Risk management efforts often involve tradeoffs between positive and negative outcomes. Having perspective on an organization or a decision maker's risk tolerance will help shape the assessments and the development of risk management alternatives that will be presented to leadership.

Availability and Quality of Information

When evaluating decision requirements, consider the availability and quality of information that can support the risk management effort, as available information will impact the design of the risk analysis approach. In engaging with decision makers at the outset of the risk management cycle, it is important to convey anticipated data limitations, including expected levels of uncertainty, so decision makers can adjust their expectations accordingly.

Designing an Approach

The above considerations shape and help define the design of the required processes to identify risks and conduct risk assessment and analysis and allow for the selection, implementation, and evaluation of risk management alternatives. By considering each of these elements systematically, decision makers and the analysts who support them are able to design an approach that is appropriate given the context.

Additionally, as the risk management process is iterative, the context may be redefined based on external events, shifting priorities, and new information. Considering such change is critical for ensuring that both the principles of flexibility and practicality are adhered to as part of risk management.

2. Identify Potential Risk

For homeland security, there is a need to consider a wide variety of risks to support decision making. As previously noted, these considerations include strategic, operational, and institutional risks. The risks that are included in any particular assessment (sometimes called the assessment's scope) are largely determined by the decision the assessment is designed to inform. The decision context established in the previous step of the process should be used to determine what individual risks should be identified and assessed.

Identifying a preliminary list of risks can generally be done from a basic knowledge of the subject matter of the decision. To do so, it is sometimes helpful to think about the risks in terms of "risk to" and "risk from." This can be a very simple exercise of defining elements affected (goals, objectives, and systems) to determine the "risk to" and capturing the things (hazards, resources, and institutional failures) that impact them to determine the "risk from." This approach will yield a fairly broad list of potentially adverse outcomes that will assist in the identification of mitigation efforts and resources.

> **Prior to conducting a risk assessment, it is valuable to make a concerted effort to identify risks beyond those usually considered.**

Unusual, Unlikely, and Emerging Risks

Prior to conducting a risk assessment, it is valuable to make a concerted effort to identify risks beyond those usually considered. For example, risks that are newly developing, even if they are poorly understood, are useful to identify. Risks that are highly unlikely but have high consequences should also be identified and incorporated into the assessment, if possible. This can even include identifying the risk of the unknown as a possible risk. Brainstorming is a common technique to identify these unusual, emerging, and rare risks. So, too, is involving a wide range of perspectives and strategic thinkers to avoid the trap of conventional wisdom and groupthink. Even when a risk is difficult to assess, it may still be important to try to understand and should be noted. It should also be acknowledged that no identification of risks is likely to capture every potential unwanted outcome — there will always be things that happen that are unanticipated.

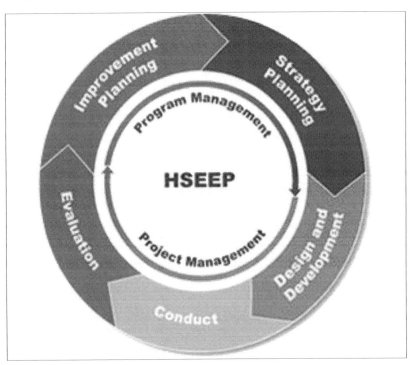

The Homeland Security Exercise and Evaluation Program (HSEEP) is a capabilities and performance-based exercise program that provides a standardized methodology and terminology for exercise design, development, conduct, evaluation, and improvement planning.

The Homeland Security Exercise and Evaluation Program (HSEEP) constitutes a national standard for all exercises. Through exercises, the National Exercise Program supports organizations to achieve objective assessments of their capabilities so that strengths and areas for improvement are identified, corrected, and shared as appropriate prior to a real incident.

The HSEEP is maintained by the Federal Emergency Management Agency's National Preparedness Directorate, Department of Homeland Security.

Scenarios

A **scenario** is a "hypothetical situation comprised of a hazard, an entity impacted by that hazard, and associated conditions including consequences when appropriate."

It is generally appropriate and helpful for homeland security risk assessments to use scenarios to divide the identified risks into separate pieces that can be assessed and analyzed individually.

When developing scenarios to identify potential risks for a risk assessment, the set of scenarios should attempt to cover the full scope of the assessment to ensure that the decision maker is provided with complete information when making a decision. Also, the scenarios should not overlap, as including multiple scenarios that contain the same event may lead to double counting the risk.

Organizing the identified risks into a framework, such as with scenarios, is helpful preparation for creating a viable methodology in the next step in the risk management cycle. In addition, examining the risks in a structured way can also be used to identify gaps where potential risks have been left out.

3. Assess and Analyze Risk

The purpose of this step is to assess the identified risks and analyze the outputs of the assessment. This step consists of several tasks:

- Determining a methodology;
- Gathering data;
- Executing the methodology;
- Validating and verifying the data; and
- Analyzing the outputs.

In practice, these tasks, like the steps of the larger risk management cycle, rarely occur linearly. Instead, risk practitioners often move back and forth between the tasks, such as refining a methodology after some data has been gathered.

Methodology

When choosing a risk assessment methodology, care should be given to remaining within the organization's capabilities.

"Methodology" is used in this document to mean any logical process by which the inputs into an assessment are processed to produce the outputs that inform the decision.

The most important factor to consider in selecting a methodology is the decision the assessment must inform. The methodology should only be as complex as necessary to properly inform the decision.

In homeland security risk analysis, there are a large number of pre-existing methodologies that may be appropriately applied to similar decisions. However, some homeland security risk management decisions will require novel methodologies, as this is a new and quickly developing field. Hence, when trying to determine the methodology, assessments that have already been completed may be a good starting point but should not be considered as the only options. Though properly informing the decision is the prime factor when selecting a methodology, other concerns will also influence the choice. Data availability, as well as time, financial, and personnel constraints also play a role.

Likelihood and Consequences

Likelihood is the chance of something happening, whether defined, measured or estimated in terms of general descriptors, frequencies, or probabilities.

Consequence, or impact, is the effect of an incident, event, or occurrence, whether direct or indirect. In homeland security risk analysis, consequences include (but are not limited to) loss of life, injuries, economic impacts, psychological consequences, environmental degradation, and inability to execute essential missions.

Homeland security risks can be assessed in terms of their likelihood and consequences.

There is no single methodology that is appropriate for measuring the likelihood and consequences of every homeland security risk, and each methodology requires independent judgment regarding its design. In some cases, it may not even be necessary to explicitly determine likelihood and consequence.

> There is no single methodology that is appropriate for measuring the likelihood and consequences of every homeland security risk, and each methodology requires independent judgment regarding its design.

Many homeland security risk assessments consider homeland security risks as a function of **Threats, Vulnerabilities, and Consequences (TVC)**. Explicitly considering each of the TVC factors is appropriate for many homeland security risks, such as those related to infrastructure protection.

However, considering TVC explicitly is sometimes not the best approach for other homeland security risk assessments — especially those that include institutional risks that can impact an organization's ability to meet operational and administrative requirements. In fact, one of the most common mistakes in homeland security risk analysis is misapplying the TVC framework. It is important that the TVC framework be applied only when appropriate to the subject matter of the analysis and the character of the assessed risks. In addition, analysts should be very careful when calculating risk by multiplying threats, vulnerabilities, and consequences, especially for terrorism, because interdependencies between the three variables, and/or poorly executed mathematical operations, can lead to inaccurate results.

Types of Methodologies

As a general rule, simple, but defensible, methodologies are preferred over more complicated methods. Simple methodologies are less prone to errors and are easier for stakeholders to understand. They are also more likely to fulfill the principles of transparency and practicality.

Homeland security risk methodologies are often sorted into **qualitative** and **quantitative** categories, but when well-designed, both types of assessments have the potential to deliver useful analytic results. Similarly, both qualitative and quantitative methodologies can be needlessly complex or poorly designed. As stated previously, the methodology that best meets the decision maker's needs is generally the best choice, whether quantitative or qualitative.

Gathering Data

Once a methodology for informing the decision has been determined, data must be gathered to populate the assessment. There are a number of potential sources for risk information. Some of the most commonly used sources for homeland security risk assessments include historical records, models, simulations, and elicitations of subject matter experts.

When collecting data, attention should be paid to all aspects of the decision that are important, regardless of whether these aspects can be readily quantified. For example, when considering the consequences of strategic homeland security risks, the assessed consequences may include difficult-to-quantify psychological impacts in addition to consequences such as lives lost and economic damage. Structured techniques, such as value focused thinking, can help the analyst determine which aspects of consequences should be included in the methodology.

Many pieces of data are not known precisely. For example, the cost estimate for damage resulting from a major earthquake in California can be estimated by a subject matter expert to fall within a range, with some values being more likely than others. The assumptions and uncertainty in the inputs should be considered in each step of the assessment's methodology to determine how they affect the outputs. Uncertainty in the outputs should then be communicated to the decision maker, as well as the assumptions that underpin the analysis. It is also useful to consider the impact of the uncertainty and how sensitive the assessment of risk is to particular pieces of uncertain data.

Validation and Presentation

Throughout the process of executing the assessment, the gathered data and evidence should be carefully studied and compared to previous work — as should the results — as doing so is part of validation and verification.

Decision makers will rarely be well-served by only a simple presentation of the outputs of a risk assessment, so the data and evidence should be analyzed to identify relevant and interesting features to the decision maker. In a broad assessment, the decision maker will often have specific areas they are particularly interested in, and will ask the analysts to focus in on those areas. Follow-up analyses will then need to be completed. In this way, analysts will regularly iterate a cycle of analyzing risks and presenting the analysis to decision makers.

Integrating Alternatives

Often, the evaluation of alternative risk management actions is part of a risk assessment methodology. Though the development of alternatives is the next step in the risk management cycle, many homeland security leaders prefer the alternatives to be integrated into the risk assessment, necessitating additional data collection and analysis. The earlier in the process the potential alternatives are known, the more efficiently their data collection can be integrated into the data collection for the rest of the assessment.

4. Develop Alternatives

In order to improve the country's ability to prevent, protect against, respond to, recover from, and mitigate a variety of manmade and natural hazards, homeland security leaders must focus their attention on identifying and executing actions to manage homeland security risks. Ultimately, the objective of homeland security risk analysis is to provide decision makers with a structured way to identify and choose risk management actions.

Identifying and Assessing Options

Within the risk management process, the step of developing alternatives involves systematically identifying and assessing available risk management options. Portions of this step may be performed by different practitioners, but the alternatives development phase brings together proposed risk management actions with the results of a risk assessment, to include course-of-action comparisons. This provides leaders with a clear picture of the risk management benefits of each proposed action or group of actions. The picture of potential benefits, when combined with an analysis of an action's costs — both monetary and non-monetary — can serve as a valuable resource for aiding decision makers in making effective and efficient homeland security choices.

- Ultimately, the development of alternative risk management actions should:

- Be understandable to participants of the process, including the decision makers and stakeholders;

- Match and comply with the organization's relevant doctrine, standards, and plans;

- Provide documentation with assumptions explicitly detailed;

- Allow for future refinements; and

- Include planning for assessment of progress toward achieving desired outcomes.

Risk Management Strategies

Risk management actions include strategies, treatments, or countermeasures for managing risks. Risks can be managed by one of four distinct methods: *risk acceptance, risk avoidance, risk control,* and *risk transfer.*

Risk Acceptance *is an explicit or implicit decision not to take an action that would affect a particular risk.*

Risk Avoidance *is a strategy or measure which effectively removes the exposure of an organization to a risk.*

Risk Control (or reduction) *is a deliberate action taken to reduce a risk's potential for harm or maintain the risk at an acceptable level.*

Risk Transfer (or deflection) *is the act of shifting some or all of the risk to another entity, asset, system, network, or geographic area.*

Methods for Developing and Evaluating Alternatives

Developing and evaluating alternative courses of action involves both technical study and applied ingenuity. While approaches for developing and evaluating alternatives are as diverse as the problem sets, considerations may include:

- Reviewing lessons learned from relevant past incidents;
- Consulting subject matter experts, best practices and government guidelines;
- Brainstorming;
- Organizing risk management actions;
- Evaluating options for risk reduction and residual risk;
- Developing cost estimates for risk management actions;
- Comparing the benefit of each risk management action with its associated cost;
- Eliminating potential options.

Evaluating risk management options should involve information generated in the context-setting and risk assessment steps of the risk management cycle. This information should be generated through analysis of the costs and other negative impacts, as well as the projected benefits of identified courses of action. It is important to note that risk management actions can be evaluated based on their potential to manage risk in the aggregate across a range of scenarios, as well as their ability to manage risks associated with a single scenario; maintaining both perspectives is crucial in identifying the most effective actions.

Needs and Constraints

Alternatives development requires consideration of the needs and constraints of an organization during the decision making process. For example, the team developing alternatives must consider the time needed to implement each risk management option; the objectives of the option, methods to achieve the objectives, and the resources required to implement the option; performance objectives, measures, and targets; and the decision making environment that would influence strategy implementation and sustainability. In a sense, the developing alternatives step is about understanding and clearly communicating the costs and benefits, expected outcomes, and likelihood of success of each strategy option.

Iterative Process

Alternatives development should be treated as a process that is iterative and evolutionary. Since risks often shift, it is important to revisit the alternatives development process, incorporate new information, and re-evaluate the options based on changed circumstances. Changes in threats or the emergence of a new risk can make a previously discarded risk management option possible, or even preferable to other options.

5. Decide Upon and Implement Risk Management Strategies

Risk management entails making decisions about best options among a number of alternatives in an uncertain environment. The key moment in the execution of any risk management process is when a decision maker chooses among alternatives for managing risks, and makes the decision to implement the selected course of action. This can include making an affirmative decision to implement a new alternative, as well as the decision to maintain the status quo.

Presenting Information

For the "Decide and Implement" phase, decision makers need to consider the feasibility of implementing options, and how various alternatives affect and reduce risk. This includes the consideration of adequate resources, capabilities, time to implement, policy imperatives, legal issues, the potential impact on stakeholders, and the potential for creating new risks for the organization.

When providing decision makers with alternatives, analysts should present options, and their strengths and weaknesses, clearly and understandably in order to ensure that decisions are informed by a common understanding of the organization's risks. Information should be tailored to the needs of leadership, and the risk analysis and management team should consider who the audience is when preparing to communicate assessments and strategies.

Document and Implement

Once a decision has been made, the decision maker must ensure that the decision is documented and communicated, and that an appropriate management structure is in place to implement the decision. Leadership should require comprehensive project management approaches that will document the planning, organizing, and managing of resources necessary for the successful implementation of the risk management strategy. This should include identifying metrics for the implementation process, which will allow the organization to track progress and improve future efforts. Additionally, leadership should develop an approach for the management of residual risk to the organization left after the decision.

6. Evaluation and Monitoring

This phase includes the evaluation and monitoring of performance to determine whether the implemented risk management options achieved the stated goals and objectives. In addition to assessing performance, organizations should guard against unintended adverse impacts, such as creating additional risk or failing to recognize changes in risk characteristics.

The evaluation phase is designed to bring a systematic, disciplined approach to assessing and improving the effectiveness of risk management program implementation. It is not just the implementation that needs to be evaluated and improved; it is the actual risk reduction measures themselves. Evaluation should be conducted in a way that is commensurate with both the level of risk and the scope of the mission.

Performance Measurement

Through effective evaluation and monitoring an organization may find it necessary to adjust its risk management options. It is crucial that a process of performance measurement be established to evaluate whether the actions taken ultimately achieved the intended performance objective. This is important not only in evaluating the success of the implemented option, but also in holding the organization accountable for progress.

A core element of evaluating and monitoring risk management options involves using effectiveness criteria to track and report on performance results with concrete, realistic metrics. In cases where the chosen course of action is to do nothing, the continued appropriateness of accepting the risk may be the best possible metric. In other cases, the best metric is often the reduction of the likelihood or consequences associated with a risk.

It is also important to monitor the larger context within which an identified risk and risk management effort exists. Good situational awareness may reveal changes in the context that require corresponding changes in the risk management effort. Both types of monitoring – effectiveness and situational awareness – are essential if risk management efforts are to be effective over time.

Logic Models

One way to develop measures that evaluate the implementation of a risk management decision is to build a performance logic model that defines causal relationships between activities and risk management goals. These logic models typically include:

Risk Management Goals: A description of the overall end-state expected to be achieved in terms of managing identified risks.

Inputs: A description of the resources that are used to carry out risk management efforts.

Efforts: A description of the types of efforts or activities that, employing the inputs, work toward achieving the risk management goals.

Output: A description of what is immediately produced by the activities, including metrics that can be used to measure that production.

Outcome Performance Measures: A description of the combined effect that delivering outputs are expected to have, including measures that evaluate the impact of the combined efforts in achieving the risk management goals.

Models of Evaluation

Models of evaluation include red teaming (scenario role-playing), exercises, external review, and surveys. Different models of evaluation will require differing levels of involvement from organization leadership and staff. For example, red teaming and exercises should be guided by leadership and analysts. External review, however, is an independent activity that should not be influenced by the risk management activity under evaluation. Leadership must provide the appropriate and requested information to the external review team, and the process should be conducted in an independent and unbiased manner.

The benefit of testing effectiveness using these methods is that it provides different perspectives on the capabilities of the risk management program. It also allows one to validate what is going well, and areas that may need improvement.

Evaluating and monitoring implemented risk management strategies should be part of considering overall performance management of homeland security activities.

7. Risk Communications

Risk communication "*is the exchange of information with the goal of improving risk understanding, affecting risk perception, and/or equipping people or groups to take appropriate actions in response to an identified risk.*"

Communications underpin the entire risk management process. As explained earlier, homeland security risk is a fluid concept affected by varying perceptions and loss tolerances, as well as uncertainty. As a result, it is imperative that risks and risk management decisions are communicated between stakeholders, partners, and customers. Communication requirements will differ, however, according to the audience and timeframe. Typically, risk communication is divided between internal and external audiences and between incident and standard timeframes.

Internal Risk Communications

Some risk communications are internal to an organization, such as that between analysts and decision makers. Maintaining two-way communication throughout the risk management process ensures that the key principles of risk management are met. For example, decision makers provide context (including values and perceptions) to bound analysts' exploration of risks and meet the organization's goals and objectives. Allowing decision makers input from the beginning of the process improves transparency, creates leadership buy-in, and sets the framework for an assessment tailored appropriately to the organization's needs and objectives. In turn, analysts provide information on risks and on possible actions to address the risks. Being transparent about methodology, limitations, and uncertainty provides decision makers with the most accurate, defensible, and practical information on which to base risk management decisions. Every internal stakeholder in the risk management process — decision makers, analysts, operational personnel, and program managers — should be included in the activities of that process through consistent, two-way communication.

External Risk Communications

The public and cross-agency nature of homeland security risk often necessitates that DHS communicate with external stakeholders, partners, and the public. Risk management decisions should be communicated to the public when appropriate in order to minimize fear while building trust. In addition, other forms of government as well as the public and the private sector often have an important role to play in reducing risk and are therefore an integral part of the risk management process.

When communicating to external parties, it is essential that varying risk perceptions and knowledge of risks be taken into account. Those outside the Department sometimes have a different perspective regarding risks than those within the Department, just as decision makers, analysts, operational personnel, and program managers have different perspectives from each other. Such differences mean that communications should be carefully tailored to the audience, but also represent an opportunity to strengthen the risk management process. External parties may help mold potential alternatives, provide context to the decision, and monitor and evaluate decisions that have been made. Thus external communications should also be two-way and should include an organization's public affairs professionals as appropriate.

Incident vs. Standard Timeframe Communications

How risk communications is defined and employed can differ based on a number of factors, including the relevance of time pressure, the purpose of the message, and the entity responsible for communicating the information. DHS communicates risks on a daily basis. Standard types of risk communications involve little time pressure and are intended to empower decision making among partners,

Members of FEMA Region 6 Incident Management Assistance Team I deploy a communications array called "The Gator" during an exercise designed to test their ability to deploy at a moment's notice. Photo credit: FEMA/Jacqueline Chandler.

stakeholders and the public.

Incident, or crisis, communications take place under different conditions than standard communications. In a crisis, empowering decision making remains a priority; however, time constraints are a critical consideration and the need to explain and persuade becomes increasingly important as a result of psychological changes in how people take in and act on information and protective guidance. Internal communications should remain bi-directional, but top-down decisiveness takes on greater importance. Externally, it is important that communications to stakeholders, partners, and the public provide clear information and, if appropriate, guidance on actions to take in a manner that is designed to minimize the anxiety that may arise in such a situation.

If the lines of communication have already been established under standard conditions, incident communications will occur more naturally and smoothly, ensuring that DHS and its partners can more effectively prevent, protect, respond, and recover. In addition, both the *National Response Framework* (January 2008) and the *National Incident Management System* (December 2008) call for a Communications Plan to be developed as one of the major components of establishing an Incident Command System and maintaining a common operating picture during an incident.

After an incident, standard communications should resume so that all stakeholders build a common understanding of what has happened, why certain decisions were made, and how to move forward. Essentially, an incident does not represent a break in the risk management process, but rather a temporary acceleration after which the process continues as normal.

Risk Communications Considerations

Risk communications will be most effective if guided by the following interrelated aims:

- **Plan for communications**. Communication efforts for decision makers and stakeholders need to be proactive as part of the risk management process; they should not be "tacked on" at the end as an afterthought. Furthermore, risk information needs to be readily available for relevant parties at all stages of the risk management cycle.

- **Maintain trust**. Past communication efforts give context to the organization's next message, shaping how it will be received. Consistency is important, but only as long as it serves to build trust. When consistency is untenable in light of emerging information, then officials need to acknowledge it, including any errors that may be involved, and explain it. Once trust is lost, it is very difficult to recover.

- **Use language appropriate to the audience**. When communicating risk, it is important to consider the intended audience and tailor the language and channels used to effectively convey the information to promote and elicit the desired actions and outcomes.

- **Be both clear and transparent**. Clarity and transparency are important to effective communications. Clarity means communicating in a direct, simple and understandable way. Transparency in communications means disclosing assumptions, methodology, and uncertainty considered.

- **Respect the audience's concerns**. Risk communications are most effective when the recipient's concerns and/or issues are acknowledged. Maintaining open channels for collaboration or feedback fosters mutual understanding. Communicators should be both receptive and responsive to queries from decision makers and stakeholders.

- **Maintain integrity of information**. Effective risk communications should acknowledge uncertainty, note any limitations of information, make assumptions explicit, and distinguish assertions from judgments supported by analysis and evidence.

Communication connects each step of the risk management process. It is also crucial for linking the risk management principles and process. One cannot overstate the importance of risk communications in risk management.

United States Department of Justice
Office of Justice Programs
Assessing and Managing the Terrorism Threat
September 2005, (Excerpts)

Criticality Assessment: Evaluating Assets

DHS defines **criticality assessment** as follows:

> *A systematic effort to identify and evaluate important or critical assets within a jurisdiction. Criticality assessments help planners determine the relative importance of assets, helping to prioritize the allocation of resources to the most critical assets.*

An essential part of the risk equation is considering the consequence of the loss of or serious damage to important infrastructure, systems, and other assets. The measure of criticality, or asset value, determines the ultimate importance of the asset. Loss of life and damage to essential assets are of paramount concern to law enforcement executives. Loss of symbolic targets, which can result in the press coverage terrorists seek, is also important; it can destroy people's faith in the ability of law enforcement and government to protect the public.

Assessing criticality can at times involve some degree of subjectivity. Assessments may rely on the intimate knowledge of law enforcement agency professionals and their colleagues in other government agencies to gauge the importance of each potential target. However, clear objective thought must prevail when loss of human life is possible. Certain facilities are inherently vulnerable and should be addressed as critical infrastructure or key assets by law enforcement:

- Transportation facilities, terminals, and other areas with concentrations of persons.

- Public utilities—electricity, water, natural gas, waste treatment.

- Public and government facilities; symbolic sites; town halls; county buildings; police, fire, and school buildings; stadiums; museums; and monuments.

- Financial and banking institutions.

- Defense and defense-related industry and research centers.

- Transportation support systems—radar, bridges, tunnels, piers, and aids to navigation.

- Health care facilities—public and private.

- Cyber/information technology service facilities and sites.

Calculating Criticality

A five point scale can be used to estimate the impact of loss of life and property, interruption of facility or other asset use, or gain to be realized by an adversary (Proteus Security Group, 1997):

Extreme (5): Substantial loss of life or irreparable, permanent, or prohibitive costly repair to a facility. Lack of, or loss of, a system or capability would provide invaluable advantage to the adversary (press coverage, the political advantage or tactical advantage to carry out further plans).

High (4): Serious and costly damage to a facility or a positive effect for the adversary. No loss of life.

Medium (3): Disruptive to facility operations for a moderate period of time; repairs—although costly—would not result in significant loss of facility capability. No loss of life.

Low (2): Some minor disruption to facility operations or capability does not materially advantage the enemy. No loss of life.

Negligible (1): Insignificant loss or damage to operations or budget. No loss of life.

Extreme and high criticality are of greatest concern. When coupled with high threat and high vulnerability, counteraction is required.

Threat Assessment

DHS defines **threat assessment** as follows:

> A systematic effort to identify and evaluate existing or potential terrorist threats to a jurisdiction and its target assets. Due to the difficulty in accurately assessing terrorist capabilities, intentions, and tactics, threat assessments may yield only general information about potential risks.

These assessments consider the full spectrum of threats, such as natural disasters, criminal activity, and major accidents, as well as terrorist activity.

Fused Intelligence

The intelligence process is the foundation of threat assessment. Systematic exploitation of crime-related information can lead to and support evaluation and analysis of terrorism and terrorist groups. The who, what, where, when, and how of terrorist groups are closely related. Intelligence efforts help produce reliable, informed responses to these questions. Without such a process, threat assessments can be unpredictable and unreliable.

The Homeland Infrastructure Threat and Risk Analysis Center (HITRAC) is the Department's infrastructure-intelligence fusion center, incorporating analysts from the Office of Infrastructure Protection and the Office of Intelligence and Analysis. HITRAC creates actionable risk-informed analysis for federal, state, local, tribal, territorial, private sector, and international partners. Photo credit: Department of Homeland Security.

Threat assessments must be compiled from comprehensive and rigorous research and analysis. Law enforcement cannot function unilaterally. Threat assessments that do not incorporate the knowledge, assessments, and understanding of state, local, and private organizations and agencies with the potential threats being assessed are inherently incomplete. For example, a threat assessment of water district facilities should include the most comprehensive data available from local police, sheriff, and fire departments; health services; emergency management organizations; and other applicable local, state, and federal agencies that may be affected by an attack on the water district's infrastructure. The threat assessment should also assimilate germane, open source, or nonproprietary threat assessments, as well as intelligence information. Lastly, the assessment must provide a high level of awareness and understanding regarding the changing threat and threat environment faced by a government entity.

Essential data to collect for analysis prior to conducting a threat assessment include (National Emergency Response and Rescue Training Center):

- **Type of adversary:** Terrorist, activist, employee, other.

- **Category of adversary:** Foreign or domestic, terrorist or criminal, insider and/or outsider of the organization.

- **Objective of each type of adversary:** Theft, sabotage, mass destruction (maximum casualties), sociopolitical statement, other.

- **Number of adversaries expected for each category:** Individual suicide bomber, grouping or "cells" of operatives/terrorists, gangs, other.

- **Target selected by adversaries:** Critical infrastructure, governmental buildings, national monuments, other.

- **Type of planning activities required to accomplish the objective:** Long-term "casing," photography, monitoring police and security patrol patterns, other.

- **Most likely or "worst case" time an adversary could attack:** When facility/location is fully staffed, at rush hour, at night, other.

- **Range of adversary tactics:** Stealth, force, deceit, combination, other.

- **Capabilities of adversary:** Knowledge, motivation, skills, weapons and tools.

To accomplish the intelligence mission of processing a threat assessment, a law enforcement executive must ensure that an officer or unit is trained and assigned to identify potential targets and can recommend enhancements for security at those targets. Action must be taken by all departments, including those with limited resources. Ideally, the entire patrol force should be trained to conduct intelligence gathering and reporting.

Calculating Threat

Threat levels are based on the degree to which combinations of these factors are present:

- **Existence:** A terrorist group is present, or is able to gain access to a given locality.

- **Capability:** The capability of a terrorist group to carry out an attack has been assessed or demonstrated.

- **Intent:** Evidence of terrorist group activity, including stated or assessed intent to conduct terrorist activity.

- **History:** Demonstrated terrorist activity in the past.

- **Targeting:** Current credible information or activity exists that indicates preparations for specific terrorist operations—intelligence collection by a suspect group, preparation of destructive devices, other actions.

- **Security environment:** Indicates if and how the political and security posture of the threatened jurisdiction affects the capability of terrorist elements to carry out their intentions. Addresses whether the jurisdiction is concerned with terrorism and whether it has taken strong proactive countermeasures to deal with such a threat.

To gauge the seriousness of a terrorist threat, the criticality, threat, and vulnerability can be quantified in the following way (Proteus Security Group, 1997):

- **Critical (5):** Existence, capability, and targeting are present. History and intentions may not be.

- **High (4):** Existence, capability, history, and intentions are present.

- **Medium (3):** Existence, capability, and history are present. Intention may not be.

- **Low (2):** Existence and capability are present. History may not be.

- **Negligible (1):** Existence or capability may not be present.

Identifying a threat is a complex process that is too often overlooked because the process of threat assessment is not well understood and is often seen as technically unreachable. Many resources are present within and outside of the law enforcement community to help law enforcement agencies complete this task, and it is important that they be used.

Vulnerability Assessment

DHS defines **vulnerability assessment** as follows:

> The identification of weaknesses in physical structures, personnel protection systems, processes, or other areas that may be exploited by terrorists. The vulnerability assessment also may suggest options to eliminate or mitigate those weaknesses.

Vulnerability is difficult to measure objectively. Progress is being made by agencies such as the National Institute of Justice in partnership with the U.S. Department of Energy's Sandia National Laboratories, as well as by studies conducted by the National Infrastructure Protection Center of DHS, to assist with these assessments. (See the list of Promising Practices/Resources in appendix I.)

Factors to consider when determining vulnerability include:

- **Location:** Geographic location of potential targets or facilities, and routes of ingress and egress; location of facility or target relative to public areas, transportation routes, or easily breached areas.

- **Accessibility:** How accessible a facility or other target is to the adversary (i.e., disruptive, terrorist, or subversive elements); how easy is it for someone to enter, operate, collect information, and evade response forces?

- **Adequacy:** Adequacy of storage facilities, protection, and denial of access to valuable or sensitive assets such as hazardous materials, weapons, vehicles or heavy equipment, and explosives or other materials that some person or organization could use deliberately or in an opportunistic manner to cause harm.

- **Availability:** Availability of equipment, adequacy of response forces and of general physical security measures.

Calculating Vulnerability

The vulnerability level is determined on a five-point scale using estimates of the sufficiency of protection or accessibility listed in the above factors (Proteus Security Group, 1997).

Highly vulnerable (5): A combination of two or more of the following with due consideration of the threat level:

- Direct access to asset or facility is possible via one or more major highway systems. Waterside access is open or adjacent land areas are unoccupied, unguarded, or allow free access.

- Asset or facility is open, uncontrolled or unlighted, or security is such that threat elements may have unimpeded access with which to collect intelligence, operate, and evade response forces. Patrols, electronic monitoring, or alarm systems are easily defeated or provide incomplete coverage.

- Individual systems within the facility, such as hazardous materials, weapons, explosives, or vehicles, are accessible with minimum force or possibility of detection.

- Response units provide minimum effective force to counter the experienced threat level. In-place physical security measures do not provide protection commensurate with the anticipated threat level.

Moderately vulnerable (3): A combination of two of the following:

- Direct access to asset or facility is possible via one or more major highway systems, but road system is restricted or patrolled. Waterside access may be open or adjacent land areas unoccupied, but mitigating geographic conditions may be present (e.g., lengthy channel access).

- Asset or facility is open, uncontrolled or unlighted, or security is such that threat elements may meet some resistance, be detected, or activate a remotely monitored alarm. Access to collect intelligence, operate, and evade response forces is at least partially hampered. Patrols, electronic monitoring, or alarm systems may be easily defeated or provide incomplete coverage.

- Individual items within the facility, such as hazardous materials, weapons, explosives, or vehicles, are accessible with moderate force, or tampering may result in detection.

- Response units provide effective force to counter the experienced threat level. Physical security measures do not provide protection commensurate with the anticipated threat level.

Low vulnerability (1): A combination of two or more of the following, provided continual awareness of the anticipated threat level is maintained:

- Asset or facility is difficult to access from major highway or road network, or outside access is limited by geography.

- Asset or facility has adequate, positive access control. Patrols, cameras, remote sensors, and other reporting systems are sufficient to preclude unauthorized entry, loitering, photography, or access to restricted areas.

- Appropriate and reasonable safeguards are taken to prevent or hinder access to sensitive materials. Protection is commensurate with degree of material sensitivity and level of threat.

- Response force is able to answer an infrastructure or facility breach with appropriate personnel, equipment, and timeliness.

Risk Assessment Calculation

Risk assessment combines all earlier assessments— criticality, threat, and vulnerability—to complete the portrait of risk to an asset or group of assets. Numerous techniques are

$$\text{Risk} = \text{Threat} \times \text{Vulnerability} \times \text{Criticality}$$

available for calculating risk, ranging from simple qualitative systems to those based on complex quantitative formulas. A common feature of most methodologies is the input on which they are based. Almost every technique addresses the following three questions to aggregate the information obtained in each of the assessment steps:

- **Criticality:** Asks what is the likely impact if an identified asset is lost or harmed by one of the identified unwanted events.

- **Threat:** Asks how likely is it that an adversary will attack those identified assets.

- **Vulnerability:** Asks what are the most likely vulnerabilities that the adversary or adversaries will use to target the identified assets.

The law enforcement executive or individual assigned to undertake these analyses can use the methods described above to determine the risk of unwanted attack on each asset.

The comprehensive results of each of the assessments can be summarized into a risk statement with an adjectival or numerical rating. The risk equation used in most systems is expressed in this basic formula:

$$\text{Risk} = \text{Threat x Vulnerability x Criticality}$$

In this equation, risk is defined as the extent to which an asset is exposed to a hazard or danger. Threat times vulnerability represents the probability of an unwanted event occurring, and criticality equals the consequence of loss or damage to the critical infrastructure or key asset.

Using this methodology in conjunction with a numerical scale or adjectival rating will produce an objective conclusion regarding the risk to an asset. Consistency in conducting the evaluations will result in a more accurate decision making process.

Risk Management

Identifying Countermeasures: Where "The Risk" Competes with "The Budget"
Countermeasures are actions, devices, or systems employed to eliminate, reduce, or mitigate risk and vulnerability. To assist in making studied decisions that can be supported over time, multiple countermeasure packages that recommend appropriate actions should be provided. Options are often characterized as follows:

- **Risk averse package:** The preferred option, unconstrained by financial or political considerations. This package provides a point of reference for the expenditure necessary to minimize risk most effectively. This option is designed to reduce risk to the greatest degree possible.

- **Risk tolerant package:** The option that strikes a balance between the needs of security and protection and the financial and political constraints of a state or municipality.

- **Risk acceptance package:** The least desired option, which typically reflects the highest acceptable amount of risk, but represents the least possible cost.

Countermeasures, such as expansion of agency staffing, installation of equipment and new technology, or target hardening, must be evaluated or tested periodically to ensure that improvements are actually working as intended. These evaluations and tests should verify that policies and procedures are in place to guide how the countermeasures will be used. Countermeasures include physical security (fencing, camera surveillance, seismic monitoring devices, barricades), cyber security (firewalls, antivirus software, secure computer networks), personnel security, and other proactive methods that industry uses to secure critical infrastructure. The California State Agency Guidance is an outstanding example of specific proactive countermeasures that the state is taking as the Homeland Security Advisory System is implemented in California.

Building Capacity

As automation technology advances, the process of conducting risk assessment and management is becoming more sophisticated, as noted in appendixes II and III. Law enforcement executives should avail themselves of the progress being made to ensure they have the ability to conduct these critical analyses.

The Office of the President of the United States
The Working Group on Financial Markets
Terrorism Risk Insurance Report
September 2006, (Excerpts)

Terrorism Risk Insurance

The Terrorism Risk Insurance Extension Act of 2005 requires the President's Working Group on Financial Markets (PWG) to perform an analysis regarding the long-term availability and affordability of insurance for terrorism risk, including group life coverage; and coverage for chemical, nuclear, biological, and radiological events; and to submit a report of its findings to Congress by September 30, 2006.

In conducting this analysis, the PWG was assisted by staff of the member agencies who reviewed academic and industry studies on terrorism risk insurance, and sought additional information and consultation through a Request for Comment published in the Federal Register. Staff also met with insurance regulators, policyholder groups, insurers, reinsurers, modelers, and other governmental agencies to gather further information.

The key findings of the PWG's analysis are set forth below. The findings are presented under three main areas: the general availability and affordability of terrorism risk insurance; coverage for group life insurance; and coverage for chemical, nuclear, biological, and radiological events. Further detail on each finding is provided in the body of the report.

Rescue crews work to clear debris from the site of the World Trade Center in New York City on September 27, 2001. Photo credit: Bri Rodriguez/FEMA.

Key Findings

Long-Term Overall Availability and Affordability of Terrorism Risk Insurance

- **The availability and affordability of terrorism risk insurance has improved since the terrorist attacks of September 11, 2001. Despite increases in risk retentions under TRIA, insurers have allocated additional capacity to terrorism risk, prices have declined, and take-up (purchase) rates have increased.** The take-up rate – or the percentage of companies buying terrorism coverage – has reportedly increased from 27 percent in 2003 to 58 percent in 2005, while the cost of coverage has generally fallen to roughly 3 to 5 percent of total property insurance costs. These improvements have transpired in a marketplace that has had access to a Federal backstop that has gradually contracted through the life of the temporary TRIA Program. Insurers' retention of risk has steadily increased under the TRIA Program: deductibles have increased from 7 percent of direct earned premium in 2003 to 17.5 percent in 2006, and other changes made to TRIA in 2005 have also increased insurer retentions. The general trend observed in the market has been that as insurer retentions have increased under TRIA and policyholder surpluses have risen, prices for terrorism risk have fallen and take-up rates have increased.

- **The improvement in the terrorism risk insurance market is due to several important factors, including better risk measurement and management, improved modeling of terrorism risk, greater reinsurance capacity, and a recovery in the financial health of property and casualty insurers. State regulation does not appear to have had a significant** impact on capacity, and a significant number of policyholders are still not purchasing terrorism coverage. How these factors continue to evolve will importantly affect further developments in the long-term availability and price of terrorism risk insurance.

o   **Insurers have made great strides in measuring and managing their risk accumulations.** The amount of capital an individual insurance company is willing to allocate to a particular risk in a given location depends on its understanding of its maximum loss under different scenarios. Since September 11, insurers have made greater use of sophisticated models that allow them to identify and manage concentrations of risk in order to avoid accumulating too much risk in any given location. This improvement in risk accumulation management has allowed insurers to better diversify and control their terrorism risk exposures, which has enhanced their ability to underwrite terrorism risk.

o   **A significant effort has been made by the insurance industry in modeling the potential frequency and severity of terrorist attacks, which helps insurers to assess their potential loss exposures.** An understanding of the potential frequency and severity of terrorist attacks is important for insurers to properly evaluate their risk exposures. Improvements in probability modeling of terrorist attacks have likely had a positive impact on insurers' willingness to provide coverage for terrorism risk following the re-evaluation of terrorism risk that took place after September 11. However, unlike other catastrophic exposures (*e.g.*, natural disasters) where there are more refined methods of modeling frequency, modeling terrorism risk frequency relies largely on analysis of terrorist behavior. Given the uncertainty of terrorism in general and, in particular, the uncertainty associated with these modeling efforts, insurers appear to have limited confidence in these models for evaluating their risk exposures.

o   **The quantity of terrorism risk reinsurance capacity has increased since the period following September 11.** Reinsurance for terrorism risk all but vanished after September 11 as reinsurers withdrew from the market. The market has since improved and reinsurers have gradually allocated more capital to terrorism risk. The key determinants in the capital allocation decisions of reinsurers include pricing, which is influenced largely by demand, loss experience, underwriting performance, and probability of loss for a given risk at a given location. These determinants also factor into the willingness of other capital providers (*e.g.*, through catastrophe bonds or other mechanisms) to allocate capital to terrorism risk. The presence of subsidized Federal reinsurance through TRIA appears to negatively affect the emergence of private reinsurance capacity because it dilutes demand for private sector reinsurance.

o   **The financial health and capacity of insurers has recovered since September 11.** There has been improvement in the financial health of the insurance industry, which plays a role in how much capacity an insurer is willing to expose to terrorism risk. Since September 11, policyholder surpluses in the property and casualty industry have risen, as the industry has remained profitable (even with the 2005 hurricane season losses) and has benefited from increased rates of return on assets.

As a result, insurers have more available capital to allocate, and they apparently have chosen to allocate additional capacity to terrorism risk as demonstrated by the increased provision of terrorism risk insurance coverage over the past few years.

    ○   **States require that some types of terrorism risk insurance be provided and otherwise regulate aspects of the terrorism risk insurance market. However, it is unclear whether these requirements have reduced capacity significantly.** State laws and regulations govern various aspects of the insurance marketplace (*e.g.*, mandating certain types of coverage, approving forms and rates, and monitoring financial solvency), and the provision of terrorism risk insurance falls within this general structure. In terms of pricing, although states regulate commercial insurance rates to various degrees (to a larger extent with workers' compensation insurance), commercial terrorism risk insurance for large property risks may be exempt from state price regulation or not subject to state price regulation (or other state mandates) when purchased from non-admitted surplus lines insurers. In addition, some insurers do not even charge for the terrorism coverage that is included in their policies. In lines of insurance with the greatest amount of price regulation and coverage mandates (such as workers' compensation insurance), insurers have generally remained in the market, even as their TRIA retentions have increased, despite not having the flexibility to fully price for terrorism risk. Therefore, while state regulations have the potential to significantly interfere with the operation of the insurance markets, it does not appear that such restrictions have had a significant impact in the market for terrorism risk insurance in the post-TRIA environment.

    ○   **While take-up rates have increased as prices have fallen, a significant number of policyholders are still not purchasing coverage. The willingness of consumers to pay for terrorism risk insurance is a determinant of how much capital insurers will allocate.** It is unclear why approximately 40 percent of all policyholders do not purchase coverage, although the Treasury's 2005 study and others have found that the primary reasons were price and assessment of their individual risk to terrorist attack. Individual perceptions of low risk are likely related to the lack of a successful terrorist attack within the U.S. since 2001, and perhaps to some degree an expectation that Federal aid might be available if a significant attack occurs.

• **Further improvements in insurers' ability to model and manage terrorism risk will likely contribute to the long-term development of the terrorism risk insurance market. However, the high level of uncertainty currently associated with predicting the frequency of terrorist attacks, along with what appears to be a general unwillingness of some insurance policyholders to purchase insurance coverage, makes any prediction of the potential degree of long-term development of the terrorism risk insurance market somewhat difficult.** The post-September 11 terrorism insurance market has developed in the presence of a Federal backstop (*albeit* a progressively less generous one over time), which creates inherent difficulties in evaluating the long-term development of the terrorism risk insurance market.

Group Life Insurance

- **Coverage for terrorism risk insurance in group life insurance policies has remained generally available and prices have declined, even though group life insurance is not part of TRIA. Given these market signals, there is no reason to expect negative developments in the group life insurance market.** Group life insurance is generally sold to employers as part of employee benefit packages along with other benefits, such as medical, dental, vision, and disability. In some cases group life insurers partner with other providers of employee benefit services. The group life insurance market is highly competitive and insurers appear to be unwilling in the face of such competition to raise prices (states do not regulate group life insurance rates), or to decline to provide terrorism coverage. Even though group life insurance has not had access to the Federal backstop under TRIA, private market forces (high competitiveness and extreme price sensitivity) have ensured the continued availability and affordability of group life insurance to employers and their participating employees.

- **As in the market for property and casualty reinsurance, there have also been improvements in the availability of catastrophic life reinsurance, and there is the potential for continued market development.** Just as with the property and casualty reinsurance, catastrophic life reinsurance all but disappeared after September 11, even though by most industry metrics, September 11 was not a catastrophe in terms of either individual or group life insurance losses. Still, the lack or limited availability of catastrophic life reinsurance following September 11 had no disruptive effect on the availability and affordability of group life insurance to consumers largely due to competitive market forces. Since then, some catastrophic life reinsurance has again become available in the marketplace, *albeit* at higher cost when compared to pre-September 11 pricing. Today, group life insurers are deciding whether to purchase reinsurance, or to forego and retain most of the risk – a decision that has not had any impact on the availability and cost of group life insurance to consumers.

- **Similar to the situation with property and casualty insurers, group life insurers have developed an increased ability to measure and manage their accumulation of terrorism exposure through the use of modeling, and there appears to be potential for additional improvements.** While group life insurers face aggregation exposure (the risk of multiple losses from a terrorist-related mass casualty event due to concentrations of insured lives), they are capable of managing this risk to some degree by managing risk accumulations. Property and casualty insurers have made great strides in modeling techniques, but it is unclear to what extent group life insurers have made use of these tools. The highly competitive environment in the group life market, the general wider dispersion of overall life insurance risks (for companies that sell both group and individual life), and some institutional arrangements regarding how policies are sold, may all influence how group life insurers view their need and ability to manage accumulation risk.

Chemical, Nuclear, Biological and Radiological ("CNBR") Coverage

- Historically, insurance coverage for losses associated with chemical, nuclear, biological, and radiological risks has generally not been widely available unless it was mandated. Insurers generally did not provide CNBR coverage even before September 11, and for the most part they do not provide such terrorism coverage even with a Federal backstop in place. Given the general reluctance of insurance companies to provide coverage for these types of risks, there may be little potential for future market development. The factors determining the availability and affordability of CNBR coverage in the marketplace have more to do with the nature, scale, and uncertainty of

Chemical, biological, radiological, and nuclear (CBRN) protective gear. Photo credit: Department of Homeland Security.

the damage and losses from CNBR events – however caused – and less to do with terrorism specifically. What coverage exists today is mostly tied to state mandates, most prominently workers' compensation insurance, as well as some aspects of fire insurance through the Standard Fire Policy. In addition, a Federal mandate requires some nuclear coverage for reactor operators and some specialty coverage exists. There is virtually no CNBR reinsurance available, and the modeling issues both for exposure and probability become even more complicated for CNBR.

- **Some insurance consumers have expressed an interest in purchasing CNBR coverage, but due to limited capacity and relatively high prices, many have decided to forgo such purchases. Policyholder expectations regarding their own potential terrorism exposure and likelihood of post-disaster Federal aid are probably higher for CNBR risks than for relatively smaller-scale conventional terrorist attacks.** The 2005 Treasury study found that the number of policyholders that purchased CNBR terrorism coverage was relatively small (except in the case of workers' compensation insurance where coverage is mandated). Among the main reasons for not purchasing CNBR terrorism coverage were that policyholders believed either that they were not at risk or that the premiums were too high. Most commercial policyholders remain generally uninsured (except where coverage is mandated, such as with workers' compensation). Some consumers may equate CNBR coverage with other coverages that are not generally available (*e.g.*, war risk)

Finally, there may be an even greater market expectation that the Federal government would respond post-loss to a CNBR event through Federal disaster aid than would be the case for a smaller-scale conventional terrorist attack.

Editor's Comments

One of the primary tools employed during the risk management process is the "security assessment". A security assessment (or security survey) is a process whereby data is collected and analyzed for potential risk. The security assessment focuses on actual vulnerabilities associated within a system, asset, or facility. The principal requirement associated with the survey is the need for the subject of the assessment to be examined in its actual or typical state. There should be no special preparation in anticipation of an assessment. This will give the most accurate representation and point out flaws within the security system.

A security assessment should be tailored to the specific subject. Even repeat surveys need customization since previous deficiencies need to be highlighted in all subsequent efforts. Although a customized process, some of the more common elements found within a facility survey could be:

- Adjacent buildings
- Areas containing assets
- Computer systems
- Fire and emergency systems
- Keys and key control
- Parking lot
- Perimeter
- Shared occupancy
- The control and supervision of entry into the facility
- The off-hours when the facility is not in operation
- Video surveillance
- Windows, doors, basement, and roof

Further Discussion

1. Discuss the **value of risk management**.

2. Discuss all of the **risk management applications**.

3. Discuss the **key principles** for effective risk management .

4. Discuss the **Homeland Security Risk Management Process**.

5. Discuss the **Risk Assessment Calculation**.

Chapter 09

Emergency Management

"In these really big disasters, the initial response is generally not government. It's individuals helping each other, trying to find out what's going on".

Craig Fugate, Administrator of FEMA

United States Department of Homeland Security
Federal Emergency Management Agency
Public Website (Excerpts)

History of FEMA

The Federal Emergency Management Agency coordinates the federal government's role in preparing for, preventing, mitigating the effects of, responding to, and recovering from all domestic disasters, whether natural or man-made, including acts of terror. FEMA can trace its beginnings to the **Congressional Act of 1803**. This act, generally considered the first piece of disaster legislation, provided assistance to a New Hampshire town following an extensive fire. In the century that followed, ad hoc legislation was passed more than 100 times in response to hurricanes, earthquakes, floods and other natural disasters.

The FEMA logo attached to a podium with microphones and flags in the background before a town hall meeting in the District of Comlumbia, 2009. Photo credit: FEMA/Bill Koplitz.

By the 1930s, when the federal approach to problems became popular, the Reconstruction Finance Corporation was given authority to make disaster loans for repair and reconstruction of certain public facilities following an earthquake, and later, other types of disasters. In 1934, the Bureau of Public Roads was given authority to provide funding for highways and bridges damaged by natural disasters. The Flood Control Act, which gave the U.S. Army Corps of Engineers greater authority to implement flood control projects, was also passed. This piecemeal approach to disaster assistance was problematic and it prompted legislation that required greater cooperation between federal agencies and authorized the President to coordinate these activities.

The 1960s and early 1970s brought massive disasters requiring major federal response and recovery operations by the Federal Disaster Assistance Administration, established within the Department of Housing and Urban Development (HUD). Hurricane Carla struck in 1962, Hurricane Betsy in 1965, Hurricane Camille in 1969 and Hurricane Agnes in 1972. The Alaskan Earthquake hit in 1964 and the San Fernando Earthquake rocked Southern California in 1971. These events served to focus attention on the issue of natural disasters and brought about increased legislation. In 1968, the National Flood Insurance Act offered new flood protection to homeowners, and in 1974 the Disaster Relief Act firmly established the process of Presidential disaster declarations.

However, emergency and disaster activities were still fragmented. When hazards associated with nuclear power plants and the transportation of hazardous substances were added to natural disasters, more than 100 federal agencies were involved in some aspect of disasters, hazards and emergencies. Many parallel programs and policies existed at the state and local level, compounding the complexity of federal disaster relief efforts. The National Governor's Association sought to decrease the many agencies with which state and local governments were forced work. They asked President Jimmy Carter to centralize federal emergency functions.

Executive Order 12127

President Carter's 1979 executive order merged many of the separate disaster-related responsibilities into the Federal Emergency Management Agency (FEMA). Among other agencies, FEMA absorbed: the Federal Insurance Administration, the National Fire Prevention and Control Administration, the National Weather Service Community Preparedness Program, the Federal Preparedness Agency of the General Services Administration and the Federal Disaster Assistance Administration activities from HUD. Civil defense responsibilities were also transferred to the new agency from the Defense Department's Defense Civil Preparedness Agency.

John Macy was named as FEMA's first director. Macy emphasized the similarities between natural hazards preparedness and the civil defense activities. FEMA began development of an Integrated Emergency Management System with an all-hazards approach that included "direction, control and warning systems which are common to the full range of emergencies from small isolated events to the ultimate emergency - war."

The new agency was faced with many unusual challenges in its first few years that emphasized how complex emergency management can be. Early disasters and emergencies included the contamination of Love Canal, the Cuban refugee crisis and the accident at the Three Mile Island nuclear power plant. Later, the Loma Prieta Earthquake in 1989 and Hurricane Andrew in 1992 focused major national attention on FEMA. In 1993, President Clinton nominated James L. Witt as the new FEMA director. Witt became the first agency director with experience as a state emergency manager. He initiated sweeping reforms that streamlined disaster relief and recovery operations, insisted on a new emphasis regarding preparedness and mitigation, and focused agency employees on customer service. The end of the Cold War also allowed Witt to redirect more of FEMA's limited resources from civil defense into disaster relief, recovery and mitigation programs.

In 2001, President George W. Bush appointed Joe M. Allbaugh as the director of FEMA. Within months, the terrorist attacks of Sept. 11th focused the agency on issues of national preparedness and homeland security, and tested the agency in unprecedented ways. The agency coordinated its activities with the newly formed Office of Homeland Security, and FEMA's Office of National Preparedness was given responsibility for helping to ensure that the nation's first responders were trained and equipped to deal with weapons of mass destruction.

A New Mission: Homeland Security

Billions of dollars of new funding were directed to FEMA to help communities face the

threat of terrorism. Just a few years past its 20th anniversary, FEMA was actively directing its "all-hazards" approach to disasters toward homeland security issues. In March 2003, FEMA joined 22 other federal agencies, programs and offices in becoming the Department of Homeland Security. The new department, headed by Secretary Tom Ridge, brought a coordinated approach to national security from emergencies and disasters - both natural and man-made.

FEMA's Emergency Management Institute in Emmitsburg, Maryland. The EMI provides national leadership in developing and delivering training to ensure that individuals and groups having key emergency management responsibilities, including FEMA employees, possess the requisite skills to effectively perform their jobs.

On October 4, 2006, President George W. Bush signed into law the Post-Katrina Emergency Reform Act. The act significantly reorganized FEMA, provided it substantial new authority to remedy gaps that became apparent in the response to Hurricane Katrina in August 2005, the most devastating natural disaster in U.S. history, and included a more robust preparedness mission for FEMA.

As it has for almost 30 years, FEMA's mission remains: to lead America to prepare for, prevent, respond to and recover from disasters with a vision of "A Nation Prepared."

FEMA's Organization Structure

Office of the Administrator
- National Advisory Council
- Office of Regional Operations

Components
- Recovery
- Response
- Logistics Management
- Mission Support Bureau
- Federal Insurance and Mitigation Administration (FIMA)
- Protection and National Preparedness
  - Grant Programs Directorate
  - Office of National Capital Region Coordination
  - National Continuity Programs Directorate
  - National Preparedness Directorate
- United States Fire Administration

Offices
- Center for Faith Based and Neighborhood Partnerships
- Office of Chief Financial Officer
- Office of Disability Integration and Coordination
- Office of Equal Rights
- Office of the Executive Secretariat
- Office of External Affairs (includes Disaster Operations, Intergovernmental Affairs, International Affairs, Legislative Affairs, Private Sector Outreach, and Public Affairs, Resource Management and Administration)
- Office of Chief Counsel
- Office of Federal Coordinating Officer Operations
- Office of Policy and Programs Analysis
- Defense Production Act Program Division

Regions
- **Region I** (Connecticut, Maine, Massachusetts, New Hampshire, Rhode Island, Vermont)
- **Region II** (New Jersey, New York, Puerto Rico, and the Virgin Islands)
- **Region III** (Delaware, District of Columbia, Maryland, Pennsylvania, Virginia and W. Virginia)
- **Region IV** (Alabama, Florida, Georgia, Kentucky, Mississippi, N. Carolina, S. Carolina and Tennessee)
- **Region V** (Illinois, Indiana, Michigan, Minnesota, Ohio and Wisconsin)
- **Region VI** (Arkansas, Louisiana, New Mexico, Oklahoma and Texas)

- **Region VII** (Iowa, Kansas, Missouri and Nebraska)
- **Region VIII** (Colorado, Montana, N. Dakota, S. Dakota, Utah and Wyoming)
- **Region IX** (Arizona, California, Hawaii, Nevada, American Samoa, Guam, Commonwealth of the Northern Mariana Islands, Republic of the Marshall Islands, and Federated States of Micronesia)
- **Region X** (Alaska, Idaho, Oregon and Washington)

Agency Spotlight

FEMA's National Advisory Council Overview

The National Advisory Council (NAC) advises the Administrator of the Federal Emergency Management Agency (FEMA) on all aspects of emergency management. The NAC incorporates State, local, and Tribal governments, private sector, and nongovernmental partners' input in the development and revision of FEMA policies and strategies. FEMA's NAC Office serves as the focal point for all NAC coordination.

Nancy Ward, FEMA Region IX Administrator, presents at the National Advisory Council meeting in San Francisco, Feb. 2012. Photo credit: FEMA.

The NAC was formed, as mandated in the Post-Katrina Emergency Management Reform Act of 2006 (PL 109-295), to ensure effective and ongoing coordination of national preparedness, protection, response, recovery, and mitigation for natural disasters, acts of terrorism and other man-made disasters by:

- Engaging State, local, and Tribal governments, the private sector; and nongovernmental partners in a continuous dialogue about emergency management to expand our common strategic understanding; and

- Providing a formal and transparent avenue for feedback, suggestions, and advice from our diverse partners involved in disaster activities.

NAC Membership

The membership of the NAC may consist of up to 35 members appointed by and serving at the discretion of the FEMA Administrator. NAC members serve for a term of 3 years, with one-third of the membership's terms ending each year. The NAC's membership is made up of influential, senior leaders from a diverse cross-section of professional and geographic areas from State, local, and Tribal governments, the private sector, and nongovernmental organizations. This diversity provides the FEMA Administrator with the best possible input from the customer and partner community of emergency management and homeland security.

NAC Accomplishments

Since the NAC's creation in 2007, the NAC's accomplishments include:

- Supplying key input on the development, implementation, and revision of the National Response Framework, the National Incident Management System, and the National Disaster Housing Strategy;

- Providing valuable feedback on the revised National Exercise Program, including recommendations on how to successfully implement the revised program;

- Maintaining open lines of communication to help engage the private sector in emergency management;

- Recommending the creation of a Regional Disability Coordinator position within each of the 10 FEMA regions; and

- Reviewing and providing input on regulatory and policy Robert T. Stafford Disaster Relief and Emergency Assistance Act issues that might help ease administrative burdens on jurisdictions.

United States Department of Homeland Security
Federal Emergency Management Agency
National Response Framework
January 2008, (Excerpts)

This *National Response Framework (NRF)* [or *Framework*] is a guide to how the Nation conducts all-hazards response. It is built upon *scalable, flexible, and adaptable coordinating structures* to align key roles and responsibilities *across the Nation*. It describes specific authorities and best practices for managing incidents that range from the serious but purely local, to large-scale terrorist attacks or catastrophic natural disasters.

This document explains the common discipline and structures that have been exercised and matured at the local, tribal, State, and national levels over time. It describes key lessons learned from Hurricanes Katrina and Rita, focusing particularly on how the Federal Government is organized to support communities and States in catastrophic incidents. Most importantly, it builds upon the *National Incident Management System (NIMS)*, which provides a consistent template for managing incidents.

The term "response" as used in this *Framework* includes immediate actions to save lives, protect property and the environment, and meet basic human needs. Response also includes the execution of emergency plans and actions to support short-term recovery. The *Framework* is always in effect, and elements can be implemented as needed on a flexible, scalable basis to improve response.

Response: The Who

An effective, unified national response requires layered, mutually supporting capabilities. The *Framework* systematically incorporates public-sector agencies, the private sector, and NGOs. It also emphasizes the importance of personal preparedness by individuals and households.

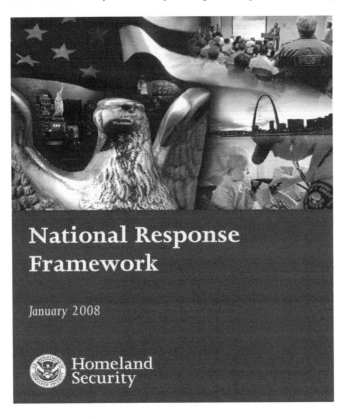

Communities, tribes, States, the Federal Government, NGOs, and the private sector should each understand their respective roles and responsibilities, and complement each other in achieving shared goals. Each governmental level plays a prominent role in developing capabilities needed to respond to incidents. This includes developing plans, conducting assessments and exercises, providing and directing resources and capabilities, and gathering lessons learned. These activities require that involved organizations understand their roles and responsibilities, and how they fit within and are supported by the *Framework*.

It is important that each level of government adapt and apply the general roles outlined in the *Framework*. To do this, organizations should define key leadership and staff functions, adopt capabilities-based planning as the method to build response capabilities, and impose the discipline needed to plan and operate effectively. Partner Guides that summarize core *Framework* concepts and are tailored specifically to leaders at different levels and types of organizations are provided through the online **NRF Resource Center**.

Even when a community is overwhelmed by an incident, there is still a core, sovereign responsibility to be exercised at this local level, with unique response obligations to coordinate with State, Federal, and private-sector support teams. Each organization or level of government therefore has an imperative to fund and execute its own core emergency management responsibilities.

Below is a brief summary of emergency management roles at the local, tribal, State, and Federal levels, as well as the roles of private-sector organizations. Emergency management is the coordination and integration of all activities necessary to build, sustain, and improve the capability to prepare for, protect against, respond to, recover from, or mitigate against threatened or actual natural disasters, acts of terrorism, or other manmade disasters.

Local Governments. Resilient communities begin with prepared individuals and depend on the leadership and engagement of local government, NGOs, and the private sector. Individuals, families, and caregivers to those with special needs should enhance their awareness of risk and threats, develop household emergency plans that include care for pets and service animals, and prepare emergency supply kits. Individuals can also volunteer in their communities.

Local police, fire, emergency medical services, public health and medical providers, emergency management, public works, environmental response professionals, and others in the community are often the first to detect a threat or hazard, or respond to an incident. They also are often the last to leave an incident site or otherwise to cope with the effects of an incident. The local senior elected or appointed official (the mayor, city manager, or county manager) is responsible for ensuring the public safety and welfare of residents. In today's world, senior officials and their emergency managers build the foundation for an effective response. They organize and integrate their capabilities and resources with neighboring jurisdictions, the State, NGOs, and the private sector. Increasingly, businesses are vital partners within communities wherever retail locations, service sites, manufacturing facilities, or management offices are located. NGOs and not-for-profit organizations also play a key role in strengthening communities' response efforts through their knowledge of hard-to-reach populations, outreach, and services.

States, Territories, and Tribal Governments. States, territories, and tribal governments have responsibility for the public health and welfare of the people in their jurisdiction. State and local governments are closest to those impacted by incidents, and have always had the lead in response and recovery. During response, States play a key role coordinating resources and capabilities throughout the State and obtaining resources and capabilities from other States. States are sovereign entities, and the Governor has responsibility for public safety and welfare. While U.S. territories, possessions, freely associated states, and tribal governments also have sovereign rights, there are unique factors involved in working with these entities. Stafford Act assistance is available to States and to Puerto Rico, the Virgin Islands, Guam, American Samoa, and the Commonwealth of the Northern Mariana Islands, which are included in the definition of "State" in the Stafford Act.

States have significant resources of their own, including State emergency management and homeland security agencies, State police, health agencies, transportation agencies, incident management teams, specialized teams, and the National Guard. The role of the State government in response is to supplement local efforts before, during, and after incidents. **If a State anticipates that its resources may be exceeded, the Governor can request assistance from the Federal Government and/or from other States through mutual aid and assistance agreements such as the Emergency Management Assistance Compact (EMAC).**

The Federal Government. The Federal Government maintains a wide array of capabilities and resources that can be made available upon request of the Governor. When an incident occurs that exceeds or is anticipated to exceed State, tribal, or local resources, the Federal Government may provide resources and capabilities to support the State response. For incidents involving primary Federal jurisdiction or authorities (e.g., on a military base or a Federal facility or lands), Federal departments or agencies may be the first responders and first line of defense, coordinating activities with State, territorial, tribal, and local partners. The Federal Government also maintains working relationships with the private sector and NGOs.

Pursuant to the Homeland Security Act of 2002 and Homeland Security Presidential Directive (HSPD) 5, the Secretary of Homeland Security is the principal Federal official for domestic incident management. Incident management refers to how incidents are managed across all homeland security activities, including prevention, protection, and response and recovery. Other Federal departments and agencies have key responsibilities to support national response activities and carry out those responsibilities within the overarching coordinating mechanisms of this *Framework*. DHS coordinates with other agencies to surge Federal support at the headquarters, regional, and field levels.

The Private Sector and NGOs. The private sector and NGOs contribute to response efforts through engaged partnerships with each level of government. Private-sector organizations and NGOs are encouraged to develop contingency plans and to work with State and local planners to ensure that their plans are consistent with pertinent plans, the *NIMS*, and this *Framework*.

Private-sector organizations play an essential role in protecting critical infrastructure systems and implementing plans for the rapid restoration of normal commercial activities and critical infrastructure operations in the event of disruption. The protection of critical infrastructure and the ability to rapidly restore normal commercial activities can mitigate the impact of an incident, improve the quality of life of individuals, and accelerate the pace of recovery for communities and the Nation. There are not-for-profit owners/operators of critical infrastructure and key resources (CIKR) facilities, notably in healthcare and power generation.

NGOs also serve a vital role at the local, State, and national levels by performing essential service missions in times of need. They provide sheltering, emergency food supplies, and other vital support services. NGOs bolster and support government efforts at all levels.

Response: The What and How

The *National Response Framework* is always in effect, and elements can be implemented at any level at any time. The *Framework* is capabilities based, which is to say that local governments, tribes, States, and the Federal Government all develop functional capabilities and identify resources that may be required based on hazard identification and risk assessment, threats, and other potential incidents such as those represented by the National Planning Scenarios.

The *Framework* describes *what we do* and *how we respond.* In short, the *National Response Framework* explains how, at all levels, the Nation effectively manages all-hazards response consistent with the *National Strategy for Homeland Security.* The remainder of this Introduction explains the *Framework's* scope, the response doctrine that animates it, and the preparedness strategy of which it is a part. It correlates with an outline of the overall document.

> In short, the National Response Framework explains how, at all levels, the Nation effectively manages all-hazards response consistent with the National Strategy for Homeland Security.

Scope

The *Framework* provides structures for implementing nationwide response policy and operational coordination for all types of domestic incidents. It can be partially or fully implemented in the context of a threat, in anticipation of a significant event, or in response to an incident. Selective implementation allows for a scaled response, delivery of the resources needed, and an appropriate level of coordination.

In this document, incidents include actual or potential emergencies or all-hazards events that range from accidents and natural disasters to actual or potential terrorist attacks. They include events wholly contained within a single jurisdiction and others that are catastrophic in nature and national in their scope or consequences.

It is not always obvious at the outset whether a seemingly minor event might be the initial phase of a larger, rapidly growing threat. The *Framework* incorporates standardized organizational structures that promote on-scene initiative, innovation, and sharing of essential resources drawn from all levels of government, NGOs, and the private sector. Response must be quickly scalable, flexible, and adaptable.

The *Framework* is also intended to accelerate the assessment and response to incidents that may require Federal assistance. In practice, many incidents require virtually reflexive activation of interagency coordination protocols to forestall the incident from becoming worse or to surge more aggressively to contain it. A Federal department or agency acting on independent authority may be the initial and the primary Federal responder, but incidents that require more systematic Federal response efforts are now actively coordinated through the appropriate *Framework* mechanisms described in this document and in its supporting annexes. This initial coordination of Federal incident assessment and response efforts is intended to occur seamlessly, without the need for any formal trigger mechanism.

This *Framework*, therefore, eliminates the Incident of National Significance declaration. No such declaration is required by the *Framework* and none will be made. The authorities of the Secretary of Homeland Security to coordinate large-scale national responses are unaltered by this change. Elimination of this declaration will, however, support a more nimble, scalable, and coordinated response by the entire national emergency management community.

Response Doctrine

Response doctrine defines basic roles, responsibilities, and operational concepts for response across all levels of government and with NGOs and the private sector. The overarching objective of response activities centers upon saving lives and protecting property and the environment. Five key principles of operations define response actions in support of the Nation's response mission. Taken together, these five principles of operation constitute **national response doctrine.**

Response doctrine is rooted in America's Federal system and the Constitution's division of responsibilities between Federal and State governments. Because this doctrine reflects the history of emergency management and the distilled wisdom of responders and leaders at all levels, it gives elemental form to the *Framework*.
This doctrine "evolves in response to changes in the political and strategic landscape, lessons learned from operations, and the introduction of new technologies. Doctrine influences the way in which policy and plans are developed, forces are organized and judgment, and enables responders to best fulfill their responsibilities."

Response doctrine evolves slowly. Response strategy and the *Framework* merit periodic review and revision, while operational plans supporting the *Framework* must be tested and improved through a process of continuous innovation. The last is especially true regarding operational plans to counter the threat of a terrorist attack.

Response doctrine is comprised of five key principles: (1) engaged partnership, (2) tiered response, (3) scalable, flexible, and adaptable operational capabilities, (4) unity of effort through unified command, and (5) readiness to act. An introductory word about each follows.

Engaged Partnership

Leaders at all levels must communicate and actively support engaged partnerships by developing shared goals and aligning capabilities so that no one is overwhelmed in times of crisis. Layered, mutually supporting capabilities at Federal, State, tribal, and local levels allow for planning together in times of calm and responding together effectively in times of need. Engaged partnership includes ongoing communication of incident activity among all partners to the *Framework*, and shared situational awareness for a more rapid response. In particular, the potential for terrorist incidents requires *a heightened state of readiness* and nimble, practiced capabilities baked into the heart of our preparedness and response planning.

Engaged partnerships are essential to preparedness. Effective response activities begin with a host of preparedness activities conducted well in advance of an incident. Preparedness involves a combination of planning, resources, training, exercising, and organizing to build, sustain, and improve operational capabilities. Preparedness is the process of identifying the personnel, training, and equipment needed for a wide range of potential incidents, and developing jurisdiction-specific plans for delivering capabilities when needed for an incident.

Preparedness activities should be coordinated among all involved agencies within the jurisdiction, as well as across jurisdictions. Integrated planning will assist in identifying gaps in capability and developing strategies to fill those gaps.

Nationwide preparedness is described in the *National Preparedness Guidelines* and the *National Exercise Program*. These documents lay out 15 National Planning Scenarios that form the basis of the newly coordinated national exercise schedule and priorities, and identify 37 core capabilities that are needed to support response across the Nation. The *Guidelines* identify core local, tribal, community, and State capabilities that will be supported by the DHS homeland security grant programs.

Tiered Response

> Incidents begin and end locally, and most are wholly managed at the local level.

Incidents must be managed at the lowest possible jurisdictional level and supported by additional capabilities when needed. It is not necessary that each level be overwhelmed prior to requesting resources from another level.

Incidents begin and end locally, and most are wholly managed at the local level. Many incidents require unified response from local agencies, NGOs, and the private sector, and some require additional support from neighboring jurisdictions or the State. A small number require Federal support. National response protocols recognize this and are structured to provide additional, tiered levels of support when there is a need for more resources or capabilities to support and sustain the response and initial recovery. All levels should be prepared to respond, anticipating resources that may be required.

Scalable, Flexible, and Adaptable Operational Capabilities

As incidents change in size, scope, and complexity, the response must adapt to meet requirements. The number, type, and sources of resources must be able to expand rapidly to meet needs associated with a given incident. The *Framework*'s disciplined and coordinated process can provide for a rapid surge of resources from all levels of government, appropriately scaled to need. Execution must be flexible and adapted to fit each individual incident. For the duration of a response, and as needs grow and change, responders must remain nimble and adaptable. Equally, the overall response should be flexible as it transitions from the response effort to recovery.

This *Framework* is grounded in doctrine that demands a tested inventory of common organizational structures and capabilities that are scalable, flexible, and adaptable for diverse operations. Adoption of the *Framework* across all levels of government and with businesses and NGOs will facilitate interoperability and improve operational coordination.

Unity of Effort Through Unified Command

Effective *unified command* is indispensable to response activities and requires a clear understanding of the roles and responsibilities of each participating organization. Success requires *unity of effort*, which respects the chain of command of each participating organization while harnessing seamless coordination across jurisdictions in support of common objectives.

Use of the Incident Command System (ICS) is an important element across multijurisdictional or multiagency incident management activities. It provides a structure to enable agencies with different legal, jurisdictional, and functional responsibilities to coordinate, plan, and interact effectively on scene. As a team effort, unified command allows all agencies with jurisdictional authority and/or functional responsibility for the incident to provide joint support through mutually developed incident objectives and strategies established at the command level. Each participating agency maintains its own authority, responsibility, and accountability. This *Framework* employs the *NIMS* standardized structures and tools that enable a unified approach to be effective both on scene and at the emergency operations centers.

The Department of Defense (DOD) is a full partner in the Federal response to domestic incidents, and its response is fully coordinated through the mechanisms of this *Framework*. Concepts of "command" and "unity of command" have distinct legal and cultural meanings for military forces and military operations. For Federal military forces, command runs from the President to the Secretary of Defense to the Commander of the combatant command to the DOD on-scene commander. Military forces will always remain under the operational and administrative control of the military chain of command, and these forces are subject to redirection or recall at any time. The ICS "unified command" concept is distinct from the military chain of command use of this term. And, as such, military forces do not operate under the command of the Incident Commander or under the unified command structure.

The *NIMS* supports response through the following elements of unified command: (1) developing a single set of objectives; (2) using a collective, strategic approach; (3) improving information flow and coordination; (4) creating common understanding of joint priorities and restrictions; (5) ensuring that no agency's legal authorities are compromised or neglected; and (6) optimizing the combined efforts of all agencies under a single plan.

Readiness to Act

Effective response requires readiness to act balanced with an understanding of risk. From individuals, households, and communities to local, tribal, State, and Federal governments, national response depends on the instinct and ability to act. A forward-leaning posture is imperative for incidents that have the potential to expand rapidly in size, scope, or complexity, and for no-notice incidents.

Once response activities have begun, on-scene actions are based on *NIMS* principles. To save lives and protect property and the environment, decisive action on scene is often required of responders. Although some risk may be unavoidable, first responders can effectively anticipate and manage risk through proper training and planning.

Command, single or unified, is responsible for establishing immediate priorities for the safety of not only the public, but the responders and other emergency workers involved in the response, and for ensuring that adequate health and safety measures are in place. The Incident Commander should ensure that each incident has a designated safety officer who has been trained and equipped to assess the operation, identify hazardous and unsafe situations, and implement effective safety plans.

Acting swiftly and effectively requires clear, focused communication and the processes to support it. Without effective communication, a bias toward action will be ineffectual at best, likely perilous. An effective national response relies on disciplined processes, procedures, and systems to communicate timely, accurate, and accessible information on the incident's cause, size, and current situation to the public, responders, plans help to ensure that lifesaving measures, evacuation routes, threat and alert systems, and other public safety information are coordinated and communicated to numerous diverse audiences in a consistent, accessible, and timely manner.

Part of a Broader Strategy

The *National Response Framework* is required by, and integrates under, a larger *National Strategy for Homeland Security* (*Strategy*) that serves to guide, organize, and unify our Nation's homeland security efforts. The *Strategy* reflects our increased understanding of the threats confronting the United States, incorporates lessons learned from exercises and real-world catastrophes, and articulates how we should ensure our long-term success by strengthening the homeland security foundation we have built. It provides a common framework by which our entire Nation should focus its homeland security efforts on achieving the following four goals:

1. **Prevent and disrupt terrorist attacks.**

2. **Protect the American people and our critical infrastructure and key resources.**

3. **Respond to and recover from incidents that do occur.**

4. **Continue to strengthen the foundation to ensure our long-term success.**

While the first three goals help to organize our national efforts, the last goal entails creating and transforming our homeland security principles, systems, structures, and institutions. This includes applying a comprehensive approach to risk management, building a culture of preparedness, developing a comprehensive Homeland Security Management System, improving incident management, better utilizing science and technology, and leveraging all instruments of national power and influence.

The *Framework* primarily focuses on the third goal: respond to and recover from incidents that do occur. The *Strategy* also provides the context that given the certainty of catastrophes on our soil – no matter how unprecedented or extraordinary – it is our collective duty to provide the best response possible. It states that, when needed, we will bring to bear the Nation's full capabilities and resources to save lives, mitigate suffering, and protect property. The *Strategy* also reminds us that as the Nation responds to an incident, we must also begin to lay the foundation not only for a strong recovery over the short term but also for the rebuilding and revitalization of affected communities and regions over the long term.

The *Strategy* calls for a *National Response Framework* that helps to strengthen the foundation for an effective national response, rapidly assess emerging incidents, take initial actions, expand operations as needed, and commence recovery actions to stabilize the area. It also calls for the *Framework* to be clearly written, easy to understand, and designed to be truly national in scope, meeting the needs of State, local, and tribal governments and the private sector and NGOs, as well as the Federal Government. In addition, the *Strategy* underscores the need to ensure that those communities devastated or severely affected by a catastrophic incident are set on a sustainable path for long-term rebuilding and revitalization. The *Framework* is designed to respond to and support the *Strategy* and is intended to be informed by and tie seamlessly to national, State, tribal, and local preparedness activities and investments.

The *Strategy* further describes how the other three national goals are supported through other strategies, plans, and ongoing efforts. For example, the national goal to prevent and disrupt terrorist attacks is further supported by the updated *National Strategy for Combating Terrorism*, released in September 2006, which articulates our Nation's strategy for winning the War on Terror. The sections in both on preventing and disrupting terrorist attacks are complementary and mutually reinforcing. In order to prevent and disrupt terrorist attacks in the United States, we are working to deny terrorists and terrorist-related weapons and materials entry into our country and across all international borders, disrupt their ability to operate within our borders, and prevent the emergence of violent Islamic radicalization in order to deny terrorists future recruits and defeat homegrown extremism.

The national goal to protect the American people and our critical infrastructure and key resources is also supported by existing plans. The *Strategy* sets forth that to protect the lives and livelihoods of the American people, we must undertake measures to deter the threat of terrorism, mitigate the Nation's vulnerability to acts of terror and the full range of manmade and natural catastrophes, and minimize the consequences of an attack or disaster should it occur. Safeguarding the American people also includes the preservation of the Nation's CIKR. Guiding our efforts to protect the Nation's CIKR is the 2006 *National Infrastructure Protection Plan (NIPP)* and its supporting Sector-Specific Plans, which were developed pursuant to HSPD-7, issued on December 17, 2003. The *NIPP* sets forth a comprehensive risk management framework and provides a coordinated approach to CIKR protection roles and responsibilities for Federal, State, local, and private-sector security partners. It sets national priorities, goals, and requirements for the effective distribution of funding and resources that will help ensure that our government, economy, and public services continue to function in the event of a manmade or natural disaster.

The last national goal is to continue to strengthen the foundation to ensure our long-term success. To fulfill these responsibilities over the long term, we will continue to strengthen the principles, systems, structures, and institutions that cut across the homeland security enterprise and support our activities to secure the homeland. Ultimately, this will help ensure the success of our *Strategy* to secure the Nation.

United States Department of Homeland Security
Overview: ESF and Support Annexes
Coordinating Federal Assistance in Support
of the National Response Framework
January 2008, (Excerpts)

Federal Support to States

Stafford Act

Federal support to States and local jurisdictions takes many forms. The most widely known authority under which assistance is provided for major incidents is the Stafford Act.

When an incident occurs that exceeds or is anticipated to exceed local, tribal, or State resources, the Governor can request Federal assistance under the Stafford Act. The Stafford Act authorizes the President to provide financial and other assistance to State and local governments, certain private nonprofit organizations, and individuals to support response, recovery, and mitigation efforts following Presidential emergency or major disaster declarations.

Most incidents are not of sufficient magnitude to warrant a Presidential declaration. However, if State and local resources are insufficient, a Governor may ask the President to make such a declaration. Before making a declaration request, the Governor must activate the State's emergency plan and ensure that all appropriate State and local actions have been taken or initiated, including but not limited to:

- Surveying the affected areas to determine the extent of private and public damage.

- Conducting joint preliminary damage assessments with Federal Emergency Management Agency (FEMA) officials to estimate the types and extent of Federal disaster assistance required.

Ordinarily, only the Governor can initiate a request for a Presidential emergency or major disaster declaration. In extraordinary circumstances, the President may unilaterally make such a declaration. The Governor's request is made through the FEMA Regional Administrator and based on a finding that the disaster is of such severity and magnitude that effective response is beyond the capabilities of the State and affected local governments, and that Federal assistance is necessary.

Members of the Connecticut National Guard work with FEMA to provide drinking water and meals-ready-to-eat to residents recovering from the effects of a severe storm that dumped snow in many parts of the state, downing trees and utility lines. Photo credit: Norman Lenburg/FEMA.

The Governor's request includes:

- Information on the extent and nature of State resources that have been or will be used to address the consequences of the disaster.

- A certification by the Governor that State and local governments will assume all applicable non-Federal costs required by the Stafford Act.

- An estimate of the types and amounts of supplementary Federal assistance required.

- Designation of the State Coordinating Officer.

The FEMA Regional Administrator evaluates the damage and requirements for Federal assistance and makes a recommendation to the FEMA Administrator. The FEMA Administrator, acting through the Secretary of Homeland Security, then recommends a course of action to the President. The Governor, appropriate Members of Congress, and Federal departments and agencies are immediately notified of a Presidential declaration.

Non-Stafford Federal Support to State and Local Jurisdictions

While the Stafford Act is the most familiar mechanism by which the Federal Government may provide support to State, tribal, and local governments, it is not the only one. Often, Federal assistance does not require coordination by DHS and can be provided without a Presidential major disaster or emergency declaration.

In these instances, Federal departments and agencies provide assistance to States, as well as directly to tribes and local jurisdictions, consistent with their own authorities. For example, under the Comprehensive Environmental Response, Compensation, and Liability Act, local and tribal governments can request assistance directly from the Environmental Protection Agency and/or the U.S. Coast Guard.

This support is typically coordinated by the Federal agency with primary jurisdiction rather than DHS. The Secretary of Homeland Security may monitor such incidents and may, as requested, activate *Framework* mechanisms to support Federal departments and agencies without assuming overall leadership for the incident.

National Defense and Defense Support of Civil Authorities

The primary mission of the Department of Defense (DOD) and its components is national defense. Because of this critical role, resources are committed after approval by the Secretary of Defense or at the direction of the President. Many DOD components and agencies are authorized to respond to save lives, protect property and the environment, and mitigate human suffering under imminently serious conditions, as well as to provide support under their separate established authorities, as appropriate. The provision of defense support is evaluated by its legality, lethality, risk, cost, appropriateness, and impact on readiness. When Federal military and civilian personnel and resources are authorized to support civil authorities, command of those forces will remain with the Secretary of Defense. DOD elements in the incident area of operations and National Guard forces under the command of a Governor will coordinate closely with response organizations at all levels.

In rare circumstances, the President can federalize National Guard forces for domestic duties under Title 10 (e.g., in cases of invasion by a foreign nation, rebellion against the authority of the United States, or where the President is unable to execute the laws of the United States with regular forces (10 U.S.C. 12406)). When mobilized under Title 10 of the U.S. Code, the forces are no longer under the command of the Governor. Instead, DOD assumes full responsibility for all aspects of the deployment, including command and control over National Guard forces.

Federal Law Enforcement Assistance

Each State has jurisdiction for enforcement of State laws, using State and local resources, including the National Guard (to the extent that the National Guard remains under State authority and has not been called into Federal service or ordered to active duty).

State governments may request Federal law enforcement assistance under the Emergency Federal Law Enforcement Assistance Act without a Presidential emergency or major disaster declaration. In addition, Federal agencies may request public safety and security or general law enforcement support from another Federal agency during a large-scale incident. The ESF #13 – Public Safety and Security Annex provides further guidance on the integration of public safety and security resources to support the full range of incident management functions.

Federal-to-Federal Support

Interagency Agreements

Federal departments and agencies routinely manage the response to incidents under their statutory or executive authorities. For example, the Department of Agriculture/Forest Service and various agencies of the Department of the Interior conduct wildland firefighting activities under existing memorandums of agreement (MOAs) with other Federal, State, and local entities.

These types of responses do not require DHS coordination and are led by the Federal entity with primary jurisdiction. In these instances, the Secretary of Homeland Security may monitor such incidents and may, as requested, activate *Framework* mechanisms to provide support to departments and agencies without assuming overall leadership for the incident.

Federal-to-Federal Support Coordinated By DHS

When a Federal entity with primary responsibility and authority for handling an incident requires Federal assistance above and beyond its interagency mechanisms (e.g., Executive orders, memorandums of understanding (MOUs), MOAs, etc.), that department or agency can request additional Federal assistance through DHS. When this happens, this support is:

- Coordinated by DHS using the multiagency coordination structures established in the *Framework* and in accordance with the *NIMS*.

- Generally funded by the Federal entity with primary responsibility and statutory authority for the incident in accordance with provisions of the Economy Act, unless other statutory authorities exist.

- Facilitated by the interagency MOU for Mutual Aid, and executed at the time of the incident through interagency agreements.

Public Law 104-321
Emergency Management Assistance Compact
October 19, 1996, (Excerpts)

EMAC is a national interstate mutual aid agreement that enables states to share resources during times of disaster. Since the 104th Congress ratified the compact, EMAC has grown to become the nation's system for providing mutual aid through operational procedures and protocols that have been validated through experience. EMAC is administered by NEMA, the National Emergency Management Association, headquartered in Lexington, KY.

EMAC acts as a complement to the federal disaster response system, providing timely and cost-effective relief to states requesting assistance from assisting member states who understand the needs of jurisdictions that are struggling to preserve life, the economy, and the environment. EMAC can be used either in lieu of federal assistance or in conjunction with federal assistance, thus providing a "seamless" flow of needed goods and services to an impacted state. EMAC further provides another venue for mitigating resource deficiencies by ensuring maximum use of all available resources within member states' inventories.

The thirteen (13) articles of the Compact sets the foundation for sharing resources from state to state that have been adopted by all 50 states, the District of Columbia, the U.S. Virgin Islands, Puerto Rico, and has been ratified by Congress (PL-104-321).

The four more commonly referenced articles of the compact (Article V, IV, VIII, and IX) address the primary concerns of personnel and states offering and receiving assistance:

Article V - Licenses and Permits

Whenever any person holds a license, certificate, or other permit issued by any state party to the compact evidencing the meeting of qualifications for professional, mechanical, or other skills, and when such assistance is requested by the receiving party state, such person shall be deemed licensed, certified, or permitted by the state requesting assistance to render aid involving such skill to meet a declared emergency or disaster, subject to such limitations and conditions as the governor of the requesting state may prescribe by executive order or otherwise.

Article VI - Liability

Officers or employees of a party state rendering aid in another state pursuant to this compact shall be considered agents of the requesting state for tort liability and immunity purposes; and no party state or its officers or employees rendering aid in another state pursuant to this compact shall be liable on account of any act or omission in good faith on the part of such forces while so engaged or on account of the maintenance or use of any equipment or supplies in connection therewith. Good faith in this article shall not include willful misconduct, gross negligence, or recklessness.

Article VIII - Compensation

Each party state shall provide for the payment of compensation and death benefits to injured members of the emergency forces of that state and representatives of deceased members of such forces in case such members sustain injuries or are killed while rendering aid pursuant to this compact, in the same manner and on the same terms as if the injury or death were sustained within their own state.

Article IX - Reimbursement

Any party state rendering aid in another state pursuant to this compact shall be reimbursed by the party state receiving such aid for any loss or damage to or expense incurred in the operation of any equipment and the provision of any service in answering a request for aid and for the costs incurred in connection with such requests; provided, that any aiding party state may assume in whole or in part such loss, damage, expense, or other cost, or may loan such equipment or donate such services to the receiving party state without charge or cost; and provided further, that any two or more party states may enter into supplementary agreements establishing a different allocation of costs among those states. Article VIII expenses shall not be reimbursable under this provision.

United States Department of Homeland Security
National Incident Management System
December 2008, (Excerpts)

What Is the National Incident Management System?

The *National Incident Management System* (NIMS) provides a systematic, proactive approach to guide departments and agencies at all levels of government, nongovernmental organizations, and the private sector to work seamlessly to prevent, protect against, respond to, recover from, and mitigate the effects of incidents, regardless of cause, size, location, or complexity, in order to reduce the loss of life and property and harm to the environment. NIMS works hand in hand with the *National Response Framework* (NRF). NIMS provides the template for the management of incidents, while the NRF provides the structure and mechanisms for national-level policy for incident management.

On February 28, 2003, the President issued Homeland Security Presidential Directive 5 (HSPD-5), "Management of Domestic Incidents," which directed the Secretary of Homeland Security to develop and administer a *National Incident Management System* (NIMS). This system provides a consistent nationwide template to enable Federal, State, tribal, and local governments, nongovernmental organizations (NGOs), and the private sector to work together to prevent, protect against, respond to, recover from, and mitigate the effects of incidents, regardless of cause, size, location, or complexity. This consistency provides the foundation for utilization of NIMS for all incidents, ranging from daily occurrences to incidents requiring a coordinated Federal response.

NIMS is not an operational incident management or resource allocation plan.

NIMS represents a core set of doctrines, concepts, principles, terminology, and organizational processes that enables effective, efficient, and collaborative incident management.

HSPD-5 also required the Secretary of Homeland Security to develop the *National Response Plan*, which has been superseded by the *National Response Framework* (NRF). The NRF is a guide to how the Nation conducts all-hazards response. The NRF identifies the key principles, as well as the roles and structures, that organize national response. In addition, it describes special circumstances where the Federal Government exercises a larger role, including incidents where Federal interests are involved and catastrophic incidents where a State would require significant support.

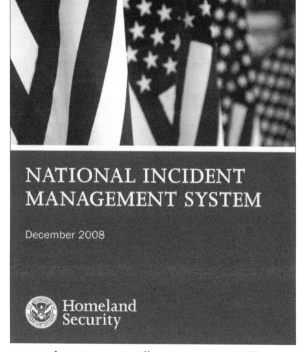

NATIONAL INCIDENT MANAGEMENT SYSTEM

December 2008

Homeland Security

HSPD-5 requires all Federal departments and agencies to adopt NIMS and to use it in their individual incident management programs and activities, as well as in support of all actions taken to assist State, tribal, and local governments. The directive requires Federal departments and agencies to make adoption of NIMS by State, tribal, and local organizations a condition for Federal preparedness assistance (through grants, contracts, and other activities). NIMS recognizes the role that NGOs and the private sector have in preparedness and activities to prevent, protect against, respond to, recover from, and mitigate the effects of incidents.

Building on the foundation provided by existing emergency management and incident response systems used by jurisdictions, organizations, and functional disciplines at all levels, NIMS integrates best practices into a comprehensive framework for use nationwide by emergency management/response personnel in an all-hazards context. These best practices lay the groundwork for the components of NIMS and provide the mechanisms for the further development and refinement of supporting national standards, guidelines, protocols, systems, and technologies. NIMS fosters the development of specialized technologies that facilitate emergency management and incident response activities, and allows for the adoption of new approaches that will enable continuous refinement of the system over time.

The Secretary of Homeland Security, through the National Integration Center (NIC), Incident Management Systems Integration Division (formerly known as the NIMS Integration Center), publishes the standards, guidelines, and compliance protocols for determining whether a Federal, State, tribal, or local government has implemented NIMS.

Additionally, the Secretary, through the NIC, manages publication and collaboratively, with other departments and agencies, develops standards, guidelines, compliance procedures, and protocols for all aspects of NIMS.

A. Introduction

The September 11, 2001, terrorist attacks and the 2004 and 2005 hurricane seasons highlighted the need to focus on improving emergency management, incident response capabilities, and coordination processes across the country. A comprehensive national approach, applicable at all jurisdictional levels and across functional disciplines, improves the effectiveness of emergency management/response personnel across the full spectrum of potential incidents and hazard scenarios (including but not limited to natural hazards, terrorist activities, and other manmade disasters). Such an approach improves coordination and cooperation between public and private agencies/organizations in a variety of emergency management and incident response activities. The *National Incident Management System* (NIMS) framework sets forth the comprehensive national approach.

Incidents typically begin and end locally, and are managed on a daily basis at the lowest possible geographical, organizational, and jurisdictional level. However, there are instances in which successful incident management operations depend on the involvement of multiple jurisdictions, levels of government, functional agencies, and/or emergency responder disciplines. These instances require effective and efficient coordination across this broad spectrum of organizations and activities.

NIMS uses a systematic approach to integrate the best existing processes and methods into a unified national framework for incident management. Incident management refers to how incidents are managed across all homeland security activities, including prevention, protection, and response, mitigation, and recovery.

This framework forms the basis for interoperability and compatibility that will, in turn, enable a diverse set of public and private organizations to conduct well-integrated and effective emergency management and incident response operations. Emergency management is the coordination and integration of all activities necessary to build, sustain, and improve the capability to prepare for, protect against, respond to, recover from, or mitigate against threatened or actual natural disasters, acts of terrorism, or other manmade disasters. It does this through a core set of concepts, principles, procedures, organizational processes, terminology, and standard requirements applicable to a broad community of NIMS users.

B. Concepts and Principles

NIMS is based on the premise that utilization of a common incident management framework will give emergency management/response personnel a flexible but standardized system for emergency management and incident response activities. NIMS is flexible because the system components can be utilized to develop plans, processes, procedures, agreements, and roles for all types of incidents; it is applicable to any incident regardless of cause, size, location, or complexity. Additionally, NIMS provides an organized set of standardized operational structures, which is critical in allowing disparate organizations and agencies to work together in a predictable, coordinated manner.

1. Flexibility

> **The components of NIMS are adaptable to any situation, from routine, local incidents to incidents requiring the activation of interstate mutual aid to those requiring a coordinated Federal response, whether planned, notice or no-notice.**

The components of NIMS are adaptable to any situation, from routine, local incidents to incidents requiring the activation of interstate mutual aid to those requiring a coordinated Federal response, whether planned (e.g., major sporting or community events), notice (e.g., hurricane) or no-notice (e.g., earthquake). This flexibility is essential for NIMS to be applicable across the full spectrum of potential incidents, including those that require multiagency, multijurisdictional (such as incidents that occur along international borders), and/or multidisciplinary coordination. Flexibility in the NIMS framework facilitates scalability of emergency management and incident response activities. NIMS also provides the flexibility for unique implementation in specified areas around the Nation. The National Integration Center (NIC), as appropriate, will review and support implementation plans, which reflect these individual requirements and organizational structures, for consistency with NIMS concepts and principles.

2. Standardization

Flexibility to manage incidents of any size requires coordination and standardization among emergency management/response personnel and their affiliated organizations. NIMS provides a set of standardized organizational structures that improve integration and connectivity among jurisdictions and disciplines, starting with a common foundation of preparedness and planning. Personnel and organizations that have adopted the common NIMS framework are able to work together, thereby fostering cohesion among the various organizations involved in all aspects of an incident. NIMS also provides and promotes common terminology, which fosters more effective communication among agencies and organizations responding together to an incident.

C. Overview of NIMS Components

NIMS integrates existing best practices into a consistent, nationwide, systematic approach to incident management that is applicable at all levels of government, nongovernmental organizations (NGOs), and the private sector, and across functional disciplines in an all-hazards context. Five major components make up this systems approach: Preparedness, Communications and Information Management, Resource Management, Command and Management, and Ongoing Management and Maintenance.

1. NIMS Components

The components of NIMS were not designed to stand alone, but to work together in a flexible, systematic manner to provide the national framework for incident management.

a. Preparedness

Effective emergency management and incident response activities begin with a host of preparedness activities conducted on an ongoing basis, in advance of any potential incident. Preparedness involves an integrated combination of assessment; planning; procedures and protocols; training and exercises; personnel qualifications, licensure, and certification; equipment certification; and evaluation and revision.

b. Communications and Information Management

Emergency management and incident response activities rely on communications and information systems that provide a common operating picture to all command and coordination sites. NIMS describes the requirements necessary for a standardized framework for communications and emphasizes the need for a common operating picture. This component is based on the concepts of interoperability, reliability, scalability, and portability, as well as the resiliency and redundancy of communications and information systems.

c. **Resource Management**

Resources (such as personnel, equipment, or supplies) are needed to support critical incident objectives. The flow of resources must be fluid and adaptable to the requirements of the incident. NIMS defines standardized mechanisms and establishes the resource management process to identify requirements, order and acquire, mobilize, track and report, recover and demobilize, reimburse, and inventory resources.

d. **Command and Management**

The Command and Management component of NIMS is designed to enable effective and efficient incident management and coordination by providing a flexible, standardized incident management structure. The structure is based on three key organizational constructs: the Incident Command System, Multiagency Coordination Systems, and Public Information.

e. **Ongoing Management and Maintenance**

Within the auspices of Ongoing Management and Maintenance, there are two components: the NIC and Supporting Technologies.

National Integration Center

Homeland Security Presidential Directive 5 required the Secretary of Homeland Security to establish a mechanism for ensuring the ongoing management and maintenance of NIMS, including regular consultation with other Federal departments and agencies; State, tribal, and local stakeholders; and NGOs and the private sector. The NIC provides strategic direction, oversight, and coordination of NIMS and supports both routine maintenance and the continuous refinement of NIMS and its components. The NIC oversees the program and coordinates with Federal, State, tribal, and local partners in the development of compliance criteria and implementation activities. It provides guidance and support to jurisdictions and emergency management/response personnel and their affiliated organizations as they adopt or, consistent with their status, are encouraged to adopt the system. The NIC also oversees and coordinates the publication of NIMS and its related products. This oversight includes the review and certification of training courses and exercise information.

Supporting Technologies

As NIMS and its related emergency management and incident response systems evolve, emergency management/response personnel will increasingly rely on technology and systems to implement and continuously refine NIMS. The NIC, in partnership with the Department of Homeland Security Science and Technology Directorate, oversees and coordinates the ongoing development of incident management-related technology, including strategic research and development.

Editor's Comments

There has been some debate over whether the study of emergency management is separate and distinct from the study of homeland theory. This seems to be a premise with little or no merit. Aside from the obvious inclusion of the Federal Emergency Management Agency in the Department of Homeland Security family of federal agencies, emergency management principles are deeply embedded in the foundations of homeland security.

The foundations of homeland security include Security, Resilience, and Customs and Exchange. It is the theory of Resilience which necessitates an academic alliance between homeland security and emergency management. Resiliency, the ability to recover from a terrorist or natural event, incorporates the ability to mitigate vulnerability and react to events should they occur. They are the beginning stages of any successful Resiliency model. These mitigation and reaction processes depict emergency management in its most fundamental form. Therefore, it is difficult to envision a homeland security program which does not include a thorough and complete examination of the emergency management process.

Further Discussion

1. Discuss the significance of **Executive Order 12127**.

2. Discuss the role of **FEMA's National Advisory Council**.

3. Discuss the objectives of the **National Response Framework (NRF)**.

4. Discuss the **Stafford Act** and how it influences governmental relationships.

5. Discuss the role of the **National Incident Management System (NIMS)**.

Chapter 10

The Terrorist Threat

"Today, we operate under the premise that individuals prepared to carry out terrorist acts might already be in the country, and could carry out further acts of terrorist violence with little or no warning. We must all work to gain a better understanding of the behaviors, tactics, and other indicators that could point to terrorist activity".

Janet Napolitano, Secretary of the Department of Homeland Security

Office of the President of the United States
Securing the Homeland Strengthening the Nation
2002, (Excerpts)

The Terrorist Threat: A Permanent Condition

Today's terrorists can strike at any place, at any time, and with a wide variety of weapons. The most urgent terrorist threat to America is the Al Qaeda network. We will prosecute our war with these terrorists until they are routed from the Earth. But we will not let our guard down after we defeat Al Qaeda. The terrorist threat to America takes many forms, has many places to hide, and is often invisible. We can never be sure that we have defeated all of our terrorist enemies, and therefore we can never again allow ourselves to become overconfident about the security of our homeland.

> **Today's terrorists can strike at any place, at any time, and with a wide variety of weapons.**

There are two inescapable truths about terrorism in the 21st century.

- First, the characteristics of American society that we cherish – our freedom, our openness, our great cities and towering skyscrapers, our modern transportation systems – make us vulnerable to terrorism of catastrophic proportions. America's vulnerability to terrorism will persist long after we bring justice to those responsible for the events of September 11.

- Second, the technological ability to launch destructive attacks against civilian populations and critical infrastructure spreads to more and more organizations and individuals with each passing year. This trend is an unavoidable byproduct of the technological, educational, economic, and social progress that creates jobs, wealth, and a good quality of life.

The combination of these two facts means the threat of terrorism is an inescapable reality of life in the 21st century. It is a permanent condition to which America and the entire world must adjust.

The need for homeland security, therefore, is not tied to any specific terrorist threat. Instead, the need for homeland security is tied to the underlying vulnerability of American society and the fact that we can never be sure when or where the next terrorist conspiracy against us will emerge. The events of September 11 were a harsh wake-up call to all citizens, revealing to us the danger we face. Not since World War II have our American values and our way of life been so threatened. The country is now at war, and securing the homeland is a national priority.

Office of the Director of National Intelligence
National Counterterrorism Center Report on Terrorism
2010, (Excerpts)

Over 11,500 terrorist attacks occurred in 72 countries in 2010, resulting in approximately 50,000 victims, including almost 13,200 deaths. Although the number of attacks rose by almost 5 percent over the previous year, the number of deaths declined for a third consecutive year, dropping 12 percent from 2009. This decline reflected a combination of two factors: a decrease in the number of attacks causing more than five deaths along with an increase in attacks causing no deaths. For the second year in a row, the largest number of reported attacks occurred in South Asia which also had the largest number of victims for the third consecutive year. More than 75 percent of the world's terrorist attacks and deaths took place in South Asia and the Near East.

United States General Accounting Office
Justice Department: Better Management Oversight
and Internal Controls Needed to Ensure Accuracy of
Terrorism-Related Statistics - GAO-03-266
January 2003, (Excerpts)

Summaries of Selected Statutory Terrorism Definitions

U.S. Code Citation	Terrorism Definition
8 U.S.C. 1182(a)(3)(B)(iii),(iv)	Generally defines "terrorist activity" as an unlawful activity, undertaken with the intent to endanger the safety of one or more individuals or to cause substantial damage to property, which involves the hijacking or sabotaging of any conveyance; hostage-taking; violent attacks upon internationally protected persons; assassinations; the use of weapons or dangerous devices, including explosives, firearms, biological, chemical, or nuclear weapons; or a threat, attempt, or conspiracy to do any of the foregoing. The statute further defines the term "engage in terrorist activity"— conduct that can render an alien inadmissible to the United States. The term encompasses not only the commission of terrorist activities, but a broad range of conduct in support of terrorist activities, generally involving such things as preparation or planning; gathering information on potential targets; soliciting funds or members; or affording material support.

18 U.S.C. 2331(1),(5)	Generally defines terrorism as unlawful acts that are dangerous to human life and that appear intended to intimidate or coerce a civilian population; to influence the policy of a government by intimidation or coercion; or to affect the conduct of a government by mass destruction, assassination, or kidnapping. Terrorism may be domestic or international under 18 U.S.C. 2331 depending on whether the crime occurred primarily outside or within the territorial jurisdiction of the United States, or whether the crime transcended national boundaries in certain respects defined by the statute.
18 U.S.C. 2332b(g)(5)	Lists numerous offenses in defining the term "Federal crime of terrorism" where the offense was calculated to influence or affect the conduct of government by intimidation or coercion or to retaliate against government conduct.
22 U.S.C. 2656f(d)	Defines "terrorism" for purposes of the State Department's annual country reports as premeditated, politically motivated violence perpetrated against noncombatant targets by sub-national groups or clandestine agents. Further defines "international terrorism" as terrorism involving citizens or the territory of more than one country.
22 U.S.C. 2708(j)	Defines an "act of international terrorism" for purposes of the State Department's rewards program as any act substantially contributing to the acquisition of unsafeguarded special nuclear material or any nuclear explosive device by individuals, groups, or non-nuclear weapon states, or any act that materially supports the conduct of international terrorism, including the counterfeiting of U.S. currency or the illegal use of other monetary instruments.

The State of Delaware
The Delaware Criminal Justice Council
Public Website, (Excerpts)

The Nature of Terrorism

There are six basic components to all terrorism. Terrorism is (1) an intentional and (2) rational (3) act of violence to (4) cause fear (5) in the target audience or society (6) for the purpose of changing behavior in that audience or society. Terrorism is a political act, the goal of which is to make a change. The terrorist is not driven by personal desires or ambitions.

Terrorism is about impact on society. There are three types of terrorist attacks: (1) attacks that involve weapons of mass destruction, (2) weapons of mass casualty and (3) weapons of mass disruption. These distinctions are made to focus on the intent of the terrorist act rather than the means per se.

A weapon of mass destruction is a weapon that causes damage to buildings, dams, bridges, computer systems or other structures of a society. A weapon of mass casualty is a weapon that causes massive sickness and/or death. Biological and chemical weapons are weapons of mass casualty. It is these types of weapons that are generally referred to as weapons of mass destruction. Weapons of mass disruption are weapons that cause social, political and/or economic damage to society. Magnetic pulse weapons (to disrupt computer operations), agro terrorism (disrupt food supply or manufacturing) or cyber terrorism (hacking into computers and destroying bank records or government records) are examples of weapons of mass disruption. The distinctions explain how terrorist goals can be achieved and that any act of violence is not terrorism. A terrorist act can involve a weapon that achieves all three goals, such as September 11th. The attack was one of mass destruction of infrastructure (the WTC and Pentagon), mass casualty (an estimated 3000 people killed) and mass disruption (airports shut down, new laws passed, heightened fear of future attack, loss of millions of dollars due to the loss of the WTC as an economic center).

> There are three types of terrorist attacks: (1) attacks that involve weapons of mass destruction, (2) weapons of mass casualty and (3) weapons of mass disruption. These distinctions are made to focus on the intent of the terrorist act rather than the means per se.

While terrorism is goal centered in creating fear in a society to achieve a political goal, a terrorist act can be placed in one of two general groupings. The act is either objective driven or terror driven.

An objective driven act of terrorism is committed in order for the terrorist group to get certain demands met by a government. Hostage taking is an example. The taking of the U.S. Embassy in Iran in 1980 was committed to get the United States to change its behavior in regard to Iran and the Middle East in general. An objective driven act of terrorism is committed to give the government a chance to negotiate or change policy. Terror driven acts are committed as retaliation for a perceived wrong or as a warning of future acts of terror if the government does not change its policies. The acts of terrorism in the Gaza Strip and West Bank are examples of terror driven attacks. Israel kills a leader of Hamas and Hamas bombs the Hebrew University and kills settlers in the West Bank. Threats follow that for every one Hamas leader that is killed, one hundred Israelis will be killed.

The nature of terrorism is the indiscriminate and indirect targeting of individuals with a specific goal and purpose. Terrorism is indiscriminate and indirect in that the people killed are not targeted specifically and the people killed, per se, are of no account to the terrorist. Who gets killed is of no consequence but the fact that people are killed is of consequence. Terrorism is not an irrational act. The targets are chosen because they will cause a desired impact (either the destruction of infrastructure, the causing of massive death, or disruption of a society). The nature of modern terrorism is that anyone can be a victim, but terrorism is not random. The apparently random target is not random, buts its appearance as random causes public anxiety and fear and change in behavior, which is exactly what the terrorist wants to accomplish. Terrorism is also a public act. The act must be such that the greater society will see it and react to the attack. The terrorist will choose targets that have symbolic value and/or economic value (WTC for example) or targets that have public value (buses, restaurants, etc.) in order to get public attention and public behavior change.

Terrorism should not be confused with traditional warfare. In war, the target is selected for its military value. In war groups of people are selected for attack because the people themselves have some specific value and attacking the group will achieve a military objective. In terrorism, the group is of little account per se, but the fact that they are killed is the point. Terrorism should not be confused with war crimes. An example of a war crime is an army going into a town with the objective of purging the town of enemy forces, and while doing so they kill unarmed civilians and non-combatants. Although such action is illegal and a crime, it is not considered terrorism; the dead were killed because the army lost control of itself, not because the destruction was designed to intimidate other towns or the society as a whole. In distinguishing the difference between war and terrorism, the focus is on the reason for the attack and the impact of the attack, not the target of the attack itself.

In summary, terrorism should be understood as a political act to achieve a desired goal through the use of violence. Terrorism is not an irrational act committed by the insane. The terrorist does not act for personal gain or gratification, thus the terrorist is not a criminal in the traditional sense. A terrorist believes in what he, and now with female suicide bombers, she is doing. The objective is worth the life of the terrorist and the lives of the people he/she will take. The intent is not to kill those who die in an attack, but to affect the larger society as a whole. An attack can be committed to destroy the buildings and operations of a society, to kill or injure people or to disrupt the peaceful existence of the society. The attack can seek to achieve all three or a combination of the three. The objective can be to force a government to negotiate or to seek revenge for a government action. Terrorism does not seek specific victims but it does seek out specific targets for a specific outcome.

The History of Terrorism: More Than 200 Years of Development

The history of terrorism dates back at least 1500 years when Jewish resistance groups (66 - 72 A.D.) known as Zealots killed Roman soldiers and destroyed Roman property. The term assassin comes from a Shi'ite Muslim sect (Nizari Isma'ilis - also known as hashashins "hashish-eaters") fighting Sunni Muslims (1090 - 1275) and during Medieval Christendom resisting occupation during the Crusades (1095-1291). The hashashins were known to spread terror in the form of murder, including women and children. The brotherhood of Assassins committed terror so as to gain paradise and seventy-two virgins if killed and to receive unlimited hashish while on earth. The modern development of terrorism began during the French Revolution's Reign of Terror (1793 - 1794). During this period the term terrorism was first coined. Through the past two hundred years, terrorism has been used to achieve political ends and has developed as a tool for liberation, oppression, and international global politics. This essay is designed to provide an overview of the development of terrorism over the past 200 years.

> The history of terrorism dates back at least 1500 years when Jewish resistance groups (66 - 72 A.D.) known as Zealots killed Roman soldiers and destroyed Roman property.

In summary, the development of terrorism as a tool to achieve political goals is as follows:

Late 18th Century - The French Revolution
Government Sponsored Terrorism.
Goal: Eliminate opposition and consolidate power. The word terrorism was coined.

Late 19th and Early 20th Century - The Anarchists
Individual Terrorism.
Propaganda by deeds.
Goal: Use terror to bring down a government.

Early 20th Century - Russian Revolution
Government Sponsored Terrorism.
Goal: Use terror to maintain power and control an entire population. Added systematic society wide use of terror to the concept of government-sponsored terrorism.

Early 20th Century - Irish Rebellion
Selective terrorism.
Sustained terrorism.
Cell operations.
Goal: Use terror to gain independence.

Middle 20th Century
Terror to end colonialism.
Goal: Use of selective terrorism on sympathizers and civilians between the French Revolution and the end of WWII. Terrorism was local and organization of terror was confined to a specific area of conflict.

The Middle East / Cold War -Late 1960's
The internationalization of terrorism and state-sponsored terrorism.
The unification of different terrorist groups as a worldwide network. Additionally, due to the Cold War different countries supporting different terrorist groups in order to destabilize rival governments. Terrorist groups allied in order to bring attention to the Arab-Israeli conflict.

The Middle East / Islamism (Militant Islam) - 1979
Religious Based Terrorism.
Expansion of Islam and the protection of Islam against Jews, Christians and the West formed a justification for the use of terror independent of the Arab-Israeli conflict.

Discussion

Over the past two centuries terrorism has been used for various reasons to achieve various goals. Terrorism has been used by religious zealots and by non-religious ideologues. The historical development of terrorism shows that it is a tool of change.

Pre-Modern Use of Terrorism - Terrorism is nothing new in the Middle East and its use is not new to Jews or Muslims. Jewish Zealots used terrorism to resist the Romans and Muslims used terrorism to resist each other (Shi'ites vs Sunni) and against the crusades. Terror during this period was used kill religious enemies. From the beginning terrorism and religion were companions. The concept of Suicide Martyrdom, dying in the service of God - dying while killing the enemies of God - dates back more than a thousand years ago. From the earliest days, terrorism encompassed the idea of dying in the service of God as a divine duty which would be rewarded in the afterlife. Terrorism against an enemy was a religious act which was considered a good and worthy act.

The French Revolution's Reign of Terror (1793 - 1794) - Modern terrorism began with the Reign of Terror by Maximilien Robespierre and the Jacobin Party. Robespierre brought to terrorism the concept that terrorism has virtue in that it can be a tool to bring about "legitimate" governmental ends. He used terror systematically to suppress opposition to the government. Robespierre introduced Government-sponsored terrorism: the use of terror to maintain power and suppress rivals. Before his reign was over hundreds of people met their end with the sound of the guillotine.

Anarchists (1890 - 1910) - Anarchists were very active during the late 19th and early 20th century. Russian anarchists sought to overthrow the Russian Czar Alexander II by assassination and eventually succeeded in 1881. The Anarchists believed that killing the Czar and other kings and nobles of Europe would bring down governments. To this end the anarchist introduced to the development of terrorism, Individual terrorism. Individual terrorism is the use of selective terror against and individual or group in order to bring down a government. The use of terror was selective because targets were selected based on their position within the governmental system. Terrorist acts were limited to ensure that innocent bystanders were not hurt. This concept of limited collateral damage to innocents, not targeting innocents, did not survive the second half of the 20th century.

Anarchists also introduced the observation that terrorism has a communicative effect. When a bomb explodes, society asks why. The need to know why an act was committed provides the perpetrators of the terrorist act a stage to which an audience is ready to listen. Thus the concept of propaganda by deeds was added to the development of modern terrorism. Terrorism was a tool of communication.

Between 1890 and 1908 anarchists were responsible for killing the kings and queens of Russia, Austria Hungry, Italy and Portugal. Anarchists were also active in the U.S. between 1890 and 1910 setting off bombs on Wall Street. The two most famous acts by anarchists were the assassinations of President McKinley (1901) and Archduke Ferdinand (1914) which resulted in the Great War.

> ## The Irish War of 1919 brought three concepts to the development of terrorism: (1) selective terrorism; (2) sustained terror over time; and (3) cell operations.

The Soviet Revolution (1917) - Lenin, followed by Stalin, expanded the idea of government-sponsored terrorism as a tool to maintain governmental control. Both used terror against an entire class of people within society (as supposed to use against one's enemies), systematically. Terror was used to control the entire society in order to build society. Fear was used as a motivational factor for governmental operations and public compliance with government. Terror was used as a way to organize and control a society.

The Irish Rebellion (1919 - 1921) - The Irish War of 1919 brought three concepts to the development of terrorism (1) selective terrorism, (2) sustained terror over time and (3) cell operations.

The goal of the war was to gain Irish independence from England. Led by Michael Collins, terrorism was applied to representatives of England (police, soldiers, judges, government officials, etc.) in an effort to make the cost of continued occupation too high to maintain. Thus to terrorism was added the concept of selective terrorism, acts of terror against representatives of government to force their departure from an area. A tactic that has been adopted and used in the West Bank and the Gaza Strip since 1967 with the loss of one key concept, the selective aspect. Today's terrorism involves attacks on civilians and non-governmental officials.

Also added to the development of the use of terrorism is the concept that to make a change in a society, the acts of terror must be sustained over a long period of time. The sustained terror will, over time, break down the will of the targeted government and they will eventually seek to an accommodation.

The Irish war also provided the concept of cell operation to terrorism. Cell operation decentralizes the implementation of terrorist acts and prevents the discovery and destruction of the terrorist organization. Each cell has a specific goal or objective. Each cell only knows its members and its specific task. Thus the capture of one cell does not provide avenues to other terrorists. Terrorist groups like Al-Qaeda operated with this decentralized design to implement the attack on September 11th. Cells in Europe, the Middle East and the U.S. had specific objectives (transfer funds, learn to fly planes, create false documents, etc.). It has been estimated that $500,000 was spend to implement the attacks of September 11th with cells operating in Europe and the Middle East providing organization, operation and financial assistance to the main cell that carried out the attack.

After WWII terrorism continued to be used as a tool for liberation and for ending colonialism in the Third World. Selective terror changed from targeting government officials to civilians and sympathizers of occupation.

Terrorism entered a new phase of development and use during the late 1960's. The 1960's brought to terrorism an international scope and a focus on the Middle East. With the 1967 war in which Israel defeated Jordan, Egypt and Syria, taking control of the Golan Heights (from Syria), East Jerusalem, the West Bank (from Jordan), the Gaza Strip and the Sinai Peninsula (from Egypt), the use of conventional war as a means to destroy Israel ended and the use of terror with the purpose of focusing attention on Israel and the Palestinians (the occupied territories) began.

Cuba and the Tri-Continental Conference (1966) - In 1966 Cuba hosted the Tri-Continental Conference which was sponsored by the Soviet Union. This conference was the beginning of the internationalization of terrorism. Terrorist and "liberation" groups from Europe, Asia, Africa, the Middle East and Latin America began to work together and build alliances. Financial, political, operation and intelligence cooperation connected terrorist groups across the world. International terrorism flourished over the preceding two decades. Europe suffered a decade of terrorist activity as European and Middle Eastern terrorist groups worked together to bring attention to the Palestinian cause. In Germany, the Red Army Faction (German group) allied itself with Black September (Palestinian group); in France, Action Direct (French group) allied with the Red Army Faction and the Red Army Brigade (Italian group); in Japan, the Japanese Red Army allied with the Popular Front for the Liberation of Palestine. Cuba became a training ground for terrorist groups.

Terrorism, the Middle East and the Cold War - As the Cold War escalated in the 1960's and the world become polarized between the East and the West, a new dynamic was added to terrorism; State-Sponsored Terrorism: governments exporting terrorism to other parts of the world for their own political interests. Iran supported Hizballah, Libia supported Abu Nidal, Iraq, Cuba, Sudan and Algeria provided training camps, economic and political support to other terrorist groups. The focus of terrorism moved to the Middle East, the Arab-Israeli / Israeli- Palestinian conflict with the U.S. supporting Israel and the Soviet Union supporting various Arab countries.

The 1970's was the decade of air terrorism with more than 20 events of terrorism directed at European and American airlines involving hijackings, bombings and hostage taking. The 1970's also involved bombings, kidnappings and other types of terrorist activity throughout Europe.

Terrorism, the Middle East and Islamism - The last twenty years of the 20th century brought terrorism full circle from its earliest history 1500 years prior. With the rise of the Ayatollah Khomeini in Iran (1979), religious based terrorism returned. Militant Islam and the protection of Islam against Jews, Christians, and the West formed an independent justification for terrorism. Religious suicide martyrdom in which young men and women die in the service of Allah is evidenced in the West Bank, the Gaza Strip and New York City.

The 1980's was the decade of hostage taking and terrorism found a target in U.S. interests around the world. Between 1979 and 1988 there were at least twelve incidents of terrorism directed at the U.S. and her interests. These incidents included the hostages in 1979, the bombing of U.S. Embassies, kidnapping of American citizens, and the bombing of airplanes.

The last decade of the 20th century made another change to the development of terrorism. Terrorism in the 1960's through the 1980's was about exposure to one's cause. A terrorist act was followed by credit taking or a warning to the U.S. that future attacks would occur if the U.S. did not change its policies or a way to gain the world's attention to the Palestinian cause. The 1990's brought to terrorism, indiscriminate killing and high mass casualty counts for its own sake. Between 1993 and September 11, 2001

On November 4, 1979, Iranian students seized the U.S. embassy in Tehran and detained more than 50 Americans. The Iranians held the American diplomats hostage for 444 days. Photo credit: U.S. Department of State.

seven terrorist attacks were committed against the U.S. in which the destruction was the point of the attack. The 1990's returned to terrorism, religious extremism and hate being enough to justify the use of terror. 1993 WTC - 6 dead, major damage to the WTC 1995 Saudi Arabia - 5 dead - bombing of the U.S. Military Headquarters 1996 Saudi Arabia - 19 dead - Khobar Towers 1997 Egypt - 58 tourist dead - terrorists open fire in the Temple of Hatshepsut 1998 Kenya and Tanzania - 224 dead - bombing of two U.S. Embassies at the same time 2000 Yemen - 17 sailors killed - U.S.S. Cole 2001 WTC / Pentagon - 3000 dead After two hundred years, terrorism has changed and has been used for a variety of different purposes to achieve various goals. Ultimately terrorism is a tool to change behavior.

Hearing before the House Armed Services Committee
"Unconventional Threats and Capabilities"
Jarret Brachman, Director
Combating Terrorism Center
February 14, 2007, (Excerpts)

Chairman Smith, Congressman Thornberry, distinguished members of the Subcommittee:

It is an honor and privilege to discuss with you the future challenges facing the nation by the global Jihadi Movement. My comments will focus on fighting the ideological and strategic dimensions of this war. I will begin by mapping the emergent trends with regards to the Jihadi Movement's ideology, then review some approaches that may improve our ability to combat those trends in the short-term, and finally conclude by proposing the establishment of a new research center, which I believe would further bolster our ability to lead us to long-term victory against the Jihadi Movement.

Emergent Trends

Our principal enemy in the global war on terrorism is the Jihadi Movement, which, at the most basic level, consists of like-minded individuals and groups worldwide who are loosely bound by a shared ideological worldview and a collectively held identity. Many of the Jihadi Movement's participants can be considered, without question, terrorists, insurgents and enemy combatants and, therefore, dealt with as such. That said, there are a growing number of participants in the Jihadi Movement that do not fit into our existing characterizations. This category includes Jihadi-minded webmasters, graphics designers, social activists, software engineers, Internet bloggers and translators.

> In the past three years, our enemy's chief priority seems to be giving more people from more places more ways and more reasons to join their Movement, whether that be in the streets of Baghdad or on websites in cyberspace.

In the past three years, our enemy's chief priority seems to be giving more people from more places more ways and more reasons to join their Movement, whether that be in the streets of Baghdad or on websites in cyberspace. In so doing, they have pioneered new tactics, techniques and procedures on the battlefield and they have learned to leverage technology in more creative and sophisticated ways online.

We have seen Jihadi activists develop heightened media savvy in terms of using propaganda for strategic image manipulation. Jihadi propagandists, whom we still know relatively little

about, have improved their abilities to spin the unpopular aspects of their Movement –
attacks that kill Muslim women, children and the elderly, for instance – while drawing the
broader Muslim world's attention to what they view as the more resonant dimensions of
their activities – such as fighting American forces in Iraq and Afghanistan.

This proliferation of ways to support the Jihadi Movement is due to the fact that al-Qa`ida
and its associated networks have focused on fomenting a grassroots social movement. This is
an important permutation in the strategic look of our enemy. Simultaneously combating al-
Qa`ida as a hierarchical organizations, as a decentralized network and as a worldview poses
both unique challenges to the nation's efforts to contain, diminish and eventually defeat the
Jihadi Movement around the world.

Since Jihadi thinkers see themselves waging a series of interconnected insurgencies, the key
to their victory, they argue, is winning the hearts and minds of various Muslim
constituencies. The two primary ways in which the chief Jihadi thinkers have sought to do
this is by: 1) indoctrinating successive generations of Muslim youth with the Jihadi value-
system; 2) creating as many possible new avenues for Muslims to participate in the Jihadi
Movement.

1. Educating the Youth

With regards to the inculcation of new generations, we have seen an intense emphasis being
placed on ideological education in the past several years among high-level Jihadi authors.
Jihadi scholars, pundits and propagandists have leveraged the Internet to establish and
maintain a rich distance-learning curriculum that instructs Jihadi candidates on all
dimensions of warfare. In fact, one of the Jihadi Movement's most prominent thinkers, Abu
Muhammad al-Maqdisi, maintains a website that serves as al-Qa`ida's library.

This online library serves as a dynamic repository for over 3,000 books and articles written
by Jihadi authors on various dimensions of the Jihadi ideology and strategy. We know that
these texts have been downloaded tens-of-thousands of times. We know that these texts have
been found in the possession of both dead and aspiring terrorists. We also know that these
texts are being actively translated from their original Arabic into a variety of languages.

Take for example the book written by Jihadi strategist, Abu Bakr Naji, called the *Management
of Savagery*. Writing as a high-level insider, Naji explains in painstaking detail how al-Qa`ida
plans to defeat the U.S. and its allies in the Middle East, establish sanctuaries in security
vacuums around the world and create propaganda that resonates better with local Muslim
populations. It has become essential reading for anyone who wants to understand the
strategic thinking of al-Qa`ida's leadership and the future of the Jihadi Movement.

Or consider the 1,600 page treatise written by Jihadi historian, Abu Musab al-Suri, which
clearly spells out the operational and strategic lessons-learned by Jihadi groups over the past
century, highlights the present obstacles that current Jihadi participants need to overcome,
and articulates a number of strategic goals for the Jihadi Movement's aspiring leadership to
understand.

2. Increasing Accessibility

Jihadis have been aggressive in identifying new ways for members of the wider Islamic community to participate in their movement. The popular Jihadi book entitled, *39 Ways to Serve and Participate in Jihad,* perhaps best encapsulates how this process manifests itself. The book's author introduces a variety of ways in which Muslims, who may not be able to fight on the frontlines because they are too young or too sick, for instance, could still prepare for and support active Jihadi insurgent campaigns around the world.

Some of those ways include urging women to socialize their children with a Jihadi mindset from an earlier age by reading them bedtime stories of the great Jihadi fighters or playing them videos of successful attacks against American forces.

> Jihadis have been aggressive in identifying new ways for members of the wider Islamic community to participate in their movement.

Other ways in which Jihadi thinkers have sought to increase participation is by encouraging members to study anthropology, sociology and public administration in universities. Having this knowledge, one Jihadi strategist argues, will help the Movement become more effective in exploiting and co-opting local tribal politics throughout the Middle East. It will help them know how to provide social services and establish governing institutions in areas where Jihadis seize control.

A particularly disturbing book recently released by Muhammad Khalil al-Hakaymah, a rising star in the Jihadi movement, is an exhaustively researched exposition on the structure, practices and vulnerabilities of America's law enforcement and intelligence communities, particularly with regards to information sharing and policy coordination. Although Hakaymah's analysis is riddled with errors, due largely to his inability to discriminate among sources, he still makes his point: Jihadi minded Muslims should innovate new ways to exploit America's existing vulnerabilities.

In short, these various writings are but a sample of the Jihadi Movement's broader effort to capitalize on the broader knowledge, creativity and insights of its membership. By doing this, our enemy hopes to catalyze the transformation of the various local insurgent and revolutionary efforts into an organic, global social movement, one that transcends organizational limitations, adapts to changes on the ground and allows for anyone to support these efforts at any level of commitment.

Short-Term Improvements

As a government, we now know that the Jihadi Movement's ideological goals and strategic objectives have been methodically articulated by the Movement's brightest thinkers. In fact, their public and private writings of these Jihadi scholars, which can be viewed as today's

Mein Kampf, hold the key for America's ability to formulate effective strategy against the Jihadi Movement.

Given the importance of these operational, strategic and ideological texts for our enemy's recruitment, educational and propaganda purposes, a more concentrated national effort to exploit these texts for policymaking is vital. Specifically, the United States should consider following two courses of action.

First, we should raise overall expectations within the government about how it is both possible and desirable to leverage knowledge against our enemy. USSOCOM has already proven itself to be among the most forward thinking agencies in this regard. By making previously restricted al Qa'ida, and other terrorist groups' internal documents from the Harmony Database, available to the broader terrorism research community, USSOCOM has exponentially increased its analytical power. This process could achieve even more significant results if additional resources were dedicated to translating, processing, and releasing these documents and making more of them available to analysts and scholars in a more timely fashion.

By setting a new standard for the granularity with which we understand our enemy's strategic and ideological strengths and weaknesses, we will be much better able to operationalize the second recommendation; namely, to deepen the ways in which America integrates insights from the study of these works into its strategy formulation.

We are increasingly seeing the need to implement flexible, synchronized multidimensional policies aimed at intelligently combating the Jihadi Movement, leveraging those key thinkers, immunizing the Jihadi Movement's target constituencies, degrading its strengths and exploiting its vulnerabilities.

The Jihadi Movement's scholars have dedicated decades of deep thought to analyzing their internal fractures and debates. They have paid careful attention to the types of counterterrorism and counterinsurgency tactics have hurt their movement in the past. They also discuss how Jihad organizations have adapted their tactics and strategies to overcome those challenges. By extracting these insights from their works, the United States will be able to more effectively and efficiently deploy its resources in this fight. The role of the broader academic community in helping the overall national effort to formulate such nuanced strategic approaches cannot be underestimated.

Toward a Long-Term Solution

During the Cold War, a similarly protracted conflict involving both aggressive military and ideological campaigns, the United States found ways to involve scholars from all disciplines in its efforts. To date, the United States government has not found a way to parallel that sweeping effort in our fight against the global Jihadi Movement. On the flip side, however, the Jihadi Movement has made their scholars and substantive experts the cornerstone of their strategies against us.

The United States government should lead this fight in combating the ideas driving the Jihadi Movement by establishing an interagency research center whose sole purpose would be to identify influential advocates of terrorism, analyze their strategic and ideological works and disseminate their analysis to other government agencies involved in this fight.

By standing up this kind of strategic research center, under the direction of USSOCOM or another agency in government, the United States would be making a public commitment to empowering our warfighters with the intellectual tools that they need to win the long-term fight. Such an entity can only be successful, however, if it resists bureaucratic temptations to classify or restrict the external distribution of this material, and if it aggressively draws upon the world's leading substantive experts on this movement, most of whom are in the country's graduate programs and teaching in our universities. Beyond the immediate benefit having such experts involved with government thinking, the establishment of a strategic research entity proposed here would serve to rebuild a positive working relationship between academe and the military.

Thank you very much for the opportunity to testify before this committee and for your devoting your time and attention to this important issue. We are keenly aware of the importance of this issue because the cadets that we teach every day at the U.S. Military Academy at West Point, will be the lieutenants serving on the front lines in a few short months. They will certainly benefit from your efforts as we strive to better confront the enemy that we face.

Editor's Comments

The following information concerning the **National Terrorism Advisory System** was taken directly from the Department of Homeland Security website:

National Terrorism Advisory System

The National Terrorism Advisory System, or NTAS, replaces the color-coded Homeland Security Advisory System (HSAS). This new system will more effectively communicate information about terrorist threats by providing timely, detailed information to the public, government agencies, first responders, airports and other transportation hubs, and the private sector.

It recognizes that Americans all share responsibility for the nation's security, and should always be aware of the heightened risk of terrorist attack in the United States and what they should do.

NTAS Alerts

Imminent Threat Alert - warns of a credible, specific, and impending terrorist threat against the United States.

Elevated Threat Alert - warns of a credible terrorist threat against the United States.

After reviewing the available information, the Secretary of Homeland Security will decide, in coordination with other Federal entities, whether an NTAS Alert should be issued.

NTAS Alerts will only be issued when credible information is available.

These alerts will include a clear statement that there is an **imminent threat** or elevated **threat**. Using available information, the alerts will provide a concise summary of the potential threat, information about actions being taken to ensure public safety, and recommended steps that individuals, communities, businesses and governments can take to help prevent, mitigate or respond to the threat.

The NTAS Alerts will be based on the nature of the threat: in some cases, alerts will be sent directly to law enforcement or affected areas of the private sector, while in others, alerts will be issued more broadly to the American people through both official and media channels.

Sunset Provision

An individual threat alert is issued for a specific time period and then automatically expires. It may be extended if new information becomes available or the threat evolves.

NTAS Alerts contain a **sunset provision** indicating a specific date when the alert expires - there will not be a constant NTAS Alert or blanket warning that there is an overarching threat. If threat information changes for an alert, the Secretary of Homeland Security may announce an updated NTAS Alert. All changes, including the announcement that cancels an NTAS Alert, will be distributed the same way as the original alert.

Further Discussion

1. Discuss the **two inescapable truths** about terrorism in the 21st century (are there more?).

2. Discuss the many definitions of **terrorism**.

3. Discuss **the nature of terrorism** and its basic components.

4. Briefly discuss the **history of terrorism**.

5. Discuss the significant **emergent trends in terrorism**.

Chapter 11

American Jihadists

"The terror threat has evolved and in many ways is more challenging now than at any time since 9/11. We are seeing an increasing number of attacks and plots resulting from radicalization of individuals already residing in the United States".

Congressman Peter King

Hearing before the Senate Committee on
Homeland Security and Governmental Affairs
"Ten Years After 9/11: Are We Safer?"
The Honorable Matthew G. Olsen, Director
National Counterterrorism Center
September 13, 2011, (Excerpts)

Homegrown Violent Extremists Activity Remains Elevated

Homegrown violent extremists (HVEs) inspired by al-Qaida's global extremist agenda are a key element of the evolution and diversification of the threat since 9/11. The growth of online English-language violent extremist content during the past three years has fostered greater cohesion, but not necessarily collaboration, among HVEs. Plots disrupted during the past year were unrelated operationally, but are indicative of a common cause rallying independent extremists to want to attack the homeland.

A key feature of this trend has been the development of a U.S. specific narrative a blend of al-Qaida inspiration, perceived victimization, and glorification of past Homegrown plotting— that addresses the unique concerns of U.S.-based violent extremists. HVEs who independently plan attacks with no direction from associates in the U.S. or overseas are difficult to detect and disrupt and could advance plotting with little or no warning.

- Arrests of HVEs in the United States in 2010 and 2011 remained at elevated levels. The arrest of U.S. Army PFC Naser Jason Abdo—who allegedly planned to kill American soldiers near Ft. Hood—underscores our concerns about the ongoing threat from lone offender HVEs. U.S.-based extremists continue to be motivated to carry out violence on the basis of a variety of personal rationales, highlighting the continued intent by some HVEs to take part in violence despite having no operational connections to terrorists overseas.

- Al-Qaida's core and some of its regional affiliates have repeatedly encouraged independent attacks, which could further encourage HVEs toward violent acts. Increasingly sophisticated English-language propaganda, including *Inspire* magazine, that provides extremists with guidance to carry out homeland attacks remains easily available via the Internet. English-language web forums also foster a sense of community and further indoctrinate new recruits, both of which can lead to increased levels of violent activity.

Although al-Qaida's Pakistan-based senior leaders previously encouraged self-initiated attacks in propaganda, their video released on June 3rd titled, -Thou Art Held Responsible Only for Thyself, marked the group's most explicit endorsement of individual terrorist acts and first public encouragement of cyber attacks.

Congressional Research Service
Report for Congress
American Jihadist Terrorism: Combating a Complex Threat
November 2011, (Excerpts)

Homegrown Jihadists

As part of a much-discussed apparent uptick in terrorist activity in the United States, from May 2009 through October 2011, arrests were made for 32 "homegrown," jihadist-inspired terrorist plots by American citizens or legal permanent residents of the United States. Two of these resulted in attacks—U.S. Army Major Nidal Hasan's alleged assault at Fort Hood in Texas and Abdulhakim Muhammed's shooting at the U.S. Army-Navy Career Center in Little Rock, AR— produced 14 deaths. By comparison, in more than seven years from the September 11, 2001, terrorist strikes (9/11) through April 2009, there were 21 such plots. Two resulted in attacks, and never more than six occurred in a single year (2006). The apparent spike in such activity after April 2009 suggests that at least some Americans—even if a tiny minority—are susceptible to ideologies supporting a violent form of jihad.

> ...from May 2009 through October 2011, arrests were made for 32 "homegrown," jihadist-inspired terrorist plots by American citizens or legal permanent residents of the United States.

How serious is the threat of homegrown, violent jihadists in the United States? Experts differ in their opinions. In May 2010 congressional testimony, terrorism expert Bruce Hoffman emphasized that it is, "difficult to be complacent when an average of one plot is now being uncovered per month over the past year or more—and perhaps even more are being hatched that we don't know about." By contrast, a recent academic study of domestic Muslim radicalization supported by the National Institute of Justice reveals that "the record over the past eight years contains relatively few examples of Muslim-Americans that have radicalized and turned toward violent extremism" and concludes that "homegrown terrorism is a serious but limited problem." Another study has suggested that the homegrown terrorist threat has been exaggerated by federal cases that "rely on the abusive use of informants." Moreover, the radicalization of violent jihadists may not be an especially new phenomenon for the United States. Estimates suggest that between 1,000 and 2,000 American Muslims engaged in violent jihad during the 1990s in Afghanistan, Bosnia, and Chechnya. More broadly, terrorism expert Brian Michael Jenkins notes that during the 1970s domestic terrorists "committed 60-70 terrorist incidents, most of them bombings, on U.S. soil every year—a level of activity 15-20 times that seen in most years since 9/11." Few of the attacks during the 1970s appear to have involved individuals motivated by jihadist ideas.

But as Dr. Hoffman's comments suggest, the November 2009 Fort Hood shootings, which killed, and the other plots and arrests in 2009, 2010, and 2011, are worrying. Secretary of Homeland Security Janet Napolitano has said that authorities are "just beginning to confront the reality that we have this issue ... and that we really don't have a very good handle on how you prevent someone from becoming a violent extremist." A single successful attack can incur scores of casualties and cause considerable socioeconomic disruption. Regardless of their novelty, frequency, or lethality, violent attacks fostered by violent jihadists radicalized in the United States remain a security concern.

The bulk of the 2009-2011 homegrown plots likely reflect a trend in jihadist terrorist activity away from schemes directed by the core leaders of Al Qaeda or other significant terrorist groups. Marc Sageman, a forensic psychiatrist and former Central Intelligence Agency (CIA) operations officer who writes about terrorism, has noted a global shift in terrorism toward decentralized, autonomously radicalized, violent jihadist individuals or groups who strike in their home countries. Global counterterrorism efforts have made it harder for international terrorist networks to formulate plots, place their recruits in targeted countries, and carry out violent strikes in locations far from their bases of operation. A senior counterterrorism official told the *Los Angeles Times* that Al Qaeda and affiliated groups are moving "away from what we are used to, which are complex, ambitious, multilayered plots."

Homegrown Violent Jihadists

This report focuses on geography and citizenship in its characterization of homegrown terrorism by defining the phenomenon as jihadist terrorist activity or plots perpetrated within the United States or abroad by American citizens, legal permanent residents, or visitors radicalized largely within the United States. These homegrown groups or individuals can focus their plots on foreign targets. They can have operational ties to foreign terrorist groups, but most of the plots after April 2009 have not. Homegrown violent jihadists potentially either come from Muslim immigrant communities or are converts to Islam. A review of the numerous arrests of homegrown violent jihadists on terrorism-related charges since 9/11 suggests a wide array of incidents. There have been those who have plotted or attempted terrorist attacks. Others have provided material support to terrorist groups. Some have recruited individuals to travel abroad—or have gone themselves—to acquire terrorist training, conduct terrorism, or join in other forms of jihadist conflict, such as the fighting in Somalia or Afghanistan.

Shortcomings and Strengths

Homegrown violent jihadists may exhibit a number of conventional shortcomings when compared to international terrorist networks such as Al Qaeda. Because some homegrown terrorists are not tied to international groups, some say they possibly lack deep, hands-on understanding of specialized tradecraft such as bomb making and may not have the financing, training camps, support networks, and broad expertise housed in international organizations with extensive rosters and greater resources. Also, homegrown groups tend to be much less formally structured than international organizations. A former CIA case officer recently commented that the threat posed by self-radicalized "lone" bombers lacking support networks, "even those who have been in contact with either Al Qaeda or the Taliban, will be hit or miss at best."

These apparent shortcomings may keep some homegrown violent jihadists from independently planning, coordinating, and implementing large-scale suicide strikes such as 9/11 or the Mumbai attacks of November 2008. Because of this, they may turn to violence involving less planning and preparation, such as assaults using firearms.

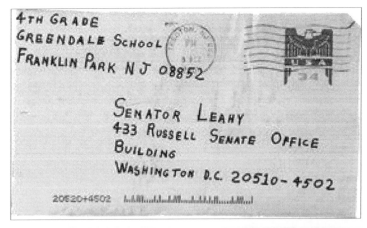

A letter addressed to Senator Patrick Leahy being opened by experts at the Army's Ft. Detrick, Maryland, biomedical research laboratory in November 2001. The envelope and letter, which were laced with anthrax, were decontaminated and examined using a number of sophisticated scientific and forensic procedures. Photo credit: FBI.

Al Qaeda appears to have embraced such homegrown lone wolf terrorist plots. In March 2010, *As Sahab*, Al Qaeda's media wing, released an English language video titled "A Call to Arms" featuring American-born spokesperson Adam Gadahn. In the video directed toward jihadists in the United States, Israel, and the United Kingdom, Gadahn extols alleged Fort Hood shooter Nidal Hasan as a "trailblazer" who did not attract law enforcement attention by training abroad or relying on conspirators. Gadahn encourages would-be terrorists to select realistically hittable targets that are familiar to them and have some broadly symbolic— especially economic— resonance. In an early June 2011 English language video message titled "Do Not Rely on Others, Take the Task Upon Yourself," Al Qaeda's American-born spokesperson Adam Gadahn even more clearly emphasized lone wolf operations.

Gadahn stresses "targeting major institutions—after a clip showing the logos of such firms as Exxon, Merrill Lynch and Bank of America—and 'influential public figures.'" At about the same time as this video was released, users of jihadist websites apparently began posting potential targets and developing hit lists.

In the same vein as Gadahn's video, Al Qaeda in the Arabian Peninsula (an Al Qaeda affiliate) has issued an English language propaganda magazine titled *Inspire*. The magazine has encouraged homegrown violent jihadist activity in the West, focusing on smaller scale strategies such as using a vehicle to run over victims. It has featured articles attributed to three prominent violent jihadist propagandists with strong American ties: Gadahn, radical U.S.-born imam Anwar al-Awlaki, and Saudi-born American citizen Samir Khan. In September 2011, the latter two died in a widely reported U.S. air strike in Yemen.

This does not mean that homegrown terrorists are incapable of sophisticated, coordinated action or linking up with international groups. For example, in 2008 foiled New York City subway bomber Najibullah Zazi received explosives instruction from Al Qaeda in Pakistan. He and coconspirators then tried to implement this training in the United States. U.S. authorities allege that senior Al Qaeda official Adnan el-Shukrijumah possibly recruited Zazi and his fellow plotters. Shukrijumah—a Saudi-born, naturalized American citizen who spent part of his youth in Brooklyn—and others involved in Al Qaeda's "external operations" program allegedly planned the attack. The relative sophistication of Zazi's plot may have actually exposed it to greater law enforcement scrutiny. Authorities likely learned of the plot while monitoring a known Al Qaeda e-mail account.

The conventionally perceived shortcomings of homegrown terrorists may actually pose some challenges for law enforcement, intelligence, and security officials charged with detecting, preventing, or disrupting terrorist plots. According to terrorism analyst Steve Emerson, "The smaller cells tend to be less powerful than a central terrorist organization like Al Qaeda, but they are harder to detect.... When the group of conspirators are [sic] small it's much more difficult for the FBI.... The larger the group, the greater the chances the FBI can infiltrate." Former Director of National Intelligence Dennis C. Blair noted that many of the terrorist schemes disrupted in 2009—including homegrown activity—relied on short-term planning. These quickly generated schemes are harder to identify and disrupt than more traditional and more highly organized international terrorist conspiracies, which can gestate for years.

According to at least one study, homegrown terrorists can be nimble adversaries, because as U.S. citizens or legal permanent residents, they can travel easily between the United States and foreign countries. While abroad, they could receive training from foreign terrorist organizations, conduct surveillance operations against foreign targets, and plan attacks. In the case of recent immigrants to the United States, they are particularly comfortable moving between American and foreign cultural contexts. English language skills, the ability to navigate Western culture, society, and context are likely key ingredients for successful strikes. Three recent cases involving alleged or actual homegrown terrorists illustrate how these factors possibly facilitate terrorist plotting:

- In February 2011, Colleen LaRose (aka "Jihad Jane") pled guilty "to all counts of a superseding indictment charging her with conspiracy to provide material support to terrorists, conspiracy to kill in a foreign country, making false statements, and attempted identity theft." She allegedly discussed with her coconspirators how her mainstream American physical appearance would allow her to "blend in with many people."

- On March 18, 2010, David Headley, born Daood Sayed Gilani to an American mother and Pakistani father, pled guilty to helping plan the 2008 terrorist attacks in Mumbai, India, and for plotting to attack the offices of a newspaper in Copenhagen, Denmark. Headley was able to use his American citizenship and Pakistani heritage to move between the United States and abroad for seven years during which time he received terrorist training in Pakistan and scouted locations in India and Denmark for terrorist attacks.

- For 10 years prior to his involvement in a September 2009 plot to trigger explosive devices in New York City's subways, Najibullah Zazi, an Afghan immigrant legally present in the United States, lived in the New York City borough of Queens and had family in Pakistan.

In 2010, the Department of Homeland Security's (DHS's) Office of Intelligence and Analysis warned, "probable terrorist perception of success in challenging the U.S. even through failed attacks, suggest[s] Al Qaeda and associated groups will try to conduct operations in the United States with increased frequency." It appears that for the foreseeable future, American citizens and legal permanent residents of the United States radicalized within the nation's borders will continue to pose a sizeable violent jihadist threat.

Radicalization and Violent Extremism

Radicalization and violent extremism are terms that are sometimes used interchangeably but do not mean the same thing. Radicalization has been described as the exposure of individuals to ideological messages and the movement of those individuals from mainstream beliefs to extremist viewpoints. Others say radicalization consists of changes in belief and behavior to justify intergroup violence and personal or group sacrifice to forward specific, closely held ideas. Still others use the term to more closely link extremist beliefs to violent action, as in this working definition by the DHS, which states that radicalization "entails the process of adopting an extremist belief system, including the willingness to use, support, or facilitate violence, as a method to effect societal change.

**U.S. House of Representatives
Committee on Homeland Security
Homegrown Terrorism:
The Threat to Military Communities Inside The United States
December 2011, Excerpts**

Insider Homegrown Terror Attacks on Military Targets inside the U.S.

June 2011

> **U.S. Marine Corps Reservist LCpl. Yonathan Melaku,** a naturalized U.S. citizen from Ethiopia, was allegedly motivated by Al Qaeda propaganda and ideology, has been charged with destruction of property and firearm violations after a series of five shootings at military installations in the Washington, D.C. area.

November 2009

> **Army Maj. Nidal Malik Hasan,** a psychiatrist, killed 13 and wounded 32 during an attack on the Soldier Readiness Center at the Army's Fort Hood, where he was stationed. AQAP leader Anwar al-Awlaki said in a news media interview that he communicated with Hasan.26

March 2003

> **Army Sgt. Hasan Akbar,** in an attack at a U.S. Army camp in Kuwait, killed two Army officers and wounded 14 others by tossing grenades into the tents of his fellow troops and then ambushed them with an M4 rifle as they ran out. The attack took place two days after the U.S. invasion of Iraq at a base located 25 miles from the Kuwait-Iraq border.

External Homegrown Terror Attacks on Military Targets inside the U.S.

June 2009

> **Abdulhakim Muhammad, born Carlos Bledsoe,** a U.S. citizen and Muslim convert, was arrested and charged with killing Army Pvt. William Long after attacking an Army recruiting office in Little Rock, Arkansas. Bledsoe allegedly specifically targeted the U.S. military to avenge its mistreatment of Muslims and he has claimed to be an AQAP operative.

But there is an important distinction between the terms "radicalization" and "violent extremism" as it relates to the threshold of U.S. law enforcement interest and action. This is because Americans have the right under the First Amendment to adopt, express, or disseminate ideas, even hateful and extremist ones. But when radicalized individuals mobilize their views (i.e., they move from a radicalized viewpoint to membership in a terrorist group, or to planning, materially supporting, or executing terrorist activity) then the nation's public safety and security interests are activated. Thus, the terms may be differentiated as follows:

- "Radicalization" describes the process of acquiring and holding radical, extremist, or jihadist *beliefs*.

- "Violent extremism," for this report, describes *violent action* taken on the basis of radical or extremist beliefs. For many, this term is synonymous with "violent jihadist" and "jihadist terrorist."

> ## "Radicalization" describes the process of acquiring and holding radical, extremist, or jihadist *beliefs*.

From Radicalization to Violent Extremism

As the terrorist threat becomes increasingly homegrown, a key way to fight it is to develop an understanding of how radicalization works and formulate ways to prevent the radicalization from morphing into violent extremism. In 2007, the New York City Police Department's (NYPD's) Intelligence Division released a study of domestic jihadist radicalization that has been widely circulated within the law enforcement community.

The study describes a general four-step process of radicalization leading to violent extremism. First, individuals exist in a **pre-radicalization** phase in which they lead lives unaware of or uninterested in either violent jihad or fundamentalist Salafi Islam. Next, they go through **self-identification** in which some sort of crisis or trigger (job loss, social alienation, death of a family member, international conflict) urges them to explore Salafism. Third, individuals undergo **indoctrination** or adoption of jihadist ideals combined with Salafi views. The study indicates that, typically, a "spiritual sanctioner" or charismatic figure plays a central role in the indoctrination process. Finally, radicalizing individuals go through "**jihadization**," where they identify themselves as violent jihadists, and are drawn into the planning of a terrorist

> ## "Violent Extremism," for this report, describes violent action taken on the basis of radical or extremist beliefs. For many, this term is synonymous with "violent jihadist" and "jihadist terrorist."

attack. At this point, according to the NYPD, they can be considered violent extremists. The FBI's own four-stage model of radicalization closely follows that of the NYPD.

This model and the process it describes—though useful—should, however, be read with caution, according to some observers. The radicalization process is best depicted in broad brush strokes. Some experts have warned against viewing the radicalization process as a "conveyer belt," somehow starting with grievances and inevitably ending in violence. The NYPD report itself acknowledges that individuals who begin this process do not necessarily pass through all the stages nor do they necessarily follow all the steps in order, and not all individuals or groups who begin this progression become terrorists. Studies by the DHS Office of Intelligence and Analysis indicate that the radicalization dynamic varies across ideological and ethno-religious spectrums, different geographic regions, and socio-economic conditions. Moreover, there are many diverse "pathways" to radicalization and individuals and groups can radicalize or "de-radicalize" because of a variety of factors.

New York State Intelligence Center
The Vigilance Project:
An Analysis of 32 Terrorism Cases
Against the Homeland
December 2010, (Excerpts)

This first iteration of the Vigilance Project reviews thirty-two terrorism cases investigated post 9/11

32 "homegrown," jihadist-inspired terrorist plots by American citizens or legal permanent residents of the United States.

1. December 2001: "Shoe Bomber" Bombing Attempt
2. May 2002: Jose Padilla, Dirty Bomb Plot
3. August 2002: Columbus Shopping Mall Plot
4. September 2002: The Lackawanna Cell
5. May 2003: Brooklyn Bridge Plot
6. June 2003: Virginia Jihad Cell
7. August 2004: Financial Centers Plot
8. August 2004: The Herald Square Plot
9. August 2004: Albany Assassination Plot
10. June 2005: Lodi, CA Cell
11. August 2005: JIS Plot
12. December 2005: Pipeline Plot
13. February 2006: Toledo Cell
14. April 2006: Atlanta Cell
15. April 2006: PATH Tunnels Plot
16. May 2006: Sears Tower Plot
17. August 2006: Liquid Explosives Airliner Plot
18. December 2006: The Illinois Shopping Mall Plot
19. May 2007: Fort Dix Plot
20. June 2007: JFK Plot
21. August 2007: Goose Creek, South Carolina Traffic Stop
22. January 2009: Long Island Railroad Plot
23. May 2009: Bronx Synagogue & Newburgh Air Base Plot
24. June 2009: Little Rock, Arkansas Recruiting Station Shooting
25. July 2009: Quantico Marine Base Plot
26. September 2009: Denver/NYC Plot
27. September 2009: Foundation Place Dallas Plot
28. September 2009: Illinois Courthouse Plot
29. November 2009: Fort Hood Shooting
30. October 2009: Massachusetts Shopping Mall Plot
31. December 2009: Christmas Day Bombing Attempt
32. May 2010: Times Square Car Bombing Attempt

that resulted in federal terrorism charges and arrests. Ninety individuals were associated with these cases, which comprise twenty-one thwarted attacks, six significant groups or cells, three failed bombing attempts and two successful attacks. All but one case involve individuals who expressed support for radical Islamic ideology, or had affiliations with foreign terrorist organizations and key terrorist figures. Additionally, most cases demonstrate the subjects' willingness or actual participation in pre-operational activities—such as explosives and weapons training, surveillance and overseas travel—in order to advance their plots and increase the likelihood of success. **Over half of the individuals studied in this report were legal United States citizens at the time of their arrest, with 70% of them natural-born citizens.**

United States Senate Committee on Homeland Security and Governmental Affairs
Majority & Minority Staff Report
Violent Islamist Extremism, The Internet, and the Homegrown Terrorist Threat
May 8, 2008, (Excerpts)

The Terrorist Internet Campaign

Propaganda has always been integral to the violent Islamist movement, especially for the purpose of attracting followers. Printed materials, videos of terrorist activities, including operations and training, and recordings of sermons and speeches espousing the virtues of the violent Islamist ideology have been distributed and sold around the world for decades. But today, for an individual seeking information on this ideology, the Committee found that the Internet provides the most accessible source of information – both passive, in the form of static Web pages, and interactive, in the form of chat rooms and discussion forums that can connect interested individuals with extremists around the world.

The use of the Internet by violent Islamist extremists is constantly in flux, with websites appearing and disappearing regularly. Yet despite the dynamic nature of the websites, there is a generally organized framework for the dissemination of the core terrorist enlistment message. For those who want to know more about violent Islamist ideology, immense caches of information and propaganda are available online. Some material is produced by organized groups committed to advancing this ideology around the world, while other material is produced by self-starting individuals, who themselves may have "signed on" to the ideology's virtual network. These self-appointed amplifiers of the violent Islamist message may not be part of a known terrorist organization, but they choose to advance the cause, not necessarily with guns but with propaganda. Much of this material is readily available through web searches and is often discussed in chat rooms and other online forums where those interested in learning more about the violent Islamist ideology begin the radicalization process and seek out like-minded individuals.

Al-Qaeda's Operation

Today, al-Qaeda manages a multi-tiered online media operation in which a number of production units associated with al-Qaeda or allied violent Islamist organizations produce content consistent with the core terrorist enlistment message. This sophisticated structure is a natural outgrowth of al-Qaeda's previous multimedia efforts. Al-Qaeda has long had a media committee and once operated the now defunct www. alneda.com, which pushed the core terrorist enlistment message and disseminated official statements from al- Qaeda leadership. Al-Qaeda also recognized, prior to 9/11, the value of videotaping attacks and disseminating the statements of terrorists who kill themselves in the name of violent Islamist ideology. Post 9/11, al-Qaeda leadership has accelerated their media campaign as necessary to pursuing their global ideological cause. In what is now a well-known letter to the former al-Qaeda commander in Iraq, Abu Musab al-Zarqawi, Ayman al-Zawahiri wrote, "We are in a battle, and more than half of this battle is taking place in the battlefield of the media. And that we are in a media battle in a race for the hearts and minds of our people."

Several examples of al-Qaeda affiliated regional production centers include:

- Al-Furquan Media (affiliated with The Islamic State of Iraq)

- As-Sahab Media (affiliated with al-Qaeda High Command)

- Media Commission or Media Committee (affiliated with al-Qaeda in the Land of the Islamic Maghreb)

- Sawt al-Jihad (affiliated with al-Qaeda in the Arabian Peninsula)

These production centers, which often include an icon or logo to identify themselves and their propaganda, are highly sophisticated operations that utilize cutting-edge technology. Videos may be relatively straightforward recordings of attacks, or they may be intricate productions with graphics, sound effects, banners, subtitles, animation, and stock footage. These centers also produce online magazines, official statements, news updates, articles, white papers, and even poetry. The use of songs, symbols, and imagery is integral, adding layers of meaning and emotion to what is being seen or heard.

Once content is created by as-Sahab, al-Furquan, or one of the other production units, it is then funneled through a clearinghouse before it is posted on the Internet. One of the most active Internet clearinghouses today is the al-Fajr Media Center, which was established in January 2006. Like the production centers, al-Fajr is almost entirely virtual. The approval process for dissemination is unclear, but once approved, content is moved from al-Fajr to pre-approved websites. On a daily basis, al-Fajr issues a host of material including statements from violent Islamist groups taking credit for attacks in Iraq, Afghanistan, Algeria, and elsewhere.

These terrorist groups use clearinghouses for two primary reasons. First, along with the icons and logos that identify production centers, clearinghouses help ensure a message's authenticity.   A product released by al-Fajr is recognized as "genuine" and helps maintain message discipline.   Because the violent Islamist movement is committed to its strict interpretation of the religion and its long-term goal to destroy the West, message discipline helps prevent deviation from either.   Second, the clearinghouse process facilitates the near-instantaneous dissemination of new propaganda.   Content approved by a clearinghouse is posted on pre-approved web forums like al-Ekhlaas, al-Hesbah, al-Buraq, or al-Firdaws that include some of the most "exclusive" violent Islamist websites – where access is tightly controlled. The "approved" message is then reposted all over the Internet to become the subject of discussion and debate.

The propaganda regularly produced by this process finds its way to literally *thousands* of violent Islamist websites across the Internet, many of which are either "mirrored" versions of one another or "simply bulletin boards" that disseminate the same material created by the production houses.   This distribution system provides built-in redundancies so that propaganda remains accessible even if one or more of the sites are not available.

Twin suicide bombings in Algeria on December 11, 2007, and a subsequent suicide bombing on January 29, 2008, illustrate how this propaganda dissemination process works. Al-Zawahiri announced in 2006 that the Salafist Group for Preaching and Fighting in Algeria had officially aligned with al-Qaeda. In forming the alliance, the group assumed the new name al-Qaeda in the Land of the Islamic Maghreb and reinvigorated its online operation with the creation of the Media Commission. Very soon after the Algerian attacks, the Media Commission released statements through al-Fajr taking credit for the attacks and providing background and pictures of the suicide bombers. Al-Fajr posted the statement online where it was then viewed and disseminated around the world. The statements included quotes from the Koran, celebrated the attacks themselves, and hit all three points of the core terrorist enlistment message.

Al-Qaeda also uses its online campaign to bypass traditional media and speak "directly" to followers, in part because the terrorist groups believe their message is diluted when replayed or reported by news outlets.   In December 2007, al-Zawahiri announced in an as-Sahab produced video that he would answer questions submitted by followers via some of the more exclusive web forums. In a subsequent as-Sahab video released on April 2, 2008, al-Zawahiri tried to address certain issues that were undermining al-Qaeda's credibility among its supporters, including al-Qaeda's responsibility for killing innocent Muslims and the writings of Sayid Imam al-Sharif. In his new book, al-Sharif, a one- time proponent of violent Islamist ideology and a religious mentor to al-Zawahiri, renounced violence as ineffective and religiously unlawful for the purpose of forcing political change. Al-Zawahiri not only tried to discredit al-Sharif's new position in his video response, he also released a book on the Internet purporting to refute many of al-Sharif's arguments.

Over the last year, al-Qaeda also made a tactical decision to increase its production of online propaganda and make more of it accessible to English-speaking audiences. Al-Qaeda has sought out English translators and, according to Charlie Allen, the Chief Intelligence Officer at the Department of Homeland Security (DHS), al-Qaeda has "ratcheted up the speed and accuracy of translated statements openly marketed to U.S. and English-speaking audiences." For example, al-Qaeda has added subtitles to its video products and made appeals directly to

Americans, including specific religious, ethnic, and racial populations in the United States and elsewhere. On September 8, 2007, as-Sahab released a video of an Osama bin Laden monologue titled "Message to the American People."

This video followed the as-Sahab release of an interview with al-Zawahiri, in which he made the following plea:

> *"That's why I want blacks in America, people of color, American Indians, Hispanics, and all the weak and oppressed in North and South America, in Africa and Asia, and all over the world, to know that when we wage Jihad in Allah's path, we aren't waging Jihad to lift oppression for the Muslims only, we are waging Jihad to lift oppression from all of mankind, because Allah has ordered us never to accept oppressions, whatever it may be".*

According to Dr. Jarret Brachman, the Director of Research at the Combating Terrorism Center at West Point, one goal of this tactical decision was to attract particular groups al-Qaeda perceives as "self-starting radicals who [could] reach back to A[l] Q[aeda's] high-command, much like we saw in London with Operation Crevice and the 7/7 attacks." DHS' Chief Intelligence Officer, Mr. Allen, also recognizes a similar intent in the changes to al-Qaeda's recent propaganda campaign, which has been assisted by supporters in the United States:

Al-Qaeda's leadership has delivered over the past twelve months, an unprecedented number of audio and video messages and has increased its translation capability, diversity of subject matters, and media savvy to reach out to wider audiences globally. Its objective is to gain wide Muslim support, empathy, financing, and future recruits. ... To help al-Qaeda target U.S. citizens, several radical websites in the United States have re-packaged al-Qaeda statements with American vernacular and commentary intending to sway U.S. Muslims.

The Purveyors of ViolentIslamist Ideology

The Internet hosts a vast electronic repository of texts and treatises by the zealots who have given shape to the supposed theological justifications for violent Islamist ideology and the strategies for advancing its cause. These zealots and their ideas, which have inspired attacks in the West and elsewhere, are considered by some to be the "center of gravity" of the violent Islamist movement, more so perhaps than bin Laden or al-Zawahiri. According to testimony received by the Committee, websites that host this material "allow the Internet to function as a kind of virtual extremist *madrassa*" enlisting and inspiring followers around the world.

One such leader is Abu Muhammad al-Maqdisi, a formally trained cleric who served as the spiritual guide for al-Zarqawi, al-Qaeda's former commander in Iraq. Al-Maqdisi created, and his followers have maintained, a website dedicated to the cleric that includes a large library of downloadable books on the supposed theological justifications for violent Islamist ideology. Links to English translations of al-Maqdisi's writings and many other violent Islamist zealots like Abu Qatada al-Filistini, Abdullah Azzam, or Sayid Imam, have been made readily available online by at-Tibyan Publications, which appears to be a global distribution network of like-minded multilingual supporters of violent Islamist ideology who have taken it upon themselves to translate texts and make them available to Western audiences. At-Tibyan Publications appears to have been at least one of the organizations to translate the English version of *39 Ways to Serve and Participate in Jihad*. This online text has been one of their most popular and widely disseminated publications.

The at-Tibyan Publications website also has a list of "recommended scholars" that include al-Zarqawi, Sayid Qutb – whose writings help lay the foundation for contemporary violent Islamist ideology – and one of the leading but lesser known violent Islamist "scholars" named Abu Musab al-Suri. Al-Suri, a one-time associate of bin Laden who was connected to the March 11, 2004, bombings in Madrid, wrote a 1,600-page screed entitled *The Call for Global Islamic Resistance*. In addition to recapping the history of the violent Islamist movement, al-Suri's text, which has been heavily discussed online, prescribes ways to advance the cause of the ideology in a post 9/11 global environment. Al-Suri's propaganda includes the creation of global Islamic resistance brigades – isolated cells committed to advancing the violent Islamist extremist agenda.

Though many of the zealots whose writings have been made available by at-Tibyan Publications have been killed or captured, their ideas persist, and the Internet has played a role in keeping those ideas alive and proliferating them with increasing momentum. The organization of the Internet campaign has also helped retain message discipline outside of al-Qaeda's efforts. For example, at-Tibyan Publications did not release al-Sharif's most recent writings, which undermined the terrorists' use of violence, posting instead his earlier writings espousing violence as a necessary tactic for the global violent Islamist movement.

Other Violent Islamist Media

Other material available online may be less doctrinal or structured. However, much of it appears designed to appeal to younger audiences who may be the most vulnerable to the influence of the core terrorist enlistment message. One of the older and more prolific media organizations is the Global Islamic Media Front (GIMF). This group, which does not appear to have any official connections to al-Qaeda leadership, produces and distributes violent Islamist material designed to inform, inspire, and recruit followers into the global violent Islamist movement. GIMF tries to reach as wide an audience as possible by disseminating material in different languages and by tailoring its content to appeal to a range of nationalities, educational backgrounds, and age groups. Original content produced by GIMF may include religious, military, or ideological texts, online magazines, and videos of speeches and military operations. At one point, the GIMF also broadcast a streaming television broadcast called the Caliphate Voice Channel. One of GIMF's most popular products was a videogame called "The Night of Bush Capturing," the object of which is to hunt and kill the President of the United States.

Followers of the ideology also produce content that supports the goals of violent Islamists.

One of the most well-known examples is the rap video "Dirty Kuffar" (Kuffar means "nonbeliever"), which was downloaded onto millions of computers or watched online. In the video, the rapper, waving a gun and a Koran, praises bin Laden and the 9/11 attacks and disparages Western leaders with lyrics such as:

> *Peace to Hamas and the Hezbollah*
> *OBL pulled me like a shiny star*
> *Like the way we destroyed them two towers ha-ha*
> *The minister Tony Blair, there my dirty Kuffar*
> *The one Mr. Bush, there my dirty Kuffar Throw them on the fire.*

The song is performed against a changing backdrop of images of world leaders morphing into animals or fictional characters and scenes of terrorists engaging in military training and attacking coalition forces in Iraq.

ChatRooms

With the proliferation of violent Islamist ideology on the Internet, anyone looking to learn more about the ideology can easily find it online. For those enticed by its message, either through the Internet or from another source, a likely first stop on the web would be one of the chat rooms or other online discussion forums that "are now supplementing and replacing mosques, community centers, and coffee shops as venues for recruitment and radicalization." Access to chat rooms, however, is tightly controlled. Several layers of validation are often required before access may be granted. Topics of discussion are also restricted, and dissenting views are rarely tolerated. Chat rooms also allow for potential followers to maintain their anonymity, which helps draw in a much wider audience. Though young males constitute a solid majority of those participating in these forums, women are becoming increasingly active. Once individuals are admitted to them, chat rooms offer users access to each other and to the global violent Islamist virtual network.

Indoctrination

There is also the very popular and accessible online text *39 Ways to Serve and Participate in Jihad*, which, as noted earlier, is one of the most popular texts that was made available on the at-Tibyan website. According to *39 Ways*, a supporter of violent Islamist ideology can aid the movement in myriad ways, including joining the movement in spirit, fundraising, or pursuing what *39 Ways* refers to as "electronic jihad." Electronic jihad not only entails participating in online chat rooms or disseminating propaganda, but it can also involve cyber attacks against enemy websites, a tactic that is creating a whole new breed of terrorist.

39 Ways also encourages supporters to read and learn the teachings of violent Islamists like Abdullah Azzam, who was a spiritual mentor to bin Laden, and Abu-Qatada, who preached alongside Abu Hamza al-Masri at the now infamous Finsbury Park Mosque in London that counts Richard Reid and Zacarias Moussaoui as two of its former attendees. The text also encourages followers to engage in weapons training and to become physically fit – even laying out a suggested exercise regimen. Disturbingly, *Ways* also explains how followers of violent Islamist ideology can participate in the cause by "raising children to love jihad and those who wage it." This includes having children "[l]isten to tapes of sermons that discuss jihad-related topics such as martyrdom and the virtues of the martyr."

---

39 Ways to Serve and Participate in Jihad
Muhammad bin Ahmad as-Salim
2003, (Excerpts)

Introduction

All Praise is for Allah who has obligated Jihad upon his servants, and has promised them firm establishment on Earth and dominance over the people of disbelief. And may Prayers and Peace be upon the best of His servants, the one who truly struggled in the Path of Allah until he achieved that which was certain (death). May Allah send Prayers and Peace upon him and his household and his fine and pure Companions.

As for what follows:

My noble brothers: the times in which we live are times of tribulation and estrangement for Islam that history has not witnessed before, where strangeness has become the norm and tribulation has become widespread, and where the entire Earth has become a stage for this conflict and for the expulsion of those who are firm upon their Din and hold onto it and defend it with their tongues and weapons. . . therefore, the entire world has announced its war on terrorism - or, rather, on Jihad - and its opposition to it and its various forms from being utilized by the Muslims.

So, Islam attacked from a single bow, and the nations of disbelief and their helpers from every corner of the Earth gathered against at-Ta'ifah al-Mansurah that took upon its shoulders this war against disbelief and the disbelievers - a clear and intense war void of any rest or mercy - until the Command of Allah arrives while they are upon that, and they will not be harmed by those who betray them from

Muhammad bin Ahmad as-Salim
('Isa al-'Awshin)
19/5/1424 H

39 **to Serve and Participate in Jihad**

At-Tibyan Publications

the treacherous or defeated Muslims or those who have drowned in the mud of this lowly worldly life. And they will not be harmed by those who oppose them from the groups of disbelief and the gangs of apostates and deniers, or from the misguided innovators. And there is no doubt that Jihad today is from the most virtuous of means of gaining nearness to Allah. In fact, it is an obligation that Allah has obligated upon us, and there is nothing more obligatory upon the Muslims after having belief in Allah than Jihad and repelling the invader who has occupied the lands of the Muslims.

*If you turned towards Islam in a land * You would find it to be like a bird whose wings have been cut off*

Jihad today is the Ummah's only choice, as the enemy today has occupied the lands of the Muslims - one by one - as Allah the Exalted said: "... And they will never cease fighting you until they cause you to turn back from your Din, if they are able to do so...

So, the Muslims today are left with no choice but that of Jihad and the language of weaponry.

Tell me, by your Lord: an invading enemy who has occupied lands, violated honor, made orphans out of children and widows out of women, has begun to strike at Islam in every valley. . . after all of this, is there a doubt that the only way to come to an understanding with this enemy is through the language of force and revenge?

So, iron is not to be fought except with iron, and force is not to be met except with force...

And it has been established for us in the Qur'an and the Sunnah - and reality bears witness to this and confirms it - that negotiations and peace do not bring back upon those who seek them anything except clear loss and dismal failure, and an increase in servitude to other than Allah and submission to the transgressors. You are warned of those who seek them in the name of the Muslims from the treacherous rulers who are not from us and whom we are not from them. Rather, they are an archenemy to us, as through them, the disbelievers have toyed with us, and through their plans and deceptions, our rights have been taken and usurped.

How can it be otherwise while Allah has said in His Book and has informed that they have started the war with us for one specific goal, and that is : "... until they cause you to turn back from your Din if they are able to... ?"

*There is no solution except for the greatest Jihad * World peace no longer satisfies us,*

*There is no peace for the enemy. This is a legislation * and belief in every Muslim heart.*

From this standpoint, and since Jihad is the choice of the Ummah and the necessary and ordained obligation, I decided - after consulting one of the brothers - to write about some steps that everyone can take to serve the Jihad and its people, and to energize the train of Jihad that is moving quickly despite the overwhelming arrogance of the transgressors.

And we have titled this document:

'39 Ways to Serve and Participate in the Jihad'

1. Make Your Intention for Jihad
2. Truthfully Ask Allah for Martyrdom
3. Go for Jihad Yourself
4. Make Jihad With Your Wealth
5. Help Prepare the Fighter Who Is Going For Jihad
6. Take Care of the Family Left Behind By the Fighter
7. Provide for the Families of the Martyrs
8. Providing for the Families of the Injured and Imprisoned
9. Collect Funds for the Mujahidin
10. Pay Zakah to Them
11. Cooperate In Treating the Wounded
12. Praise the Mujahidin and Mention Their Accounts and Call the People to Follow In Their Footsteps
13. Encourage the Mujahidin and Incite Them to Continue
14. Speak Out For the Mujahidin and Defend Them
15. Expose the Hypocrites and Traitors
16. Call and Incite the People to Jihad
17. Advise the Muslims and the Mujahidin
18. Hide the Secrets of the Mujahidin that the Enemy Can Benefit From
19. Supplicate For Them
20. The Supplication of Distress (Qunut an-Nawazil
21. Follow and Spread the News of the Jihad
22. Participate in Spreading Their Releases of Books and Publications
23. Issue Fatawa That Aide Them
24. Stay Connected With the Scholars and Preachers and Inform Them of the Situation of the Mujahidin
25. Become Physically Fit
26. Train With Weapons and Learn How To Shoot
27. Learn to Swim and Ride Horses
28. Learn First-Aid
29. Learn the Fiqh of Jihad
30. Giving Shelter to the Mujahidin and Honoring Them
31. Have Enmity Towards the Disbelievers and Hate Them
32. Expend Effort to Free Our Captives
33. Spread the News About the Captives and Be Concerned With their Affairs
34. Electronic Jihad
35. Stand in Opposition to the Disbelievers
36. Raise Your Children to Love Jihad and Its People
37. Abandon Luxury
38. Boycott the Goods of the Enemy
39. Do Not Hire Workers from the War Wagers (Harbiyyin)

Editor's Comments

Today's domestic terror threats are not limited to the traditional religious-based violent extremism associated with al-Qa'ida and other similar terrorist organizations. In fact, these "other" types of domestic terror plots are far more common and are occurring throughout the entire United States. It is interesting to note that a person has a greater chance of witnessing one of these "other" terrorist schemes, then an official al-Qa'ida sanctioned operation.

When examining these "other" forms of domestic terror, one only has to look for:

- Abortion extremists
- Anarchist extremism
- Eco-terrorists and animal rights extremists
- Militia extremism
- School and workplace mass-shootings
- Sovereign citizens movement
- White supremacy extremism

_____

Further Discussion

1. Discuss the theory of **Homegrown Jihadists**.

2. Discuss **"lone wolves"** and their impact on terrorist operations in the United States.

3. Discuss the theories of **R**adicalization and **Violent Extremism**.

4. Discuss **terrorist propaganda** and their **internet campaign**.

5. Discuss '**39 Ways to Serve and Participate in the Jihad**' and its impact on radicalization.

Chapter 12

Combating Terrorism

"The gravest danger our Nation faces lies at the crossroads of radicalism and technology. Our enemies have openly declared that they are seeking weapons of mass destruction, and evidence indicates that they are doing so with determination. The United States will not allow these efforts to succeed. History will judge harshly those who saw this coming danger but failed to act. In the new world we have entered, the only path to peace and security is the path of action."

President George W. Bush

Henry Crumpton, Coordinator for Counterterrorism
U.S. Department of State, January 2006

"Our global interdependence makes us stronger, but also in some aspects, more vulnerable. There is also a backlash from those who view globalization as a threat to traditional culture and their vested interests. Some discontented, illiberal non-state actors perceive themselves under attack and, therefore, resort to offensive action. This is the case with Al Qaeda and affiliated organizations. Yet, these enemies face a strategic environment featuring nation states with an overwhelming dominance in conventional military forces. This includes but is not limited to the U.S. It's no surprise, then, that our actual and potential enemies have taken note of our conventional superiority and acted to dislocate it. State actors, such as North Korea and Iran, seek irregular means to engage their foes. Iran uses proxies such as Hizballah. Non-state actors like Al Qaeda have also developed asymmetric approaches that allow them to side-step conventional military power. They embrace terror as a tactic, but on such a level as to provide them strategic impact. Toward that end, they seek to acquire capabilities that can pose catastrophic threats, such as WMD, disruptive technologies, or a combination of these measures."

United States Executive Office of the President
National Strategy for Counterterrorism
June 2011, (Excerpts)

Principles That Guide our Counterterrorism Efforts

Although the terrorist organizations that threaten us are far from monolithic, our CT efforts are guided by core principles: Adhering to U.S. Core Values; Building Security Partnerships; Applying CT Tools and Capabilities Appropriately; and Building a Culture of Resilience

We are committed to upholding our most cherished values as a nation not just because doing so is right but also because doing so enhances our security. Adherence to those core values—respecting human rights, fostering good governance, respecting privacy and civil liberties, committing to security and transparency, and upholding the rule of law—enables us to build broad international coalitions to act against the common threat posed by our adversaries while further delegitimizing, isolating, and weakening their efforts. The United States is dedicated to upholding the rule of law by maintaining an effective, durable legal framework for CT operations and bringing terrorists to justice. U.S. efforts with partners are central to achieving our CT goals, and we are committed to building security partnerships even as we recognize and work to improve shortfalls in our cooperation with partner nations.

Our CT efforts must also address both near- and long-term considerations—taking timely action to protect the American people while ensuring that our efforts are in the long-term security interests of our country. Our approach to political change in the Middle East and

North Africa illustrates that promoting representative and accountable governance is a core tenet of U.S. foreign policy and directly contributes to our CT goals.

At the same time, we recognize that no nation, no matter how powerful, can prevent every threat from coming to fruition. That is why we are focused on building a culture of resilience able to prevent, respond to, or recover fully from any potential act of terror directed at the United States.

Adhering to U.S. Core Values

The United States was founded upon a belief in a core set of values that is written into our founding documents and woven into the very fabric of our society. Where terrorists offer injustice, disorder, and destruction the United States must stand for freedom, fairness, equality, dignity, hope, and opportunity. The power and appeal of our values enables the United States to build a broad coalition to act collectively against the common threat posed by terrorists, further delegitimizing, isolating, and weakening our adversaries.

- **Respect for Human Rights**. Our respect for universal rights stands in stark contrast with the actions of al-Qa'ida, its affiliates and adherents, and other terrorist organizations. Contrasting a positive U.S. agenda that supports the rights of free speech, assembly, and democracy with the death and destruction offered by our terrorist adversaries helps undermine and undercut their appeal, isolating them from the very population they rely on for support. Our respect for universal rights must include living them through our own actions. Cruel and inhumane interrogation methods are not only inconsistent with U.S. values, they undermine the rule of law and are ineffective means of gaining the intelligence required to counter the threats we face. We will maximize our ability to collect intelligence from individuals in detention by relying on our most effective tool—the skill, expertise, and professionalism of our personnel.

- **Encouraging Responsive Governance**. Promoting representative, responsive governance is a core tenet of U.S. foreign policy and directly contributes to our CT goals. Governments that place the will of their people first and encourage peaceful change directly contradict the al-Qa'ida ideology. Governments that are responsive to the needs of their citizens diminish the discontent of their people and the associated drivers and grievances that al-Qa'ida actively attempts to exploit. Effective governance reduces the traction and space for al-Qa'ida, reducing its resonance and contributing to what it fears most—irrelevance.

- **Respect for Privacy Rights, Civil Liberties, and Civil Rights**. Respect for privacy rights, civil liberties, and civil rights is a critical component of our Strategy. Indeed, preservation of those rights and liberties is essential to maintain the support of the American people for our CT efforts. By ensuring that CT policies and tools are narrowly tailored and applied to achieve specific, concrete security gains, the United States will optimize its security and protect the liberties of its citizens.

Murder of U.S. Nationals Outside the United States; Conspiracy to Murder U.S.
Nationals Outside the United States; Attack on a Federal Facility Resulting in Death

AYMAN AL-ZAWAHIRI

Aliases:

Abu Muhammad, Abu Fatima, Muhammad Ibrahim, Abu Abdallah, Abu al-Mu'iz, The Doctor, The Teacher, Nur, Ustaz, Abu Mohammed, Abu Mohammed Nur al-Deen, Abdel Muaz, Dr. Ayman al Zawahiri

DESCRIPTION

Date(s) of Birth Used:	June 19, 1951	Hair:	Brown/Black
Place of Birth:	Egypt	Eyes:	Dark
Height:	Unkown	Complexion:	Olive
Weight:	Unknown	Sex:	Male
Build:	Unknown	Citizenship:	Egyptian
		Languages:	Arabic; French

Scars and Marks: None known

Remarks: Al-Zawahiri is a physician and the founder of the Egyptian Islamic Jihad (EIJ). This organization opposes the secular Egyptian Government and seeks its overthrow through violent means. In approximately 1998, the EIJ led by Al-Zawahiri merged with Al Qaeda.

CAUTION

Ayman Al-Zawahiri has been indicted for his alleged role in the August 7, 1998, bombings of the United States Embassies in Dar es Salaam, Tanzania, and Nairobi, Kenya.

REWARD

The Rewards For Justice Program, United States Department of State, is offering a reward of up to $25 million for information leading directly to the apprehension or conviction of Ayman Al-Zawahiri.

SHOULD BE CONSIDERED ARMED AND DANGEROUS

If you have any information concerning this person, please contact your local FBI office or the nearest American Embassy or Consulate.

- **Balancing Security and Transparency**. Democratic institutions function best in an environment of transparency and open discussion of national issues. Wherever and whenever possible, the United States will make information available to the American people about the threats we face and the steps being taken to mitigate those threats. A well-informed American public is a source of our strength. Information enables the public to make informed judgments about its own security, act responsibly and with resilience in the face of adversity or attack, and contribute its vigilance to the country's collective security. Yet at times, some information must be protected from disclosure—to protect personnel and our sources and methods of gathering information and to preserve our ability to counter the attack plans of terrorists.

- **Upholding the Rule of Law**. Our commitment to the rule of law is fundamental to supporting the development of an international, regional, and local order that is capable of identifying and disrupting terrorist attacks, bringing terrorists to justice for their acts, and creating an environment in every country around the world that is inhospitable to terrorists and terrorist organizations.

  o **Maintaining an Effective, Durable Legal Framework for CT Operations**. In the immediate aftermath of the September 11, 2001 attacks, the United States Government was confronted with countering the terrorist threat in an environment of legal uncertainty in which long-established legal rules were applied to circumstances not seen before in this country. Since then we have refined and applied a legal framework that ensures all CT activities and operations are placed on a solid legal footing. Moving forward, we must ensure that this legal framework remains both effective and durable. To remain effective, this framework must provide the necessary tools to defeat U.S. adversaries and maintain the safety of the American people. To remain durable this framework must withstand legal challenge, survive scrutiny, and earn the support of Congress and the American people as well as our partners and allies. It must also maintain sufficient flexibility to adjust to the changing threat and environment.

  o **Bringing Terrorists to Justice**. The successful prosecution of terrorists will continue to play a critical role in U.S. CT efforts, enabling the United States to disrupt and deter terrorist activity; gather intelligence from those lawfully held in U.S. custody; dismantle organizations by incarcerating key members and operatives; and gain a measure of justice by prosecuting those who have plotted or participated in attacks. We will work with our foreign partners to build their willingness and capacity to bring to justice suspected terrorists who operate within their borders. When other countries are unwilling or unable to take action against terrorists within their borders who threaten the United States, they should be taken into U.S. custody and tried in U.S. civilian courts or by military commission.

Building Security Partnerships

The United States alone cannot eliminate every terrorist or terrorist organization that threatens our safety, security, or interests. Therefore, we must join with key partners and allies to share the burdens of common security.

- **Accepting Varying Degrees of Partnership**. The United States and its partners are engaged in the full range of cooperative CT activities—from intelligence sharing to joint training and operations and from countering radicalization to pursuing community resilience programs. The United States partners best with nations that share our common values, have similar democratic institutions, and bring a long history of collaboration in pursuit of our shared security. With these partners the habits of cooperation established in other security-related settings have transferred themselves relatively smoothly and efficiently to CT.

    In some cases partnerships are in place with countries with whom the United States has very little in common except for the desire to defeat al-Qa'ida and its affiliates and adherents. These partners may not share U.S. values or even

Coalition special operations forces assault a building in search of a mock high-value target in Darwsko, Poland, Sept. 20, 2010, during the opening ceremony for exercise Jackal Stone 2010. Photo credit: United States Department of Defense.

our broader vision of regional and global security. Yet it is in our interest to build habits and patterns of CT cooperation with such partners, working to push them in a direction that advances CT objectives while demonstrating through our example the value of upholding human rights and responsible governance. Furthermore, these partners will ultimately be more stable and successful if they move toward these principles.

- **Leveraging Multilateral Institutions**. To counter violent extremists who work in scores of countries around the globe, the United States is drawing on the resources and strengthening the activities of multilateral institutions at the international, regional, and sub-regional levels. Working with and through these institutions can have multiple benefits: It increases the engagement of our partners, reduces the financial burden on the United States, and enhances the legitimacy of our CT efforts by advancing our objectives without a unilateral, U.S. label. The United States is committed to strengthening the global CT architecture in a manner that complements and reinforces the CT work of existing multilateral bodies. In doing so, we seek to avoid duplicating and diluting our own or our partners' efforts, recognizing that many of our partners have capacity limitations and cannot participate adequately across too broad a range of multilateral fora.

Applying CT Tools and Capabilities Appropriately

As the threat from al-Qa'ida and its affiliates and adherents continues to evolve, the United States must continually evaluate the tools and capabilities we use to ensure that our efforts are appropriate and consistent with U.S. laws, values, and long-term strategic objectives.

- **Pursuing a "Whole-of-Government" Effort:** To succeed at both the tactical and strategic levels, we must foster a rapid, coordinated, and effective CT effort that reflects the full capabilities and resources of our entire government. That is why this Strategy integrates the capabilities and authorities of each department and agency, ensuring that the right tools are applied at the right time to the right situation in a manner that is consistent with U.S. laws.

- **Balancing Near- and Long-Term CT Considerations.** We need to pursue the ultimate defeat of al-Qa'ida and its affiliates without acting in a way that undermines our ability to discredit its ideology. The exercise of American power against terrorist threats must be done in a thoughtful, reasoned, and proportionate way that both enhances U.S. security and delegitimizes the actions of those who use terrorism. The United States must always carefully weigh the costs and risks of its actions against the costs and risks of inaction, recognizing that certain tactical successes can have unintended consequences that sometimes contribute to costs at the strategic level.

Building a Culture of Resilience

To pursue our CT objectives, we must also create a culture of preparedness and resilience2 that will allow the United States to prevent or—if necessary—respond to and recover successfully from any potential act of terror directed at our nation.

- Building Essential Components of Resilience. Al-Qa'ida believes that it can cause the United States to change course in its foreign and national security policies by inflicting economic and psychological damage through terrorist attacks. Denying success to al-Qa'ida therefore means, in part, demonstrating that the United States has and will continue to construct effective defenses to protect our vital assets, whether they are critical infrastructure, iconic national landmarks, or—most importantly—our population. Presenting the United States as a "hardened" target is unlikely to cause al-Qa'ida and its affiliates and adherents to abandon terrorism, but it can deter them from attacking particular targets or persuade them that their efforts are unlikely to succeed. The United States also contributes to its collective resilience by demonstrating to al-Qa'ida that we have the individual, community, and economic strength to absorb, rebuild, and recover from any catastrophic event, whether manmade or naturally occurring.

Our Overarching Goals- Combating Terrorism

With our core principles as the foundation of our efforts, the United States aims to achieve eight overarching CT goals. Taken together, these desired end states articulate a framework for the success of the United States global counterterrorism mission.

- **Protect the American People, Homeland, and American Interests**. The most solemn responsibility of the President and the United States Government is to protect the American people, both at home and abroad. This includes eliminating threats to their physical safety, countering threats to global peace and security, and promoting and protecting U.S. interests around the globe.

- **Disrupt, Degrade, Dismantle, and Defeat al-Qa'ida and Its Affiliates and Adherents**. The American people and interests will not be secure from attacks until this threat is eliminated—its primary individuals and groups rendered powerless, and its message relegated to irrelevance.

- **Prevent Terrorist Development, Acquisition, and Use of Weapons of Mass Destruction.** The danger of nuclear terrorism is the greatest threat to global security. Terrorist organizations, including al-Qa'ida, have engaged in efforts to develop and acquire weapons of mass destruction (WMD)—and if successful, they are likely to use them. Therefore, the United States will work with partners around the world to deter WMD theft, smuggling, and terrorist use; target and disrupt terrorist networks that engage in WMD-related activities; secure nuclear, biological, and chemical materials; prevent illicit trafficking of WMD-related materiel; provide multilateral nonproliferation organizations with the resources, capabilities, and authorities they need to be effective; and deepen international cooperation and strengthen institutions and partnerships that prevent WMD and nuclear materials from falling into the hands of terrorists. Success will require us to work with the international community in each of these areas while establishing security measures commensurate with the

Interviewing Saddam: Teasing Out the Truth

Imagine sitting across from Saddam Hussein every day for nearly seven straight months—slowly gaining his trust, getting him to spill secrets on everything from whether he gave the order to gas the Kurds (he did) to whether he really had weapons of mass destruction on the eve of war (he didn't). All the while gathering information that would ultimately be used to prosecute the deposed dictator in an Iraqi court.

That was the job of FBI Special Agent George Piro, who told his story on the TV news program *60 Minutes* in January 2008.

Soon after Saddam was pulled out of a spider hole on December 13, 2003, the CIA—knowing the former dictator would ultimately have to answer for his crimes against the Iraqi people—asked the FBI to debrief Hussein because of its respected work in gathering statements for court.

That's when the Bureau turned to Piro, an experienced counterterrorism investigator who was born in Beirut and speaks Arabic fluently. Piro was supported by a team of CIA analysts, as well as FBI agents, intelligence analysts, language specialists, and a behavioral profiler.

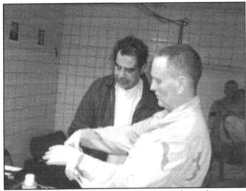

Piro knew getting Saddam to talk wouldn't be easy. He prepped by studying the former dictator's life so he could better connect with Saddam and more easily determine if he was being honest. It worked: during the first interview on January 13, 2004, Piro talked with the dictator about his four novels and Iraqi history. Hussein was impressed and asked Piro to come back.

From that day forward, everything Piro did was designed to build an emotional bond with Saddam to get him to talk truthfully. To make Hussein dependent on him and him alone, Piro became responsible for virtually every aspect of the ex-ruler's life, including his personal needs. He always treated Saddam with respect, knowing he would not respond to threats or tough tactics. As part of his plan, Piro also never told Hussein that he was an FBI field agent, instead letting him believe, for the sake of building credibility, that he was a high-level official who reported directly to the President.

It took time. Piro spent 5 to 7 hours a day with Saddam for months, taking advantage of every opportunity that presented itself, including listening to Hussein's poetry. Eventually, Saddam began to open up.

Among Saddam's revelations:

- Saddam misled the world into believing that he had weapons of mass destruction in the months leading up to the war because he feared another invasion by Iran, but he did fully intend to rebuild his WMD program.
- Saddam considered Usama bin Laden "a fanatic" and a threat who couldn't be trusted.
- The former dictator admitted "initially miscalculating President Bush and President Bush's intentions," Piro said, thinking the war would be more like the shortened air campaign of the Gulf War.
- Saddam never used look-alikes or body doubles as widely believed, thinking no one could really play his part.
- Hussein made the decision to invade neighboring Kuwait in 1990 following an insulting comment by one of its emirs.

Piro was so successful at befriending Saddam that the former dictator was visibly moved when they said goodbye. "I saw him tear up," Piro said during the television interview. And for the FBI, which gathered vital intelligence and evidence along the way, it was time well spent.

http://www.fbi.gov/about-us/history/a-centennial-history/a_new_era_of_national_security_2001-2008 threat, reinforcing counter-smuggling measures, and ensuring that all of these efforts are sustained over time.

- **Eliminate Safe-havens**. Al-Qa'ida and its affiliates and adherents rely on the physical sanctuary of ungoverned or poorly governed territories, where the absence of state control permits terrorists to travel, train, and engage in plotting. In close coordination with foreign partners, the United States will continue to contest and diminish al-Qa'ida's operating space through mutually reinforcing efforts designed to prevent al-Qa'ida from taking advantage of these ungoverned spaces. We will also build the will and capacity of states whose weaknesses al-Qa'ida exploits. Persistent insecurity and chaos in some regions can undermine efforts to increase political engagement and build capacity and provide assistance, thereby exacerbating chaos and insecurity. Our challenge is to break this cycle of state failure to constrict the space available to terrorist networks.

- **Build Enduring Counterterrorism Partnerships and Capabilities**. Foreign partners are essential to the success of our CT efforts; these states are often themselves the target of—and on the front lines in countering—terrorist threats. The United States will continue to rely on and leverage the capabilities of its foreign partners even as it looks to contribute to their capacity and bolster their will. To achieve our objectives, partners must demonstrate the willingness and ability to operate independently, augmenting and complementing U.S. CT efforts with their unique insights and capabilities in their countries and regions. Building strong enduring partnerships based on shared understandings of the threat and common objectives is essential to every one of our overarching CT objectives. Assisting partners to improve and expand governance in select instances is also critical, including strengthening the rule of law so that suspected terrorists can be brought to justice within a respected and transparent system. Success will depend on our ability to work with partners bilaterally, through efforts to achieve greater regional integration, and through multilateral and international institutions.

- **Degrade Links between al-Qa'ida and its Affiliates and Adherents**. Al-Qa'ida senior leaders in Pakistan continue to leverage local and regional affiliates and adherents worldwide through formal and informal alliances to advance their global agenda. Al-Qa'ida exploits local grievances to bolster recruitment, expand its operational reach, destabilize local governments, and reinforce safe-havens from which it and potentially other terrorist groups can operate and attack the United States. Together with our partners, we will degrade the capabilities of al-Qa'ida's local and regional affiliates and adherents, monitor their communications with al-Qa'ida leaders, drive fissures between these groups and their bases of support, and isolate al-Qa'ida from local and regional affiliates and adherents who can augment its capabilities and further its agenda.

- **Counter al-Qa'ida Ideology and Its Resonance and Diminish the Specific Drivers of Violence that al-Qa'ida Exploits.** This Strategy prioritizes U.S. and partner efforts to undercut al-Qa'ida's fabricated legitimization of violence and its efforts to spread its ideology. As we have seen in the Middle East and North Africa, al-Qa'ida's calls for perpetual violence to address longstanding grievances have met a devastating rebuke in the face of nonviolent mass movements that seek solutions through expanded individual rights. Along with the majority of people across all religious and cultural traditions, we aim for a world in which al-Qa'ida is openly and widely rejected by all audiences as irrelevant to their aspirations and concerns, a world where al-Qa'ida's ideology does not shape perceptions of world and local events, inspire violence, or serve as a recruiting tool for the group or its adherents. Although achieving this objective is likely to require a concerted long-term effort, we must retain a focus on addressing the near-term challenge of preventing those individuals already on the brink from embracing al-Qa'ida ideology and resorting to violence. We will work closely with local and global partners, inside and outside governments, to discredit al-Qa'ida ideology and reduce its resonance. We will put forward a positive vision of engagement with foreign publics and support for universal rights that demonstrates that the United States aims to build while al-Qa'ida would only destroy. We will apply focused foreign and development assistance abroad. At the same time, we will continue to assist, engage, and connect communities to increase their collective resilience abroad and at home. These efforts strengthen bulwarks against radicalization, recruitment, and mobilization to violence in the name of al-Qa'ida and will focus in particular on those drivers that we know al-Qa'ida exploits.

> **"As extremists try to inspire acts of violence within our borders, we are responding with the strength of our communities, with the respect for the rule of law, and with the conviction that Muslim Americans are part of our American family."**
>
> President Barack Obama, State of the Union, January 2011

- **Deprive Terrorists of their Enabling Means.** Al-Qa'ida and its affiliates and adherents continue to derive significant financial support from donors in the Persian Gulf region and elsewhere through kidnapping for ransom and from exploitation of or control over lucrative elements of the local economy.

Terrorist facilitation extends beyond the financial arena to those who enable travel of recruits and operatives; acquisition and movement of materiel; and electronic and non-electronic communication. The United States will collaborate with partner nations around the world to increase our collective capacity to identify terrorist operatives and prevent their travel and movement of supplies across national borders and within states. We will continue to expand and enhance efforts aimed at blocking the flow of financial resources to and among terrorist groups and to disrupt terrorist facilitation and support activities, imposing sanctions or pursuing prosecutions to enforce violations and dissuade others. We will also continue our focus on countering kidnapping for ransom, which is an increasingly important funding source for al-Qa'ida and its affiliates and adherents. Through our diplomatic outreach, we will continue to encourage countries—especially those in Europe—to adopt a policy against making concessions to kidnappers while using tailored messages unilaterally and with our partners to delegitimize the taking of hostages. Mass media and the Internet in particular have emerged as enablers for terrorist planning, facilitation, and communication, and we will continue to counter terrorists' ability to exploit them.

The Homeland

For the past decade, the preponderance of the United States' CT effort has been aimed at preventing the recurrence of an attack on the Homeland directed by al-Qa'ida. That includes disrupting plots as well as working to constrain al-Qa'ida's ability to plan and train for attacks by shrinking the size and security of its safe-havens. Offensive efforts to protect the Homeland have been complemented by equally robust defensive efforts to prevent terrorists from entering the United States or from operating freely inside U.S. borders. To support the defensive side of this equation, we have made massive investments in our aviation, maritime, and border-security capabilities and information sharing to make the United States a hardened and increasingly difficult target for terrorists to penetrate.

These efforts must continue. We know al-Qa'ida and its affiliates continue to try to identify operatives overseas and develop new methods of attack that can evade U.S. defensive measures. At the same time, plots directed and planned from overseas are not the only sort of terrorist threat we face. Individuals inspired by but not directly connected to al-Qa'ida have engaged in terrorism in the U.S. Homeland. Others are likely to try to follow their example, and so we must remain vigilant.

We recognize that the operating environment in the Homeland is quite different from any other country or region. First, the United States exercises sovereign control and can apply the full strength of the U.S. legal system, drawing on the capabilities of U.S. law enforcement and homeland security communities to detect, disrupt, and defeat terrorist threats. Second, in the Homeland, the capabilities and resources of state, local, and tribal entities serve as a powerful force multiplier for the Federal government's CT efforts.

Integrating and harmonizing the efforts of Federal, state, local and tribal entities remains a challenge. As the threat continues to evolve, our efforts to protect against those threats must evolve as well.

The United States will rely extensively on a broad range of tools and capabilities that are essential to our ability to detect, disrupt, and defeat plots to attack the Homeland even though not all of these tools and capabilities have been developed exclusively for CT purposes. Such tools include capabilities related to border protection and security; aviation security and screening; aerospace control; maritime/port security; cargo security; cyber security; nuclear, radiological, biological, and chemical materials and the ability to detect their illicit use; biometrics; critical infrastructure protection; force protection; all hazards preparedness; community engagement; and information sharing among law enforcement organizations at all levels.

We are working to bring to bear many of these capabilities to build resilience within our communities here at home against al-Qa'ida inspired radicalization, recruitment, and mobilization to violence. Although increasing our engagement and partnership with communities can help protect them from the influence of al- Qa'ida and its affiliates and adherents, we must ensure that we remain engaged in the full range of community concerns and interests. Just as the terrorist threat we face in the United States is multifaceted and cannot be boiled down to a single group or community, so must our efforts to counter it not be reduced to a one-size-fits-all approach. Supporting community leaders and influential local stakeholders as they develop solutions tailored to their own particular circumstances is a government, we will continue to institutionalize successful practices and provide advice and guidance where appropriate, with the goal of preventing al-Qa'ida inspired radicalization.

Although this Strategy focuses predominantly on the al-Qa'ida linked and inspired threats, we also need to maintain careful scrutiny of a range of foreign and domestic groups and individuals assessed as posing potential terrorist threats, including those who operate and undertake activities in the United States in furtherance of their overseas agendas. We must be vigilant against all overseas-based threats to the Homeland, just as we must be vigilant against U.S. based terrorist activity—be it focused domestically or on plotting to attack overseas targets.

To ensure that we are constantly addressing any deficiencies or weaknesses in our CT system, the President ordered comprehensive reviews and corrective actions in the immediate aftermath of attempted attacks. Following the tragic attack at Fort Hood, the failed attempt to bomb a Detroit-bound airliner, and the attempted bombing of Times Square, we have taken numerous steps to address information sharing shortfalls within the government, strengthen analysis and the integration of intelligence, and enhance aviation security, including by implementing a new, real-time, threat-based screening policy for all international flights to the United States. Such reviews and attendant corrective actions need to be a constant feature of our CT effort.

**Hearing before the Senate Committee on
Homeland Security and Governmental Affairs
"Ten Years After 9/11: Are We Safer?"
The Honorable Matthew G. Olsen, Director
National Counterterrorism Center
September 13, 2011, (Excerpts)**

Introduction

Chairman Lieberman, Ranking Member Collins, members of the Committee, thank you for the opportunity to appear before you today—along with Homeland Security Secretary Napolitano and FBI Director Mueller—to discuss the evolution of the terrorist threat facing our nation over the last decade and how we are addressing that threat. I also want to thank the Committee for your support of the National Counterterrorism Center, and for the strong working relationship this Committee has developed with NCTC.

It is appropriate that we continue this week to reflect on the day that our nation suffered the single most destructive terrorist attack in our history. In so doing, we honor those who perished and the sacrifices made by the families and loved ones left behind.

The Committee's hearing is entitled, Ten Years After 9/11: Are We Safer? The short answer to that question is yes. While al-Qaida and its affiliates continue to pose a significant threat, we are safer than we were on September 11, 2001. Thanks to the skill and hard work of thousands of dedicated men and women in the intelligence, homeland security, diplomatic, and law enforcement communities as well as our men and women in uniform—we have made significant progress in the fight against terrorism.

With the support and guidance of Congress, we have built an enduring counterterrorism framework by creating new institutions to address terrorist threats. This framework including the National Counterterrorism Center (NCTC)—has increased the sharing of terrorism-related information within the government, and between federal, state, local and tribal law enforcement, as well as with the public. The government has prevented attacks by disrupting terrorists in the United States and abroad, and prosecuting those arrested for supporting terrorists or their operations. The United States has worked with its partners internationally to promote governance and deny safe haven to terrorists, as well as to counter the flow of funds to terror groups, including designating terrorist entities to cut off funding worldwide.
Al-Qaida as an organization is weakened. We have placed relentless pressure on its leadership and worked to deny it safe haven, resources, and the ability to plan and train. Usama Bin Ladin, who more than anyone was responsible for the September 11, 2001, terrorist attacks, is dead—killed by U.S. forces in one of the most bold and challenging counterterrorism operations in our history.

At the same time, al-Qaida, its affiliates and adherents around the world, as well as other terrorist organizations, continue to pose a significant threat to our country. This threat is resilient and adaptive and will persist for the foreseeable future. America's campaign against terrorism did not end with the mission at Bin Ladin's compound in Abbottabad, Pakistan in May. A decade after the September 11th attacks, we remain at war with al-Qaida and face an evolving threat from its affiliates and adherents. Confronting this threat and working with resolve to prevent another terrorist attack is NCTC's focus, first and foremost.

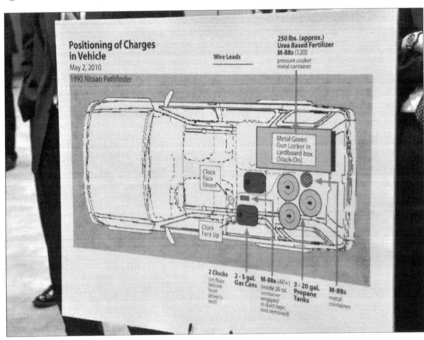

Faisal Shahzad was arrested in connection with an attempted car bombing in New York City on May 2, 2010. A schematic of the attempted car bomb is displayed, showing the positioning of the explosive charges that were placed in the vehicle. Photo credit: Craig Crawford for The Department of Justice.

In my statement, I will begin by examining the evolution of the terrorist threat. I will then describe the role of NCTC and the recent reforms we have adopted. Finally, I will identify some of the challenges we face going forward.

The Evolving Terrorist Threat

Al-Qa'ida Core and its Allies in Pakistan Pose Threat Despite Degradation

Counterterrorism successes and sustained pressure have left al-Qaida at its weakest point in the last ten years, and significantly degraded the group's ability to conduct attacks outside of South Asia. This is exemplified by the lack of a successful operation in the West since the 7 July 2005 transportation bombings in London. Further, the killing of Usama bin Ladin in May and last month's killing of al-Qaida's newest deputy, Atiyah abd al Rahman, mark strategic milestones in our fight against al-Qaida, and are likely to accelerate al-Qaida's decline, but does not mute the impact of its narrative.

Al-Qa'ida Core

Al-Qaida core's capability to recruit, train, and deploy operatives for anti-Western attacks has been reduced. Yet the group remains the ideological leader of the global extremist movement and continues to influence extremists through public media statements. Core al-Qaida's advancement of several unsuccessful smaller-scale Western plots in the past two years, including against the homeland and Europe, highlight its ability to continue some attack preparations while under sustained counterterrorism pressure, and we remain concerned al-Qaida may be plotting an attack against the United States at home or overseas. Moreover, while most observers view the non-violent successful tactics of the Arab Spring demonstrators in Egypt and Tunisia as a repudiation of al-Qaida message and approach, the group's leadership continues to seek openings for its destructive narrative. Since January they have prepared at least 12 propaganda messages related to the Arab Spring, making it a key theme of their media strategy.

In the aftermath of Bin Ladin's death, al-Qaida leaders moved quickly to name his long-time deputy, Ayman al-Zawahiri, as his successor. Al-Zawahiri is the only active leader remaining from that core group of al-Qaida leaders who were in Afghanistan in the lead-up to 9/11. Since this announcement, some affiliates have publicly sworn allegiance and pledged support to Zawahiri, reinforcing the importance of al-Qaida core's leadership role in the global movement.

While al-Qaida core's capabilities to attack the United States are diminished, and they have failed to conduct another homeland attack in the 10 years since 9/11, the group's intent to strike us at home remains strong. In advance of the 9/11 anniversary this year, al-Qaida leader al-Zawahiri issued a public statement encouraging sympathizers to attack the United States.

Recently obtained information suggests that as of February 2010, al-Qaida was contemplating large attacks in the homeland on symbolic dates, specifically the tenth anniversary of 9/11. However, degraded external operational capabilities suggest al-Qaida may seek smaller scale, achievable tactics and targets of opportunity. As of spring 2010, al-Qaida core believed targets worthy of the group's focus included prominent transportation, infrastructure, economic, and political targets.

Al-Qa'ida's Pakistan-Based Militant Allies

The success of Operation Enduring Freedom after 9/11 in expelling al-Qaida from its Afghanistan safe haven forced the group to rely on local allies and new hosts across the border in Pakistan. Since its relocation, al-Qaida has consistently encouraged its local militant allies to expand their operational agendas to include U.S. and Western targets—both within the region and overseas. Faisal Shahzad's May 2010 attempted bombing in Times Square is a stark reminder that al-Qaida allies such as Tehrik-e-Taliban Pakistan

The compound in Abbottabad, Pakistan, where Usama Bin Ladin was mortally wounded by Special Forces units of the United States of America on May 1, 2011. Photo credit: United States Central Intelligence Agency.

(TTP) continue to threaten U.S. interests in the Afghanistan and Pakistan region. Such threats—including threats to avenge Bin Ladin's death—have the stated intent and demonstrated capability to attempt attacks in the in the United States.

- TTP in mid-June said the group supports Ayman al-Zawahiri as al-Qaida new leader and further claimed Zawahiri is TTP's –chief and supreme leader; TTP's spokesman described al-Zawahiri as a capable person who would inspire the group to take on the West. A TTP deputy claimed in an AP interview that TTP would complete [bin Ladin's mission] with a new zeal and a separate leader vowed to hit American targets outside Pakistan.

- Other al-Qaida allies in Pakistan and Afghanistan, notably the Afghan Taliban and the Haqqani Network, have close ties to al-Qaida. These groups have demonstrated the intent and capability to conduct attacks against U.S. persons and targets in Afghanistan, and we are looking closely for any indicators of attack planning in the West. Both groups also continue to provide safe haven to al-Qaida and neither has publicly disavowed tiesto the terrorist group despite sustained counterterrorism pressure.

- Lashkar-e-Tayyiba (LT)—perpetrators of the November 2008 coordinated armed assault against multiple targets in Mumbai—is one of the largest and most dangerous of the militant groups and poses a threat to a range of interests in South Asia. LT has been implicated in multiple attacks in India, including the 11 July 2006 attack on Mumbai commuter trains and the December 2001 armed assault on the Indian Parliament building. Attacks in Kashmir and India have had a destabilizing effect on the region, increasing tensions between India and Pakistan. LT is increasing its operational role in attacks against coalition forces in Afghanistan. LT has not previously conducted attacks in the United States or the West; however, LT, or individuals who trained with LT in the past but have adopted a more global extremist agenda, could pose a threat to the homeland and the West, particularly if they were to work in collaboration with al-Qaida, its allies and affiliates, or other like-minded terrorists.

The Evolution of al-Qa'ida's Regional Affiliates and the Increasing Threat to the West

Ten years after 9/11, we face a much more diffuse and diversified threat, largely due to the emergence and evolution of regional affiliates who support al-Qaida core's strategy of creating a self-sustaining global extremist movement. To varying degrees, the affiliates have increased the scope of their operations, seeking to strike some U.S. and Western targets both inside and outside of their respective regions.

Al-Qa'ida in the Arabian Peninsula (AQAP)

Yemen was already a key battleground and regional base of operations from which AQAP could plan attacks, train recruits, and facilitate the movement of operatives prior to the outbreak of the Arab Spring related violence earlier this year. AQAP's gains and the regime's governing challenges are increasing our concerns about the group's capability to conduct additional attacks targeting the homeland and U.S. interests overseas, as well as our concerns about the group's continuing propaganda efforts designed to inspire like-minded Western extremists to conduct attacks in their home countries.

- AQAP's two attempted attacks against the homeland—the attempted airliner attack during December 2009, and its follow-on effort to down two U.S. bound cargo planes in October 2010 using explosives-laden printer cartridges were indicative of a determined enemy capable of adjusting tactics to achieve success.

- AQAP also is encouraging extremists in the United States to strike here. Each of AQAP's first six issues of Inspire magazine has featured a section titled, Open Source Jihad, which aims to provide easily followed instructions on weapons use, explosives construction, and targeting ideas.

Al-Qa'ida Operatives in East Africa and Al-Shabaab

East Africa remains a key operating area for the Somalia-based terrorist and insurgent group al-Shabaab and other al- Qaida associates. Despite recent setbacks in Mogadishu, al-Shabaab is still a significant threat to U.S. interests and remains committed to al-Qaida's ideology. At least 20 U.S. persons—the majority of whom are ethnic Somalis-- have traveled to Somalia since 2006 to fight and train with al-Shabaab. The impact of the famine on the fighting in Somalia is not yet clear.

- In the past year, at least two young men who left the United States and traveled to Somalia were killed while fighting with al-Shabaab.

- The June death in Somalia of al-Qaida veteran Fazul Abdullah Muhammad, a.k.a. Harun Fazul, removes one of the most capable operatives in the region. Nonetheless, we remain concerned that foreign fighters associated with his network continue to train and plot against U.S. and Western targets.

Al-Qa'ida in the Lands of the Islamic Maghreb (AQIM)

AQIM has had limited success in exploiting the Arab Spring in North Africa, and there is no indication their propaganda has found a receptive audience. AQIM threatens U.S. and other Western interests in North and West Africa, primarily through kidnap-for-ransom operations and small arms attacks; though, the group's recent execution of several French hostages and first suicide bombing attack in Niger last year demonstrate AQIM's lethality and attack range. Sustained Algerian efforts against AQIM have degraded the organization's ability to conduct high-casualty attacks in the country and compelled the group to shift its operational focus from northern Algeria to the vast, ungoverned Sahel region in the south.

- AQIM continues to hold multiple European hostages, most recently kidnapping an Italian woman in February.

Al-Qa'ida in Iraq (AQI)

Ongoing counterterrorism successes against AQI--to include the deaths of the group's top two leaders last year in a joint Iraqi/U.S. military operation--have continued to put pressure on the organization. AQI's recent public statement claiming 65 separate attacks in May and June indicate the group remains an active and capable al-Qaida affiliate. Immediately following UBL's death the current leader of AQI publically reaffirmed his group's support for al-Qaida and Ayman al-Zawahiri. The arrests in May of two AQI-affiliated Kentucky-based Iraqi refugees highlight the potential threat posed by U.S.-based AQI-associates. We assess that AQI remains committed to al-Qaida's global agenda and are concerned they may be intent on conducting external operations, to include in the homeland.

- Al-Qaida in Iraq has released two Arabic-language propaganda statements encouraging individual terrorist acts, including a January video that called for lone offender attacks against Western infrastructure and students and an early April interview in which AQI's leader generally reiterated the January call for attacks and noted that weapons used in Iraq are available in most countries.

State Sponsors of Terrorism

In September 2001, seven countries—Cuba, Iran, Iraq, Libya, North Korea, Sudan, and Syria—were on the State Sponsors of Terrorism List. Today, only Cuba, Iran, Sudan, and Syria remain.

Iran is still the foremost state sponsor, and since 9/11 the regime has expanded its involvement with terrorist and insurgent groups—primarily in Iraq and Afghanistan that target U.S. and Israeli interests. Iran's Islamic Revolutionary Guard Corps-Qods Force and Ministry of Intelligence and Security have been involved in the planning and execution of terrorist acts and the provision of lethal aid—such as weapons, money, and training—to these groups, particularly Lebanese Hizballah.

- Iran's relationship with Hizballah since 9/11 has evolved from a traditional state sponsor- proxy relationship to a strategic partnership that provides a unified front against Israel and the U.S.

- During the past decade, Syria has narrowed and shifted how and who it supports as a result of such events as the 9/11 attacks, the Palestinian intifadahs, the death of Arafat, and the Iraq war. The Assad regime limits support to groups directly relevant to Syrian interests in Lebanon, the Occupied Territories, and Iraq.

- Since 2001, Sudan has taken action against several terrorist groups within Sudan and gradually improved cooperation with the U.S. and regional partners. We remain concerned about permanent improvements in Khartoum's counterterrorism legislation, HAMAS, and Palestinian Islamic Jihad remaining in Sudan.

The National Counterterrorism Center

Created in the aftermath of the attacks on 9/11, the overarching mission of the NCTC is to lead the effort to combat international terrorism. In its 2004 report, the 9/11 Commission observed that, the United States confronts a number of less visible challenges that surpass the boundaries of traditional nation-states and call for quick, imaginative and agile responses. That observation—as true today as it was when the 9/11 Commission issued its report—led the Commission to recommend the creation of a National Counterterrorism Center. As the 9/11 Commission proposed: Breaking the mold of national government organization, this NCTC should be a center for joint operational planning and joint intelligence.

The National Counterterrorism Center in Washington, DC. Photo credit: Office of the Director of National Intelligence.

In December 2004, Congress established NCTC. The Intelligence Reform and Terrorism Prevention Act of 2004 set forth NCTC's key responsibilities. These responsibilities are captured in NCTC's mission statement: Lead our nation's effort to combat terrorism at home and abroad by analyzing the threat, sharing that information with our partners, and integrating all instruments of national power to ensure unity of effort.

Intelligence Analysis and Integration

By law, NCTC serves as the primary organization in the U.S. government for analyzing and integrating all intelligence possessed or acquired by the government pertaining to terrorism and counterterrorism, except intelligence pertaining exclusively to domestic terrorism and domestic counterterrorism. NCTC has a unique responsibility to examine all international terrorism issues, spanning geographic boundaries and allowing for intelligence to be analyzed regardless of whether it is collected inside or outside the United States. NCTC has access to the entire catalogue of reporting—both foreign and domestic—on terrorism issues.

NCTC's strategic analyses are vetted and coordinated throughout the intelligence community, which adds multiple analytic perspectives. NCTC produces coordinated assessments on such critical terrorism issues as terrorist safe havens, state sponsors of terrorism, counterterrorism cooperation worldwide, and regional terrorism issues and groups. NCTC also regularly prepares intelligence assessments that are integrated into NCTC's Directorate of Strategic Operational Planning to inform policymakers on the progress of U.S. counterterrorism efforts.

NCTC's strong analytic cadre, which includes detailees and assignees from across the intelligence community, means that NCTC products reflect the diversity of the entire intelligence community and not the analytic view of one group or agency.

Watch-listing

NCTC also serves as the central and shared knowledge bank on known and suspected terrorists and international terror groups, as well as their goals, strategies, capabilities, and networks of contacts and support. As the federal government's central and shared knowledge bank, NCTC has developed and maintains the Terrorist Identities Datamart Environment (TIDE) on known and suspected terrorists and terrorist groups. In this role, NCTC advances the most complete and accurate information picture to our partners to support terrorism analysts. We also support screening activities that ultimately help prevent terrorist plans and operations against U.S. interests.

Strategic Operational Planning

NCTC is charged with conducting strategic operational planning for counterterrorism activities, integrating all instruments of national power, including diplomatic, financial, military, intelligence, homeland security, and law enforcement activities. In this role, NCTC looks beyond individual department and agency missions toward the development of a single, unified counterterrorism effort across the federal government. NCTC develops interagency counterterrorism plans to help translate high level strategies and policy direction into coordinated department and agency activities to advance the President's objectives. These plans address a variety of counterterrorism goals, including regional issues, weapons of mass destruction-terrorism, and countering violent extremism. The strategic operational planning process integrates all phases of the planning cycle—developing a plan, monitoring its implementation, and assessing its effectiveness and resource allocations—and creates communities of interest to coordinate and integrate implementation.

For example, NCTC is joining with the Department of Homeland Security and the Federal Bureau of Investigation to conduct workshops across the United States that enable cities to better develop and refine their response plans to evolving terrorist threats. These -Joint Counterterrorism Awareness Workshops increase the ability of federal, state, local and private sectors partners to respond to a threat by discovering gaps in capabilities, planning, training and resources; and identify existing programs or resources that can close those gaps. The workshops also provide a venue to share best practices at the state and local levels and serve as a basis for identifying issues and gaps that may subsequently be addressed nationwide.

Interagency Threat Assessment and Coordination Group

In 2007, this Committee played an integral role in creating the Interagency Threat Assessment and Coordination Group, or ITACG. Located at NCTC, the ITACG is led by DHS in partnership with the FBI. The group brings together federal and nonfederal intelligence, law enforcement and first responder communities and is dedicated to bridging the intelligence information gap between traditional intelligence agencies and state, local, tribal and private sector partners. The ITACG's role in the intelligence community is to advocate for the intelligence and information needs of these key partners and to help federal intelligence agencies improve the way in which they produce and disseminate intelligence information to intelligence customers. The ITACG has representatives from a geographically diverse set organizations and agencies, with expertise in law enforcement, fire and rescue, and health services.

Key NCTC Initiatives

With the support of Congress, NCTC and the rest of the government have made strides in the fight against terrorism, but much work remains. We face threats from a dynamic and complex terrorist environment. NCTC is committed to changing and adapting to meet these threats and the challenges they present. In particular, over the last two years—with lessons learned from the failed airline bombing in December 2009–NCTC has implemented several initiatives to improve our ability to identify and prevent terrorist attacks.

Pursuit Group

In January 2010, NCTC created the Pursuit Group to develop tactical leads and pursue terrorism threats. The formation of the Pursuit Group has provided the counterterrorism community with a group of co-located analysts that have unparalleled data access and expertise, which enables Pursuit Group to focus exclusively on information that could lead to the discovery of threats aimed against the homeland or U.S. interests abroad. With teams comprised of personnel from across the intelligence community, with access to the broadest range of terrorism information available, Pursuit Group analysts are able to identify actionable leads that could otherwise remain disconnected or unknown. While the majority of the intelligence community understandably follows current threats, Pursuit Group analysts can ensure that terrorism cases are examined as thoroughly as possible by pursuing non-obvious and unresolved connections, identifying unknown, known or suspected terrorists, and focusing on seemingly unimportant details that could yield relevant information.

The Pursuit Group provides investigative leads, collection requirements, and potential source candidates to operational elements like the FBI, CIA, or DHS for intelligence purposes or action.   During the first 3 quarters of Fiscal Year 2011, the Pursuit Group completed over 800 actions that provided the counterterrorism partners, including the federal law enforcement community, with new knowledge and analysis on tactical terrorism threats. These actions range from communicating directly with other agencies via cable to providing information for TIDE, watch-listing, and no-fly nominations.

Watch-listing and TIDE

NCTC has adopted important reforms in the watch-listing process and has improved NCTC's receipt, processing, and the quality of information sharing in support of the Center's watch-listing and screening responsibilities.   Specifically, the intelligence community adjusted the minimum identifying information necessary to allow additional individuals to be entered into the Terrorist Identities Datamart Environment (TIDE) and took other measures to ensure more effective record and database searches, correlation of data, and processing of encounters.   In July 2010, the community watch-listing guidance was revised to provide flexibility to push forward information that previously had not met the requirements.

The added features include a bulk ingest application, automatic processing of the nominations, and exporting records to the Terrorist Screening Center in near-real time. We also increased our ability to store, compare, match, and export biometrics such as fingerprint, facial images, and iris scans. At the same time, however, we have taken great care to ensure that our core civil liberties and privacy protections are preserved.   Nominations of U.S. persons to a watch-list must still be supported by reasonable suspicion that the person is a -known or suspected terrorist, and a person cannot be watch-listed based solely upon First Amendment protected activity, or based solely upon race, ethnicity, or religious affiliation.

> **NCTC has developed and maintains the Terrorist Identities Datamart Environment (TIDE) on known and suspected terrorists and terrorist groups.**

One of the key gaps we identified in the watch-listing process was the need to enhance existing TIDE records with additional information. NCTC is now taking a more aggressive and innovative approach to seek methodologies and data repositories to ingest biographic, biometric, and derogatory information. We also are conducting large scale data correlation efforts on a nightly basis, enabling discovery of previously unknown terrorist connections and attributes. As the threat continues to evolve, our watch-listing experts are proactively partnering with NCTC's Pursuit Group and the counterterrorism community to expedite the sharing of information to build more complete terrorist identities.

Information Technology

NCTC has implemented several significant improvements to its information technology. These include:

- Expanding advanced data correlation services to process and filter massive data sets.

- Improving technology supporting the development of leads to identify non watch-listed names or aliases.

- Updating NCTC's integrated data repository with several country-specific data sets.

For example, prior to December 2009, analysts were required manually to search and integrate information—data from multiple networks residing in specific databases had to be searched, selected, and copy/pasted to get the relevant information to the analyst's primary workspace. Now, NCTC's Counterterrorism Data Layer is being developed to ingest relevant data and to allow NCTC analysts to search, exploit, and correlate terrorism information in a single environment. Thanks to the efforts of the DNI, Secretary Napolitano, Director Mueller, and the Directors of the CIA, NSA, and DIA, NCTC is acquiring priority data sets for ingestion, and for the first time, NCTC analysts can search across key homeland security and intelligence information and get back a single list of relevant results. Moreover, sophisticated analytical tools are in place to permit analysts to conduct Google-like searches, conduct link analysis and data visualization, and to triage information. These efforts are being pursued with careful consideration of legal, policy, and technical issues to protect privacy and civil liberties.

Countering Violent Extremism

Over the past ten years, the government has expanded its counterterrorism efforts to include a focus on preventing al-Qaida and its adherents from recruiting and radicalizing the next generation of terrorists, both overseas and at home. Efforts to prevent and counter violent extremism focus on undercutting the terrorist narrative, improving government and law enforcement expertise for understanding the threat, and building more resilient communities—making radicalization and recruitment to violence more difficult for al-Qaida's and its allies and affiliates. Because this new approach takes a more holistic view of the threat, it requires the active engagement of departments and agencies whose missions go beyond traditional counterterrorism and law enforcement missions.

In this framework, the National Security Council (NSC) is leading a whole of government approach for the U.S. Government's efforts to counter violent radicalization, as described in the August 2011 domestic radicalization strategy, *Empowering Local Partners to Prevent Violent Extremism in the United States*. NCTC supports the NSC implementation of the strategy by working closely with our federal partners, as well as with state, local and tribal partners to build and support programs, activities, and efforts that directly and indirectly counter violent extremism.

NCTC Workforce

As NCTC re-doubles its efforts to meet the challenges posed by al- Qaida, its affiliates and adherents, our progress is dependent on our dedicated and diverse workforce. The talented men and women who work at NCTC perform a unique and vital service to the nation, NCTC has benefitted from the integration of analysts and planners from across the intelligence community, the U.S. military, and other federal, state, and local partners. Maintaining this diversity through continued commitment from intelligence agencies and other organizations is a priority for NCTC. We continue to strengthen this workforce by providing the training, resources, and leadership needed to ensure the Center's continued success.

Challenges Ahead

We continue to address challenges in dealing with the dynamic and adaptive terrorist threat environment. The nature of the threat challenges our analysts' ability to sort and connect critical bits of information across disparate data sets. The rapid change and proliferation in communications technologies require a proactively postured intelligence community, while effectively balancing the protection of sources and methods, and the need to share information.

The drawdown of U.S. military forces in Iraq and changes in relationships with key partners, such as Egypt, may affect our ability to maintain access to long-term targets. The potential impacts of the Arab Spring and upheaval in the Middle East are not yet fully understood, particularly as they relate to the al-Qaida narrative and key relationships.

While remaining vigilant against foreign-inspired threats, efforts to build resilience within our communities are essential to continuing progress against al-Qaida inspired radicalization recruitment, and mobilization to violence here at home. Engagement and partnerships with communities remain important to protecting them from the influence of al-Qaida, its affiliates and adherents. Integrating and harmonizing the efforts of federal, state, local, and tribal entities will remain a challenge—one we must continue to pursue.

Finally, all of our efforts must be consistent with our core values. We must carry out the mission of NCTC in a manner that retains the trust of the American people and remains true to the oaths we have taken to support and defend the Constitution. NCTC is committed to fulfilling this solemn responsibility by protecting civil liberties and privacy and respecting the rule of law. While we work to protect the Nation, we are dedicated to upholding the trust of the American people and exemplifying the values on which the nation was founded.

Chairman Lieberman, Ranking Member Collins and members of the Committee, I thank you for the opportunity to testify before the committee today. Your support has made it possible to reduce the likelihood of a successful terrorist attack. As you know, perfection is no more possible in counterterrorism than it is in any other endeavor. NCTC, in partnership with the entire counterterrorism community, continues to work tirelessly to reduce the likelihood of an attack, but we cannot guarantee safety. We must continue to foster the resilience of the American people to prepare for a potential attack.

With your determined leadership, NCTC and our key partners—sitting here with me today—we have established a strong posture against the enemies who seek to do us harm, and will continue to make progress in this fight. Every day, the threat information we review underscores the fluid and dynamic terrorist threat to the United States. We must work relentlessly to reduce that threat to our nation. In the months and years to come, I look forward to working with this Committee and the rest of Congress to keep the American people safe.

United States Department of State
Office of the Coordinator for Counterterrorism
Foreign Terrorist Organizations
Public Website, (Excerpts)

Foreign Terrorist Organizations (FTOs) are designated by the Secretary of State in accordance with section 219 of the Immigration and Nationality Act (INA). FTO designations play a critical role in the fight against terrorism and are an effective means of curtailing support for terrorist activities.

Legal Criteria for Designation under Section 219 of the INA as amended:

1. It must be a *foreign organization*.

2. The organization must *engage in terrorist activity*, as defined in section 212 (a)(3)(B) of the INA (8 U.S.C. § 1182(a)(3)(B)), or *terrorism*, as defined in section 140(d)(2) of the Foreign Relations Authorization Act, Fiscal Years 1988 and 1989 (22 U.S.C. § 2656f(d)(2)), *or retain the capability and intent to engage in terrorist activity or terrorism.*

3. The organization's terrorist activity or terrorism must threaten the security of U.S. nationals or the national security (national defense, foreign relations, or the economic interests) of the United States.

U.S. Government Designated Foreign Terrorist Organizations as of 9/15/2011

- Abu Nidal Organization (ANO)
- Abu Sayyaf Group (ASG)
- Al-Aqsa Martyrs Brigade (AAMS)
- Al-Shabaab
- Ansar al-Islam (AAI)
- Asbat al-Ansar
- Aum Shinrikyo (AUM)
- Basque Fatherland and Liberty (ETA)

- Communist Party of the Philippines/New People's Army (CPP/NPA)
- Continuity Irish Republican Army (CIRA)
- Gama'a al-Islamiyya (Islamic Group)
- HAMAS (Islamic Resistance Movement)
- Harakat ul-Jihad-i-Islami/Bangladesh (HUJI-B)
- Harakat ul-Mujahidin (HUM)
- Hizballah (Party of God)
- Islamic Jihad Union (IJU)
- Islamic Movement of Uzbekistan (IMU)
- Jaish-e-Mohammed (JEM) (Army of Mohammed)
- Jemaah Islamiya organization (JI)
- Kahane Chai (Kach)
- Kata'ib Hizballah (KH)
- Kongra-Gel (KGK, formerly Kurdistan Workers' Party, PKK, KADEK)
- Lashkar-e Tayyiba (LT) (Army of the Righteous)
- Lashkar i Jhangvi (LJ)
- Liberation Tigers of Tamil Eelam (LTTE)
- Libyan Islamic Fighting Group (LIFG)
- Moroccan Islamic Combatant Group (GICM)
- Mujahedin-e Khalq Organization (MEK)
- National Liberation Army (ELN)
- Palestine Liberation Front (PLF)
- Palestinian Islamic Jihad (PIJ)
- Popular Front for the Liberation of Palestine (PFLP)
- PFLP-General Command (PFLP-GC)
- al-Qaida in Iraq (AQI)
- al-Qa'ida (AQ)
- al-Qa'ida in the Arabian Peninsula (AQAP)
- al-Qaida in the Islamic Maghreb (formerly GSPC)
- Real IRA (RIRA)
- Revolutionary Armed Forces of Colombia (FARC)
- Revolutionary Organization 17 November (17N)
- Revolutionary People's Liberation Party/Front (DHKP/C)
- Revolutionary Struggle (RS)
- Shining Path (Sendero Luminoso, SL)
- United Self-Defense Forces of Colombia (AUC)
- Harakat-ul Jihad Islami (HUJI)
- Tehrik-e Taliban Pakistan (TTP)
- Jundallah

- Army of Islam (AOI)
- Indian Mujahideen (IM)

Identification

The Office of the Coordinator for Counterterrorism in the State Department (S/CT) continually monitors the activities of terrorist groups active around the world to identify potential targets for designation. When reviewing potential targets, S/CT looks not only at the actual terrorist attacks that a group has carried out, but also at whether the group has engaged in planning and preparations for possible future acts of terrorism or retains the capability and intent to carry out such acts.

Designation

Once a target is identified, S/CT prepares a detailed "administrative record," which is a compilation of information, typically including both classified and open sources information, demonstrating that the statutory criteria for designation have been satisfied. If the Secretary of State, in consultation with the Attorney General and the Secretary of the Treasury, decides to make the designation, Congress is notified of the Secretary's intent to designate the organization and given seven days to review the designation, as the INA requires. Upon the expiration of the seven-day waiting period and in the absence of Congressional action to block the designation, notice of the designation is published in the *Federal Register*, at which point the designation takes effect. By law an organization designated as an FTO may seek judicial review of the designation in the United States Court of Appeals for the District of Columbia Circuit not later than 30 days after the designation is published in the *Federal Register*.

Until recently the INA provided that FTOs must be redesignated every 2 years or the designation would lapse. Under the Intelligence Reform and Terrorism Prevention Act of 2004 (IRTPA), however, the redesignation requirement was replaced by certain review and revocation procedures. IRTPA provides that an FTO may file a petition for revocation 2 years after its designation date (or in the case of redesignated FTOs, its most recent redesignation date) or 2 years after the determination date on its most recent petition for revocation. In order to provide a basis for revocation, the petitioning FTO must provide evidence that the circumstances forming the basis for the designation are sufficiently different as to warrant revocation. If no such review has been conducted during a 5 year period with respect to a designation, then the Secretary of State is required to review the designation to determine whether revocation would be appropriate. In addition, the Secretary of State may at any time revoke a designation upon a finding that the circumstances forming the basis for the designation have changed in such a manner as to warrant revocation, or that the national security of the United States warrants a revocation. The same procedural requirements apply to revocations made by the Secretary of State as apply to designations. A designation may be revoked by an Act of Congress, or set aside by a Court order.

Effects of Designation/Legal Consequences

1. With limited exceptions set forth in the Order, or as authorized by OFAC, all property and interests in property of designated individuals or entities that are in the United States or that come within the United States, or that come within the possession or control of U.S. persons are blocked.

2. With limited exceptions set forth in the Order, or as authorized by OFAC, any transaction or dealing by U.S. persons or within the United States in property or interests in property blocked pursuant to the Order is prohibited, including but not limited to the making or receiving of any contribution of funds, goods, or services to or for the benefit of individuals or entities designated under the Order.

3. Any transaction by any U.S. person or within the United States that evades or avoids, or has the purpose of evading or avoiding, or attempts to violate, any of the prohibitions in the Order is prohibited. Any conspiracy formed to violate any of the prohibitions is also prohibited.

4. Civil and criminal penalties may be assessed for violations.

Other Effects

1. Deters donations or contributions to designated individuals or entities.

2. Heightens public awareness and knowledge of individuals or entities linked to terrorism.

3. Alerts other governments to U.S. concerns about individuals or entities aiding terrorism, and promotes due diligence by such governments and private sector entities operating within their territories to avoid associations with terrorists.

4. Disrupts terrorist networks, thereby cutting off access to financial and other resources from sympathizers.

5. Encourages designated entities to get out of the terrorism business.

Terrorism Spotlight

AL-QA'IDA

Variant spelling of al-Qa'ida, including al Qaeda; translation "The Base"; Qa'idat al-Jihad (The Base for Jihad); formerly Qa'idat Ansar Allah (The Base of the Supporters of God); the Islamic Army; Islamic Salvation Foundation; the Base; The Group for the Preservation of the Holy Sites; The Islamic Army for the Liberation of the Holy Places; the World Islamic Front for Jihad Against Jews and Crusaders; the Usama Bin Ladin Network; the Usama Bin Ladin Organization; al-Jihad; the Jihad Group; Egyptian al-Jihad; Egyptian Islamic Jihad; New Jihad

Description

Al-Qa'ida (AQ) was designated as a Foreign Terrorist Organization on October 8, 1999. AQ was established by Usama bin Ladin in 1988 and originally consisted of members who fought in Afghanistan against the Soviet Union. The group helped finance, recruit, transport, and train Sunni Islamist extremists for the Afghan resistance. AQ's strategic objectives include uniting Muslims to fight the United States and its allies, overthrowing regimes it deems "non-Islamic," and expelling Westerners and non-Muslims from Muslim countries. Its ultimate goal is the establishment of a pan-Islamic caliphate throughout the world. AQ leaders issued a statement in February 1998 under the banner of "The World Islamic Front for Jihad against the Jews and Crusaders," saying it was the duty of all Muslims to kill U.S. citizens, civilian and military, and their allies everywhere. AQ merged with al-Jihad (Egyptian Islamic Jihad) in June 2001.

Activities

AQ is the most significant terrorist threat to the United States and it developed stronger relationships with its affiliates in the Middle East, North Africa, and Europe in 2010. AQ, its allies, and those inspired by the group were involved attacks in Africa, Europe, the Middle East, and South Asia including suicide bombings and vehicle-borne improvised explosive devices in Iraq, Afghanistan, and Pakistan.

AQ and its supporters claim to have shot down U.S. helicopters and killed U.S. servicemen in Somalia in 1993, and to have conducted three bombings that targeted U.S. troops in Aden in December 1992. AQ also carried out the August 1998 bombings of the U.S. Embassies in Nairobi and Dar es Salaam, killing up to 300 individuals and injuring more than 5,000. In October 2000, AQ conducted a suicide attack on the USS Cole in the port of Aden, Yemen, with an explosive-laden boat, killing 17 U.S. Navy sailors and injuring 39.

On September 11, 2001, 19 AQ members hijacked and crashed four U.S. commercial jets – two into the World Trade Center in New York City, one into the Pentagon near Washington, DC; and the last into a field in Shanksville, Pennsylvania – leaving over 3,000 individuals dead or missing.

In November 2002, AQ carried out a suicide bombing of a hotel in Mombasa, Kenya that killed 15. AQ probably provided financing for the October 2002 Bali bombings by Jemaah Islamiya that killed more than 200. In 2003 and 2004, Saudi-based AQ operatives and associated extremists launched more than a dozen attacks, killing at least 90 people, including 14 Americans in Saudi Arabia. Bin Ladin's deputy al-Zawahiri claimed responsibility on behalf of AQ for the July 7, 2005 attacks against the London public transportation system. AQ likely played a role in the 2006 failed plot to destroy several commercial aircraft flying from the United Kingdom to the United States using liquid explosives.

The Government of Pakistan accused AQ, along with Tehrik-e Taliban Pakistan (TTP), of being responsible for the October 2007 suicide bombing attempt against former Pakistani Prime Minister Benazir Bhutto that killed at least 144 people in Karachi, Pakistan. The Government of Pakistan stated that Baitullah Mehsud, a now-deceased TTP leader with close ties to AQ, was responsible for Bhutto's December 27, 2007 assassination.

In January 2009, Bryant Neal Vinas – a U.S. citizen who traveled to Pakistan, allegedly trained in explosives at AQ camps, and was eventually captured in Pakistan and extradited to the United States – was charged with providing material support to a terrorist organization and conspiracy to commit murder. Vinas later admitted his role in helping AQ plan an attack against the Long Island Rail Road in New York and confessed to having fired missiles at a U.S. base in Afghanistan. In September 2009, Najibullah Zazi, an Afghan immigrant and U.S. lawful permanent resident, was charged with conspiracy to use weapons of mass destruction, to commit murder in a foreign country, and with providing material support to a terrorist organization as part of an AQ plot to attack the New York subway system. Zazi later admitted to contacts with AQ senior leadership, suggesting they had knowledge of his plans. In February 2010, Zazi pled guilty to charges in the United States District Court for the Eastern District of New York. U.S. officials have described the alleged bombing plot as one of the most serious terrorist threats to the United States since the 9/11 attacks.

Strength

AQ's organizational strength is difficult to determine in the aftermath of extensive counterterrorism efforts since 9/11. The arrests and deaths of mid-level and senior AQ operatives have disrupted communication, financial, facilitation nodes, and a number of terrorist plots. Additionally, supporters and associates worldwide who are "inspired" by the group's ideology may be operating without direction from AQ central leadership; it is impossible to estimate their numbers. AQ serves as a focal point of "inspiration" for a worldwide network that is comprised of many Sunni Islamic extremist groups, including some members of the Gama'at al-Islamiyya, the Islamic Movement of Uzbekistan, the Islamic Jihad Union, Lashkar i Jhangvi, Harakat ul-Mujahidin, the Taliban, and Jemaah Islamiya. TTP also has strengthened its ties to AQ.

Location/Area of Operation

AQ was based in Afghanistan until Coalition Forces removed the Taliban from power in late 2001. Since then, they have resided in Pakistan's Federally Administered Tribal Areas. AQ has a number of regional affiliates, including al-Qa'ida in Iraq (AQI), al-Qa'ida in the Arabian Peninsula, and al-Qa'ida in the Islamic Maghreb.

External Aid

AQ primarily depends on donations from like-minded supporters as well as from individuals who believe that their money is supporting a humanitarian cause. Some funds are diverted from Islamic charitable organizations. In addition, parts of the organization raise funds through criminal activities; for example, AQI raises funds through hostage-taking for ransom, and members in Europe have engaged in credit card fraud. U.S. and international efforts to block AQ funding have hampered the group's ability to raise money.

HAMAS

aka the Islamic Resistance Movement; Harakat al-Muqawama al-Islamiya; Izz al-Din al Qassam Battalions; Izz al-Din al Qassam Brigades; Izz al-Din al Qassam Forces; Students of Ayyash; Student of the Engineer; Yahya Ayyash Units; Izz al-Din al-Qassim Brigades; Izz al-Din al-Qassim Forces; Izz al-Din al-Qassim Battalions

Description

Hamas was designated as a Foreign Terrorist Organization on October 8, 1997. Hamas possesses military and political wings, and was formed in late 1987 at the onset of the first Palestinian uprising, or Intifada, as an outgrowth of the Palestinian branch of the Muslim Brotherhood. The armed element, called the Izz al-Din al-Qassam Brigades, conducts anti-Israeli attacks, previously including suicide bombings against civilian targets inside Israel. Hamas also manages a broad, mostly Gaza-based network of "Dawa" or ministry activities that include charities, schools, clinics, youth camps, fund-raising, and political activities. A Shura Council based in Damascus, Syria, sets overall policy. After winning Palestinian Legislative Council elections in January 2006, Hamas seized control of significant Palestinian Authority (PA) ministries in Gaza, including the Ministry of Interior. Hamas subsequently formed an expanded militia called the Executive Force, subordinate to the Interior Ministry. This force and other Hamas cadres took control of Gaza in a military-style coup in June 2007, forcing Fatah forces to either leave Gaza or go underground.

Activities

Prior to 2005, Hamas conducted numerous anti-Israeli attacks, including suicide bombings, rocket launches, improvised explosive device attacks, and shootings. Hamas has not directly targeted U.S. interests, though the group has conducted attacks against Israeli targets frequented by foreigners. The group curtailed terrorist attacks in February 2005 after agreeing to a temporary period of calm brokered by the PA and ceased most violence after winning control of the PA legislature and cabinet in January 2006. After Hamas staged a June 2006 attack on Israeli Defense Forces soldiers near Kerem Shalom that resulted in two deaths and the abduction of Corporal Gilad Shalit, Israel took steps that severely limited the operation of the Rafah crossing. In June 2007, after Hamas took control of Gaza from the PA and Fatah, an international boycott was imposed along with the closure of Gaza borders. Hamas has since dedicated the majority of its activity in Gaza to solidifying its control, hardening its defenses, tightening security, and conducting limited operations against Israeli military forces.

Hamas fired rockets from Gaza into Israel in 2008 but focused more on mortar attacks targeting Israeli incursions. In June 2008, Hamas agreed to a six-month cease-fire with Israel and temporarily halted all rocket attacks emanating from Gaza by arresting Palestinian militants and violators of the agreement. Hamas claimed responsibility for killing nine civilians, wounding 12 children and 80 other civilians in an attack at the residence of Fatah's Gaza City Secretary in Gaza in August 2008. Hamas also claimed responsibility for driving a vehicle into a crowd in Jerusalem, wounding 19 soldiers and civilians in September 2008. Hamas fought a 23-day war with Israel from late December 2008 to January 2009, in an unsuccessful effort to break an international blockade on Gaza and force the openings of the international crossings. Since Israel's declaration of a unilateral ceasefire on January 18, 2009, Hamas has largely enforced the calm, focusing on rebuilding its weapons caches, smuggling tunnels, and other military infrastructure in Gaza. Hamas carried out multiple rocket attacks on Israel in 2009 but was relatively inactive in 2010. In September 2010, Hamas claimed responsibility for carrying out a series of drive-by shootings in the West Bank that killed four Israelis near Hebron.

Strength

Hamas is believed to have several thousand Gaza-based operatives with varying degrees of skills in its armed wing, the Izz al-Din al-Qassam Brigades, along with its reported 9,000-person Hamas-led paramilitary group known as the "Executive Force."

Location/Area of Operation

Hamas has a presence in every major city in the Palestinian territories. The group retains a cadre of leaders and facilitators that conduct diplomatic, fundraising, and arms-smuggling activities in Lebanon, Syria, and other states. Hamas also increased its presence in the Palestinian refugee camps in Lebanon, probably with the goal of eclipsing Fatah's long-time dominance of the camps.

External Aid

Hamas receives the majority of its funding, weapons, and training from Iran. In addition, the group raises funds in the Persian Gulf countries and receives donations from Palestinian expatriates around the world. Some fundraising and propaganda activity takes place in Western Europe and North America. Syria provides safe haven for its leadership.

HIZBALLAH

aka the Party of God; Islamic Jihad; Islamic Jihad Organization; Revolutionary Justice Organization; Organization of the Oppressed on Earth; Islamic Jihad for the Liberation of Palestine; Organization of Right Against Wrong; Followers of the Prophet Muhammed

Description

Hizballah was designated as a Foreign Terrorist Organization on October 8, 1997. Formed in 1982, in response to the Israeli invasion of Lebanon, the Lebanese-based radical Shia group takes its ideological inspiration from the Iranian revolution and the teachings of the late Ayatollah Khomeini. The group generally follows the religious guidance of Khomeini's successor, Iranian Supreme Leader Ali Khamenei. Hizballah is closely allied with Iran and often acts at its behest, though it also acts independently. Hizballah shares a close relationship with Syria, and like Iran, the group is helping advance its Syrian objectives in the region. It has strong influence in Lebanon, especially with the Shia community. The Lebanese government and the majority of the Arab world still recognize Hizballah as a legitimate "resistance group" and political party.

Hizballah provides support to several Palestinian terrorist organizations, as well as a number of local Christian and Muslim militias in Lebanon. This support includes the covert provision of weapons, explosives, training, funding, and guidance, as well as overt political support.

Activities

Hizballah's terrorist attacks have included the suicide truck bombings of the U.S. Embassy and U.S. Marine barracks in Beirut in 1983; the U.S. Embassy annex in Beirut in 1984; and the 1985 hijacking of TWA flight 847, during which a U.S. Navy diver was murdered. Elements of the group were responsible for the kidnapping, detention, and murder of Americans and other Westerners in Lebanon in the 1980s. Hizballah was also implicated in the attacks on the Israeli Embassy in Argentina in 1992 and on the Argentine-Israeli Mutual Association in Buenos Aires in 1994. In 2000, Hizballah operatives captured three Israeli soldiers in the Sheba'a Farms area and, separately, kidnapped an Israeli non-combatant in Dubai. Although the non-combatant survived, on November 1, 2001, Israeli army rabbi Israel Weiss pronounced the soldiers dead. The surviving non-combatant, as well as the bodies of the IDF soldiers, were returned to Israel in a prisoner exchange with Hizballah on January 29, 2004.

Since at least 2004, Hizballah has provided training to select Iraqi Shia militants, including the construction and use of shaped charge improvised explosive devices (IEDs) that can penetrate heavily-armored vehicles. Senior Hizballah operative, Ali Mussa Daqduq, was captured in Iraq in 2007 while facilitating Hizballah training of Iraqi Shia militants attacking U.S. and coalition forces. When captured, Daqduq had detailed documents that discussed tactics to attack Iraqi and coalition forces. In July 2006, Hizballah attacked an Israeli Army patrol, kidnapping two soldiers and killing three, starting a conflict with Israel that lasted into August.

Senior Hizballah officials have repeatedly vowed retaliation for the February 2008 killing in Damascus of Imad Mughniyah, Hizballah's military and terrorism chief, who was suspected of involvement in many attacks. Rawi Sultani was arrested in 2009 for providing targeting information to Hizballah on the Israeli Defense Chief of Staff.
The group's willingness to engage in violence and its increasing stockpile of weapons continues to threaten stability in the region. In a two-week period in May 2008, Hizballah's armed takeover of West Beirut – which occurred after the Lebanese government announced its plan to remove Hizballah's telephone network – resulted in

more than 60 deaths. Egyptian authorities in late 2008 disrupted a Hizballah cell that was charged with planning to attack Israeli interests including tourists in the Sinai Peninsula, and Israeli ships passing through the Suez Canal. The network was also engaged in smuggling weapons, supplies, and people through tunnels to Gaza. Twenty-six men belonging to this Hizballah cell were convicted in April 2010. In November 2009, the Israeli navy seized a ship carrying an estimated 400-500 tons of weapons originating in Iran and bound for Hizballah, via Syria.

Strength

Several thousands of supporters and members.

Location/Area of Operation

Operates in the southern suburbs of Beirut, the Bekaa Valley, and southern Lebanon.

External Aid

Hizballah receives training, weapons, and explosives, as well as political, diplomatic, monetary, and organizational aid from Iran; and training, weapons, diplomatic, and political support from Syria. Hizballah also receives funding from private donations and profits from legal and illegal businesses. Hizballah also receives financial support from Lebanese Shia communities in Europe, Africa, South America, North America, and Asia.

Editor's Comments

A basic counter-terrorism model taken directly from the United States Department of State website:

Defeating the Terrorist Enemy
Links between global, regional & local actors allow extremists to aggregate local complaints into ideological grievance and local actions into strategic impact. Breaking links hastens the isolation and fragmentation of extremist groups, and contributes to reducing the threat over time - ultimately marginalizing terrorists who can then be dealt with by local governments.

Defeating the Terrorist Enemy: Attack All Levels of the Threat Complex Simultaneously
The "enemy" comprises a three-fold threat complex:

- **Leaders** - Global Actors, including al-Qaida and associated networks, which provide leadership, resources, inspiration and guidance to extremists.

- **Safe Havens** - Space that provide a secure base for extremist action, including:

  o **Physical space** - failed/failing states, under-governed areas and sponsors who provide safe areas where terrorists train and organize. Many safe havens sit astride international borders, demanding a regional, rather than solely national response.

- o **Cyber space**- electro-magnetic and internet-based means for communication, planning, resource transfer and intelligence collection. These means allow terrorists to organize, communicate, spread propaganda and transfer money.

- o **Ideological space** - belief systems, ideas and cultural norms that enhance the enemy's freedom of action. These include ethnic identities, religious attitudes and political cultures.

- **Underlying conditions** - Local groups, grievances, communal conflicts and societal structures that provide fertile soil in which extremism flourishes, and provide the "fuel" that the enemy exploits. Many of these grievances and conflicts are pre-existing and resolving them is a related but separate issue to combating terrorism, per se.

Further Discussion

1. Discuss **U.S. core values** in relation to counterterrorism operations.

2. Discuss the implications of **state-sponsored terrorism**.

3. Discuss the core functions of the **National Counterterrorism Center**.

4. Discuss the legal criteria for designation as a **Foreign Terrorist Organization**.

5. Discuss the activities of the terrorist organization **HAMAS**.

President Barack Obama, Address to the Nation, May 1, 2011

"Good evening. Tonight, I can report to the American people and to the world that the United States has conducted an operation that killed Osama bin Laden, the leader of al Qaeda, and a terrorist who's responsible for the murder of thousands of innocent men, women, and children. It was nearly 10 years ago that a bright September day was darkened by the worst attack on the American people in our history. The images of 9/11 are seared into our national memory ~ hijacked planes cutting through a cloudless September sky; the Twin Towers collapsing to the ground; black smoke billowing up from the Pentagon; the wreckage of Flight 93 in Shanksville, Pennsylvania, where the actions of heroic citizens saved even more heartbreak and destruction. And yet we know that the worst images are those that were unseen to the world. The empty seat at the dinner table. Children who were forced to grow up without their mother or their father. Parents who would never know the feeling of their child's embrace. Nearly 3,000 citizens taken from us, leaving a gaping hole in our hearts. On September 11, 2001, in our time of grief, the American people came together. We offered our neighbors a hand, and we offered the wounded our blood. We reaffirmed our ties to each other, and our love of community and country. On that day, no matter where we came from, what God we prayed to, or what race or ethnicity we were, we were united as one American family. We were also united in our resolve to protect our nation and to bring those who committed this vicious attack to justice. We quickly learned that the 9/11 attacks were carried out by al Qaeda ~ an organization headed by Osama bin Laden, which had openly declared war on the United States and was committed to killing innocents in our country and around the globe. And so we went to war against al Qaeda to protect our citizens, our friends, and our allies. Over the last 10 years, thanks to the tireless and heroic work of our military and our counterterrorism professionals, we've made great strides in that effort. We've disrupted terrorist attacks and strengthened our homeland defense. In Afghanistan, we removed the Taliban government, which had given bin Laden and al Qaeda safe haven and support. And around the globe, we worked with our friends and allies to capture or kill scores of al Qaeda terrorists, including several who were a part of the 9/11 plot. Yet Osama bin Laden avoided capture and escaped across the Afghan border into Pakistan. Meanwhile, al Qaeda continued to operate from along that border and operate through its affiliates across the world. And so shortly after taking office, I directed Leon Panetta, the director of the CIA, to make the killing or capture of bin Laden the top priority of our war against al Qaeda, even as we continued our broader efforts to disrupt, dismantle, and defeat his network. Then, last August, after years of painstaking work by our intelligence community, I was briefed on a possible lead to bin Laden. It was far from certain, and it took many months to run this thread to ground. I met repeatedly with my national security team as we developed more information about the possibility that we had located bin Laden hiding within a compound deep inside of Pakistan. And finally, last week, I determined that we had enough intelligence to take action, and authorized an operation to get Osama bin Laden and bring him to justice. Today, at my direction, the United States launched a targeted operation against that compound in Abbottabad, Pakistan. A small team of Americans carried out the operation with extraordinary courage and capability. No Americans were harmed. They took care to avoid civilian casualties. After a firefight, they killed Osama bin Laden and took custody of his body. For over two decades, bin Laden has been al Qaeda's leader and symbol, and has continued to plot attacks against our country and our friends and allies. The death of bin Laden marks the most significant achievement to date in our nation's effort to defeat al Qaeda. Yet his death does not mark the end of our effort. There's no doubt that al Qaeda will continue to pursue attacks against us. We must ~ and we will - remain vigilant at home and abroad. As we do, we must also reaffirm that the United States is not - and never will be - at war with Islam. I've made clear, just as President Bush did shortly after 9/11, that our war is not against Islam. Bin Laden was not a Muslim leader; he was a mass murderer of Muslims. Indeed, al Qaeda has slaughtered scores of Muslims in many countries, including our own. So his demise should be welcomed by all who believe in peace and human dignity. Over the years, I've repeatedly made clear that we would take action within Pakistan if we knew where bin Laden was. That is what we've done. But it's important to note that our counterterrorism cooperation with Pakistan helped lead us to bin Laden and the compound where he was hiding. Indeed, bin Laden had declared war against Pakistan as well, and ordered attacks against the Pakistani people. Tonight, I called President Zardari, and my team has also spoken with their Pakistani counterparts. They agree that this is a good and historic day for both of our nations. And going forward, it is essential that Pakistan continue to join us in the fight against al Qaeda and its affiliates. The American people did not choose this fight. It came to our shores, and started with the senseless slaughter of our citizens. After nearly 10 years of service, struggle, and sacrifice, we know well the costs of war. These efforts weigh on me every time I, as Commander-in-Chief, have to sign a letter to a family that has lost a loved one, or look into the eyes of a service member who's been gravely wounded. So Americans understand the costs of war. Yet as a country, we will never tolerate our security being threatened, nor stand idly by when our people have been killed. We will be relentless in defense of our citizens and our friends and allies. We will be true to the values that make us who we are. And on nights like this one, we can say to those families who have lost loved ones to al Qaeda's terror: Justice has been done. Tonight, we give thanks to the countless intelligence and counterterrorism professionals who've worked tirelessly to achieve this outcome. The American people do not see their work, nor know their names. But tonight, they feel the satisfaction of their work and the result of their pursuit of justice. We give thanks for the men who carried out this operation, for they exemplify the professionalism, patriotism, and unparalleled courage of those who serve our country. And they are part of a generation that has borne the heaviest share of the burden since that September day. Finally, let me say to the families who lost loved ones on 9/11 that we have never forgotten your loss, nor wavered in our commitment to see that we do whatever it takes to prevent another attack on our shores. And tonight, let us think back to the sense of unity that prevailed on 9/11. I know that it has, at times, frayed. Yet today's achievement is a testament to the greatness of our country and the determination of the American people. The cause of securing our country is not complete. But tonight, we are once again reminded that America can do whatever we set our mind to. That is the story of our history, whether it's the pursuit of prosperity for our people, or the struggle for equality for all our citizens; our commitment to stand up for our values abroad, and our sacrifices to make the world a safer place. Let us remember that we can do these things not just because of wealth or power, but because of who we are: one nation, under God, indivisible, with liberty and justice for all. Thank you. May God bless you. And may God bless the United States of America."

And the fight against terrorism continues...

Appendix

U.S. Department of Homeland Security
Office of Public Affairs
A Day in the Life of the
Department of Homeland Security
2010, (Excerpts)

On the 8th anniversary of the Department of Homeland Security, our nation is more secure than it was two years ago, and more secure than when DHS was founded. Every day, DHS works with first responders, state, local, tribal and territorial governments, community groups, international partners and the private sector to secure our nation and to counter the evolving threats we face. Securing our homeland requires our constant vigilance, hard work, and determination to prepare for, prevent, respond to, and recover from terrorism and other threats.

Below is a sampling of what the men and women of DHS do over the course of a typical day – working across the country and around the world – to keep Americans safe and secure.*

To prevent terrorism and enhance security, TODAY, DHS will:

- Screen approximately 2 million passengers and their checked baggage before they board commercial aircraft;

- Intercept 90 prohibited items at checkpoints (TSA outbound and CBP inbound) and prevent 1,945 prohibited items from entering federal facilities;

- Deploy thousands of transportation security officers and federal air marshals to protect the traveling public;

- Minimize the wait times of passengers' security screening to an average of less than 10 minutes;

- Conduct 135 armed waterborne patrols near maritime critical infrastructure and key resources;

- Monitor 1,428 radiation portal monitors to scan 100 percent of all containerized cargo entering from Canada and Mexico; 100 percent of the personally owned vehicles entering from Canada and Mexico; and 99 percent of all arriving seaborne containerized cargo for illicit radiological/nuclear materials;

- Train 3,400 federal officers and agents from 89 different federal agencies, as well as state, local, tribal and international officers and agents, in one or more of the 469 basic and advanced training programs available;

- Train 12 state and local law enforcement officials on how to use preventive radiological/nuclear detection equipment;

- Review all-source intelligence information, conduct analysis, and develop products to disseminate to federal, state, local, tribal, territorial and private sector partners regarding current and developing threats, as well as potential indicators of the threat; and

- Provide resources and expertise to support the nation's 72 state and major urban area fusion centers to engage law enforcement and homeland security agencies across the country in reporting suspicious activities and implementing protective measures.

To secure and manage our borders, TODAY, DHS will:

- Process nearly 1 million travelers entering the United States at air, land and sea ports of entry;

- Inspect more than 47,000 truck, rail and sea containers;

- Process more than $88 million in fees, duties and tariffs;

- Seize 11,435 pounds of narcotics at or near ports of entry nationwide;

- Seize or remove 1,100 pounds of illegal drugs via maritime routes;

- Issue 200 credentials to qualified merchant mariners to ensure the safety, security and efficiency of the maritime supply chain; and

- Manage 3,500 commercial vessel transits through the Marine Transportation System to facilitate the safe and efficient movement of goods and people.

To enforce and administer our immigration laws, TODAY, DHS will:

- Make an average 728 administrative arrests and 638 criminal alien arrests;

- Seize approximately $400,000 in undeclared or illicit currency at and between U.S. ports of entry nationwide;

- Litigate nearly 1,500 cases in immigration court and obtain 6,161 final orders of removal including 933 for criminal aliens;

- House 33,429 illegal aliens in detention facilities nationwide;

- Process 24,371 applications for immigration benefits; and

- Naturalize nearly 2,583 new U.S. citizens.

To safeguard and secure cyberspace, TODAY, DHS will:

- Protect U.S. information systems (the federal *.gov* domain) through the United States Computer Emergency Readiness Team (US-CERT), which detects, responds and issues warnings to an average of more than 18 incidents per month arising from almost 15,000 daily alerts;

- Work closely with government and private sector partners to defend against and respond to a range of cyber threats, and when necessary, provide onsite support to owners and operators of the nation's critical infrastructure on incident response, forensic analysis, site assessments and training; and

- Promote the development of a world-class cybersecurity workforce by supporting initiatives such as Scholarship for Service and developing education curriculum designed to ensure our cyber professionals are educated in every aspect of cyber risk mitigation.

To ensure resilience to disasters, TODAY, DHS will:

- Provide $22 million to states and local communities for disaster response, recovery, and mitigation activities;

- Help save $4.6 million in damages from flooding across the country through FEMA's Flood Plain Management;

- Help protect 104 homes from the devastating effects of flooding through flood insurance policies issued by the National Flood Insurance Program;

- Strengthen citizen preparedness and participation through funding and technical assistance to the nearly 2,400 tribal, state, territorial, and local Citizen Corps Councils in every state and five U.S. territories;

- Train 951 emergency responders to improve capabilities across all-hazards, to include weapons of mass destruction, cybersecurity, agriculture and food protection, and citizen preparedness; and

- Save 13 lives, respond to 64 search and rescue cases and prevent loss of $260,000 in property damage.

*Data contained in this section is approximate and represents daily averages based on annual DHS Department-wide statistics

Glossary

U.S. Department of Homeland Security, National Incident Management System Selected Definitions, 2008

Actual Event: A disaster (natural or man-made) that has warranted action to protect life, property, environment, public health or safety. Natural disasters include earthquakes, hurricanes, tornadoes, floods, etc.; man-made (either intentional or accidental) incidents can include chemical spills, terrorist attacks, explosives, biological attacks, etc.

After Action Reports (AAR): The AAR documents the performance of exercise related tasks and makes recommendations for improvements. The Improvement Plan outlines the actions that the exercising jurisdiction(s) plans to take to address recommendations contained in the AAR.

Agency: A division of government with a specific function offering a particular kind of assistance. In ICS, agencies are defined either as jurisdictional (having statutory responsibility for incident management) or as assisting or cooperating (providing resources or other assistance).

All Hazards: Any incident caused by terrorism, natural disasters, or any chemical, biological, radiological, nuclear, or explosive (CBRNE) accident. Such incidents require a multi-jurisdictional and multi-functional response and recovery effort.

Assessment: The evaluation and interpretation of measurements and other information to provide a basis for decision-making.

Audit: A formal examination of an organization's or individual's accounts; a methodical examination and review.

Available Resources: Resources assigned to an incident, checked in, and available for a mission assignment, normally located in a Staging Area.

CBRNE: Chemical, biological, radiological, nuclear, and high yield explosive categories normally associated with weapons of mass destruction.

Chain of Command: A series of command, control, executive, or management positions in hierarchical order of authority.

Check-In: The process through which resources first report to an incident. Check-in locations include the incident command post, Resources Unit, incident base, camps, staging areas, or directly on the site.

Chief: The ICS title for individuals responsible for management of functional sections: Operations, Planning, Logistics, Finance/Administration, and Intelligence (if established as a separate section).

Command Staff: In an incident management organization, the Command Staff consists of the Incident Command and the special staff positions of Public Information Officer, Safety Officer, Liaison Officer, and other positions as required, who report directly to the Incident Commander. They may have an assistant or assistants, as needed.

Command: The act of directing, ordering, or controlling by virtue of explicit statutory, regulatory, or delegated authority.

Committed Activities: Actions that an individual or an agency/department have agreed to see through until completion.

CONUS: Continental United States.

Coordinate: To advance systematically an analysis and exchange of information among principals who have or may have a need to know certain information to carry out specific incident management responsibilities.

Corrective Action: Improved procedures that are based on lessons learned from actual incidents or from training and exercises.

Counter-terrorism: Offensive measures taken to prevent, deter, and respond to terrorism.

Critical Infrastructure: Systems and assets, whether physical or virtual, so vital to the United States that the incapacity or destruction of such systems and assets would have a debilitating impact on security, national economic security, national public health or safety, or any combination of those matters.

Cyber-terrorism: A criminal act perpetrated by the use of computers and telecommunications capabilities, resulting in violence, destruction and/or disruption of services to create fear by causing confusion and uncertainty within a given population, with the goal of influencing a government or population to conform to a particular political, social, or ideological agenda.

Designated Foreign Terrorist Organization (DFTO): A political designation determined by the U.S. Department of State. Listing as a DFTO imposes legal penalties for membership, prevents travel into the U.S., and proscribes assistance and funding activities within the U.S. or by U.S. citizens.

DHS: Department of Homeland Security.

Dispatch: The ordered movement of a resource or resources to an assigned operational mission or an administrative move from one location to another.

Emergency Incident: An urgent need for assistance or relief as a result of an action that will likely lead to grave consequences.

Emergency Operations Centers (EOCs): The physical location at which the coordination of information and resources to support domestic incident management activities normally takes place. An EOC may be a temporary facility or may be located in a more central or permanently established facility, perhaps at a higher level of organization within a jurisdiction. EOCs may be organized by major functional disciplines (e.g., fire, law enforcement, and medical services), by jurisdiction (e.g., Federal, State, regional, county, city, tribal), or some combination thereof.

Emergency Operations Plan (EOP): The "steady-state" plan maintained by various jurisdictional levels for managing a wide variety of potential hazards.

Emergency Response Provider: Includes state, local, and tribal emergency public safety, law enforcement, emergency response, emergency medical (including hospital emergency facilities), and related personnel, agencies, and authorities.

Emergency: A human-caused or natural event, which requires responsive action to protect life or property.

Entry-level First Responder: Entry-level first responders are defined as any responders who are not a supervisor or manager.

Equipment Acquisition: The process of obtaining resources to support operational needs.

Equipment: The set of articles or physical resources necessary to perform or complete a task.

Evacuation: Organized, phased, and supervised withdrawal, dispersal, or removal of civilians from dangerous or potentially dangerous areas, and their reception and care in safe areas.

Evaluation: The process of observing and recording exercise activities, comparing the performance of the participants against the objectives, and identifying strengths and weaknesses.

Exercise: Exercises are a planned and coordinated activity allowing homeland security and emergency management personnel—from first responders to senior officials—to demonstrate training, exercise plans, and practice prevention, protection, response, and recovery capabilities in a realistic but risk-free environment. Exercises are a valuable tool for assessing and improving performance, while demonstrating community resolve to prepare for major incidents.

Failed State: A dysfunctional state which also has multiple competing political factions in conflict within its borders, or has no functioning governance above the local level. This does not imply that a central government facing an insurgency is automatically a failed state. If essential functions of government continue in areas controlled by the central authority, it has not "failed."

FEMA: Federal Emergency Management Agency.

Framework: A conceptual structure that supports or contains set of systems and/or practices.

Function: Function refers to the five major activities in the Incident Command System: Command, Operations, Planning, Logistics, and Finance/Administration. The term function is also used when describing the activity involved, e.g., the planning function. A sixth function, Intelligence, may be established, if required, to meet incident management needs.

General Staff: A group of incident management personnel organized according to function and reporting to the Incident Commander. The General Staff normally consists of the Operations Section Chief, Planning Section Chief, Logistics Section Chief, and Finance/Administration Section Chief.

Grantee: A person/group that has had monies formally bestowed or transferred.

Group: Established to divide the incident management structure into functional areas of operation. Groups are composed of resources assembled to perform a special function not necessarily within a single geographic division. Groups, when activated, are located between branches and resources in the Operations Section.

Hazard: Something that is potentially dangerous or harmful, often the root cause of an unwanted outcome.

Homeland Security Exercise and Evaluation Program (HSEEP): A capabilities- and performance-based exercise program that provides a standardized policy, methodology, and language for designing, developing, conducting, and evaluating all exercises. HSEEP also facilitates the creation of self- sustaining, capabilities-based exercise programs by providing tools and resources such as guidance, training, technology, and direct support.
HUMINT: Human intelligence

Improvement Plan: The After Action Report documents the performance of exercise related tasks and makes recommendations for improvements. The Improvement Plan outlines the actions that the exercising jurisdiction(s) plans to take to address recommendations contained in the AAR.

Incident Action Plan (IAP): An oral or written plan containing general objectives reflecting the overall strategy for managing an incident.

Incident Command Post (ICP): The field location at which the primary tactical-level, on-scene incident command functions are performed. The ICP may be collocated with the incident base or other incident facilities and is normally identified by a green rotating or flashing light.

Incident Command System (ICS): A standardized on-scene emergency management system which provides for the adoption of an integrated organizational structure. ICS is the combination of facilities, equipment, personnel, procedures, and communications operating within a common organizational structure, designed to aid in the management of resources during incidents. It is used for all kinds of emergencies, and is applicable to small as well as large and complex incidents.

Incident Objectives: Statements of guidance and direction necessary for selecting appropriate strategy(s) and the tactical direction of resources. Incident objectives are based on realistic expectations of what can be accomplished when all allocated resources have been effectively deployed. Incident objectives must be achievable and measurable, yet flexible enough to allow strategic and tactical alternatives.

Incident: An occurrence or event, natural or human-caused, that requires an emergency response to protect life or property. Incidents can, for example, include major disasters, emergencies, terrorist attacks, terrorist threats, wildland and urban fires, floods, hazardous materials spills, nuclear accidents, aircraft accidents, earthquakes, hurricanes, tornadoes, tropical storms, war-related disasters, public health and medical emergencies, and other occurrences requiring an emergency response.

Incident-Specific Hazards: Anticipated events that may or may not occur that require coordinated response to protect life or property, e.g., pandemic flu, avian flu, etc.

Initial Action: The actions taken by those responders first to arrive at an incident site.

Initial Response: Resources initially committed to an incident.

Institutionalize ICS: Government officials, incident managers and emergency response organizations at all jurisdictional levels adopt the Incident Command

System (ICS) and launch activities that will result in the use of the ICS for all incident response operations. Actions to institutionalize the use of ICS take place at two levels - policy and organizational/operational.

Insurgency: An organized movement aimed at the overthrow of a constituted government through the use of subversion and armed conflict.

Intelligence Officer: The intelligence officer is responsible for managing internal information, intelligence, and operational security requirements supporting incident management activities. These may include information security and operational security activities, as well as the complex task of ensuring that sensitive information of all types (e.g., classified information, law enforcement sensitive information, proprietary information, or export-controlled information) is handled in a way that not only safeguards the information, but also ensures that it gets to those who need access to it to perform their missions effectively and safely.

Interagency: An organization or committee comprised of multiple agencies.

Interoperability & Compatibility: A principle that holds that systems must be able to work together and should not interfere with one another if the multiple jurisdictions, organizations, and functions that come together are to be effective in domestic incident management. Interoperability and compatibility are achieved through the use of such tools as common communications and data standards, digital data formats, equipment standards, and design standards.

Interstate: A region comprised of multiple states.

Intrastate: A region within a single state.

Inventory: An itemized list of current assets such as a catalog of the property or estate, or a list of goods on hand.

Joint Information Center (JIC): A facility established to coordinate all incident-related public information activities. It is the central point of contact for all news media at the scene of the incident. Public information officials from all participating agencies should collocate at the JIC.

Joint Information System (JIS): Integrates incident information and public affairs into a cohesive organization designed to provide consistent, coordinated, timely information during crisis or incident operations. The mission of the JIS is to provide a structure and system for developing and delivering coordinated interagency messages; developing, recommending, and developing and delivering coordinated interagency messages; developing, recommending, and executing public information plans and strategies on behalf of the IC; advising the IC concerning public affairs issues that could affect a response effort; and controlling rumors and inaccurate information that could undermine public confidence in the emergency response effort.

Jurisdiction: A range or sphere of authority. Public agencies have jurisdiction at an incident related to their legal responsibilities and authority. Jurisdictional authority at an incident can be political or geographical (e.g., city, county, tribal, State, or Federal boundary lines) or functional (e.g., law enforcement, public health).

Lessons Learned: Knowledge gained through operational experience (actual events or exercises) that improve performance of others in the same discipline.

Leverage: Investing with borrowed money as a way to amplify potential gains.

Liaison: A form of communication for establishing and maintaining mutual understanding and cooperation.

Local Government: A county, municipality, city, town, township, local public authority, school district, special district, intrastate district, council of governments (regardless of whether the council of governments is incorporated as a nonprofit corporation under State law), regional or interstate government entity, or agency or instrumentality of a local government; an Indian tribe or authorized tribal organization, or in Alaska a Native village or Alaska Regional Native Corporation; a rural community, unincorporated town or village, or other public entity.

Logistics: Providing resources and other services to support incident management.

Major Disaster: A major disaster is any natural catastrophe (including any hurricane, tornado, storm, high water, wind-driven water, tidal wave, tsunami, earthquake, volcanic eruption, landslide, mudslide, snowstorm, or drought), or, regardless of cause, any fire, flood, or explosion, in any part of the United States, which in the determination of the President causes damage of sufficient severity and magnitude to warrant major disaster assistance under this Act to supplement the efforts and available resources of States, tribes, local governments, and disaster relief organizations in alleviating the damage, loss, hardship, or suffering caused thereby.

Management by Objective: A management approach that involves a four-step process for achieving the incident goal. The Management by Objectives approach includes the following: establishing overarching objectives; developing and issuing assignments, plans, procedures, and protocols; establishing specific, measurable objectives for various incident management functional activities and directing efforts to fulfill them, in support of defined strategic objectives; and documenting results to measure performance and facilitate corrective action.

Measure: A determination of a jurisdiction's specific level of compliance, evaluated according to that jurisdiction's responses to the metrics that have been established.

Metric: Metrics are measurements in the form of questions that were derived from implementations activities. These metrics are separated into two categories; tier 1 and tier 2.

Millenarian: Apocalyptic; forecasting the ultimate destiny of the world; foreboding imminent disaster or final doom; wildly unrestrained; ultimately decisive.

Mitigation: The activities designed to reduce or eliminate risks to persons or property or to lessen the actual or potential effects or consequences of an incident. Mitigation measures may be implemented prior to, during, or after an incident. Mitigation measures are often informed by lessons learned from prior incidents. Mitigation involves ongoing actions to reduce exposure to, probability of, or potential loss from hazards. Measures may include zoning and building codes, floodplain buyouts, and analysis of hazard-related data to determine where it is safe to build or locate temporary facilities. Mitigation can include efforts to educate governments, businesses, and the public on measures they can take to reduce loss and injury.

Mobilization: The process and procedures used by all organizations-state, local, and tribal-for activating, assembling, and transporting all resources that have been requested to respond to or support an incident.

Multiagency Coordination: A Multi-Agency Coordination System is a combination of facilities, equipment, personnel, procedures, and communications integrated into a common system with responsibility for coordinating and supporting domestic incident management activities.

Multijurisdictional Incident: An incident requiring action from multiple agencies that each have jurisdiction to manage certain aspects of an incident. In ICS, these incidents will be managed under Unified Command.

Mutual-Aid Agreement (MAA): A written agreement between agencies, organizations, and/or jurisdictions that they will assist one another, on request, by furnishing personnel, equipment, and/or expertise in a specified manner.

Narco-Terrorism: Terrorism conducted to further the aims of drug traffickers. It may include assassinations, extortion, hijackings, bombings, and kidnappings directed against judges, prosecutors, elected officials, or law enforcement agents, and general disruption of a legitimate government to divert attention from drug operations.

National Incident Management System (NIMS): A system mandated by HSPD-5 that provides a consistent nationwide approach for state, local, and tribal governments; the private-sector, and nongovernmental organizations to work effectively and efficiently together to prepare for, respond to, and recover from domestic incidents, regardless of cause, size, or complexity. To provide for interoperability and compatibility among state, local, and tribal capabilities, the NIMS includes a core set of concepts, principles, and terminology. HSPD-5 identifies these as the ICS; multiagency coordination systems; training; identification and management of resources (including systems for classifying types of resources); qualification and certification; and the collection, tracking, and reporting of incident information and incident resources.

National Response Plan (NRP): The *National Response Plan* is an all-discipline, all-hazards plan that establishes a single, comprehensive framework for the management of domestic incidents. It provides the structure and mechanisms for the coordination of Federal support to State, local, and tribal incident managers and for exercising direct Federal authorities ad responsibilities.

Nongovernmental Organization (NGO): An entity with an association that is based on interests of its members, individuals, or institutions and that is not created by a government, but may work cooperatively with government. Such organizations serve a public purpose, not a private benefit. Examples of NGOs include faith-based charity organizations and the American Red Cross.

No-Notice Events: An occurrence or event, natural or human-caused, that requires an emergency response to protect life or property (i.e. terrorist attacks and threats, wildland and urban fires, floods, hazardous materials spills, nuclear accident, aircraft accident, earthquakes, hurricanes, tornadoes, public health and medical emergencies etc).

Operational Period: The time scheduled for executing a given set of operation actions, as specified in the Incident Action Plan. Operational periods can be of various lengths, although usually not over 24 hours.

Operations Security (OPSEC): A process of identifying critical information and subsequently analyzing friendly actions attendant to military operations and other activities to: a. Identify those actions that can be observed by adversary intelligence systems. b. Determine indicators hostile intelligence systems might obtain that could be interpreted or pieced together to derive critical information in time to be useful to adversaries. c. Select and execute measures that eliminate or reduce to an acceptable level the vulnerabilities of friendly actions to adversary exploitation.

Pathogen: Any organism (usually living) capable of producing serious disease or death, such as bacteria, fungi, and viruses.

Personnel Accountability: The ability to account for the location and welfare of incident personnel. It is accomplished when supervisors ensure that ICS principles and processes are functional and that personnel are working within established incident management guidelines.

Physical security: That part of security concerned with physical measures designed to safeguard personnel; to prevent unauthorized access to equipment, installations, material and documents; and to safeguard them against espionage, sabotage, damage, and theft.

Planning: A method to developing objectives to be accomplished and incorporated into an Emergency Operations Plan (EOP).

Preparedness: The range of deliberate, critical tasks and activities necessary to build, sustain, and improve the operational capability to prevent, protect against, respond to, and recover from domestic incidents. Preparedness is a continuous process. Preparedness involves efforts at all levels of government and between government and private-sector and nongovernmental organizations to identify threats, determine vulnerabilities, and identify required resources. Preparedness is operationally focused on establishing guidelines, protocols, and standards for planning, training and exercises, personnel qualification and certification, equipment certification, and publication management.

Prevention: Actions to avoid an incident or to intervene to stop an incident from occurring. Prevention involves actions to protect lives and property.

Private Sector: Organizations and entities that are not part of any governmental structure. It includes for-profit and not-for-profit organizations, formal and informal structures, commerce and industry, and private voluntary organizations (PVO).

Processes: Systems of operations that incorporate standardized procedures, methodologies, and functions necessary to provide resources effectively and efficiently. These include resource typing, resource ordering and tracking, and coordination.

Public Information Systems: The processes, procedures, and systems for communicating timely and accurate information to the public during crisis or emergency situations.

Qualification and Certification: This subsystem provides recommended qualification and certification standards for emergency responder and incident management personnel. It also allows the development of minimum standards for resources expected to have an interstate application. Standards typically include training, currency, experience, and physical and medical fitness.

Reception Area: This refers to a location separate from staging areas, where resources report in for processing and out-processing. Reception Areas provide accountability, security, situational awareness briefings, safety awareness, distribution of IAPs, supplies and equipment, feeding, and bed down.

Recovery Plan: A plan developed by a State, local, or tribal jurisdiction with assistance from responding Federal agencies to restore the affected area.

Recovery: The development, coordination, and execution of service- and site-restoration plans; the reconstitution of government operations and services; individual, private- sector, nongovernmental, and public-assistance programs to provide housing and to promote restoration; long-term care and treatment of affected persons; additional measures for social, political, environmental, and economic restoration; evaluation of the incident to identify lessons learned; post-incident reporting; and development of initiatives to mitigate the effects of future incidents.

Resource Management: Efficient incident management requires a system for identifying available resources at all jurisdictional levels to enable timely and unimpeded access to resources needed to prepare for, respond to, or recover from an incident. Resource management includes mutual-aid agreements; the use of special state, local, and tribal teams; and resource mobilization protocols.

Resource Typing Standard: Categorization and description of response resources that are commonly exchanged in disasters through mutual aid agreements.

Resources: Personnel and major items of equipment, supplies, and facilities available or potentially available for assignment to incident operations and for which status is maintained. Resources are described by kind and type and may be used in operational support or supervisory capacities at an incident or at an EOC.

Response Asset Inventory: An inventory of the jurisdiction's resources that have been identified and typed according to NIMS Resource Typing Standards. Development of a Response Asset Inventory requires resource typing of equipment, personnel, and supplies identified in the inventories of State resources.

Response Assets: Resources that include equipment, personnel and supplies that are used in activities that address the effect of an incident.

Response: Activities that address the short-term, direct effects of an incident. Response includes immediate actions to save lives, protect property, and meet basic human needs. Response also includes the execution of emergency operations plans and incident mitigation activities designed to limit the loss of life, personal injury, property damage, and other unfavorable outcomes.

Safety Officer: A member of the Command Staff responsible for monitoring and assessing safety hazards or unsafe situations and for developing measures for ensuring personnel safety.

Scalability: The ability of incident managers to adapt to incidents by either expanding or reducing the resources necessary to adequately manage the incident, including the ability to incorporate multiple jurisdictions and multiple responder disciplines.

Self-certification: Attest as being true or as meeting a standard based on an agency's or department's own evaluation of itself.

Setback: Distance between outer perimeter and nearest point of buildings or structures within. Generally referred to in terms of explosive blast mitigation.

Span of Control: The number of individuals a supervisor can effectively manage, usually expressed as the ratio of supervisors to individuals.

Staging Area: Location established where resources can be placed while awaiting a tactical assignment. The Operations Section manages Staging Areas.

Standard Equipment List (SEL): A list issued annually to promote interoperability and standardization across the response community at the local, state, and federal levels by offering a standard reference and a common set of terminology. It is provided to the responder community by the Inter-Agency Board for Equipment Standardization and Interoperability (IAB). The SEL contains a list of generic equipment recommended by the IAB to organizations in preparing for and responding to all-hazards.

Standard Operating Procedures (SOPs): A complete reference document that details the procedures for performing a single function or a number of independent functions.

Standardization: A principle that provides a set of standardized organizational structures—such as the Incident Command System (ICS), multi-agency coordination systems, and public information systems—as well as requirements for processes, procedures, and systems designed to improve interoperability among jurisdictions and disciplines in various area, including: training; resource management; personnel qualification and certification; equipment certification; communications and information management; technology support; and continuous system improvement.

Strategic: Strategic elements of incident management are characterized by continuous long- term, high-level planning by organizations headed by elected or other senior officials. These elements involve the adoption of long-range goals and objectives, the setting of priorities; the establishment of budgets and other fiscal decisions, policy development, and the application of measures of performance or effectiveness.

Strategy: Plans, policies, procedures for how to achieve a stated goal or initiative.

Task Force: Any combination of resources assembled to support a specific mission or operational need. All resource elements within a Task Force must have common communications and a designated leader.

Technical Assistance (TA): Support provided to State, local, and tribal jurisdictions when they have the resources but lack the complete knowledge and skills needed to perform a required activity (such as mobile-home park design and hazardous material assessments).

Territory: A geographical area belonging to or under the jurisdiction of a governmental authority; a part of the United States (U.S.) not included within any State but organized with a separate legislature.

Terrorism: Terrorism is defined as activity that involves an act dangerous to human life or potentially destructive of critical infrastructure or key resources and is a violation of the criminal laws of the United States or of any State or other subdivision of the United States in which it occurs and is intended to intimidate or coerce the civilian population or influence a government or affect the conduct of a government by mass destruction, assassination, or kidnapping.

Threat: An indication of possible violence, harm, or danger.

Tools: Those instruments and capabilities that allow for the professional performance of tasks, such as information systems, agreements, doctrine, capabilities, and legislative authorities.

Training Curriculum: A course or set of courses designed to teach personnel specific processes, concepts, or task-oriented skills.

Training: Specialized instruction and practice to improve performance and lead to enhanced emergency management capabilities.

Tribal: Any Indian tribe, band, nation, or other organized group or community, including any Alaskan Native Village as defined in or established pursuant to the Alaskan Native Claims Settlement Act (85 stat. 688) [43 U.S.C.A. and 1601 et seq.], that is recognized as eligible for the special programs and services provided by the United States to Indians because of their status as Indians.

Type: A classification of resources in the ICS that refers to capability. Type 1 is generally considered to be more capable than Types 2, 3, or 4, respectively, because of size; power; capacity; or, in the case of incident management teams, experience and qualifications.

Unified Command (UC): An application of ICS used when there is more than one agency with incident jurisdiction or when incidents cross political jurisdictions. Agencies work together through the designated members of the UC, often the senior person from agencies and/or disciplines participating in the UC, to establish a common set of objectives and strategies and a single IAP.

Unity of Command: The concept by which each person within an organization reports to one and only one designated person. The purpose of unity of command is to ensure unity of effort under one responsible commander for every objective.

Volunteer: A volunteer is any individual in performance of services without promise, expectation, or receipt of compensation for services performed.

WMD: Weapons of Mass Destruction. Weapons that are capable of a high order of destruction and/or of being used in such a manner as to destroy large numbers of people. Weapons of mass destruction can be high explosives or nuclear, biological, chemical, and radiological weapons, but exclude the means of transporting or propelling the weapon where such means is a separable and divisible part of the weapon.

WOT: War on terrorism.

Resources

Brachman, Jarret. "Statement of Jarret Brachman Before the House Armed Services Subcommittee on Terrorism, Unconventional Threats and Capabilities." Washington. 14 February 2007.

Bush, George W. "Address to the Nation." Washington. 11 September 2001.

Congressional Research Service. Report For Congress: American Jihadist Terrorism, Combating A Complex Threat. Washington: Congressional Research Service, 2011.

Crumpton, Henry "Remarks by Amb. Henry A. Crumpton, U.S. Coordinator for Counterterrorism at RUSI Conference on Transnational Terrorism." 16 January 2006.

Emergency Management Assistance Compact, Public Law 104–321, 110 Stat. 3877. 1996.

Muhammad bin Ahmad as-Salim, 39 Ways to Serve and Participate in Jihad. At-Tibyan Publications, 2003.

Obama, Barrack. "Address to the Nation." Washington. 1 May 2011.

Office of the Director of National Intelligence. National Counterterrorism Center Report on Terrorism. Washington: Office of the Director of National Intelligence, 2010.

Olsen, Matthew G. "Statement of Matthew G. Olsen Before the Senate Committee on Homeland Security and Governmental Affairs: Ten Years After 9/11, Are We Safer?" Washington. 13 September 2011.

The State of Delaware. The Nature of Terrorism. Public web site. Accessed 4 September 2011. cjc.delaware.gov/terrorism/nature.shtml

The State of New York. The Vigilance Project: An Analysis of 32 Terrorism Cases Against the Homeland. New York: New York State Intelligence Center, 2010.

U. S. Communications Sector Coordinating Council. Background. Public web site. Accessed 5 September 2011. http://www.commscc.org

U.S. Department of Homeland Security. A Day in the Life of the Department of Homeland Security. Washington: Department of Homeland Security, 2010.

U.S. Department of Homeland Security. Brief Documentary History of the Department of Homeland Security, 2001 to 2008. Washington: Department of Homeland Security, 2008.

U.S. Department of Homeland Security. Building Resilience Through Public-Private Partnerships. Washington: Federal Emergency Management Agency, 2012.

U.S. Department of Homeland Security. <u>Civil Defense and Homeland Security: A Short History of National Preparedness Efforts</u>. Washington: Department of Homeland Security, 2006.

U.S. Department of Homeland Security. Critical Infrastructure Sector Partnerships. Public web site. Accessed 2 September 2011. http://www.dhs.gov/files/partnerships/editorial_0206.shtm

U.S. Department of Homeland Security. Department Structure. Public web site. Accessed 5 September 2011. http://www.dhs.gov/xabout/structure/

U.S. Department of Homeland Security. History of FEMA. Public web site. Accessed 4 September 2011. http://www.fema.gov/about/history.shtm

U.S. Department of Homeland Security. <u>National Incident Management System</u>. Washington: Department of Homeland Security, 2008.

U.S. Department of Homeland Security. <u>National Infrastructure Protection Plan: Partnering to Enhance Protection and Resiliency</u>. Washington: Department of Homeland Security, 2009.

U.S. Department of Homeland Security. <u>National Response Framework</u>. Washington: Federal Emergency Management Agency, 2008.

U.S. Department of Homeland Security. <u>Overview: ESF and Support Annexes Coordinating Federal Assistance in Support of the National Response Framework</u>. Washington: Federal Emergency Management Agency, 2008.

U.S. Department of Homeland Security. <u>Quadrennial Homeland Security Review Report: A Strategic Framework for a Secure Homeland</u>. Washington: Department of Homeland Security, 2010.

U.S. Department of Homeland Security. <u>Risk Management Fundamentals: Homeland Security Risk Management Doctrine</u>. Washington: Department of Homeland Security, 2011.

U.S. Department of Justice. <u>Assessing and Managing the Terrorism Threat</u>. Washington: Department of Justice, 2005.

U.S. Department of Justice. <u>Engaging the Private Sector to Promote Homeland Security: Law Enforcement-Private Security Partnerships</u>. Washington: Department of Justice, 2005.

U.S. Department of Justice. Highlights of the USA Patriot Act. Public web site. Accessed 4 September 2011. http://www.justice.gov/archive/ll/highlights.htm

U.S. Department of State. Foreign Terrorist Organizations. Public web site. Accessed 25 September 2011. http://www.state.gov/j/ct/rls/other/des/123085.htm

U.S. Executive Office of the President. <u>Presidential Decision Directive 63: The Clinton Administration's Policy on Critical Infrastructure Protection</u>. Washington: The White House, 1998.

U.S. Executive Office of the President. <u>Presidential Executive Order 13228: Establishing the Office of Homeland Security and the Homeland Security Council</u>. Washington: The White House, 2001.

U.S. Executive Office of the President. <u>National Strategy for Counterterrorism</u>. Washington: The White House, 2011.

U.S. Executive Office of the President. <u>Securing the Homeland, Strengthening the Nation</u>. Washington: The White House, 2002.

U.S. Executive Office of the President. <u>Terrorism Risk Insurance Report</u>. Washington: The White House, 2006.

U.S. Executive Office of the President. <u>The Department of Homeland Security</u>. Washington: The White House, 2002.

U.S. General Accounting Office. <u>Justice Department: Better Management Oversight and Internal Controls Needed to Ensure Accuracy of Terrorism-Related Statistics</u>. Washington: General Accounting Office, 2003.

U.S. Senate. <u>Violent Islamist Extremism, the Internet, and the Homegrown Terrorist Threat</u>. Washington: U.S. Senate Committee on Homeland Security and Governmental Affairs, 2008.